PERGAMON INTERNATIONAL LIBRARY
of Science, Technology, Engineering and Social Studies
The 1000-volume original paperback library in aid of education,
industrial training and the enjoyment of leisure
Publisher: Robert Maxwell, M.C.

Teaching Social Skills to Children
(PGPS — 89)

THE PERGAMON TEXTBOOK
INSPECTION COPY SERVICE

An inspection copy of any book published in the Pergamon International Library
will gladly be sent to academic staff without obligation for their consideration for
course adoption or recommendation. Copies may be retained for a period of 60 days
from receipt and returned if not suitable. When a particular title is adopted or
recommended for adoption for class use and the recommendation results in a sale
of 12 or more copies, the inspection copy may be retained with our compliments.
The Publishers will be pleased to receive suggestions for revised editions and new
titles to be published in this important International Library.

Related Titles

Teaching Social Skills to Children

Innovative Approaches

Edited by
Gwendolyn Cartledge,

Department of Specialized
Instruction

and **JoAnne Fellows Milburn,**
Starr Commonwealth/Hannah
Neil Center for Children,
Columbus, Ohio

Pergamon Press
New York • Oxford • Toronto • Sydney • Frankfurt • Paris

Foreword*

Teaching socially desirable behavior will no doubt be the Zeitgeist of the next decade. Already, this rising tide can be seen in recently published texts concerning theoretical and practical aspects of positive social behavior: Staub's two volumes (1978 & 1979) are concerned with theory, rationale, and applications for teaching social behavior and morality; Phillips (1978) presents teaching alternatives to psychopathology; and my text focuses on teaching classroom social behavior (Stephens, 1978). These are just a few of the many books which are needed for practitioners to deal effectively with our changing social conditions. The present text adds to the repertoire of needed information on this important and relatively recent subject: Its concern is with teaching social behavior to children, including special populations.

What has caused this great interest in social behavior? Why do we find it necessary to *teach* behaviors which at one time were acquired in less direct ways? Clear answers to such questions are not readily available. But three major conditions within our society suggest how and why we have arrived at the need to teach social skills and concepts.

First, our basic *social institutions* are undergoing great changes. The family has served as the primary socializing agency for many years. Yet, its present changes have resulted in a lessening of influence on our young. The rise in single-parent homes; high rates of marital separation and divorce; and an increase in remarriages have contributed to a weakening of social instruction in homes. Single parents are often also working parents; they simply have less time to devote to parenting. Divorce and separation frequently confuse the young, divide their loyalties, and drain parents of the emotional stability often needed to be effective social models. It has been estimated that about 25 percent of children under the age of 18 are living in what has been termed synergistic families—families of remarriage (Mayleas, 1977). As a result, sexual relations between stepparents and stepchildren have increased, causing sexual abuse and surely not contributing to healthy social adjustments.

*References appear at end of chapter 4.

The church—another basic socializing agent—is in a state of flux. Religious values have become more fluid in keeping with our casual life styles. And organized religion is less influential, touching a smaller proportion of the population.

While almost the entire population is now processed through elementary and secondary schools, the school's role as a socializing agency has also diminished. The entertainment industry, coupled with the increased bureaucratization of schools, has contributed to the lessening influence of the educational system.

Network television has moved into these vacuums, providing an influence in tastes, values, and behavior of magnitudes unheard of previously. Exercising their rights to freedom of expression, commercial broadcasters rely upon protection under the United States Constitution's First Amendment as a license to impose their values on the public. Recently on network television a prominent producer of family shows (Norman Lear, *All in the Family Special* (telecast) March 4, 1979) used the logic that children are exposed to explicit sex and four letter words on the playgrounds of America as a rationale for being permitted to do the same during TV prime time.

Should the airways be licensed for producers and others to impose their political and social values upon the public? Should First Amendment rights be exercised under a license from the federal government? Should television producers be allowed the same freedoms as those in the print media? Such issues are fundamental to our society and are not easily resolved.

Second, our *mobile population* also contributes to changes in socialization. On the average, the family in the United States moves about once every five years. Moving at this rate provides a sense of anonymity with less commitment to places, neighborhoods and localities. Destructive behavior —vandalizing public property and littering—is believed to be higher among highly mobile groups. And feelings of obligations to others are at best tentative. Acquaintances replace friends and peers. All of these factors contribute to the dissolution of group values.

Third, the increasing emphasis on *individuality* (do your own thing) encourages us to be even less responsive to the needs of others. Insensitivity to people, animals and the environment has become commonplace. How are freedom of expression and other rights to be exercised in a society which must increasingly depend upon group efforts? How will we be governed without group standards? Is there a way to have our individual freedoms and a strong society too? Can we educate the young for such a society? Perhaps not. Yet, in this age of rapid change, educational needs are greater than ever, for people must exercise increasingly finer judgments about more complex situations. But we now know that information alone will seldom change behavior and attitudes. Rather, the society shapes our responses; built into the environment are powerful incentives which "encourage" us to choose, and the choices may not always be good for individuals or for this society.

Obviously, no single book can address these complex issues. Some are legalistic, others are educational and psychological. Many issues require political as well as educational considerations. This text, however, will aid in recognizing the need to change our views on how social behavior is acquired and to formulate rationales for identifying those behaviors to be taught. It should serve as a valuable resource to practitioners who wish to add social skills teaching to their repertoire of ways to help children become better citizens in today's complex society.

Thomas M. Stephens
Professor and Chairman
Exceptional Children
and
Executive Director
National Center, Educational Media
and Materials for the Handicapped
The Ohio State University

Acknowledgments

We would like to thank the many people who helped us with various aspects of this book. Some of those who should receive special thanks include: typists Linda Juzkiewicz and Wanda Tucker for their competent help with the preparation of the manuscript; teachers, clinicians, and academicians Nancy Klein, Shirley Joseph, Nancy B. Miller, Tom Milburn, and Michael Milburn for reading and critiquing parts of the manuscript, with particular gratitude to Christine Kring for reviewing Part One of the manuscript and compiling the Resource Materials Section; graduate student, Darryl Smith for his contribution to the manuscript; and department chair, Diana Jordan for providing encouragement and means for producing a book.

Publishers and authors who gave us permission to reproduce copyrighted material, including:

Edleson, J.L. *A behavioral roleplay test for assessing children's social skills: Testing booklet.* Unpublished manual, University of Wisconsin-Madison, 1978.

Edleson, J.L., and Cole-Kelly, K. *A behavioral roleplay test for assessing children's social skills: Scoring manual.* Unpublished manual, University of Wisconsin-Madison, 1978.

Edleson, J.L., and Rose, S.D. *A behavioral roleplay test for assessing children's social skills.* Paper presented at the annual convention of the Association for the Advancement of Behavior Therapy, Chicago, 1978.

Fagen, Stanley; Long, Nicholas; and Stevens, Donald. *Teaching children self-control.* Columbus, Ohio: Charles E. Merrill, 1975.

Gambrill, E.D. *Behavior modification.* San Francisco: Jossey-Bass, 1977.

Harrison, Marta. *For the fun of it: Selected cooperative games for children and adults,* pp. 10, 11, 15, 16 as in appendix to *A manual on non-violence and children,* compiled and edited by Stephanie Judson. Philadelphia: Friends Peace Committee, 1515 Cherry Street, 1977.

Hill, Walker, and Buckley, Nancy. *Token reinforcement techniques.* Eugene, Ore.: E.B. Press, 1974.

Kanfer, Fredrick, and Goldstein, Arnold. *Helping people change.* Elmsford, N.Y.: Pergamon Press, 1975.

Krathwhol, David; Bloom, Benjamin; and Masia, Bertram. *Taxonomy of educational objectives: The classification of educational goals: Handbook 2: Affective domain.* Copyright © 1964 by Longman Inc. Reprinted with permission of Longman.

Orlick, Terry. *The cooperative spirit and games book: Challenge without competition.* Pantheon Books, Division of Random House, Inc., New York, copyright 1978.

Spivack, G., and Shure, M. *Social adjustment of young children: A cognitive approach to solving real-life problems.* San Francisco: Jossey-Bass, 1978.

Stephens, Thomas. *Social skills in the classroom.* © Copyright 1978, Cedars Press, Inc., P.O. Box 29351, Columbus, Ohio. Reproduced with permission, all rights reserved.

Turnbull, Ann; Strickland, Bonnie; and Brantley, John. *Developing and implementing IEP's: Individualized education programs.* Columbus, Ohio: Charles E. Merrill, 1978.

Wood, Mary. *Developmental therapy.* Baltimore: University Park Press, 1975.

We would also like to thank our families and friends for all the less tangible but equally appreciated kinds of help and support.

Part I: Steps In Teaching Social Skills

Introduction to Part I*

This book is designed as an aid to people who are directly charged with the socialization of children and youth, both normal and handicapped. The audience could be the regular classroom teachers, special education teachers, or clinicians in school, residential, or outpatient settings; and possibly parents who wish to improve their socializing impact on their child. (Parents are, after all, the child's first teachers and are the first sources for social skill training.) This book is intended to be used as a text in preservice programs for teacher training and the training of clinicians such as social workers, psychologists, and guidance counselors.

The book is concerned with social behaviors broadly considered as skills to be taught, and the emphasis is placed on the building of prosocial, adaptive, new behaviors rather than on the elimination of problem behaviors or the development of motivational systems to increase the performance of behaviors already in the child's repertoire. The authors were encouraged to develop this book through a series of personal experiences with children, teachers, and clinicians in several schools and treatment settings. We have become convinced that social behaviors can and should be specifically taught as part of a school curriculum or remedial therapy program, and that the skills for such teaching should be in the repertoires of all teachers and clinicians. Although parents may less often feel the need to provide systematic teaching in the home, some knowledge of how social skills are taught, both purposefully and inadvertently, can add immeasurably to their effectiveness as parents. In addition, parents have an important role in the maintenance and generalization of social skills taught to children in other settings and should be knowledgeable about social skills training carried out by teachers and clinicians.

In clinical settings, a case may be made for teaching social skills to children for the prevention of later psychological disorders. There is evidence that many adults suffering from psychiatric illnesses—particularly anxiety states, reactive depressions, and personality disorders—are also characterized by social inadequacy (Trower, Bryant & Argyle, 1978). Some longitudinal research (Kagan & Moss, 1962) indicates that childhood defi-

---

*References for chapters 1 through 4 appear at the end of chapter 4.

3

ciencies in social interaction are carried into adulthood. Phillips (1978) suggests that if needed social skills are not learned, "current problems will remain and later ones will be more likely to develop or become exacerbated. As and when social skills are learned, at whatever time in life, they are a basis for present adequacy and prevention of future inadequacy" (p. 141).

The most data supporting the need for teaching social skills comes from studies of the relationship between social behaviors and school achievement (Cartledge & Milburn, 1978). It has been suggested that the teaching of social skills goes on all the time in the classroom as a "hidden curriculum" even when the teacher does not deliberately engage in social skills instruction. The teacher, like the parent, is a powerful and influential person in the child's life and, as such, serves as a model for social behaviors. In addition, the teacher shapes the child's social behaviors, intentionally or not, through the process of reinforcement. Studies of teacher attitudes and behavior suggest that social behaviors on the part of the student are an important determinant of how the teacher interacts with him. Students with positive social behaviors (for example, those who seek out the teacher, initiate contacts about work assignments, answer or try to answer questions, smile at the teacher, and are attentive during lessons), generally receive more positive teacher attention and have a higher rate of academic success. A series of studies by Cobb and his colleagues (Hops & Cobb, 1973, 1974; Cobb & Hops, 1973; Walker & Hops, 1976) have identified specific social "survival skills" which predict achievement from one academic area to another and have demonstrated that training in these survival skills could bring about an increase in academic achievement.

There is some controversy in research circles about whether the most efficient target for classroom behavior change efforts may be academic responses rather than social behaviors since, for some populations, improvement in academic achievement appears to result in improved social skills as well as the reverse. Something of a reciprocal relationship appears to exist between improved curriculum, reinforcement of academic responses, and the development of relevant social behaviors. Social behaviors and academic behaviors are so highly correlated that it is difficult to reinforce academic responses without also reinforcing the social behaviors that make the academic responses possible, e.g., attention to the required stimuli, complying with teacher directions, responding under circumstances specified by the teacher. Focusing specifically on social behaviors for direct instruction seems particularly relevant for children possessing very low levels of the social behaviors that have been determined to be essential for academic success. Again looking at prevention of later adjustment problems as a rationale for teaching social skills, a survey of social-vocational adjustment of adult mentally-retarded individuals by Goldstein (1972) seems relevant. He found that vocational adjustment problems appeared more related to social behaviors than to task performance per se, implying that for adult job competence it is as important to arrive at work on time, channel anger constructively, or approach coworkers appropriately, as it is to perform the task itself.

There is an underlying model that serves as a framework to produce the dimensions the authors used to develop the chapters for the book that follows. The model exists in a number of versions variously called "perspective teaching," "diagnostic teaching," or "directive teaching" (Stephens, 1977). Essentially, the elements are: (1) define in specific behaviorally-stated terms the behavior to be taught; (2) assess the level of competence possessed by the learner in order to determine his initial level of performance; (3) teach the behaviors defined through assessment as lacking in the learner's repertoire; (4) evaluate or reassess for results of teaching; and (5) provide opportunities for practice and generalization or transfer of behaviors to new situations. In the teaching of social skills, all these steps need to be present to some degree. The chapters are thus identified under headings corresponding to these steps, including (1) a chapter on selection of skills, (2) a chapter on assessment and evaluation, (3) a chapter on teaching procedures, and (4) a chapter on maintenance and transfer. Because of the close relationship between assessment and evaluation, the book does not contain separate chapters on each. Rather, the two processes, which often involve the same materials or procedures, are combined in Chapter 2.

In addition to the organizing model, two assumptions guided the construction of the book. One was that social skills contain cognitive and affective as well as overt behavioral aspects. A child may have, for example, a social behavior in his repertoire that he seldom exhibits. Such cognitive dimensions as negative expectations, the presence of self-defeating thoughts, deficits in social perception and discrimination, and such affective dimensions as anxiety and fear of failure may interfere with the performance of appropriate social skills. An attempt is made to include approaches to social skills teaching involving cognitive and affective dimensions as well as the behavioral aspects of social skills. The other assumption was that the teaching of social skills differs as one deals with different populations. The developmental level of the child needs to be considered, for example, as well as handicapping conditions that may interfere with learning. The authors have, therefore, included chapters dealing with specific handicapping conditions and different developmental levels as they relate to the teaching of social skills, written by contributors with expertise in these areas.

Although throughout the book the authors use such evaluative terms as "appropriate," "desirable," "proper," "positive," and so forth, when speaking of a social behavior, it should be understood that the social and cultural context of a behavior ultimately defines those terms, as further discussed in Chapter 1.

The material presented in this volume does not constitute a comprehensive review of current literature on social skills for children, but represents, instead, a set of ideas for practice that can be applied by those working therapeutically with children. Most of the approaches suggested here have empirical foundations or have been demonstrated to be effective with children and youth in bringing about improved social functioning.

Chapter 1
Selecting Social Skills

To begin with, what are "social skills"? These can be defined broadly or narrowly, and terms like "social competence" and "social skills" are sometimes used interchangeably. Combs and Slaby (1977) define social skill as "the ability to interact with others in a given social context in specific ways that are societally acceptable or valued and at the same time personally beneficial, mutually beneficial, or beneficial primarily to others" (p. 162). Another useful definition is that of Libet and Lewinsohn (1973) in which social skill is defined as "the complex ability both to emit behaviors that are positively or negatively reinforced and not to emit behaviors that are punished or extinguished by others" (p. 304). Social skills conceptualized in terms of social consequences can be regarded further as behaviors that are emitted in response to environmental events presented by another person or persons (e.g., cues, demands, or other communications) and are followed by positive environmental responses. In many programs involving social skills for children, self-help skills (e.g., grooming) are also regarded as social skills, since they initially are taught in a social context and involve positive consequences from others. The goal of teaching self-help skills, however, is eventual performance of those behaviors independent of others. Social skills discussed in this volume will be limited, for the most part, to those behaviors which involve interaction between the child and his peers or adults where the primary intent is the achievement of the child's or adult's goals through positive interactions. As may be seen in Chapter 7, however, with handicapped populations, some simple, nonsocial behaviors may need to be taught as prerequisites to make subsequent social skills possible.

FACTORS IN SOCIAL SKILL SELECTION

In determining what social skills should be taught to children, the problem can be approached both as a general set of norms defined by various experts as behaviors necessary for competence as a child in our culture and specifically in

7

terms of what behaviors are needed by an individual child to be regarded as competent.

Social skill instruction in many ways is similar to the teaching of academic behaviors. Tyler (1949), in a discussion of curriculum development, suggests that instructional objectives should emerge from the three sources of *the learner, contemporary society,* and *subject specialists* or *experts.* That is, first one must consider the characteristics of the learner which may influence what is taught and the manner it is presented. Second, the immediate and larger society present conditions which mandate particular learning experiences in order to insure eventual adjustment in that environment. And finally, within any teaching area, there exists a resource of basic information as identified by subject specialists that should be used as the basis for the instructional content.

Developmental Theories

Looking at learner characteristics as a way of identifying social skills to be taught, one relevant set of criteria is that suggested by developmental theories. It may be debated whether behavior always develops according to the stages outlined by various theorists, whether some behaviors can be more easily taught and maintained at one stage than at another, and which behaviors need to be taught or simply result inevitably from maturation. At the same time, the stage theories do provide broad indexes for social development and assist in the task of determining the sequence in which social behaviors are taught. The developmental theories briefly outlined below include those of Freud, Erikson, and Piaget, along with Kohlberg's model for moral development and Hewett's application of developmental theory to the education process.

Freud, through psychoanalytic theory, provides a five-stage developmental system based on psycho-sexual constructs. Stressing biological functions (oral, first year; anal, 1-3 years; phallic or oedipal, 3-5 years; latency, 5-12 years; genital, 12 years to adult), each stage reflects common human experiences that produce conflicts to be resolved. The social implications are that, according to this model, positive attributes or behaviors are acquired by children who successfully progress through each crisis stage. The reverse is the case for those unable to resolve the respective conflicts. For example, early social behaviors are centered around the mother or other principal caretaker with a gradual widening of relationships to others in the home and outside. Central to Freudian theory is the concept of necessary conflict resolution through which the child learns to share relationships and handle feelings of jealousy and anger, theoretically through identification with the same-sex parent (a process which might be said to involve the social skill of imitation or modeling). During "latency," the period when peers and

school interests increase in importance, one criterion for successful development would be an increased emphasis on peer relations as opposed to child-
adult interactions.

In an extension of Freud's psychoanalytic model, Erikson (1963) presents
an eight-stage developmental system of socialization extending from infancy through adulthood, with a set of conflicts to be mastered at each stage,
primarily through the development of social behaviors. The first year of life
is marked by the stage of *Trust versus Mistrust* where a sense of trust
emerges from a secure relationship with parents. During the second year,
the child enters the stage of *Autonomy versus Shame and Doubt.* As parental control is relaxed, the child begins to gain greater control over his own
actions; insecurity, shame, and doubt may occur if too much negative external control is exercised. The *Initiative versus Guilt* stage at approximately
three years of age is characterized by the child's increased physical mobility
and greater freedom in exploring the environment. Successful progression
through this stage will increase the likelihood that the child will emerge an
initiating individual, tending to pursue interests without fear or guilt. During the school years, the child enters the *Industry versus Inferiority* stage.
At this point, school tasks and relationships outside the family gain importance. Failure to achieve in learning tasks and/or to establish good peer
relationships may contribute to a sense of inferiority. The next stage of
Identity versus Role Diffusion occurs from puberty through adolescence.
This is the period during which the child must find his own identity and
determine personal roles that are compatible with the larger society. The
adult stages are *Intimacy versus Isolation, Generativity versus Stagnation,*
and *Integrity versus Despair* and respectively address the issues of one's
ability to enter mutual relationships based on trust, to engage in various
forms of parenting and, during aging, to view one's life with a sense of integrity or acceptance rather than despair.

Erikson suggests that the appropriately-socialized child successfully
moves through a series of stages that begin with trust in others and
culminate in adulthood with a realistic, socially-approved sense of himself.
In Erikson's frame of reference, early social behaviors that develop through
the relationship with parents and early caretakers involve the infant's ability
to take, to give, and to get others to care for his needs. Also important is the
young child's ability to accept adult demands for regulation in various bodily functions as well as in his movement around his environment. Social
responses developed with early caretakers become expressed in widening
circles with siblings, peers, and other adults; and behaviors involving independence and initiative take on increasing value. In any process of
socialization, early social behaviors are taught by parents and caretakers
through their responses and their examples. A social skills curriculum for
the older child can only attempt to recapitulate early stages of development

as they are reflected in the classroom or therapeutic setting. An example of a program involving the application of developmental concepts in a socialization curriculum is that of Wood (1975) described later in this chapter.

While the preceding developmental theories stressed psychological factors contributing to eventual socialization, Piaget (Inhelder & Piaget, 1964) presents a theory that focuses on cognitive development. Most relevant to the contents of this book, is the Piagetian (1965) developmental sequence for moral development. In this system, Piaget analyzes children's play behavior relative to rules and games and specifies four stages: (1) motor development, (2) egocentric, (3) mutual cooperation, and (4) development of moral principles. During the first stage of motor development, the child's play is largely motor and individualistic in nature. By the time the child nears the second (i.e., egocentric stage), occurring approximately between the ages of two and five, the child has begun to apply rules to daily activities. This use of rules is not based on moral judgment, but rather results from the external control of adults and older children, whose standards the child views at this point as absolute and correct. As the child moves into the third stage of mutual cooperation, the belief in the absolute nature of external rules is modified, and the child begins to establish rules according to the particular social circumstances. However, at this stage, the interests of others are an important consideration in rule formulation. At approximately 11 or 12 years of age, the child enters the last stage with the recognition of moral principles in the establishment of social order. During this period, the child begins to recognize the functional importance of rules, the importance of the rights of others, and the importance of rules in the social order, i.e., as a mechanism for protecting individual rights. Although this model presents moral development in stages, these stages are not considered to be mutually exclusive for elements of each exist at all levels, e.g. aspects of cooperation and motor development occur during the egocentric stage. The difference, according to Piaget, is in the degree in which specific behavior patterns are found in the respective stages.

Kohlberg (1969) builds on these ideas with a six-stage developmental theory suggesting that morality evolves from primarily egotistical considerations (stages 1 & 2), to interest in maintaining order and stability (stages 3 & 4), to the highest levels (stages 5 & 6) where the individual adheres to inner principles, defining his behavior according to conscience and convictions rather than simply by laws and regulations. Within Kohlberg's model, children with delinquent behaviors are operating at the lower egotistical levels where the emphasis is on personal gain and the avoidance of punishment. Using this framework, direct instruction, gradually moving through the developmental stages, would be recommended in order to improve social behaviors. An application of this model in social skill instruction is discussed by Bash and Camp in Chapter 5.

If one accepts these hierarchies related to moral development as presented by Piaget and Kohlberg, the implications for selection of social skills would be, for example, that behaviors such as sharing and cooperative play could most easily be taught after the age of two, and that acceptance of authority through following directions and understanding consequences can be taught much earlier than behaviors involving independent decision making. Also implied is that social skills involving empathy or understanding of another's point of view could most easily be taught at a later stage, and that principles based on one's inner beliefs probably are best established after one recognizes the importance of order and regulation.

Hewett (1968), in an effort to make developmental theories more educationally relevant, presents a developmental sequence of educational goals consisting of: Attention, Response, Order, Exploratory, Social Mastery, and Achievement. The first stage of *Attention* is characterized by the child's ability to attend to relevant stimuli, a prerequisite for all learning. Once the child learns to attend, learning cannot proceed until some response is made to the stimuli. In the second or *Response* stage, emphasis is placed upon helping the child to interact actively with the environment in order to facilitate learning. In the third, *Order* stage, the child must learn to follow rules or to proceed according to an established routine. The *Exploratory* stage is the next step in the learning process which is enhanced through exploring and investigating one's environment. The *Social* stage of this hierarchy considers the social factors that affect learning. Since learning is a social event, especially in school, children must learn the mode for interacting with both adults and peers. The ultimate goal of all learning experiences is mastery. At the *Mastery* level the learner is expected to perform the task independently and with proficiency. The final and highest level is *Achievement*. Self-motivation gains importance at the achievement level where the child attempts to perfect and elaborate on learning beyond the point of mastery. At this level, the child takes pride in accomplishment.

An early step in determining social skill instruction is to view the child according to developmental standards and identify the progression needed for desired performance. For example, the elementary-aged child who should be competent in school tasks but is experiencing particular difficulty may first need to learn how to attend before engaging in higher level activities. In order to respond to social skills training, the child may need to learn first to attend, to identify relevant stimuli, and to make required responses to the stimuli. A developmental hierarchy like that of Hewett which makes it possible to define skill sequences according to learning stages can presumably make instruction more relevant for a particular child.

Social Criteria in Skill Selection

The models cited above do not provide precise specifications for teaching but, rather, standards for emotional, social, cognitive and moral development that enable the practitioner to gauge levels of development. In selecting skills for a particular child or group of children, a number of social criteria in addition to developmental stages need to be considered. There is much variety of opinion in different parts of society, among groups of professionals, even within families, and certainly over time, about how children should act. For example, rather than being "seen and not heard" as in days of yore, children are now being taught assertiveness, measured in terms of loudness of speech, eye contact, duration of speech, and ability to make requests (Bornstein, Bellack, & Hersen, 1977). On the other hand, in rating social skills they considered important for success in their class, a group of teachers valued more highly the skills concerned with order, cooperative behavior, accepting consequences, following rules and directions, avoiding conflict, and basic self-help behavior. They valued relatively less the skills which involved initiating contact with others, greeting and conversation skills, being assertive in interpersonal relationships, and performing for others (Milburn, 1974). Critics of the use of behavior modification techniques point out that these procedures are being used too often to develop quiet, controlled, docile, conforming behaviors, the "model" child:

who stays glued to his seat and desk all day, continually looks at his teacher or his text/workbook, does not talk to or in fact look at other children, does not talk unless asked to by the teacher, hopefully does not laugh or sing (or at the wrong time), and assuredly passes silently in the halls. [Winnett and Winkler, 1972, p. 501]

This criticism notwithstanding, a number of studies have identified specific classroom "survival skills" which are highly correlated with academic success. These include attending, volunteering answers, complying with teacher requests, following teacher directions, and remaining on task.

The cultural context of social behaviors is another important consideration for the selection of social skills to teach a given child. Numerous examples exist of cultural differences: people from different cultures stand at different distances from one another; children in some cultural groups are taught not to look at others directly; children in some families or subcultures are taught to hit back rather than engage in some alternative to counteraggression. Clearly, the teacher or therapist who is concerned with helping the child to be more effective in interpersonal relationships must consider what adult and peer behavior norms exist in the child's wider environment. The views of the child himself and those in his peer group about what social behaviors are most desirable need to be considered, and these change with age. For example, Rotheram (1978) found that, among adolescents, ninth graders were more concerned with relationships with authority figures (parents and teachers), than were twelfth grade students for whom peer relationships were most salient. The child's opinions are particularly important for providing motivation to engage in social skills learning tasks.

Most often, the need for social skills training for an individual child arises because of an excess of some behavior considered to be undesirable, where the problem is seen to exist because the child does not have the related acceptable behaviors in his repertoire. The selection of what more desirable behaviors should be taught to replace the problematic ones depends, as suggested above, on many factors, often including subjective assessment on the part of the concerned adult. Techniques exist to teach children almost anything that is within their comprehension and capabilities. For that reason, in selecting social skills for children it seems particularly important to choose those behaviors that will have value to them. The "Relevance of Behavior Rule" of Allyon and Azrin (1968) states "Teach only those behaviors that will continue to be reinforced after training." In the selection of social skills, application of this rule would help to assure that the behaviors required have some intrinsic value to the child, will benefit the child, and are valued by others in the child's environment who will reward their occurrence.

Some bases for selecting social skills are implied in Wolf's (1978) discussion of social validity as a criterion for determining what are socially significant problems for behavior change efforts. Social validity, according to Wolf, can best be established by consumers or representatives of the relevant community according to such criteria as whether the behaviors have social significance in relation to goals desired by society, whether the procedures used to bring about behavior change are acceptable, and whether the effects or results of behavior change are satisfactory to the relevant consumers. As is pointed out in Chapter 4, the extent to which social skills are generalized and maintained depends to a great extent on environmental responses that keep the behaviors going. Selection and teaching of social skills that are meaningful to the consumers or audiences (i.e., the child, his peers, parents, and significant others in his environment) should assist considerably in the task of maintaining the skills over time.

SOCIAL SKILLS INVENTORIES

In order to teach social skills, the skills must first be identified. Several lists or inventories of social behaviors have been developed which can be useful to the practitioner in selecting skills to teach to an individual child or group.

Because of the many variables involved in determining the selection of social behaviors, it may be difficult to find a social skills inventory that meets all the needs of the individual child or specific group, and the practitioner may need to add more behaviors or delete some that are not relevant to the child or the social situation. Inventories do provide a useful place to start, however, and can aid in the assessment of social skills deficits. Samples of social skills inventories are presented below, including one by Wood (1975) for the young, emotionally-disturbed child, one by Stephens (1978) for the elementary age child, and a primary-level inventory by Turnbull, Strickland, and Brantley (1978). These inventories are all generated specifically for use in school settings and serve as the basis for teaching curricula. There is currently a lack of social skills inventories with behaviors more broadly oriented toward the home or residential setting and the community.

The teaching model developed by Wood (1975) for young, handicapped children incorporates many of the principles of the previously mentioned developmental theorists. It attempts to provide a functional system to be used in teaching the emotionally disturbed child. The model presents specific behavior goals according to the five stages of development, each of which includes the four "curriculum" areas of Behavior, Communication, Socialization and (pre) Academics. See table 1.1.

The behavior goals are further broken down into specific objectives. For example, the stage II socialization goal of participating successfully in activities with others includes the following skills:

STAGE II - SOCIALIZATION GOAL:
TO PARTICIPATE IN ACTIVITIES WITH OTHERS

1. to *participate spontaneously* in specific parallel activities with another child using similar materials but not interacting.
2. to *wait* without physical intervention by teachers. (Verbal support or touch may be used.)
3. to initiate appropriate minimal movement toward another child within the classroom routine. (Child, through gesture and action, begins minimal appropriate social interaction with another child.)
4. to participate in a verbally directed sharing activity. (Child passes materials or gives toy to another.)

    Examples:
    a. Child passes cookies within the classroom structure.
    b. Child gives toy to another. (Verbal cues may be used.)
    c. Child can use same paint, water, or box of crayons that another child is using.

5. to *participate* in cooperative activities or projects with another child during play time, indoor or outdoor. (Child is involved actively with another child; verbal support or touch may be used.)
6. to *participate* in cooperative activities or projects with another child during organized class activities. (Child is involved actively with others; verbal support or touch may be used.)
[Wood, 1975, p. 278]

Table 1.1. Developmental Therapy Goals for Each Curriculum Area at Each Stage of Therapy

Stage	Behavior	Communication	Socialization	Academic Skills
I	To trust own body and skills	To use words to gain needs	To trust an adult sufficiently to respond to him	To respond to the environment with processes of classification, discrimination, basic receptive language concepts and body coordination
II	To successfully participate in routines and activities	To use words to affect others in constructive ways	To participate in activities with others	To participate in classroom routines with language concepts of similarities and differences, labels, use color; numerical processes of ordering and classifying; and body coordination
III	To apply individual skills in group processes	To use words to express oneself in the group	To find satisfaction in group activities	To participate in the group with basic expressive language concepts; functional semi-concrete concepts; of conservation; of conservation; and body coordination
IV	To contribute individual effort to group success	To use words to express awareness of relationship between feelings and behavior in self and others	To participate spontaneously and successfully as a group member	To successfully use signs and symbols in formalized school work and in group experiences
V	To respond to critical life experiences with adaptive constructive behavior	To use words to establish and enrich relationships	To initiate and maintain effective peer group relationships independently	To successfully use signs and symbols for formalized school experiences and personal enrichment

Source: Wood, 1975, p. 9.

15

A similar skill listing is provided for each goal presented in the developmental therapy curriculum, essentially analyzing each goal into specific responses which comprise that behavior class. Another feature underscoring the utility of the Wood inventory is the fact that the objectives are listed as observable behaviors, and conditions for performance are specified.

While the Wood inventory was developed primarily for young children in special settings with "serious emotional and behavioral disorders," Stephens (1978) has published a social skills curriculum for the classroom that encompasses a greater age range and is not restricted to special populations. Using a task analysis model, the behaviors are grouped into four major categories—Environmental, Interpersonal, Self-Related, and Task-Related behaviors—which are further analyzed into 30 subcategories and 136 specific skills. Subcategory headings include:

SELF-RELATED BEHAVIORS

Accepting Consequences
Ethical Behavior
Expressing Feelings
Positive Attitude toward Self
Responsible Behavior
Self Care

ENVIRONMENTAL BEHAVIORS

Care for the Environment
Dealing with Emergency
Lunchroom Behavior
Movement around Environment

TASK-RELATED BEHAVIORS

Asking and Answering Questions
Attending Behavior
Classroom Discussion
Completing Tasks
Following Directions
Group Activities
Independent Work
On-Task Behavior
Performing Before Others
Quality of Work

INTERPERSONAL BEHAVIORS

Accepting Authority
Coping with Conflict
Gaining Attention
Greeting Others
Helping Others
Making Conversation
Organized Play
Positive Attitude Toward Others
Playing Informally
Property: Own and Others [Pp. 30-38]

Specific responses have been identified for each subcategory. A sample category, subcategory and skill listing follows:

Major Category: INTERPERSONAL BEHAVIORS

Sub-Category: Coping with Conflict (CC)

Skills: To respond to teasing or name-calling by ignoring, changing the subject, or using some other constructive means.

To respond to physical assault by leaving the situation, calling for help, or using some other constructive means.

To walk away from peer when angry to avoid hitting.

To refuse the request of another politely.

To express anger with nonaggressive words rather than physical action or aggressive words.

To handle constructively criticism or punishment perceived as undeserved. [P. 121]

The Stephens skill listings were developed through a social validation process. The inventory was generated from classroom observation and teacher interviews, along with a content analysis of 13 problem behavior checklists or behavior scales for elementary age children. It was then submitted to a large number of regular and special education teachers to identify which behaviors they considered most important for success in the school environment (Milburn, 1974). For a complete skill listing the reader is referred to *Social Skills in the Classroom* (Stephens, 1978).

Another inventory of social competence skills has been provided by Turnbull, Strickland, and Brantley (1978). Like that of Stephens, this listing is divided according to categories, subcategories, and specific skills. A special feature of this inventory is that the skills are identified according to primary, intermediate, junior high, and senior high levels. The following is a sample from the primary level:

SOCIAL COMPETENCE–PRIMARY LEVEL

I. Socialization
   1. Has good group relationships:
      _____ a. Shares books, crayons, pencils, etc.
      _____ b. Takes turns in group games, at water fountain, etc.
      _____ c. Accepts limits set by teacher, principal, and janitor.
      _____ d. Avoids unnecessary tattling.
      _____ e. Avoids using physical force against others.
      _____ f. Takes care of property.
      _____ g. Begins to be aware of feelings of others.
      _____ h. Has a friendly disposition.
      _____ i. Obeys rules at home and school.
      _____ j. Treats others as he would like to be treated.
      _____ k. Begins to develop a sense of right and wrong.

   2. Engages in courteous behavior:
      _____ a. Uses terms such as please, thank you, and excuse me at appropriate times.
      _____ b. Demonstrates knowledge of when and where to place hands on others.
      _____ c. Greets teacher and peers pleasantly in the morning.

II. Understanding and Accepting Oneself
  1. Understands self emotionally and physically:
    _____ a. Recognizes and tells full name.
    _____ b. Recognizes and tells address, birth date, age, and telephone number.
    _____ c. Knows and tells race and religion.
    _____ d. Verbalizes things he likes and dislikes.
    _____ e. Engages in play activities appropriate to age and sex.
    _____ f. Identifies times when he is happy and sad.
    _____ g. Says people differ in appearance.
    _____ h. Explains that his physical and emotional well-being affect the way he does school work.
    _____ i. Begins to accept any physical limitation.

  2. Understands assets and limitations:
    _____ a. Explains that everyone has strengths and weaknesses.
    _____ b. Recognizes and tells about individual differences within class.
    _____ c. Identifies his own major strengths and weaknesses.

  3. Establishes feelings of self-respect:
    _____ a. Takes pride in accomplishment.
    _____ b. Continues to try after experiencing failure. [P. 308]

Developed primarily as an aid for special education teachers in designing individualized education programs, this skill listing is not as extensive or precise as those of Stephens or Wood and points out some of the difficulties in generating and categorizing lists of behavior. A practitioner using this checklist would, for example, undoubtedly wish to add more items in every category, might question the placement of items, and would certainly want to further operationalize such statements as "takes pride in accomplishment" in order to define behavior to teach.

The three preceding social skills inventories were developed primarily for younger children in educational settings. An example of an inventory generated by Goldstein, Sprafkin, Gershaw, and Klein for use with adolescents in either a classroom or clinical setting is presented in Chapter 9. This group of skills has aggressive adolescents as a target population but is applicable to younger children as well. These skills form the basis for the Structured Learning curriculum which Goldstein and his colleagues describe in Chapter 9. As in the preceding inventories, each skill is analyzed into a set of behavioral steps that can be translated into specific teaching objectives. There is considerable similarity among all these inventories, even taking into consideration the differing intended populations.

The inventories described above encompass a broad range of social skills that to varying degrees include behaviors related to affective and cognitive processes. Some additional lists of behaviors that are specific to cognitive or affective dimensions of social skills are described below.

Cognitive Behaviors

Cognitive processes are being increasingly recognized as important deter-minants of social functioning and, therefore, necessary elements in the development and use of social skills. For example, negative self-defeating or negative cognitions and mental images may interfere with the child's will-ingness to learn or perform newly-learned social skills. The child's ability to assess contingencies, as well as his ability to discriminate salient aspects of social situations, may determine his social responses. His social competence is also enhanced by the possession of cognitive problem-solving skills. One cognitive program is presented by Spivack and Shure (1974) in their book, *Social Adjustment of Young Children.* The purpose of this program is to help children conceptualize social problems accurately, to identify alter-native solutions to the problem, and to perceive the possible consequences to their behavior. Although Spivack and Shure do not provide an inventory, they do specify general and specific abilities that constitute the problem solving process.

General Abilities
1. sensitivity to human problems
2. ability to imagine alternative courses of action
3. ability to conceptualize means to solve a problem
4. sensitivity to consequences and cause and effects in human behavior (pp. 20, 21)

Specific Skills
1. Prerequisite language and thinking skills*
   a. Words for alternatives
      * or
      * not
      * and
   b. Words for people's preferences
      * some
      * same
      * different
   c. Words describing emotions/feelings
      * happy
      * sad
      * mad
2. Learning new content with familiar words, focusing on people rather than objects
   a. People words
      * boy
      * girl
3. Developing concepts with previously listed words, i.e., emphasis placed on using words in various contexts to demonstrate understanding, grammatical accuracy deemphasized
4. Seeking and evaluating alternative solutions
   a. Words for alternative solutions
      * maybe
      * might
      * if - then

b. Words for consequential thinking
  • Why - because

*Note: Although these words are listed in isolation, the program stresses their functional use. (See example in Chapter 3)

5. Evaluating own ideas and solutions, i.e. children personally assess manner in which they handled problem

The use of cognitions for positively directing overt behavior has also been stressed by Meichenbaum. He identifies a set of abilities which can be translated into self-statements to assist in problem solving. In the following example these are used for cognitive tasks:

1. ability to define the problem ("What is it that I have to do?")
2. ability to focus attention and guide responses through self-statements ("carefully . . . draw the line down")
3. ability to administer self-reinforcement ("Good, I'm doing fine.")
4. ability to evaluate and correct one's performance ("That's okay. . . . Even if I make an error I can go on slowly.")   [Meichenbaum and Goodman, 1971, p. 32]

The importance of language in cognitive models becomes obvious to reviewing the above skills and abilities. The child needs to have the functional use of various words and phrases before engaging in higher level reasoning or understanding the relationships of various events. The specific skills listed in the Spivack and Shure program emerged from an analysis of the higher level general abilities and the realization that their particular population had language deficits that limited reasoning abilities. For teaching purposes, as with other behaviors, cognitions need to be operationalized into overt responses. For example, "understands cause and effect" is not as observable as, "is able to state a reasonable consequence for wrong doing." The behaviors taken from the Meichenbaum-Goodman model are specific and observable, but they involve relatively higher level language skills, suggesting that for children functioning at lower levels exhibiting language deficits it may be necessary to analyze these responses into lower level prerequisites.

Affective Behaviors

Although emotions or feelings are private events, difficult to measure except through their overt behavioral expressions, the emotions and their manifestations have a role in social skills training. Izard (1977) has defined certain emotions, i.e., interest-excitement, joy, surprise, distress-anguish, anger-rage, disgust-revulsion, contempt-scorn, fear-terror, shame-shyness-humiliation, and guilt as "fundamental emotions," which in combination form other emotional states—anxiety, depression, love, hostility, and hate. Like negative cognitions to which they are related, fear, anxiety, and resulting shyness can interfere with learning and performing social behaviors. Social skills training dealing with emotions can have several interrelated aspects. At the most basic level it has to begin with recognizing and labeling the experiencing of feelings in oneself, followed by recognizing and labeling the expression of emotions in others. The ultimate goal involves learning appropriate or acceptable ways to express a variety of feelings under varying stimulus conditions as well as ways to eliminate or modify dysfunctional affects in order to enhance social interaction. A taxonomy developed by Krathwohl, Bloom, and Masia (1956) presents a hierarchy of affective-cognitive behaviors, progressing from the lowest to highest level behaviors. The following listing of the Krathwohl et al. taxonomy gives a brief description of the major category and a sample affective objective for the subcategories in parenthesis.

1.0 Receiving (Attending)
(The lowest level affective classification, these behaviors refer to the child's "willingness" to attend to relevant stimuli in the learning situation.)
1.1 Awareness
(Develops awareness of aesthetic factors in good art and the like.)
1.2 Willingness to Receive
(Appreciation and tolerance of cultural patterns exhibited by individuals from other religious groups.)
1.3 Controlled or selected Attention
(Alertness toward human values and judgments on life as they are recorded in literature.)
2.0 Responding
(At the next level learner begins to interact or show "interest" in relevant stimuli.)
2.1 Acquiescence in Responding
(Obeys the playground regulations.)
2.2 Willingness to Respond
(Acceptance of responsibility for his own health and for the protection of the health of others.)
2.3 Satisfaction in Response
(Takes pleasure in conversing with many different kinds of people.)
3.0 Valuing
(At this point, the individual's overt behaviors are guided more by internal "attitudes" or values than by simply observing rules and regulations.)
3.1 Acceptance of a Value
(Grows in a sense of kinship with human beings of all nations.)
3.2 Preference of a Value
(Assumes responsibility for drawing reticent members of a group into conversation.)
3.3 Commitment
(Devotion to those ideas and ideals which are the foundations of democracy.)
4.0 Organization
(As values increase in number, individual must analyze, organize, and prioritize into value system.)
4.1 Conceptualization of a Value
(Attempts to identify the characteristics of an art object which he admires.)

4.2 Organization of a Value System
(Weighs alternative social policies and practices against the standards of the public welfare rather than the advantage of specialized and narrow interest groups.)
5.0 Characterization by a Value or Value Complex
(At the highest level of this hierarchy the individual has internalized the value system as indicated by consistent behavior.)
5.1 Generalized Set
(Judges problems and issues in terms of situations, issues, purposes, and consequences involved rather than in terms of fixed, dogmatic precepts or emotionally wishful thinking.)
5.2 Characterization
(Develops a consistent philosophy of life.)

Theoretically, according to this sequence, the child's affective development follows a pattern in which he first becomes aware of his surroundings, then learns to comply with the existing rules and regulations in his environment, and finally moves through the process of developing a personal value system. One's behavior and value system are considered to be inseparable, in that our beliefs are reflected by behavior. Therefore, the instructional goal is to help the child acquire values that foster humane, positive attitudes toward others, anticipating that the child's social behaviors will develop accordingly.

Another source for identifying affective behaviors which may be useful in teaching social skills is the "Developing Understanding of Self and Others (DUSO)" program (Dinkmeyer, 1973) which was designed to facilitate social/emotional development for young children with special needs. Compared to the model designed by Krathwohl and his colleagues, which identifies general categories from which more specific objectives must be derived, the DUSO program is more applied in that teaching activities are provided for the various affective and social behaviors to be developed. The progression of learning begins with developing a sense of oneself, proceeding to an awareness of one's own feelings associated with various life experiences. This second stage is followed by the sharing of affective experiences or identification of similar feelings with others, leading to the development of sense of empathy. Finally, as a result of empathizing with others, it is felt that the child will develop a sense of equality with others ("I'm OK—You're OK"). Schematically, the model may be viewed as illustrated below:

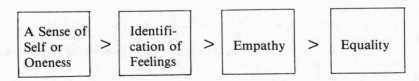

Some of the feelings or affective experiences identified in the DUSO program include:

- Identifies feelings associated with group interaction (e.g., enjoyment, shyness, recognition, etc.). etc.).
- Demonstrates feelings of self-worth and value as an individual by coping with the environment to the best of his abilities, and accepting his capabilities in just being himself.
- Demonstrates acceptance and understanding of the individuality of others, through the recognition of differing needs, purposes, and abilities.
- Demonstrates that even though people are different, they can still work together.
- Demonstrates a recognition and acceptance of personal imperfections and, at the same time, evidences discovery and building of individual strengths.
- Demonstrates the ability verbally to identify various ways of coping with rejection (e.g., sit alone and cry, find some other activity to entertain oneself).
- Demonstrates an understanding that emotions normally fluctuate, that it is not necessary to stop loving someone when he misbehaves, or that others no longer care for us when their actions displease us.
- Demonstrates a sensitivity to the feeling of others.
- Demonstrates an acceptance of one's limitations without feeling inadequate regarding one's total self.
- Demonstrates the ability to make value judgments and to accept the consequences of one's choices.
- Demonstrates a sense of equality by recognizing that each individual is a person of value, and that every other person is just as important to himself as I am to myself. (This concept facilitates empathy, courtesy, and respect for others.)

As with Krathwohl et al., the DUSO program suggests a sequence of learning for affective development. Although it is not explicitly designed for this purpose, a useful affective inventory can be devised from the DUSO program by listing the behaviors to be taught as discrete skills. A consideration for both the Krathwohl and DUSO programs is the need to specify the overt manifestations of the identified affective states. For example, what behaviors are indicative of "recognition and acceptance of personal imperfections" or "evidences discovery and building of individual strengths"? The DUSO program tends to emphasize the role and use of emotions in social development, whereas the Krathwohl taxonomy stresses values and belief systems. To varying degrees, both programs are designed to assist the child in understanding self and others, in identifying and clari-fying emotions, in identifying and clarifying values, and in developing overt behaviors that are congruent with identified affective states. Since value systems and manner of emotional expression vary among social groups, any inventory would need to be devised to reflect the orientation of a particular group, while simultaneously adhering to the regulations of the larger so-ciety.

Several criteria for evaluation can be applied by the practitioner choosing among social skills inventories and curricula related to social, cognitive, and affective behaviors. One of these is the extent to which the skills outlined have been operationalized and developed into behaviorally-stated objec-tives which facilitate instruction. Others relate to the appropriateness of the materials to the developmental level and deficits of the children involved, and the relevance to the social and cultural values of the particular target group. To be most useful, the suggested skills will be seen as valuable to the child, his peers, and the adults in his various social environments. Because of the ways in which values and situational needs differ among persons and groups, definitive all-encompassing, social skills inventories and curricula may never be possible. As mentioned earlier, the practitioner will usually want to make changes in existing approaches to fit a particular clinical or teaching situation.

INDIVIDUALIZING SKILL SELECTION

In the process of selecting and developing specific social skills for instruc-tion to meet individual needs, two sets of procedures are particularly useful. One is the formulating of behavioral objectives stated in positive terms, and the other is the analysis of broadly-stated social behaviors into subcom-ponents. As mentioned earlier, the need for social skills training often is identified because of a problem or deficit. Social skills training involves helping children discard some behaviors and substitute more acceptable ones. Many of the problem behaviors displayed by children have opposite or incompatible desirable behaviors which could be taught or increased in frequency. For example:

Problem Behaviors	*Social Skills*
1. The child calls others by uncomplimentary names	1. The child makes positive remarks to others
2. The child frequently interrupts the conversation of others	2. the child waits for pauses in the conversations before speaking

3. The child makes negative statements about his/her ability
4. The child cheats when playing games with peers
5. The child tantrums when teased by peers
6. The child laughs at or ignores individual in need of help

3. The child identifies something (s)he does well
4. The child plays games according to rules
5. The child responds to peer teasing by ignoring or some other appropriate responses
6. The child assists individual in need of help

As previously indicated, the social goals we have for children are generally conceptualized in global terms, e.g., "to play cooperatively" or "to assume responsibility." Operationalizing such goals into their subcomponents assists in the process of defining behaviors to be taught. Although there are several models for analyzing a task, the essential steps involve (1) specifying the desired behavior, (2) identifying the subskills of the composite behavior, (3) stating the subskills in terms of observable behaviors, (4) sequencing the subskills according to order of instruction, (5) identifying and implementing appropriate instructional strategies, and (6) evaluating results.

Moyer and Dardig (1978) present several practical approaches to task analysis. A method developed by Mager (1972) that is especially applicable to social or affective behaviors is summarized by Moyer and Dardig as follows:

1. Write the goal on paper.
2. List the observable behaviors a person would exhibit to show that he or she has attained the goal.
3. Review the list, discarding those behaviors that should not be included and identifying those in need of clarification.
4. Describe what is intended for each goal on the list by determining how frequently or how well the behavior must be performed.
5. Test the statements for adequacy and completeness by determining whether the behaviors in the final list represent comprehensive attainment of the goal. [P. 18]

For a practical application of these guidelines, consider the situation of primary aged children who tend to be overly aggressive and disagreeable in play situations. Stated in positive terms, the social goal would be to develop "cooperative play behaviors." An example of a systematic performance analysis of this composite behavior is presented below.

1. When presented with an informal play period, the child will approach a peer and suggest a cooperative play activity. (Example: "Let's use these blocks to build a big house.")
2. When engaged in a joint play activity with a peer, the child will suggest respective responsibilities, working toward a common goal. (Example: "I will make this wall and you can make the other one.")
3. While engaged in a cooperative play activity with a peer, the child will participate according to the established rules or procedures. (Example: If it has been previously established how the structure should be built, the child will adhere to this decision unless the matter is fairly renegotiated with all parties.)
4. While engaged in a joint play activity with another peer, the child will assist the other child, if necessary, and refrain from disrupting or abusing his/her partner. (Example: "Here is another block for your wall.")
5. While engaged in a cooperative play activity with a peer, the child will make positive comments to his/her partner. (Example: "I like the big wall you built.")
6. Following a cooperative play activity, the child will work with peer to put away play materials.

In analyzing social behaviors, certain factors become obvious. First, social behaviors do not readily lend themselves to sequential listing. For example, the subskills in the preceding analysis have been sequenced according to more temporal considerations rather than stated as prerequisites to the subsequent skill. Second, the extent and exact form of the analysis are relative to the specific population. For example, in the above listing, assumptions were made regarding the child's oral language skills. Youngsters experiencing difficulties in spontaneous oral language may need instruction in prerequisite language skills, such as extending an invitation to a peer or making positive statements, before they are expected to make these statements in play situations. Finally, by specifying the exact responses and conditions, the performance and evaluation processes are facilitated. The task analysis process enables both the child and the evaluator to know what is expected and when the responses are to occur, essential aspects of social skill instruction.

SUMMARY

Before social skill instruction can take place, it is necessary to determine what skills are important for children to learn. A number of considerations enter into the identification of social skills, among them the child's developmental level, which may facilitate or retard learning and retaining of skills, the views of persons who make up the child's environment, and the likelihood that given social skills will be valued and reinforced by others once they are learned.

Skill selection can be based on inventories of social skills that include behavioral, affective, and cognitive dimensions. Skill selection can also be based on an assessment of individual deficits in social skills.

The therapist or teacher can turn the child's problem behaviors into opportunities for social skill instruction through the development of positively stated objectives, further analyzed into specific components through a task analysis process.

Chapter 2
Assessment and Evaluation of Social Skills

Assessment can take many forms, from fleeting observational impressions to systematic recording or use of standardized instruments. Why should a social skills teaching program involve assessment? Social skills can certainly be taught without the sometimes difficult and time-consuming task of prior assessment to determine the extent to which a skill is in the child's repertoire. For researchers, rigorous assessment is, of course, a necessity in order to create a basis for measuring the effects of social skills teaching on behavior change. For teachers and clinicians, the most effective interventions also involve assessment, since they, too, must be concerned with the effectiveness of their efforts. Assessment helps provide hypotheses about what skills the child lacks and needs to be taught and some understanding about why skill deficits exist. Assessment helps determine whether the problem is that of teaching a new behavior or, instead, that of arranging the environment in such a way as to encourage the performance of a behavior the child has in his repertoire but does not display.

Mager and Pipe (1970) have presented a paradigm which is useful to consider in looking at the question of assessment for social skill instruction. They suggest that problem behavior (in this case, lack of social skill in some area) may exist because the desired behavior is not known or has not been taught, because the reinforcing conditions are not sufficient to encourage the behavior, or because reinforcement exists for the undesirable problem behavior. A social skill may, thus, be missing because the child may lack information or ability to perform the behavior, because the environment does not provide sufficient encouragement for the behavior even though he may know how to do it, or because there is a payoff for not carrying out the desired social behavior. Beyond this, another related reason for not engaging in a desirable social skill may be the existence of unpleasant feelings such as fear or anxiety associated with the behavior performance, which are avoided by avoiding the behavior. For example, a child may fail to assert himself constructively in a conflict with another child because he does not know how to go about saying or doing appropriately assertive things; because he does not perceive any benefits from saying or doing something he knows how to do; or because, by withdrawing in a nonassertive way, he is able to avoid the anxiety he may experience by taking risks in conflict situations. It could be argued that most behaviors defined as social skills have some goal associated with them, and a child may be faced with having to choose from among several competing goals. In attempting, through assessment, to determine which of these possible alternatives is operating, i.e., whether the problem is one of skill deficit or motivation, the teacher or clinician can determine at what level to pitch the intervention.

Most researchers agree that the development of effective assessment procedures for measuring social skills is still in its infancy. There are many problems associated with assessing social skills that interfere with obtaining valid and reliable measures. One of these is the fact that many behaviors are situation specific, in that a child may display a behavior in one situation but not in another. Such a discrepancy may exist because the conditions that encourage the behavior are different or are perceived by the child to be different in differing situations. In this context, the question of whether one is assessing knowledge of a social skill or ability to perform the behavior becomes an issue. As Bandura (1977a) points out in the social learning theory literature, because people learn many behaviors by observing others, a child may have some cognitive understanding of what would be desirable social behaviors but may not be able to translate the behaviors into actions. It becomes necessary, therefore, to assess both the child's knowledge of a behavior and whether he can perform it under appropriate circumstances. Because motivational factors in the form of reinforcing conditions in the environment may also have some effect on the child's performance of a social behavior, it would seem that the most accurate assessment of performance would take place under highly reinforcing circumstances. Hence, the teacher or practitioner also needs to know what contingencies of reinforcement are operating in order to structure assessment situations in a way to make them highly positive.

A further problem in the assessment of social skills is that of reliability among different persons. There are many sources of data about a child's social behavior, including a variety of adults, peers, and the child himself. Various studies have determined that there is little agreement between researchers and parents, between parents and teachers, and between adults and children in their ratings of subjects on social behavior. Children's self-perceptions about their social behavior do not correlate highly with other's perceptions, but the child's view is still an important piece of assessment information, particularly in relation to motivation for change and response to social skills teaching. The problems with validity and reliability of social skills assessment procedures exist, in part, because of the situational aspects of social skill performance and because of the subjective aspects of looking at social behavior. It was pointed out in the preceding chapter that there are wide variations among persons and groups about what is regarded as acceptable social behavior on the part of children. Such lack of agreement creates problems in establishing criteria for determining when a behavior should be taught or defining criteria for mastery of a newly-taught behavior. Developmental level must also be taken into consideration in establishing criteria. A high school student might be considered to have good greeting skills if he can (1) establish eye contact, (2) smile, (3) say "hello," (4) provide his name, (5) ask for or say the other person's name, and (6) extend his hand and shake hands. A preschool child might be considered to have adequate greeting skills with only the first three or four behaviors.

In discussing criteria, it could be argued that it is sufficient for the teacher or clinician to determine only whether the behavior occurs at all in the desired situations. If the behavior does not occur or occurs very infrequently in a given situation, then teaching of the behavior in that context seems indicated. If the behavior occurs with low frequency and with poor quality, teaching may also be indicated in order to increase the child's ease with the behavior. For example, a child who is able to greet an adult but does so with stammering and lack of eye contact may need practice in greeting skills based on the quality of the responses, even though he demonstrates that he knows what to say.

Regardless of the many difficulties and the embryo state of social skill assessment, some assessment is better than none, and there are a number of possible procedures to use. Assessment procedures selected by the practitioner depend on several factors: (1) the behavior being assessed, (2) whether he is assessing an individual child or a group of children, (3) what other resources in terms of observers and equipment are available, and (4) the developmental level of the child and his ability to read and to provide self-reports. Of the methods outlined below, some involve questionnaires or rating scales of various kinds that can be completed by those knowledgeable about the child — the teacher, parent, other children, or the child himself. Other methods involve observing the child's actual performance of various behaviors, either in the natural environment, or in a situation set up to be analogous to the natural environment. Still other procedures involve ways to test the child's knowledge of social responses, apart from whether or not he can actually perform the behaviors in social situations. Since problems of validity and reliability exist with most social skill assessment approaches, the accuracy of assessment results is enhanced by the use of multiple methods rather than a single method, more than one setting, and input from more than one person.

SCALES AND INVENTORIES

A first step in the formal assessment process may be the employment of rating measures where individuals closely associated with the child—such as parents, teachers, peers, or mental health workers—or the child himself indicate the presence or absence of certain behaviors in the child's repertoire. As an initial procedure, ratings are generally considered to be screenings for identification purposes rather than in-depth comprehensive assessment of social competence. Rating instruments may be classified according to either the person providing the behavior evaluation or the nature of the reporting form. Ratings, by teachers, parents and other adults are most commonly acquired through behavioral checklists. Behavior checklists used for this purpose can be published versions (usually backed up with data related to validity and reliability) or checklists devised by the practitioner to meet a specific need. In addition, social skills inventories can have utility as checklists for assessment, with varying degrees of reliability, depending on the specificity of the items. The Stephens (1978) inventory, for example, was demonstrated to have test-retest reliability of .89 when used for assessment purposes (Feldstein, 1975). Sociometric techniques have been utilized extensively as a method for children to rate their peers. A third rating form, especially for the older child, is the self-report procedure where the youngster completes a checklist or performs some other paper-and-pencil task in order to provide behavior information about himself.

Behavior Checklists

Behavior checklists have been employed extensively to assess child behavior, particularly as viewed by adults closely associated with children. Although in the past such ratings have been considered to have limited validity, there is evidence to suggest that teacher ratings are beneficial in screening the socially incompetent child (Greenwood, Walker, and Hops, 1977). This is especially true for children falling at the extremes. Behavior checklists have certain advantages. They are easy to administer and easy to analyze, making it possible to use copies of the same instrument to obtain responses from several different informants on the same child. For example, one child could be rated by his parents, his teacher, his school counselor, and so forth, each using different copies of the same form. A comparison of the multiple responses would aid in identifying the most salient behaviors to address and some understanding of how the child functions in various settings.

Many of the most popular checklists have been standardized and are used largely with special populations. One such scale is the Adaptive Behavior Scale (American Association on Mental Deficiency, Lambert & Associates, 1974) which has been designed to rate mentally retarded individuals on various social and functional life skills such as language, economics, and domestic activity. A children's version of this scale (The Ohio State University Research Foundation, 1979) includes many of the same categories and a similar oganization as the adult model. The classes of behavior considered under the section of *Personal Responsibility* and *Socialization* include moral development, consideration for others, awareness of others, and personal interaction. A sample subarea follows:

Consideration for Others (Circle only *ONE*)

Usually tries to help other children do the right
  things 5
Tries to get help for a child that is hurt or
  crying 4
Apologizes or tries to do something nice when he/she
  has been unkind. 3
Comforts an unhappy person by hugging him/her,
  talking to him/her, or offering something to make
  him/her feel better. 2
Helps caretaker perform small cooking or cleaning
  tasks 1
Does not help others. 0
Other _____

Part two of the AAMD Adaptive Behavior Scale focuses on maladaptive behaviors which are stated negatively, and range from self-mutilating behaviors (bites or cuts self) to peculiar mannerisms (hugs or kisses people inappropriately in public) to abuse of others (attacks others with sharp instruments). The scale should be completed by someone with a thorough knowledge of the child. It provides a rather extensive list of social behaviors, the profile of which could serve as a guide for subsequent instruction.

The Quay-Peterson Behavior Problem Checklist (Quay & Peterson, 1967) is a rating scale for children and adolescents that emerged from the identification of problem behaviors among normal public school children (grades K-8) and special populations (institutionalized juvenile delinquents, children in classes for the emotionally disturbed, and children seen in child guidance clinics). An analysis of these behaviors resulted in four major factors. The first factor, *conduct disorder*, is characterized by restlessness, attention-seeking, and disruptiveness. *Personality problem*, the second factor, refers to behaviors such as self-consciousness and feelings of inferiority. The third factor, *inadequacy-immaturity*, includes preoccupation and attentional deficits; while behaviors such as gang membership and school truancy make up the fourth factor of *socialized delinquency*. Although the authors state that the items refer to easily-observable behavior, the items tend to refer more to classes of behavior such as impertinence, irritability, and irresponsibility than to specific responses. The Quay-Peterson Checklist has been validated empirically. Its value appears to reside primarily in its usefulness for classifying children according to the four previously mentioned categories of social/emotional disturbance rather than the identification of specific behavioral deficits.

An instrument that provides for the rating of more specific behaviors is the Walker Problem Behavior Identification Checklist (WPBIC), (1976). Standardized on the fourth, fifth, and sixth grade children, this checklist is designed to identify children with behavior problems severe enough to classify them as emotionally disturbed. The checklist contains 50 items which have been factored into five scales of disturbed behavior: (1) acting-out, (2) withdrawal, (3) distractibility, (4) disturbed peer relations, and (5) immaturity. A unique feature of this scale is that it discriminates between boys and girls, allowing for more "problem" behaviors among boys since this is "typical" in the general population. A girl who receives a score of 12 or higher could be considered maladjusted, while a boy would need a score of 22 for the same classification, suggesting an interesting distinction that may change as sex roles become redefined in our culture. In terms of social skill instruction, the WPBIC provides a pupil profile according to the five previously-listed scales, enabling the examiner to identify problem areas which probably should receive further attention for both assessment and instruction. Sample items from the WPBIC include:

21. Habitually rejects the school experience through actions or comments.
22. Has enuresis. (Wets bed.)
23. Utters nonsense syllables and/or babbles to himself.
24. Continually seeks attention.
25. Comments that nobody likes him.
26. Repeats one idea, thought, or activity over and over.
27. Has temper tantrums.
28. Refers to himself as dumb, stupid, or incapable.
29. Does not engage in group activities.
30. When teased or irritated by other children, takes out his frustration(s) on another inappropriate person or thing.

A final set of checklists to be considered here is the Devereux Behavior Rating Scales. This set contains three instruments: one for the young child in a clinical setting, one for the adolescent in a clinical setting, and one for the young child in the elementary school setting. The scales for clinical use are geared toward the identification or further classification of the emotionally disturbed child or adolescent. The scoring procedure is devised so that a behavior profile is obtained, and the items are categorized according to factors such as "pathological use of senses" and "emotional detachment" for the child scale, and "defiant resistive" and "domineer sadistic" for the adolescent.

The Devereux Elementary School Behavior Rating Scale requires the teacher to use a five or seven-point scale to rate children on items such as:

Compared with the average child in the normal classroom,
how often does the child . . .

15. Give an answer that has nothing to do with the question being asked?
17. Interrupt when the teacher is talking?
26. Make irrelevant remarks during a classroom discussion?

The intent of this 47-item scale is to assess pupil behaviors that correlate highly with school success. In comparison to the clinically-oriented scale, the behavior factors deal less with pathology as indicated by categories such as "Classroom disturbance," "Impatience," and "Comprehension." The behavior rating scales discussed above are examples of some of the more commonly-used, published measures for assessing overt behaviors. For a more extensive listing for elementary-aged children, the reader is referred to other resources, for example, the *Survey of Behavior Rating Scales for Children* compiled by Rie and Friedman (1978), and *Measures of Social Skills*, an annotated bibliography developed by Henriques (1977).

Examiner-Constructed Scales

In assessing social skills, one is often concerned only with particular aspects of the child's interpersonal skills, such as the ability to participate in a group project with a peer, engage in a conversation with an adult, show a positive attitude toward others, or show appropriate affect in various situations. Here, the examiner is concerned with identifying the specific responses that constitute that general behavior or attitude and determining the presence of that response in the child's behavioral repertoire, rather than describing the child along the entire range of interpersonal social skills. For such purposes, the most useful and viable checklists are probably those developed by the practitioner. Mager (1972) provides a model for developing observable objectives for nonobservable goals. For example, perhaps the concern is for the child to demonstrate a more "positive attitude" toward his peers. Once the goal is stated, the next step is to determine the specific behaviors children exhibit that are indicative of positive peer attitudes. Responses may include: smiling at peers, giving compliments, participating in games with peers, making positive statements about peers, and helping peers when asked. After progressing through various steps of refinement, a list of observable behaviors is produced that can be used as a checklist for the designated behavioral goals. Thus, for the goal of positive attitudes, a specific behavioral listing may include the responses already identified as well as additional ones specific to the child and setting. An example of an examiner-constructed behavior checklist follows:

. DIRECTIONS: For each of the listed behaviors rate the child according to the following scale...
demonstrates

	no skill 1	little skill 2	adequate skill 3	good skill 4	considerable skill 5
Politeness					
1. Makes eye contact	1	2	3	4	5
2. Smiles	1	2	3	4	5
3. Says thank you	1	2	3	4	5
4. Says please	1	2	3	4	5
5. Offers to assist others	1	2	3	4	5
6. Makes appropriate apologies	1	2	3	4	5
7. Addresses others appropriately	1	2	3	4	5
8. Makes positive comments to others	1	2	3	4	5
Cooperation					
1. Follows group rules	1	2	3	4	5
2. Complies with reasonable requests	1	2	3	4	5
3. Takes turns	1	2	3	4	5
4. Shares appropriately	1	2	3	4	5
5. Participates in group activities	1	2	3	4	5

The above scale shows behavior categories analyzed into more specific responses on which the child is to be rated. With informally-constructed scales, the examiner would concentrate on the behaviors that are of concern for a particular child or setting; for example, assessment in a residential setting would include more domestic as opposed to the academic-related behaviors in a school setting. The model described is consistent with criterion-referenced procedures wherein the assessment focuses on the child's ability to perform the particular skill rather than comparing the child to his peers, as with the previously-described standardized scales.

Behavior checklists are quick, easy to administer, screening devices for children and adults. While they may be useful in profiling behavioral repertoires, they do have limitations. One disadvantage is that the subjectivity of the respondent may result more in information about how the child is perceived than how he really is. Checklists are least useful as pre- and post-test measures. It is generally concluded that this limitation is primarily due to the lack of specificity in the checklist items. On the other hand, there is some evidence that greater specificity appears to lead to less, rather than increased, reliability (Evans & Nelson, 1977). Despite these shortcomings, behavior checklists can be of value as an initial procedure in assessing social skills and deficits.

Sociometric Procedures

Ratings by peers are most commonly obtained through sociometric techniques. These procedures, designed to study group dynamics and relative social status, have been used in a variety of social situations. For children, they have been applied largely in the classroom where the intent was initially to identify compatible groupings in order to facilitate learning. More recently, sociometric measures have been recognized as an effective tool for identifying and predicting social maladjustment in children and adolescents.

Children experiencing high levels of peer rejection can be identified through sociometry. By indicating the degree of like or dislike for fellow students, it can be determined which children are liked least and thus most rejected. This method may be used to supplement other techniques, such as interviews (which may give distorted perceptions of how the child is viewed by others) and direct observation (which may only give interaction frequencies). Children with low peer interaction rates may not be rejected by peers, but the reverse may be true, i.e., children with high interaction frequencies may be least liked if interactions contain frequent negative encounters (Gottman, 1977). A second related use of sociometric assessment is for prediction. A relationship appears to exist between childhood peer rejection and later-life social maladjustment, such as juvenile delinquency or emotional disturbance (Roff, Sells, & Golden, 1972).

Sociometric assessments, while differing on specific procedures, generally require children to rate their peers according to degree of acceptance and nonacceptance. Positive measures and responses e.g., "whom do you like the most?" are generally preferred, but it has been determined that negative responses e.g. "whom do you like the least?" are also necessary in order to distinguish between those who are disliked and those simply ignored. It has been shown that children who are not identified when using positive measures may not necessarily be rejected but rather overlooked during the selection process. An example of a spontaneous choice test as presented by Miller (1977, p.20) follows:

Spontaneous Choice Test

Opposite each name check how you feel about persons in your group.

	Like	Dislike	Indifferent
Mary J.			
James F.			
John J.			
Others			

In addition to choosing peers based on a generalized attitude, other measures require children to specify preference according to specific activities, such as play and academic tasks. For example:

Sociometric Preference Test

Choose five persons you would most like to work with.
Mark 1st, 2nd, 3rd, 4th, 5th choice.

Mary J.	
James F.	
John J.	
Sam E.	
Etc.	

[Miller, 1977, p. 20]

Sociometric procedures also vary according to the ages and development level of the child. Responses and scoring procedures become more complex as the group increases in sophistication.

Obtaining valid peer ratings is a major consideration in using sociometric techniques, especially with young children. Moore and Updegraff (1964) developed a peer-rating procedure used with nursery school children ranging from three to five years in age. Individual interviews were conducted wherein the responding child was presented with a board containing individual pictures of each child in the group. The examiner assisted the child in identifying each picture, and then the child was asked to find someone he especially liked. After four choices were made, the child was directed to identify someone he didn't like very much for four more choices. Following this step, the examiner pointed to the pictures of children not selected and asked the responding child if he liked or disliked that child. With this method Moore and Updegraff identified four response categories:

Spontaneous Positive - Responding child points to (four) pictures of children liked

Spontaneous Negative - Responding child points to (four) pictures of children disliked

Forced Positive   - Examiner points to pictures and asks if respondent likes the child

Forced Negative   - Examiner points to pictures and asks if child is disliked

Responses were scored according to positives, negatives, and order of choice. For example, a child selected first as being liked received plus 8 points while the first disliked child selected received minus 8. Similarly, the second liked received plus 6 and second disliked minus 6, with the remaining two points being 4 and 3. Forced positive and negative children received plus and minus 1 point. Computation of the assigned points yielded composite sociometric scores for each child, with well liked children receiving the highest scores.

A method used with older children is the roster and rating sociometric questionnaire. The roster is an alternative to the more common "fill-in" instrument where the child is expected to write in names of peers. The child is presented with an alphabetized roster with a five-point scale following each name. The respondent is expected to rate each member listed on a scale from 1 to 5. Each child's score is the average of all his ratings. This method is considered to have certain advantages in that it allows for ratings by all group members and, by providing ratings on a continuum, it circumvents some of the unpleasant ethical aspects of negative ratings (Hymel & Asher, 1977). These procedures are a variation of the roster and seven-point scale rating method used by Roistacher (1974) with eighth-grade boys in a schoolwide sociometric analysis. Other sociometric procedures include activities like the "Who Are They" test developed by Bowman, DeHann, Kough and Liddle (1956) where the child is expected to identify a classmate who he feels is best described by various statements designed to measure leadership, aggression, withdrawn behavior, and friendship. Sample items include: "Who are the good leaders?" and "Who are the boys and girls who make good plans?"

Sociometric techniques can be administered in various ways. When using them with children, several considerations or cautions should be noted. For very young children, sociometric ratings should be obtained through individual interviews, making certain the child understands the directions and responds properly. Similar procedures may be necessary for somewhat older children with special needs. By third grade, the child is probably able to make sociometric ratings through paper-and-pencil tasks. Another consideration that crops up at this stage is the preference for same sex peers. For that reason, choices may be based largely on sex rather than personality factors. One technique to correct for this occurrence is to provide assessments only according to sex so that girls rate only girls and boys rate boys. Whether or not this procedure is adopted, sex must be considered when analyzing the results. In order to counter for the tendency of children to base ratings of a peer on a recent negative experience, it is recommended that the sociometric procedure be administered two or more times over a period of weeks in order to obtain accurate results. While positive ratings are generally the most preferred and the most reliable, negative ratings are necessary in order to discriminate correctly between rejected and overlooked children. One alternative to "dislike" or "least liked" statements is the use of five or seven-point scales where children are required to rate on a continuum. Finally, it seems that instruments that require children to write in the names of peers are less reliable than those which provide rosters of the entire peer group. For young children Asher, Singleton, Tinsley and Hymel (1979) recently developed a roster-type sociometric measure (children attached a happy, sad, or neutral face to a classmate's picture) which also proved more reliable than the previously-described nomination procedure.

Self Reports

Another approach to the rating or screening process is for the child to assess his own social competence using various scales and inventories. While one may question the child's ability to perceive his own social behavior or his effect on others accurately, these reports may provide valuable assessment data. The child's responses may be used to compare discrepancies between his self-perceptions and assessments of him made by others, to identify critical areas for instruction based on the child's misperceptions of his own behavior, and to determine changes in self-statements pre- and post-treatment.

Self-report measures, most commonly used with adults, are typically designed to assess personality traits rather than specific interpersonal social skills. They have been criticized for poor validity and the tendency to focus on general states as opposed to observable behaviors. These instruments also have been defended (Cautela & Upper, 1976) in that the research findings have not substantiated lower reliability with self-reports than with other measures and, as previously indicated, the self-reports are specific observable behaviors in themselves.

One kind of self-report measure which has been designed to assess overt behaviors is the assertiveness scale. Wood and Michelson (1978) developed the Children's Assertive Behavior Scale (CABS), a pencil-and-paper, multiple-choice instrument that measures specific responses reflecting behavior categories such as empathy, conversation making, requests, and compliments. For each item, the child is required to choose one of five possible choices, indicating how he would respond in that situation. The range of choices and corresponding values within each item include very passive (-2), passive (-1), assertive (0), aggressive (1) and very aggressive $(+2)$ responses so that assertive children would receive the low positive scores. The scale consists of 29 items. Listed below is a sample item with the responses labeled according to the aggressive passive continuum.

1.   Someone says to you, "I think you are a very nice person."

You would usually:
a)   Say, "No I'm not that nice."   (very passive)
b)   Say, "Yes, I think I am the Best!" (very aggressive)
c)   Say, "Thank you."   (assertive)
d)   Say nothing and blush   (passive)
e)   Say, "Thanks, I am really great." (aggressive)

Another assertiveness scale that used a self-evaluation format is the Rathus Scale (1973), originally developed for adults and adapted by Wood & Michelson (1978) for use with children. The Rathus Assertiveness Scale Revised for Children includes 38 statements to which the child is required to agree or disagree. For example:

Agree   Disagree   41. I like to argue.
Agree   Disagree   42. I like to complain when I am not satisfied.
Agree   Disagree   43. I won't hurt somebody's feelings, even if they hurt mine.
Agree   Disagree   44. It takes me a long time to get to know new people.

Self-report scales dealing with self-concept attempt to measure the child's sense of himself in terms of his feelings of self worth, acceptance, success, and so forth. These are generally paper-and-pencil tests where the child indicates the degree to which he agrees or disagrees with the given statement. One instrument that has been widely used is the Self-Esteem Inventory developed by Coopersmith (1967) for children between the ages of 8 and 10 years. The inventory contains 59 items, and for each one the child is required to check whether that statement is like or unlike him. For example:

	Like Me	Unlike Me
1. I spend a lot of time daydreaming.	_____	_____
2. I'm pretty sure of myself.	_____	_____
3. I often wish I were someone else.	_____	_____
4. I'm easy to like.	_____	_____

A self-concept instrument at the adolescent level is the Self-Esteem Scale by Rosenberg (1965). Here the youngster has to respond on a four-point scale to ten generally-stated items. Sample statements include:

I feel that I'm a person of worth, at least on an equal plane with others.

1 _____ Strongly agree
2 _____ Agree
*3 _____ Disagree
*4 _____ Strongly disagree

Responses by starred items indicate low self-esteem.

The foregoing discussion is not exhaustive in terms of the number of child and adolescent self-report measures that exist designed to assess personality and self-concept variables. Within a behavioral context, the emphasis is placed on how the child describes himself, not whether his reports actually reflect the way he feels or would respond under the stated conditions. It is significant if a child reports himself to be popular and well liked by other children and yet he is observed to be a loner and constantly teased by his peers. Thus, the child's reporting becomes a target for change. For this reason, it is recommended that self-report measures be employed in conjunction with other assessments (such as parent and teacher reports and direct observation) geared toward the same behaviors. To illustrate, Wood and Michelson (1978), in using the previously mentioned CABS measure, also developed a second instrument to be completed by teachers who rated the child on the same items on which he was rating himself. For example, item number 2 on the child's form reads:

2. Someone does something that you think is really great. You would usually:
    a) Act like it wasn't that great and say, "That was alright."
    b) Say, "That was alright, but I've seen better."
    c) Say nothing.
    d) Say, "I can do much better than that!"
    e) Say, "That was really great!"

Rating the child on the same behaviors, the teacher's form is:

2. Someone does something that the youth thinks is really great:
    The youth would usually:
    a) Act like it wasn't that great and say, "That was alright."
    b) Say, "That was alright, but I've seen better."
    c) Say nothing.
    d) Say, "I can do much better than that!"
    e) Say, "That was really great!"

The nature of self-assessment is such that self-report scales probably should not be used as the sole indicator of the child's social adjustment, but should be used in combination with other instruments and other sources such as parents, teachers, clinicians, and peers. Not only do other sources provide a check in determining the accuracy of the child's statements, but they also assist in deciding whether the initial point of intervention will be instruction in specific interpersonal social skills, the child's perception of himself in related social situations, or the child's reporting behavior itself.

OBSERVATION OF PERFORMANCE

Assessing in the Natural Environment

The most obvious (but not necessarily easiest) way of assessing performance of social behaviors is to observe the child and see what he does in his every-day surroundings. Because of the differences in behavior in different situations, it may be necessary to gather observational data from various persons who see the child in different contexts. Various methods of counting and documenting behaviors have been outlined in the research literature. Written descriptions in the form of diaries or narratives are sometimes called "continuous recording." Bijou, Peterson & Ault (1968) suggest a four-column format for this kind of recording which involves time, antecedent events, child responses, and consequent events. Recording events in a temporal sequence makes it possible not only to describe specific behaviors but also to form hypotheses about the relationships which exist between a behavior and its antecedents and consequences. Being able to make such hypotheses in relationship to social skills is particularly useful in determining the conditions that facilitate the expression of desirable social behaviors.

Narrative recording has been used to describe any behaviors that occur, without focusing on particular behavior. Methods for more systematic recording of specific behaviors include event recording by means of tally marks, wrist counters, and other counting devices — time sampling techniques involving time intervals, duration recording, and the use of coding or rating systems related to the observed behavior.

Assessing social skills, particularly as alternatives to some identified problem behaviors, usually involves dealing with nonexistent or low-frequency behaviors. Mann (1976) suggests that event recording, i.e., the recording of each occurrence of each event (behavior), is a preferred process with infrequent behaviors. It is probably the simplest method, requiring only a means of recording and a set of discrete behaviors that can be reliably identified by the observer. The kinds of social skills that might be documented using event recording could include positive remarks, sharing, compliance with requests, raising hand in class, or saying please and thank you. Cooper (1974) details a set of devices and procedures for event recording that include: (1) a counter such as a golf counter worn on the wrist, (2) a hand-tally digital counter such as the grocery store counter, (3) a "wrist tally board," which is a note pad worn on the wrist, (4) masking tape worn on the wrist or clothing of either the observer or the child on which tally marks can be made, and (5) objects such as buttons or paper clips that can be transferred from one place to another, (pockets, for example) when the event occurs. A simple clipboard, paper, and pencil could also be used. Eisler (1976) suggests that for the most reliable recording, the observer should limit the number of behaviors recorded at one time to no more than two.

Duration recording, or recording how long the behavior occurs, is more appropriate for social behaviors that occur for an extended time period and that have a clearly-defined beginning and end. It is useful when the teaching goal is to lengthen or shorten the period of time. For example, one might wish to lengthen the amount of time the child spends in constructive play or in conversation with peers, or shorten the amount of time the child delays before complying with an adult request. A watch or wall clock with a second hand or, ideally, a stop watch are generally used for duration recording, along with a means of recording the numbers obtained. Cooper (1974) suggests that duration recording may be used in two ways: as a simple time duration (e.g. five minutes); or as a percentage of some specified time period, obtained by dividing the total time into the recorded time duration. Other methods of observational recording are more complex and, thus, more appropriate to a research setting where trained observers are available. More detailed recording techniques may not be necessary for the practitioner whose main concern is determining whether or not the child has a behavior in his repertoire. Several good resources are available, however, outlining obervational methods, e.g., Cooper (1974), Mash & Terdal (1976), Hersen & Barlow (1976).

Considerable concern is expressed in empirical circles about the "reactive effect" of observation, or the possibility that the fact of observation will serve to change the observed behavior. Kent and Foster (1977), in reviewing studies on reactivity of observation procedures, conclude that, although the presence of an observer may sometimes affect the observed behavior, such findings are not always present, and not all behaviors are affected by observers. When reactivity is present, such effects usually occur at the beginning of observation but weaken over time. For social skills assessment, where the goal is to determine skills and deficits, observation effects could be considered an asset if they serve to strengthen the incentives operating in the assessment situation and, thus, motivate the child to display his most positive behaviors.

Setting Up "Contrived" Situations

Since it is sometimes inefficient to wait for a behavior to occur in the natural environment in order to collect observational data, an approach suggested by Stephens (1978) is that of arranging the natural environment in such a way as to require or facilitate the behavior, then watching for its occurrence. An example of such a contrived assessment situation would be that presented for the skill "To share toys and equipment in a play situation":

During a free-play or recess period, have the target student play with some available toys or equipment alone for a short time. Then send another student over to play with the same toys or equipment. Observe whether the first (target) student willingly allows the second to play with the toys, and if he plays together with the second student. Or, establish a small group activity, such as drawing pictures with one set of magic markers or pens given to target student for all to share: Observe target student for sharing behavior. [P. 293]

The Interview as an Assessment Situation

The interview might be considered one kind of contrived situation that potentially can provide observational data on a variety of social behaviors as well as self-report information. In the treatment of an adult, the interview is probably the primary source of information about the client. When dealing with children, the interview may present special problems. Responding to another person in a one-to-one interview situation involves a complex set of communication skills which the child may not yet possess. Children are considerably less likely than adults to be able to engage in self-monitoring of feelings and responses and to be able to report about them to someone else. In addition, children seldom present themselves to a teacher or therapist expressing concern about their own problems or behavior deficits. A discussion oriented toward identifying their difficulties is likely to engender resistance and avoidance.

Despite these difficulties there is much useful information to be gathered in an interview. A number of behaviors can be observed, for example:

- The child's ability to sit quietly, pay attention to the adult, maintain eye contact, listen;
- The child's ability to communicate about his behaviors and feelings, ability to describe situations and his role in them, his ability to put thoughts into words, his vocabulary, his voice quality and articulation, the length of his answers, the relevance of his replies, his ability to initiate as well as respond;
- The nature of affect displayed by the child, whether he is comfortable in a one-to-one situation with an adult, his greeting skills.

A small group interview reveals a different set of behaviors for observation, especially those related to peer interactions:

- The nature of the child's interaction with peers, whether he initiates or follows, whether he is easily influenced into group misbehavior, how he participates in a group task.
- The nature of the child's verbal behavior with peers, whether he initiates and carries on conversations, makes relevant comments, listens to others, is positive with peers.

A task-oriented group could potentially reveal, for example:

- The child's ability to follow rules related to the task, ask permission to use another's property, stay on task, share materials, work cooperatively, ask for and give help, use "please" and "thank you."

In addition to observational information, it is possible to assess the child's knowledge of appropriate social behaviors by structuring the content of the interview around questions related to social behaviors. Eisler (1976) has provided a partial list of interpersonal behavior situations that might be explored in an interview with adult clients related to their history of interpersonal response patterns. Adapted to children, the list could include:

1. The ability to express opinions contrary to those of peers, parents, teachers;
2. The ability to ask favors of someone;
3. The ability to initiate conversations with peers and adults;
4. The ability to refuse unreasonable requests from friends and strangers;
5. The ability to invite a peer to play;
6. The ability to compliment someone;
7. The ability to receive compliments;
8. The ability to ask for help in solving problems;
9. The ability to resist pressure from peers to behave in an unacceptable way.

Evans and Nelson (1977) have suggested that, because of the child's limited behavioral repertoire, the skill of the interviewer in communicating with children is important. Also important is setting up the situation to be non-threatening and positive. Some people who work with children find that food is useful to have available, and the presence of play materials such as clay or crayons may make an interview situation seem less formal for a child.

Permanent Products

Cooper (1974) defines permanent products as "Products that are tangible and can be measured any time after the student's behavior." Although permanent products may have more applicability in academic assessment, there are approaches to social skill assessment through observations that involve a product. Because behavior goes by quickly, and accurate observations are difficult, an increasingly practical means of assessing behaviors in the natural environment involves the use of video and audio tapes to capture the behavior and make it accessible for later evaluation. Such devices are particularly useful for the researcher where reliability of assessment is a concern. In a social skills program to increase appropriate dinnertime conversation, for example, tape recordings were made in the home during the dinner hour and analyzed according to conversational categories, making possible both assessment and ongoing evaluation (Jewett & Clark, 1976). Audio and video tapes are also valuable where the behaviors of more than one child are being assessed at a time. For the teacher and therapist, video or audio tape recording can be a useful tool in assessing the child's social skill deficits, in enabling the child to assess his own skill deficits, and in demonstrating improvements by comparing tapes before and after training.

Permanent products play a role where behaviors to be assessed in the natural environment cannot be directly observed but must be inferred from observable results; for example, assessing the degree of a child's compliance with a request to clean his room. Other social skills involve the production of a product; for example, the ability to write a "thank you" note or take a phone message, or the tangible results of a group project designed to assess ability to work cooperatively in a group and share materials.

SELF-MONITORING

Self-monitoring, or having the child observe and record his own social behavior, is included as an assessment technique even though it has a number of limitations. Self-recording has been identified as reactive, since the child knows the target behavior and the purpose of the recording, and the self-recording can, thus, result in behavior change. There are a number of studies in which self-recording has been successfully employed as an intervention to bring about positive behavior change. Self-recording can be monitored by others if the behavior is an observable one, but if the child is recording private events (such as thoughts and feelings) there is no way to assess the reliability of the data. At the same time, other than self-reports, there is no means of accessing those internal events.

Self-reporting is a skill which would need to be taught before it could become a useful means of assessment. In teaching self-monitoring, it would be necessary first to make sure the child can identify the presence of the target behavior when emitted, then provide the child with a means of recording the behavior. Any of the observation techniques included earlier could be used by the child with some instruction, e.g., using a counter or a time piece to record frequency or duration of a specific behavior. A child trying to develop the social skill of ignoring another child who teases him could, for example, record on a wrist counter his attempts at ignoring. Edelson and Rose (1978) used self-report procedures in which children developed a weekly diary of problem situations. One important aspect of self-monitoring instruction would be to teach the child to identify the situational events preceding and following the target behaviors. Kanfer (1975) suggests some steps for self-monitoring that could easily be employed with a young person. These include:

1. Discussing why it is important to keep a record and how such monitoring will be helpful;
2. Identifying the behaviors to be observed;
3. Selecting a means of recording;
4. Showing how the recording can be graphed; and
5. Role playing and rehearsing the procedures.

For children, it seems particularly important for the behavior to be simple and easily defined and for only one behavior to be selected at a time. As discussed earlier, self-reports as assessment tools have questionable validity and are most useful when combined with data from other sources. The skill of self-monitoring, however, has utility for enhancing social functioning as well as potential for assisting in the generalization of social skills over time. Self-monitoring is discussed further in Chapters 3 and 4.

ANALOGUE SITUATIONS

Naturalistic or in vivo situations are probably the most desirable conditions for assessing interpersonal social behaviors. However, considering the impracticality of continual observation for specific interpersonal events, one is led to the structuring of analogous or analogue situations. Role playing is an analogue technique that has been used for many years for the assessment of personal interaction behaviors as well as for the remediation of social skill deficiencies. As an assessment technique, role playing has the advantages of permitting the practitioner to (1) study the environmental conditions under which the response occurs as well as the response itself

(Goldfried & D'Zurilla, 1969), and (2) arrange a variety of conditions so that many responses can be assessed and studied.

As children develop socially, they learn to respond differently to different people, they learn to appreciate the feelings of others, and they develop an understanding of how their behavior determines the responses they receive from others. The development of social perception facilitates the acquisition of interpersonal social skills. Role playing assessment techniques are designed to determine the individual's ability to perceive social situations accurately and to make responses that are considered appropriate to the situation.

Definition of Role Playing

Role playing is a form of sociodrama which has been defined as a "make believe" process (Corsini, 1966). During role playing the participant is expected to either (1) step outside his usual role and take the role of another, thereby developing some understanding of the other's position; or (2) re-enact some personal experience in order to gain insight into his own behavior. Corsini (1966, p. 9) postulates five components of role playing. It

1. *Is a close representation of real life behavior.* Although staged, every effort is made to reconstruct the natural conditions as closely as possible. The situations enacted are ones which the participant has either previously encountered or will very likely experience in the near future.
2. *Involves the individual holistically.* That is, the participant is required to respond totally to the situation. In role playing the participant must *think* or employ cognitions, he must respond emotionally or use feeling, and he must *act* or use drama.
3. *Presents observers with a picture of how the patient operates in real life situations.* This aspect provides assessment information so that the observer can determine skill competence under various social conditions.
4. *Because it is dramatic, focuses attention on the problem.*
5. *Permits the individual to see himself while in action in a neutral situation.* Role playing provides a mechanism whereby the individual may analyze his own behavior and recognize how certain actions can trigger various responses (sometimes negative ones) from others.

Although role playing is a dramatic process, it takes various forms and does not necessarily involve enactment with a partner. Corsini (1966) identifies two forms of role playing which are solitary in nature. In one form, the individual role plays through imagery what will happen in certain situations, such as asking the boss for a raise or asking an acquaintance for a date. The other form is overt behavior rehearsal in which the child rehearses some future event, such as a speech or presentation. The child who is extremely anxious about events (such as making a report in class or meeting a new peer) may practice these behaviors through role playing in order to improve the performance and relieve the anxiety. Employing Corsini's first condition, the child would simply imagine how he would act in these situations, whereas with behavioral rehearsal the child would perform the behavior overtly, perhaps acting in front of a mirror in order to monitor himself. A third form, identified by Corsini as "dyadic therapeutic," involves interaction with another person to dramatize a particular event. This type of role playing is rather spontaneous and does not utilize a script or prescribed responses. It could be effectively used by a teacher or clinician to resolve conflict and to help children analyze their own behavior by having them reenact events involving various interpersonal problems such as peer-peer, teacher-pupil, or child-parent discord. A fourth form of role playing, not addressed by Corsini but which is especially valuable for assessment purposes, is a variation of the dyadic structure. Here, one member of the pair has a prepared script to which the child is expected to respond spontaneously. An example is the following scenario taken from an assessment instrument for children developed by Calpin and Kornblith (1978). The assessment conditions involve one person (in this case outside the room) reading the part of the narrator and a second person (who sits facing the child in the room) delivering the prompt. Following the prompt, the child responds in an unprescribed manner to express his reaction to the particular situation.

Narrator: "You're watching TV, but one of the kids is making so much noise that you can't hear. When you tell him to be quiet, he says:"
Prompt: "Make me."
Child's
Response

By providing prepared scenes delivered by one member of the pair, assessment conditions are held constant and allow for response comparisons across subjects. It also permits the practitioner to determine progress following social skill instruction.

Conditions for Role Playing Assessments

Increased interest in social skill instruction and role playing has resulted in the identification of some conditions that increase the validity of role playing as an assessment tool. Goldfried and D'Zurilla's (1969) behavioral-analytic guidelines for assessing social competence provide standards that can be used for developing role play instruments. The variables considered are: (1) situational analysis, (2) response enumeration, (3) response evaluation, (4) development of measurement format, and (5) evaluation of the measure.

Under *situational analysis* Goldfried and D'Zurilla suggest that an environmental survey be conducted so that the most meaningful, problematic situations which an individual typically encounters are identified. For children, this might involve having children and adults (such as parents, teachers, and mental health workers) systematically record all problem situations encountered by or with children over a specified time period (Edelson & Rose, 1978). Interviews with children and adults may also be conducted in order to identify problem situations. The second step of *response enumeration* involves determining response situations which are appropriate (i.e., not too easy or too difficult) as well as clear, so that additional elaboration is not required, and for which possible alternative responses have been specified. Response enumeration could be conducted by observing and recording responses to various problem situations. Once possible responses have been identified, it is then necessary in the third step of *response evaluation* to determine which responses are most effective (i.e., likely to receive more favorable reaction in the natural environment). The technique suggested is to employ individuals who are most likely to encounter the child under these circumstances in the natural environment to rate the responses. The fourth step, *development of measurement format*, specifies the mode of responses to be used by the child in order to assess competence in various social situations. Because of its many advantages, role playing (compared to written responses or naturalistic observations) is a frequently preferred way of assessing. Finally, as with any testing instrument, *evaluation of the measure* refers to whether the assessment procedures adhere to recognized psychometric principles. That is, the test items are valid in that they measure what they purport to measure, reliable in that they yield similar scores on repeated measures, computed according to sound scoring procedures, and standardized in that they proved for performance comparisons across populations. Situation analysis and response enumeration are particularly important in role play assessment since the assessment research demonstrates that the quality of the role-played behavior increases when the person being assessed could relate to or identify with the assessment situation.

In summary, assessment conditions using role playing should involve several considerations. The environment of the target subject should be assessed in order to include problematic, relevant situations. The response situations must be analyzed and evaluated so that the child knows exactly what is expected and the tester knows the degree to which the subject's response indicates competence.

Role Play Assessments

Presently, few assessment instruments exist that utilize role playing techniques. Although role-play assessment instruments vary according to social skill focus, settings, and population, certain commonalities do exist.

- *Practice situation*. Prior to the actual testing situation, scenes are used to determine if the child understands what is expected. They can also be used as a mechanism for warming up to the role playing situation.
- *Standard script*. In order to insure uniformity of testing conditions both within and between subjects, scripts are developed and delivered by a narrator.
- *Prompts*. Following each scene presented by the narrator, a prompt is given by a role model to which the child is expected to respond. For example, a scene is described by the narrator where the child is being teased, and then the prompt actually delivers the taunting statement to which the child directly responds. Role models (people within the child's peer group) also provide an additional element of realism to the situation.
- *Video taping and rating*. Under experimental conditions, the role-played scenes are video taped and later evaluated by objective observers.

One role-playing test incorporating the above conditions, the Behavioral Assertiveness Test for Children (BAT-C), was developed by Bornstein (Bornstein, Bellack, & Hersen, 1977). Focusing on assertive behaviors in school settings, examples from the nine-scene instrument follow:

Female Model
1. Narrator: "You're part of a small group in a science class. Your group is trying to come up with an idea for a project to present to the class. You start to give your idea when Amy begins to tell hers also."

    Prompt: "Hey, listen to my idea."

2. Narrator: "Imagine you need to use a pair of scissors for a science project. Betty is using them, but promises to let you have them next. But when Betty is done she gives them to Ellen."

    Prompt: "Here's the scissors, Ellen."

3. Narrator: "Pretend you loaned your pencil to Joannie. She comes over to give it back to you and says that she broke the point."

    Prompt: "I broke the point."   [P. 186]

Edleson and associates (Edleson & Rose, 1978; Edleson & Cole-Kelly, 1978) have standardized a role-play test for children which extends social skill assessment beyond the realm of assertiveness and investigates interpersonal skills in various situations. Adhering closely to the Goldfried and D'Zurilla procedures discussed earlier in this section, the authors identified problem conditions common to children and incorporated them into role-play assessment scenes. This test consists of twelve scenes involving peer or sibling interactions in several settings such as school, home, or the playground. An example of a situation and the corresponding directions follows:

Alright, let's go on to the first situation. Remember, just pretend you are really there and act just like you would if it was happening to you. I'll play like I'm the other person in each situation.

Situation One
Your friend got a B on a book report. You got a lower grade. Your friend comes up to you and says, "I got a B on my book report. The teacher said I did a good job."

Now I'll play your friend who says this to you and you act towards me just like you would towards a friend who said this to you. Okay? I'll read the situation once more then I'll act like your friend. Ready? (Reread situation once)

Tester: "I got a B on my book report. The teacher said I did a good job."

(TAPE ANSWER ONLY. If audiotaping, be sure to record NONVERBAL behavior on coding sheet.)

Consistent with standardized measures, the authors provide a system for response evaluation. For the above example, the scoring procedures would be:

Situation One
Pretend your friend got a B on a book report. Pretend you got a lower grade. Your friend comes up to you and says, "I got a B on my book report. The teacher said I did a good job."

Score   Criteria
4   Must include: a *praise statement* expressed in the *first person* (e.g., "I think that's great!" or I'm really happy for you"), and a statement of how the child *did or feels* about how he/she did (e.g., "I didn't do as well" or "I'm not as happy about my grade").

Example: "I think that's great you did so well. I'm not as happy about my grade. I didn't do as well."

3   Includes two of three above.

Example: "I think that's great you did so well. It's great you did well. I'm not as happy about my grade."

2   Includes one of the three above.

Example: "It's great you did so well"
"I didn't do so well"
"I'm not as happy about my grade"

As previously indicated, role playing has the advantage that it is convenient, it allows for the assessment of a wide range of behaviors, and it approximates natural response conditions. It also has disadvantages, the principle one being questionable validity. Initial research findings suggest that there may be considerable variance between the responses made in contrived, rather limited, role-playing situations and those made under natural conditions (Bellack, Hersen & Turner, 1978). While these findings are not conclusive, the implication might be that role play assessment may measure more accurately what the child knows than what the child does (an issue to be discussed later under assessing cognitions). Assuming that, at the very least, this is the case, role-playing assessment can still provide extremely valuable information about the child's social competence.

Audio and Video Tape Role-Play Assessments

In order to increase the similarity to the natural environment, role-playing assessments, such as those described in the preceding section, may be provided through audio or video tapes. Under these conditions, the individual must respond to various situations as presented on the tapes. Every effort is made to make the scenes realistic, employing theatrics such as background sound effects, actors, and confederates who are as similar as possible to the type of person being described in the scene. For example, if the assessment situation consists of one child responding to another child on the playground, then playground noises would be included in the background, and a child (confederate) would be used to record the comments to which the child being assessed would respond. Responses made by the child being assessed may be either oral or physical; it is assumed that the closer the approximations are to reality, the more natural will be the child's responses. A third alternative is paper-and-pencil responses in the form of multiple-choice questionnaires where the child must indicate which of the listed behaviors he would perform under the conditions presented. Although somewhat more difficult for children, another type of paper-and-pencil response is the open-ended format, requiring the child to generate his own natural reaction to the taped situation.

Audio and video tape assessment measures are considered to have special advantages in that (1) they more closely approximate real-life conditions, (2) it is possible to structure audio tapes to assess characteristics specific to a particular child, (3) they may be administered without the examiner being present, (4) one may employ nonverbal as well as verbal communications with video tapes (Nay, 1977), and (5) they also make it possible to present identical stimuli in assessing more than one child. The most obvious disadvantages of using video tapes as an assessment tool are equipment costs and the time involved in staging props, and so forth in order to obtain the desired effects. Another shortcoming is that responding to the taped situations requires only single responses and does not allow for ongoing interaction. In live role-playing situations the interaction may be continued beyond the initial response, resulting in a more thorough and, possibly more accurate, assessment of how the child would respond under such conditions.

Audio and video tape assessment conditions are very similar to those in the previously described role-play situation. That is, the child is instructed how he is to respond, a narrative describing the situation is provided, a confederate actor makes a comment to which the individual being assessed must respond, and the response is made according to some predetermined mode. Despite the increased interest in audio visual methods in social skill assessment, very few examples are found in the research literature, and these have been devised primarily to assess social competence in college students or adult mental patients rather than children. An example of an open-ended audio tape measure is the one developed by Arkowitz, Lichtenstein, McGovern, and Hines (1975) to assess the social competence of the dating behavior of undergraduate college males. The Taped Situations Test (TST) included ten scenes relative to various heterosexual dating situations. For each scene, the narrator presented background information, a confederate (in this case female) gave a lead-in statement, and then there was a pause where the person being assessed was required to respond to the confederate. An example of such a scene is given by Arkowitz, et al. (p. 5):

Narrator: At a party, you go over to a girl and ask her to dance.

Female
Confederate: I'm not really much of a dancer.

   [A prerecorded signal is given and the person being assessed responds:]

      [Varies according to individual. One possibility given by the authors is] Actually, neither am I. Why don't we just talk instead?

As indicated, the responses given to the confederate are open-ended, i.e., the person being assessed is given no suggestions for possible responses but is encouraged to answer the confederate in the manner he would under real-life circumstances.

An audio tape assessment procedure using a forced-choice format was devised by Goldstein, Martens, Hubben, van Belle, Schaaf, Wiersma and Goldhard (1973), Forced-choice formats involve providing the individual being assessed with two or more options and requiring them to select one. The audio tapes were designed to assess the independent behavior of adult mental patients. The format consisted of stage setting by one speaker and the delivery of a provocative statement from a second speaker. Following this statement, the individual being assessed was required to respond by selecting one of two possible alternatives provided by the examiners. For example:

E_1: "A friend asks you to go downtown to buy a special present for her mother. However, you buy a different present because the one she wanted is sold out. She says to you:"

E_2: "I think it's rubbish!"

Independent response alternative: "Then you should have gone yourself."

Dependent response alternative: "I'll change it for you."

Although not devised for children, the above examples incorporate a format and procedure that can easily be adapted for any population. As previously indicated, one strength of audio tape assessments is the relative ease with which one could develop assessment scenes based on the unique needs of the individual client or child.

ASSESSING AFFECTIVE AND COGNITIVE BEHAVIORS

The point has been made that thoughts and feelings are relevant to the instruction of social skills, because how children feel and think in social situations affects their social behavior, and because socialization involves learning culturally-defined acceptable public ways to express these inner events. Affects and cognitions are closely related. As Meichenbaum puts it, "...each cognition has an affective component and similarly, each affect a cognitive component" (1976, p. 147). Cognitive theorists hypothesize that cognitions about external events (e.g., evaluations, associations, anticipated consequences, self-praise, self-criticism) give rise to feelings followed by overt behaviors. According to cognitive theory, such cognitions take the form of "inner dialogue" which starts originally in the developmental process for the child with the external speech of others, next is reflected in the child's own spoken language, and then goes "underground" and becomes inner speech that guides his feelings and actions (Meichenbaum, 1977).

Assessing inner events usually begins with verbal self-reports, even though these are difficult to validate independently. As pointed out in the section dealing with self-monitoring, self-reporting is a complex set of be-haviors involving the ability to recognize and label one's own thoughts and feelings and report on them verbally to someone else. Programs to teach such behavior should be part of a social skills training program and may have to be taught before self-reporting can be useful as an assessment tech-nique. A program suggested by Rotheram (1978) uses an adaptation of Wolpe's (1958) Subjective Units of Discomfort Scale (SUDS) to develop the child's ability to self-report feelings. In her program, children use the con-cept of Fear Thermometer (Walk, 1956) to construct a scale from 0 to 100 to rate their responses in stressful situations. A highly-stressful situation has a SUDS of 100, while a low-stress situation is closer to 0. The child is taught to recognize the difference in his feelings and physiological reactions along the SUDS continuum from 0 to 100 in specific situations.

In assessing anxiety and fear in adults, one common approach is the Fear Survey Schedule in which the individual indicates on a scale the degree of his fear of listed objects or events. Many variations of the fear survey tech-nique have been developed for use with different populations (Hersen, 1973). These scales have differing degrees of reliability and ability to predict adult behavior in potentially fear-inducing situations, and very little infor-mation is available currently on adaptations of such schedules for use with children.

Several scales have been developed for self-reporting of anxiety by chil-dren, including the Children's Manifest Anxiety Scale (Casteneda, McCandless, & Palermo, 1956), the General Anxiety Scale for Children, and the related Test Anxiety Scale for Children, both by Sarason and associates (1960). These scales involve children in answering "Yes" or "No" to questions describing situations which could evoke anxiety, e.g., "Are you frightened by lightning and thunderstorms?" A similar self-report scale has been developed by Spielberger (1973).

Assessing affect has an advantage over assessing cognitions per se in that there are physiological manifestations of feelings that can be more directly measured. Because physiological arousal accompanies such negative emo-tions as fear, anxiety, apprehension, and anger, a number of bodily changes often take place which can be observed. Technological measures have been used in research studies with adults to measure physiological aspects of fear and anxiety, including measures of skin response and cardiac activity. Because of practical considerations, it is unlikely that these will become popular assessment procedures with children in school or clinical settings.

Observation of facial expression and various "body language" manifes-tations of affect seems to be one of the best ways to gather data on affect in children; there are many behaviors that have been interpreted to be outward signs of inner reactions. Some of these include the condition of body stiff-ness or relaxation; the tensing of muscles of neck and shoulders; flushing;

trembling hands or hand wringing; chewing fingers; nail biting; thumb sucking; stroking, twisting, or pulling out hair; biting or licking lips; frequent throat clearing; frequent trips to the bathroom or many drinks of water; heavy breathing; signs of anguish such as tears, wailing, moaning, or sobbing; signs of happiness such as giggling, smiling, laughing; speech indicators such as stammering, inability to speak out loud, hesitation in speech, voice tremors, talking to oneself; or physical symptoms such as headaches, stomach aches, or vomiting. A very stressed child may regress and wet his pants or soil. The hyperactive child may attempt to reduce feelings of anxiety through continual verbal and bodily activity. Conversely, a child in a state of panic can be immobilized and mute. And, of course, the child's face can present a variety of clues from which inferences about thoughts and feelings can be made, although using such overt manifestations to assess inner events needs to be approached cautiously, only as a basis for hypotheses to be tested in other ways.

In the process of assessing cognitive factors relating to social skills, the goals are to determine whether the child has cognitive understanding of the behaviors being taught, whether he is engaging in faulty cognitions that interfere with desirable social behavior, or whether he is lacking in problem solving strategies that would facilitate desired social interactions and overall competence. While it can be argued that a child may show behaviors under assessment conditions that he may not translate into actual behavior in the natural environment, this information is valuable for instructional purposes. As indicated previously, teaching approaches should differ considerably for the child who knows what the appropriate social response should be but for various reasons fails to perform, as opposed to the child who is inappropriate because he doesn't know what to do. Measures for assessing the child's knowledge of proper social responses generally use the format found in the analogue categories described in the preceding section. The further the assessment conditions are removed from real-life events, the greater the likelihood that one is assessing cognitions rather than the actual responses the child would make within the described situation. Therefore, paper-and-pencil analogues (more so than other analogue categories) may be important primarily for providing information about the extent to which the child is able to specify rather than perform the correct social response (Nay, 1977). Within these assessment conditions, a social situation is presented, typically in writing, to which the child must give the appropriate social response in open-ended or multiple-choice form. An example of the multiple-choice form is Wood and Michelson's Children's Assertiveness Behavior Scale, (1978) presented earlier under self-report scales. Open-ended instruments require the child to tell what should be done or how he would act under the conditions presented. Examples of the open-ended methods are the Spivack and Shure (1974) measures described later in this section.

Faulty cognitions (i.e., maladaptive self-statements, assumptions, and beliefs) are thought to be one kind of impediment to social competence. Faulty cognitions may take forms such as negative self statements ("I'm dumb," or "I hate myself") or exaggerations where, for example, the child has one negative interaction with a peer and decides that everyone hates him. Other forms of dysfunctional cognitions include perfectionistic thinking where every effort is expected to be perfect, and inaccurate attributions where the child fails to accept responsibility for his behavior but attributes his actions to external factors (Meichenbaum, 1977). For example, "I can't sit still because I didn't have my medicine today," or "My school work is not good because the teacher doesn't like me." Meichenbaum has adapted the following set of distorted thinking patterns from Beck (1970):

(1) arbitrary inference - the drawing of a conclusion when evidence is lacking or actually supports the contrary conclusion;
(2) magnification - exaggeration of the meaning of an event;
(3) cognitive deficiency - disregard for an important aspect of a life situation;
(4) dichotomous reasoning - overly simplified and rigid perception of events as good or bad, right or wrong;
(5) overgeneralization - taking a single incident such as failure as a sign of total personal incompetence and in this way generating a fallacious rule."

[Meichenbaum, 1977, p. 192]

The basic task in assessing a child's cognitions is to get the child to identify his faulty self-statements, especially those that occur while he is engaged in some maladaptive behavior. Several techniques have been identified by Meichenbaum (1976) for assessing a child's cognitions. One of these involves video taping the child while he is being assessed on some behavioral measure such as the previously-described role-play test. The tape is replayed, and the child is asked to share the thoughts he experienced during the enactment. Cognitions are probed, particularly in scenes where social skill deficits are observed. Attention is then given to other similar situations in an effort to determine to what extent this particular pattern is indicative of the child's general thought processes.

In a related procedure, imagery is used in an interview situation rather than overt behavioral enactment of the problem situation. The child is asked to imagine the scene, to close his eyes and "run a movie through his head," describing his thoughts while mentally reliving the situation. For example, the child experiencing difficulty in approaching a peer for social interaction, or talking in class, or taking a test, would visualize himself in these situations and share the things he would say to himself while so engaged. The objective is to determine if the child is emitting self-statements that are self-defeating or counterproductive to the desired behavior. The child who wants to ask a peer to participate in a social activity with him but tells himself that the peer won't do it because he doesn't like him is producing internal dialogue that will sabotage the desired goal of social interaction with a peer.

A third aspect of cognitive assessment is to determine whether the child is able to engage in constructive thinking in order to identify alternative solutions to problem situations. Children frequently display maladaptive behavior, not necessarily because they prefer conflict but because they have not realized alternative responses that would produce a more satisfactory resolution. Spivack and Shure (1974) have developed several instruments for measuring the cognitive problem-solving skills of young children. The Preschool Interpersonal Problem Solving Test (PIPS) assesses the child's ability to think of alternative solutions, the What Happens Next Game (WHNG) measures consequential thinking, and the Means-Ends Problem Solving Test (MEPS) investigates the child's ability to conceptualize means toward a goal. The PIPS test has two parts, one presenting conflict situations with a peer, the second depicting the child in a conflict situation with his mother. In the first part of the PIPS test, the child is given seven basic stories involving one child playing with a toy that is wanted by a second child. The child being assessed is required to tell what the child in the story who wants the toy might do to resolve the situation, for example:

"Here's (child A) and here's (child B). A is playing with this truck and he has been playing with it for a long time. Now B wants a chance to play with the truck but A keeps on playing with it. Who's been playing with the truck for a long time? You can point. That's right, A. (Point to A.) Who wants to play with it? That's right, B. What can B do so he can have a chance to play with the truck?" (If there is no new relevant response: "What can B say...?").

[Spivack and Shure, 1974, p. 194]

Following the completion of this section, the child is given five additional stories where the child in the story does something to anger his mother, for example: "A broke his mother's favorite flowerpot and he is afraid his mother will be mad at him. What can A do or say so his mother will not be mad?" (p. 195). Again, the child is expected to give solutions to these problems. The child is probed to give as many different solutions as possible. Each different alternative is counted as one point, yielding a total PIPS score for both parts of the test.

The second test, the What Happens Next Game, is designed to determine whether the child is able to anticipate consequences to certain behaviors. It is described as a game because the examiner begins telling a story and the child is required to complete it. The child is given five stories of peer conflicts with toys and five stories involving the child doing something without adult permission. Examples of both types follow:

(1) "A had a truck and he was playing with it. B wanted to play with that truck. So B grabbed—you know, snatched—that truck. Tell me what happens next."

(2) "Here's A and this is Mrs. Smith. A saw Mrs. Smith's little poodle dog on her porch and took it for a walk. But A did not ask Mrs. Smith if he could take it. What might happen next in the story?"   [P. 198]

In testing, the focus is on whether the child is actually able to specify realistic consequences to various events and if so, the number of different consequences identified.

The Children's MEPS involves the child in attempting to fill in the middle part of a problem situation where the child is presented with the beginning and ending; for example:

Al (Joyce) has moved into the neighborhood. He (she) didn't know anyone and felt very lonely. The story ends with Al (Joyce) having many good friends and feeling at home in the neighborhood. What happens in between Al's (Joyce's) moving in and feeling lonely, and when he (she) ends up with many good friends?   [Spivack, Platt and Shure, 1976, p. 65]

The child's response is scored in terms of "Means," i.e., inputs that lead to problem solution, "obstacles," additional problems the child adds to the script that interfere with a solution, and "time," i.e., using time as a means to solve the problem. The Children's MEPS is designed for elementary school children and is given orally in order to maintain attention and minimize problems related in inability to read. Research with this instrument reveals that children with emotional problems are less likely than normal children to be able to conceptualize means toward a goal, less likely to consider obstacles in the way of a goal, and less likely to be aware of the importance of the passing of time in the solution of a problem.

ASSESSING REINFORCERS

It has been suggested previously that the motivating conditions operating in a situation affect both the child's performance of social behaviors and his ability to learn new ones. Social skills are more likely to be exhibited when the child expects a positive outcome for his behavior, and he is more likely to participate in activities designed to teach social skills if he expects gratifying results. Knowing what the child regards as rewarding will make it easier to engage him in the social skills learning task. For that reason, the topic of assessment includes reinforcers as an area for attention, both the contingencies of reinforcement that are present in a situation and the potential reinforcers that might be used to enhance teaching.

An assessment of contingencies operating in a situation involves looking at both the conditions that exist prior to the occurrence of a behavior and those that follow the behavior. In assessing situations as to the degree to which they facilitate or inhibit the child's performance of desirable social behaviors, a number of questions may be asked, for example,

- What is the rate of the target behavior?
- What events occur that appear to trigger the behavior?
- When and under what circumstances does it occur?
- What people are present?
- What social responses follow the behavior?
- What outcomes could the child perceive as a result of his behavior?

The other facet of assessing reinforcers involves identifying those consequences for behavior that a child or group of children appear to value and which can be provided following desired behaviors to increase the probability of repetition. Since reinforcers do not have absolute value but rather are defined by their effects on behavior, it has been suggested that one speak only of assessing for "potential" reinforcers (Mash & Terdall, 1976). A dessert might seem like a potent reinforcer, for example, except when a child is completely satiated with food; praise serves as a positive reinforcer to most people, but it sometimes has an opposite effect with very disturbed children. Whether any consequence will serve to encourage a given behavior at any point in time depends on such factors as the presence of competing reinforcers, the physiological state of the child, and the child's past experience with the potential reinforcer.

Within the limitations inherent in assessing for reinforcers, there are instruments that have been developed for this purpose. Gelfand and Hartmann (1975) have devised a *Reinforcer Identification List,* a checklist on which an informant can indicate a child's preferences. The comprehensive list of items includes foods, drinks, playing games and sports, toys, books, social contacts, animals, travel, music and dancing, and hobbies. *The Children's Reinforcement Survey* by Clement and Richard (1976) asks the informant to list and then rank the child's preferred people, preferred places, things with which the child spends time, favorite foods and drinks, and most frequent activities. The informant is asked to indicate not only the persons, things, and activities with which the child spends the most time, but also those he would like to have available to him more often. Because of the highly individual and varying nature of reinforcers, there are no standardized procedures or norms for this instrument. A questionnaire of this sort could be used to gather information from an adult informant by way of paper and pencil or interview or used as content for an interview with the child himself, always with the caveat that one is only identifying possible rather than actual reinforcers.

Children will often reveal, in spontaneous conversation, those things they value. A further means of assessing reinforcers is through observation of what children do when given free choice. According to the "Premack principle," "for any pair of responses the more probable one will reinforce the less probable one" (Premack, 1965), which implies that any behavior can have reinforcing value relative to some other behavior. Applying this principle, for example, teachers have used math as a reinforcer for reading when the child enjoys math more than reading, and freedom to walk around the room as a reinforcer for sitting in one's seat and being on task. Because identifying reinforcers through observation and counting to determine more frequent behaviors is not always practical or efficient, the "reinforcement menu" has been developed as a short cut. One such menu devised by Daley (1976) for mentally-retarded children involved 22 drawings of activities that had been identified as high frequency occurrences. Children were able to indicate preferences by picking out pictures. Similar menus could easily be made for nonreading children by using cutouts from magazines.

Stephens (1976) outlines a series of related techniques for assessing reward systems. These involve: (1) individual or group interviews in which a child is asked to choose between a series of potential rewards (for example, whether he would feel better with a star on his paper or having his paper on the bulletin board); (2) a paper-and-pencil forced-choice preference schedule in which the child is asked to indicate his preferences among paired activities; and (3) a contrived task approach in which the teacher selects an easy task for the child, provides a series of reinforcers for the child's performance (for example, touch, verbal praise), and evaluates the child's response in terms of enthusiasm, persistence, and quality of performance, comparing performance under the varying reward conditions.

SUMMARY

Assessment prior to the teaching of social skills helps determine which social behaviors are missing from the child's repertoire and thus need to be taught, and which behaviors only need to be increased through altering motivational conditions. Assessment assists also in determining the effectiveness of teaching and clinical interventions.

Rating instruments such as behavior checklists, sociometric questionnaires, and paper-and-pencil self-report measures constitute a relatively simple way to gather data for screening purposes. Such measures can also help to identify problem areas that can be developed into behavioral objectives for teaching of positive alternative behaviors. In using rating instruments, caution must be taken and consideration given to the fact that the profile obtained may be largely an indication of how the child is perceived rather than how he actually is.

Observation and recording of the child's performance of social skills in various aspects of his natural environment provide the most specific and relevant information. Observational data can be gathered in a variety of spontaneous situations, or events can be structured to elicit the behavior being assessed. An interview can serve as one such contrived situation that lends itself to the observation of a number of interpersonal behaviors.

Other data can be gathered in the natural environment through permanent products, especially the use of video and audio tapes. Simulations of events in the natural environment through role playing provide another source of observational data. Assessment using role playing can be carried out using spontaneous reenactments of problem situations or through more standardized means using prepared scripts that prompt responses. Role playing scenarios can be delivered by live players or through audio or video taped presentations. The interpretation of these measures should take into consideration that behaviors emitted during role play may vary from responses under natural conditions.

Along with determining the behaviors that the child emits under various social situations, it is also important to identify the cognitions and emotions he is experiencing that may interfere with or facilitate social competence. Self monitoring can provide data about such private events but, at the same time, is limited as an assessment technique by reactive effects, along with the amount of sophistication and skill required to observe, measure, and report on one's thoughts and feelings. In addition to assessment by way of self reports related to feelings and thoughts in social situations, a series of assessment procedures have been devised to measure problem-solving skills.

Finally, it is important to assess reinforcement systems in order to determine what incentives can be used to increase the probability that the child will engage in social skill instruction and that the newly-acquired social behaviors will be maintained after being established. Social skills assessment presents many problems of validity and reliability. For this reason, multiple methods are advisable, as well as more than one informant and assessment across a variety of situations.

Chapter 3
The Teaching Process

When the social skills to be taught have been identified, and it has been determined through assessment whether the child can perform those behaviors, the practitioner is now ready for the task of teaching the skills that are lacking or are not a comfortable part of the child's repertoire of social behaviors. Learning takes place primarily through observation, imitation, and feedback from the environment; children learn social skills in much the same way they learn academic concepts. The steps in instruction can be seen as involving first the presentation of a stimulus; second, the eliciting of a response to the stimulus; and third, providing feedback about the correctness of the response, followed by further refinement of responses and practice in correct responses. In social skills instruction, the first step can be a demonstration, a verbal description, a picture or diagram, or any of many other stimuli describing the behavior. The desired response from the child is his attempt to reproduce the stimuli through imitation. The feedback provided for the response can take a variety of forms, but needs essentially to convey information about whether and how the response should be repeated or changed. Opportunities are then needed for further imitation, further feedback, and practice.

Along with these steps, at least two other elements are necessary. These are the child's attention and the child's willingness to engage in the learning task, both of which are related to the motivating conditions in the learning situation. Basic to motivation is the teacher or therapist's ability to present himself or herself as a positive stimulus. In other words, the nature of the relationship that exists with the child or children will affect the child's involvement. Along with the adult's ability to provide support and encouragement, there are other ways to set the stage or provide the stimulus conditions that will encourage the child to participate. Depending on the nature of the skills to be taught, the nature of the setting, and the ages of the children involved, a number of procedures could be used in varying combinations to create motivating conditions. Some of these are presented below:

1. Initiating a discussion about the skill in question, establishing its relevance for the child, why it is important, what benefits there are to learning this skill, what disadvantages there are from not knowing this behavior. Such a discussion could relate to specific problem situations children are experiencing, possibly disguised or put in a fantasy context.
2. Use of materials such as stories, filmstrips, films, and other audio-visual media to set the stage.
3. Use of bulletin boards for visual presentations through pictures, photographs, cartoons, or student-produced art work related to the skill. A bulletin board could highlight, for example, the "Skill of the Week" or could present a sports figure or other hero emphasizing the behavior. (For example, a picture captioned "O.J. Simpson says, 'Be a good sport' " with specific sportsmanlike behaviors outlined below.)
4. Grouping of children in ways to enhance peer support and reinforcement and provide children with peer models. A single child by himself may be harder to engage in social skills training than at least a "duo" where two children can provide motivation for each other. Elementary-age children may prefer to be in single-sex groups, while older adolescents are likely to prefer cross-sex groups. In some settings, it may be necessary to avoid stigma by using the whole class or developing groups based on criteria other than need for social skills training.
5. Using techniques appropriate to the age level of the young person, making sure the behaviors selected for development are relevant to the child. The interest of elementary-age children in forming clubs might lend itself to a "Social Skills Club" which meets under established conditions at some desirable place and time. For adolescents the use of media such as videotape feedback with opportunities to operate the equipment themselves could enhance interest, as could providing as many opportunities as possible for self direction in the selection of skills, in the development of scenarios for role playing, and in evaluating progress.
6. The establishment of expectations that some positive benefits will result from engaging in the task at hand. Such benefits could include both the future payoffs from knowing the behaviors and such immediate benefits as having refreshments or getting out of a homework assignment. It is important to schedule social skills training at times when the activity does not compete with high-interest activities. Children who are less easily motivated may need a contingency contract where activities, privileges, or tangible reinforcers can be offered in exchange for engaging in social skills training. Badges, ribbons, or certificates can serve as incentives.
7. Efforts to make the activity fun, for example, with the use of humor and game formats. Examples of some social skills games are given later in this chapter. Introducing fantasy to add a storybook quality has the benefit of lessening the anxiety that could be associated with personal

problems or deficits in social skills. Puppets lend themselves particularly well to such an effort. The making of puppets for this purpose could become a related art project, and the production of a puppet show could be a conclusion to a series of social skill training sessions.

In the chapter that follows, a variety of teaching procedures are described. Many have been described in research literature with empirically-demonstrated positive results. Procedures for teaching observable social behaviors almost always involve some aspect of learning by imitation or social modeling. Social modeling is also important for the teaching of adaptive ways of thinking and feeling in social situations, particularly where the internal events can be reflected in some overt behavior. Although strategies for teaching social skills related to affective and cognitive dimensions are separated in the chapter for ease of presentation, in practice affective, cognitive, and behavioral aspects of social skills instruction will usually be present at the same time. Relaxation procedures are included here as a social skill since they can be translated into coping methods to be used in stressful interpersonal situations, as can be various cognitive coping strategies. Also included as a section on approaching the teaching of social skills by means of games, a way to enhance interest and excitement and thus secure the child's involvement and participation.

SOCIAL MODELING—ROLE PLAYING

Social modeling is the process of producing a model of social behavior that enables another to learn by observation and imitation. An individual observes another person's behavior and then imitates that behavior by behaving similarly under similar circumstances. Social modeling is considered to be the method whereby most social behaviors are learned, especially during the developing years when children learn to imitate the behaviors of significant others in their lives, e.g., parents, teachers, and peers. For example, young children playing with dolls will be observed to care for and speak to their dolls in a manner similar to the way their parents treat them or a sibling. In later years, these same children may note aspects of their behavior that duplicate that of their parents even though, in many cases, there is a conscious desire not to emulate their parents' child-rearing practices. On a larger scale, modeling through the media (i.e., television, films) has extensively affected our lifestyles to the extent that it influences the products we consume and the entertainment we pursue. Whether through the mass media or direct observation, there is evidence that models also influence the degree to which we engage in aggressive, passive, or assertive behaviors (Bandura, 1973).

The power of social modeling in modifying behaviors and in developing new ones has been thoroughly documented under laboratory conditions. Investigators have used these procedures to help children acquire such behaviors as increased social interaction for isolated children (O'Connor, 1973), an increased tendency to give to charity and to help others (Rosenhan & White, 1967), and improved conversation skills involving asking for and giving information (Zimmerman & Pike, 1972). Social modeling also has been used extensively to develop assertive behaviors (McFall & Lillesand, 1971). In addition to facilitating the development of novel responses, modeling has been effective in eliminating or reducing such maladaptive behaviors in children as aggression (Chittenden, 1942). For developing new social behaviors, the basic elements of instruction through social modeling consist of: (1) instructions, (2) exposure to a model, (3) rehearsal, (4) performance feedback, and (5) practice. Each of these elements is described below.

Providing Instructions

Rather than simple responses, individual social skills are actually complex processes, frequently consisting of a chain of behaviors. The child must be instructed how to perform the specific subskills that make up the comprehensive social skill. For example, what responses are required in greeting someone, in making a friend, or in being assertive? In the first case, the child would be expected at least to make eye contact, say hello, give his name, and perhaps smile. Skills such as making friends and good sportsmanship are even more complex, but still lend themselves to analysis. The components of friendship making have been identified as greeting, asking the other child for some information such as, "Where are you from?", inviting the other child to do something with him, and telling the child something such as "I like to play ball" (Gottman, Gonso & Rasmussen, 1975). At the initial stage of instructions, the child is assisted in identifying the specific responses to be made, the nature of these responses, the sequence of occurrence (if applicable), and how they should be performed.

For social skill instruction, it is strongly suggested that children be helped to analyze the components of a social skill themselves rather than simply being told what they should be. For example, for the skill of friendship making, a film or story could be presented that depicts children successfully making friends, followed by a discussion to identify the specific reponses that helped the fictional characters to make friends. As the behaviors are generated, they are listed and sequenced according to order of occurrence such as:

1. Say, "Hi, how are you? My name is_____, what's yours?"

2. Ask something like, "Where are you from?" or "What are you doing?"
3. Invite him or her to do something, "I want to play checkers. Would you like to play with me?"

In specifying the behaviors, the trainer should use the child's own words as much as possible and take into consideration the developmental levels and cultural differences of the children. For example, older children (particularly boys) might include in this sequence a handshake, the complexity of which might differ from one cultural group to another. It might also be necessary to establish whether each child understands the nature of each behavior listed and whether he is able to reproduce them in a relatively natural rather than mechanical fashion. One approach might be to ask children to demonstrate their suggested responses, e.g., "George, what else might you ask a new child? Would you show us how you would ask that?" Instructions need to be tailored to the child's social skill development level. A child operating at an especially low level may not only need assistance in identifying specific responses but also in determining what they are and how they should be made. On the other hand, higher functioning children may only need minimal prompting in subskill identification and performance. Instructions in the form of "coaching" were employed by Oden and Asher (1977) to facilitate friendship-making skills in children. These procedures are described in detail in Chapter 6 of this book.

Presenting a Model

Directly related to instruction in subskill components is the exposure to the model or demonstration of how the specific responses should be made into the composite behavior. Important factors at this stage of the modeling process include: (1) model characteristics, (2) attention to the model, (3) recognition of specific responses made by the model, and (4) the mode of presentation. It has been established that characteristics of the model can either facilitate or inhibit the tendency of the observer to copy the modeled behavior. Modeling is enhanced when the observer perceives the model as being important, successful, and as someone with whom he can identify. It should be noted, however, that models representing exceptionally high standards or unfamiliar lifestyles and models with low prestige or perceived incompetence may prove to be ineffective.

Obviously, for modeling situations to be most effective, the observer must be attentive. Attention, to some extent, may be a function of the model's characteristics and the reinforcing properties of the presentation. Other ways to increase attention may include "setting the stage" where one establishes the importance of the particular social behavior and provides reinforcers or contingencies for paying attention. Related to attention is the ability to recognize and understand the exact responses produced by the model. Observation without understanding would result in inadequate or partial imitation, at best. Therefore, it is suggested that after the skill has been modeled, the observer be assisted in identifying and sequencing the exact responses exhibited by the model. One technique, as given by Marlatt and Perry (1975), is to use videotapes with a narrator's comments dubbed over the action in order to draw the child's attention to the most salient aspects of the observed behavior.

In addition to the above factors, the learning process can be facilitated by the way in which the modeling is presented. Goldstein, Sprafkin and Gershaw (1976, P. 6) provide guidelines for "modeling display," suggesting that the behaviors be presented:

a) in a clear and detailed manner,
b) in the order from least to most difficult behaviors,
c) with enough repetition to make overlearning likely,
d) with as little irrelevant (not to be learned) detail as possible, and
e) with several different models, rather than a single model, [p. 6]

In devising an instructional program, along with multiple models, the social skills trainer should consider the various sources for models. Adults may serve as effective models for young children, as may puppets and story characters. For adolescents, however, adults in their immediate environment may have less influence over their behavior than peers, rock stars, or movie idols. Outlined below are several ways of presenting models in social skills instruction, including the use of puppets, taped models, models through books, and live models.

1. *Puppets.* One method for presenting models in a group setting is through puppetry. Although generally considered most appropriate for the younger child, puppets also can serve as effective models for the older child or adolescent. The determining factor with puppets, as with other forms of models, is relevance or the extent to which the child can identify with the characters depicted. For example, one effective social skills instruction program with junior high school youngsters used puppets in the role of the school cheerleaders, athletes, and other individuals commonly found in a junior high setting. In addition to being attractive and possibly increasing attention to the learning situation, puppets can be used to depict social situations of immediate concern in a way that is less threatening and, in some cases, less embarrassing than if live models were used. Puppets provide an element of objectivity so that the child unwilling to directly deal with his own actions may be willing to view, discuss, and eventually role play the same behaviors with puppets.

Puppets may also take the form of fictional characters such as Winnie-the-Pooh or television favorites such as Sesame Street characters. In addition to commercially-available puppets, children may be assisted in making their own puppets. Personally-made puppets can contribute to model identification and attractiveness. Hand-made puppets may range from rather elaborate productions made of fabric cut from patterns, paper mache, or clay to very simple models made of socks, paper bags, boxes, tin cans, construction paper with drawn features, or figures cut out and pasted on tongue depressors.

A program that makes extensive use of puppetry is the Developing Understanding of Self and Others (DUSO) Program published by American Guidance Service. For each lesson, a variety of instructional strategies are used including problem stories, discussions with puppets, live role playing, and role playing with puppets. In this program, puppets are used to present the problem, to model desired behaviors, and to role play possible alternative responses. For example, in one lesson dealing with verbal aggression, the initial activities with the two main puppet characters help children to understand the importance of avoiding making unpleasant comments to others, while the role-playing puppet activity focuses on helping children to identify appropriate ways of expressing positive and negative feelings.

As the child develops more skill and becomes more comfortable in dramatic activities, it is to be hoped that he will prefer to engage in live role playing, discarding symbols and props such as puppets. Responses practiced under live role playing conditions should be easier to transfer to everyday situations.

2. *Taped Models.* Models may also be presented through the media, i.e., films, television, radio, audio and video tapes, magazines, and newspapers. While references can be made to positive role models found in the mass media, these sources lend themselves less easily to formal social learning instruction because of the difficulty in controlling content or ensuring that the most desirable material will be viewed or read. Greater control can be exercised with video and audio tapes designed for social skill instruction. The efficacy of film-mediated models in producing new social responses has been thoroughly documented (Bandura, 1969). The typical method of presentation is to show a model encountering and effectively resolving a conflict situation. For example, one modeling video tape described by Goodwin and Mahoney (1975) involves controlling aggression while being provoked. The tape shows the model coping with verbal aggression from peers by engaging in various self statements such as, "I will not get angry," "I will not fight." The self statements were dubbed onto the tape to illustrate the model's thought processes. While viewing the tapes, the coping mechanisms used by the models (i.e., cognitive self statements) were highlighted so that the observers were aware of the exact behaviors (in this case cognitions) that helped the model to cope successfully with the situation.

Although audio tapes have not been used as extensively for social modeling, they are particularly useful in modeling skills in verbal communication or affect. For example, audio tapes may be used to model the delivery of assertive statements with appropriate tonal quality and emotion. Modeling instructions that have been taped allow for additional presentations so that, where necessary, the behavior may be reviewed repeatedly until learned.

3. *Models Through Books.* Along with tapes and films, books may serve as another source of symbolic modeling for children and adolescents. Stories that have been realistically written with believable and significant characters can be used to teach a child how to respond to various social situations. For example, a reading series entitled *Getting It Together* (Goldberg & Greenberger, 1973) presents stories of adolescents in everyday problem situations. One story, "Now Will You Listen?" describes how high school students attempt to resolve hostilities and conflict between black and white students in the school. The story *Ira Sleeps Over,* written for younger children by Bernard Waber, describes how a young boy handles a problem after listening to the misadvice of his sister, suggesting that one should follow his own best judgment and not worry about others laughing at him.

A resource for identifying stories dealing with children's problems is the *Book Finder* published by American Guidance Service. The reader is also referred to the materials list in the appendix of this book. The following critéria are suggested by Cianciolo (1965) for selection of books for "bibliotherapy." The selections should:

1. focus on a particular need;
2. be written on the child's level;
3. center on the problem;
4. have realistic approaches;
5. have lifelike characters; and
6. accurately depict groups the characters represent.

4. *Live Models.* Live models are another option for modeling presentations. Live modeling is staged in a manner similar to that of taped presentations. In contrast to tapes, however, live procedures provide for greater flexibility so that alternative responses may be demonstrated. For example, in the social skill situation involving responses to verbal aggression, there are several viable options available to the child, e.g., engaging in certain cognitions in order to maintain control, leaving the scene, reporting the situations to an adult authority figure, and so forth. A role play situation could be structured with the practitioner and child or the child with other children acting out the various alternatives. Following each enactment a discussion would ensue to determine factors such as: (1) what response occurred (e.g., walking away), (2) whether it was effective (e.g., did it stop the

taunting), (3) how the actor(s) felt, and (4) what other responses one might use in this situation. Inappropriate responses might also be displayed in order to demonstrate relative effects. Thus, with live modeling, children could observe several alternatives and assess the consequences to these behaviors. For example, depending on the social situation, reporting to an adult may result in more taunting, suggesting that other responses should be considered. The learning experience may be enhanced by permitting children to reverse roles, e.g., being the taunter and the one taunted.

For reasons discussed previously, peers may serve as highly effective models in social skill instruction and can assist in individualizing social skill lessons. Children functioning on low levels who are unable to benefit from traditional social modeling or role playing techniques may profit from individual instruction where they are assisted in copying and reproducing the desired social responses. Ascher and Phillips (1975) describe such a procedure labeled "guided behavior rehearsal" where trained peer guides, competent in the particular social area, used modeling and behavior rehearsal to help adult clients gain greater social competence. The guide was responsible for accompanying the client to various social situations in order to model appropriate behaviors, for conducting training sessions where specific responses were rehearsed, and for providing feedback and reinforcement for approximations to desired responses. In one case, these procedures were successful in teaching a neurologically-impaired young man exactly how to initiate and engage in conversation with the result that his social skills were improved and he was enabled to sustain relationships.

Similar procedures have been successfully used with children (Csapo, 1972). A socially-skilled child is assigned to a peer with social deficits to assist in areas such as playing with peers, resisting aggression, and engaging in conversations. The peer model is trained in modeling techniques for the target behaviors to be developed and in techniques for prompting and reinforcing the incompetent child. Children selected to serve as models should be respected by the other child, should be skilled in the social behaviors to be developed, and should be similar in background, e.g., age, sex, and socioeconomic status.

Rehearsal

Observed behavior will not necessarily be learned unless some mechanism is put into operation whereby the observed behavior is retained and subsequently reproduced. The modeled behaviors must be practiced by the child before he can produce them successfully in real-life situations. Behavior rehearsal (Rose, 1972) represents a form of structured role playing that enables the child to act out and practice the new behaviors. Bandura (1977a) has suggested that practice may be conducted through covert responding, verbal responding, and motoric reproduction.

1. *Covert Responding.* Covert responding essentially refers to cognitive images about a particular event. It has been established that imagery can be used effectively to develop both academic and social behaviors. Behaviors coded through imagery can be retrieved later for appropriate responding. When engaged in social skill instruction, the use of imagery or covert responses can be prompted by helping the learner to reproduce in his mind or imagine the behavior that had previously been modeled. For example, the child has just been exposed to a modeling session designed to teach appropriate responses to verbal aggression. The child may then be directed to imagine the scene and possible responses as follows:

You are walking home from school and two pupils from your class are following you. They begin to tease you because you struck-out during the baseball game and your team lost. Imagine what you will do next. You decide to ignore them. You notice that some of your friends are ahead so you walk quickly to catch up and begin talking with them. Imagine what happens next.

Other resolutions to this scene may include:

a. Responding with an assertive statement such as, ''I know I struck out but everyone does sometimes and I won't feel badly because I did this time.''
b. Responding with an empathic statement such as, ''I know you are upset because we lost the game and I am too, but I tried my best.''
c. Responding through physical avoidance, e.g., leaving the scene by taking another route home or going into a public building such as a store or library.

Obviously, the responses employed would depend partly on the circumstances and the particular population. For example, in one situation, verbally assertive statements may serve to extinguish undesirable behavior; in another situation they may provoke more aggression. Children may generate undesirable responses, for example, a verbally aggressive statement like, ''Maybe I'm not such a good baseball player, but I'm the best speller in the class.'' Through imagining consequences, children may be helped to recognize that although the immediate results may be rewarding, the long-term effects of counter-aggression may be aversive. Rather than identifying one pat solution for each conflict situation, the aim is to help children recognize that a variety of alternatives may exist, and that the ones used should be those most likely to resolve rather than exacerbate the situation. The imagery procedure may include:

a. Child closes eyes while scene is depicted by practitioner.
b. Child is directed to imagine self performing the designated response.
c. Child is directed to imagine reactions to his response.
d. Practitioner directs child through some scene with alternative responses.
e. Child and practitioner identify the most natural and appropriate responses that the child would employ under similar circumstances in the future.

Before engaging the child in imagery, it may be advisable to use relaxation techniques in order to reduce any anxiety associated with conflict situations. Relaxation will be discussed later in this chapter.

2. *Verbal responding.* An extension of the steps used for covert responding or imagery is verbal responding. Retention and appropriate performance can be enhanced by having the child talk through the desired responses, elaborating on the previous imagery sequence. At each step, the child describes the scene again in his own words, restating the alternatives and verbalizing possible consequences to proposed resolutions.

3. *Motor responding.* Although the two previous response types may be used independently, they also may be viewed as preparation for making motor responses. Here the child is required to act out (typically in a role playing format) the responses that he has observed, that he has visualized through imagery, and that he has verbalized. Role play essentially consists of four basic parts:

a. *setting the stage* – describing the scene, selecting participants, and assigning and describing participant roles.
b. *enactment* – participants interact with each other, dramatizing respective roles.
c. *discussion/evaluation* – performances are evaluated by participants and observers, and alternative responses identified.
d. *reenactment* – scene is role played again, incorporating suggestions from step *c;* different participants may be identified.

As previously discussed, the practitioner may choose live enactments or symbolic representations such as puppets.

In addition to providing for the practice of desired behaviors, responding through role playing has other advantages. It allows for switching roles so that the participants can view both sides of the situation. This is especially important for the child who tends to exhibit behaviors that are annoying to others. For example, the child who frequently engages in teasing may be the object of taunting behavior in the role play. Another advantage is the opportunity to observe consequences of specific responses. For example, the child who chooses to counter aggression with more aggression or with extreme passivity may realize that he has simply negatively escalated rather than resolved the situation. By observing the consequences, children may begin to recognize the importance of alternative behaviors. A third advantage of enactment through role playing is that it facilitates memory. New behaviors are more effectively learned and maintained if the method of practice incorporates a motor component such as overt role playing.

Feedback

As with all learning, feedback is critical to social skill development, since by receiving information about his performance the child is able to make the necessary corrections to improve his skills. Feedback may take a variety of forms, for example, (1) verbal feedback where the child receives corrective instructions or praise, (2) reinforcement where correct responses earn tangible reinforcers, and (3) self evaluation where a system is devised whereby the child can evaluate himself. As indicated above, the typical role-play situation incorporates a discussion/evaluation phase for the purposes of either indicating better ways to perform the behavior or suggesting other ways to respond such as, "Smile when you shake hands, George" or "Another way to make friends with Marie is to ask her to play a game with you." For behaviors performed correctly, the trainer should compliment the child being careful to praise specific responses, e.g., "You really did a good job of following the rules when you played checkers, George."

Video and audio tapes are valuable self evaluation tools and may be especially effective for the adolescent who has difficulty accepting feedback from other sources. The simulated social interactions are taped and, afterward, the participants evaluate their performance according to specified criteria. The effects may be somewhat dramatic in cases where the youngster is completely unaware of how he presents himself or the effect he has on others. For example, the child who tends to scowl or yell may recognize how negative these behaviors are by observing them on tape. Teaching children how to monitor and evaluate their own behavior involves assisting them in understanding what the goals of various social interactions are and how to determine whether a particular encounter was successful. Self evaluation is another aspect of the role play discussion/evaluation phase. This may be provided by guiding the child through a sequence of questions such as (considering the previous scene of verbal aggression):

• What did you want to happen?
• Did they stop teasing you?
• What else did they do?
• Were you pleased with the way you got them to stop? (Or why do you think they didn't stop?)
• If you were being teased again, would you do the same thing?
• What would you try to do better?
• Why?
• How do you feel about yourself in this situation?
• How do you think the boys feel?
• Do you want to remain angry at these boys?
• What will you do the next time you meet these boys?

Feedback may also be provided through reinforcement systems. Contingencies frequently are attached to social behaviors so that correct performance results in desired reinforcers. If the social skills instructor determines that feedback through verbal reinforcement is insufficient to motivate the child or children to increase desirable social responses in a social modeling or role-play situation, tangible or token reinforcement systems may be established. It may be necessary to differentiate between reinforcers given for participation regardless of the quality of the responses and those that provide positive feedback for the desired responses. A suggested set of procedures is as follows:

1. Define clearly what behaviors will be rewarded. For example, in a role-playing situation to teach assertive behavior, reinforcers can be given for such target behaviors as:
   a. looking at the person you are speaking to
   b. speaking in an appropriate tone of voice
   c. smiling at the person you are relating to
   d. making verbal responses without hesitating
   e. making positive or relevant verbal statements.

2. Provide reinforcers in a form appropriate to the child, e.g.,
   a. edibles such as cereal or candy for a very young or low-functioning child
   b. poker chips or other tangible kind of token
   c. points on a chart or on the chalkboard

3. Deliver reinforcers either:

   a. during the activity immediately following the target behavior, along with verbal feedback, e.g., "good eye contact, John," or "that was a good reply," provided the giving of verbal feedback is not disruptive of the activity.

   b. or in an evaluation session after the activity individually or in a group, i.e., "In that last role play, how many points should we give John for eye contact?"

In the last situation, the discussion around the awarding of points can serve as corrective verbal feedback. For this purpose, the most ideal arrangement would be the availability of videotapes to review, discuss, and use as the basis for awarding points. Whether tokens or points need to be exchanged for backup reinforcers in the form of privileges, activities, or tangible items will have to be determined by the trainer based on an assessment of existing motivation levels. It is important to remember to reinforce liberally for steps in the right direction, since initial attempts at learning social skills are likely to be awkward and far less than perfect.

An example of the use of tokens in social skills training is an adaptation used by Rotheram (1978) of a technique suggested by Flowers (1975). Rotheram's program makes use of different colored tokens to convey different kinds of feedback in assertiveness training with children and adolescents. Passive behavior is indicated by a blue token, aggressive behavior by a red token, and assertive behavior by a green token. These tokens are held either by student "directors" or the instructor "supercoach" and are given out during role playing to identify a behavior as assertive, passive, or aggressive. These tokens are primarily intended for cueing to teach discrimination, but according to Rotheram, the tokens quickly acquire reinforcement power and are an aid in group management. In addition to the red, blue, and green tokens, her procedures include yellow tokens delivered by the instructor for behavior management and to reinforce efforts to learn the new assertive behaviors.

Practice

Once the child demonstrates the ability to perform the behavior independently (i.e., without extensive prompting or corrective feedback), he is then directed to practice this behavior in other conditions and with other people. After the child has consistently made appropriate responses to verbally aggressive statements, for example, the trainer may direct the child to practice these behaviors when teased on the playground or at home with his siblings. The child is also directed to report back to the trainer the results of these practice sessions, at which point the child is praised for his successes and receives additional instructions, if necessary. In practicing behaviors in other settings, it is important to determine if the child is able to assess the social situations and make the most appropriate responses. For example, making an assertive remark and leaving the scene may be an appropriate way to respond to verbal aggression from a peer or sibling but not necessarily from a parent or teacher. An additional consideration in such cases may be to make sure the child does not deliberately create negative situations for the purpose of practicing the assigned behaviors.

The five basic steps outlined above—(1) instructions, (2) modeling, (3) rehearsal, (4) feedback, and (5) practice in other settings—have been incorporated by Northrop, Wood, and Clark (1979) into a ten-step sequence for "social skill teaching interactions" which they apply both in structured sessions and in spontaneous "incidental teaching" following the occurrence of a problem. The steps are as follows:

Social Skill Teaching Interactions

Definitions of Teaching Interaction Components:

1. Positive approach to student-Instructor makes initial contact or opening statement in a

nonpunitive manner. May be a greeting or descriptive praise but should not include punishing statements.

2. Description of inappropriate behavior - Instructor describes inappropriate behavior in detail to student.
3. Description of appropriate behavior - Instructor describes desired or appropriate and effective behavior to student.
4. Rationale for the appropriate behavior - Instructor describes consequences, both good and bad, that could be received following appropriate and inappropriate behavior. What's the link to real world—reason for performing behavior, long-term payoff.
5. Modeling of desired behavior - Instructor demonstrates the appropriate (and may include the inappropriate) ways to perform the defined social skill.
6. Request for student to practice - Instructor requests the student to practice the desired behaviors in a role-play situation. The instructor should develop the role-play scene to include necessary social stimuli, e.g., other peers, adults.
7. Feedback during practice - Instructor provides both positive and negative feedback on student's performance by describing those behaviors which are good, adequate, or need improvement, and by offering constructive suggestions for future performance.
8. Requests for additional practice by student - Instructor requests student to attempt role-play situation again and suggests specific behavior changes and improvements to be included. Might use cues.
9. Praise for accomplishments - Instructor delivers praise to student for performance and participation.
10. Give "homework" practice assignment - Instructor requests the student to attempt the trained social skill in another setting, at another time, or with different people. Instructor should reemphasize the desired behaviors and rationales to be utilized by the student.

In the sequence outlined above, practice is carried out first through role playing and feedback in the instructional setting, then in the student's natural environment. Further steps could be added, those of reporting back results of homework and further role playing practice in the training environment to improve on the in vivo practice experience.

COGNITIVE APPROACHES

Cognitive approaches to social skill instruction focus on helping the child acquire thought patterns considered to be functional for social competence. While various models exist (Wilson, 1978), they may be grouped according to two primary intentions: (1) to alter the statements the child makes to himself, or (2) to develop cognitive problem solving skills. The common element present in all models is the theoretical position that cognitions play a major role in directing behavior and, thus, the child's maladaptive behavior may be indicative of inadequate thinking styles.

Altering Self-Statements

One theoretical framework for altering self-statements stems from the Rational Emotive Therapy (RET) model developed by Albert Ellis (1962). The basic premise is that maladaptive behaviors largely result from irrational belief systems that influence what we say to ourselves and, thereby, control our behavior. Ellis (1977) takes the position that inappropriate behavior is less a function of a particular event than it is of what one says to himself about the event. The child who receives a failing mark, for example, may exhibit more maladaptive behavior if he tells himself that he is worthless and dumb or that it is terrible and catastrophic to fail. The objective of rational models is to help the individual identify the events leading to specific behaviors, to analyze irrational belief systems considered to be controlling these reactions, and to replace these systems with rational ones that are more likely to lead to adaptive behavior. In examining irrational belief systems, Ellis (1977) suggests looking for the things one tells himself he should or must do or must have happen. Examples of these beliefs as listed by Gambrill (1977, pp. 498, 499) include:

1. The idea that it is a dire necessity for an adult human being to be loved or approved by virtually every significant other person in his community.
2. The idea that one should be thoroughly competent, adequate, and achieving all possible respects, if one is to consider oneself worthwhile.
3. The idea that certain people are bad, wicked, or villainous and that they should be severely blamed and punished for their villainy;
4. The idea that it is awful and catastrophic when things are not the way one would very much like them to be;
5. The idea that human unhappiness is externally caused and that people have little or no ability to control their sorrows and disturbances;
6. The idea that if something is or may be dangerous or fearsome, one should be terribly concerned about it and should keep dwelling on the possibility of its occurring;
7. The idea that it is easier to avoid than to face certain life difficulties and self-responsibilities;
8. The idea that one should be dependent on others and needs someone stronger than oneself on whom to rely;
9. The idea that one's past history is an all-important determinant of one's present behavior, and that because something once strongly affected one's life, it should indefinitely have a similar effect;
10. The idea that one should become quite upset over other people's problems and disturbances; and
11. The idea that there is invariably a right, precise, and perfect solution to human problems, and that it is catastrophic if this correct solution is not found.

The principles of rational-emotive therapy have been adapted by Knaus (1974) into an instructional program for children called Rational-Emotive Education (REE). Designed to be used by the classroom teacher, the objective of REE is to help the child to develop rational belief systems that foster more positive feelings and, thus, lead to more adaptive behaviors. The program contains five major learning areas that include:

a. *Feelings* - helping children become aware of feelings, their origins and various modes of expression.
b. *Challenging Irrational Beliefs* - helping children to recognize irrational belief systems, their effects and how to develop cognitive styles that would enable the children to challenge these irrational thought patterns on their own.
c. *Challenging Feelings of Inferiority* - helping children recognize the complex nature of individuals, that each person has positives as well as negatives, and that children should not view themselves or others in terms of a single attribute whether good or bad.
d. *Learning, Mistake-making and Imperfection* - helping children to understand the nature of the learning process, differences of opinion, and mistakes in order to develop a more realistic approach toward learning and to avoid the pitfalls of perfectionism.
e. *Demanding, Catastrophizing and Challenging* - teaching children to challenge irrational *must* and *should* systems which lead to "catastrophizing" and "awfulizing" and to replace them with more reasonable attitudes of *desire* and *prefer*. That is, the child will learn to think in terms of the things he would like to happen rather than the things that he demands should happen.

Also included are teaching activities for seven special topics: (a) Responsibility (roles and rules), (b) Perspective (viewing a situation from more than one perspective), (c) Stereotyping, (d) Teasing and name-calling, (e) Bullies, victims, bystanders, (f) Guided protest: The child as a consumer, and (g) Friendship. A traditional teaching model is used where a concept is presented, deductive techniques in the form of discussions, games, role plays, and skits are used to challenge an irrational belief and establish a more rational one; and the conclusion is reinforced through "homework" assignments and follow-up activities. According to the author, the program is geared to children from fourth to eighth grades but can be adapted for younger and older youngsters. It is intended to be presented several times weekly for approximately a nine-month period.

A cognitive approach similar to RET is Meichenbaum's (1977) stress-inoculation training which places more emphasis on (1) developing specific thinking skills or verbal mediators, and (2) applying these skills under stressful conditions. Meichenbaum describes stress-inoculation training as a three-step process wherein the individual is helped to conceptualize the problem, to develop cognitive coping skills, and to apply the skills under stressful conditions. In the first step, the child is aided in understanding the antecedent events and the cognitive and physiological aspects of the problem (what events provoked the emotional event), the physical responses that accompanied the emotions (increased heartbeat, sweating, etc.), and the self-statements that directed the emotional overt behaviors (such as flight in fear or fighting in anger). The techniques used to develop these understandings include engaging the child in a discussion, inquiring how he felt under these conditions, and encouraging the use of imagery. With imagery, the child is directed to relive a recent event and to "run a movie through his mind." If the problem situation involves excessive anger and extreme reactions, the child is asked to reconstruct his most recent tantrum, from which it might be determined that: (1) he gets angry whenever he makes an incorrect response in his academic work; (2) he feels hot and starts to breathe hard; (3) he feels that he is a dummy and no good when he gets something wrong; and (4) he starts to cry, to yell, to destroy his papers, and to throw things.

After the situation has been analyzed and the child realizes the events that precipitated his behavior, he is then trained to practice certain coping self statements. Meichenbaum (1977, p. 155) presents a four-phase model with sample self statements to be employed for rehearsing coping cognitions that consisted of: (1) preparing for a stressor—recognizing the nature of the situation ("What is it you have to do?" or "You can develop a plan to deal with it"); (2) confronting and handling a stressor—using statements to increase courage and self confidence ("Just 'psych' yourself up—you can meet this challenge" or "One step at a time; you can handle the situation"), (3) coping with the feeling of being overwhelmed—recognizing that reactions to the situation will occur and trying to keep these feelings under control ("You should expect your fear to rise" or "Don't try to eliminate fear totally; just keep it manageable"); and (4) reinforcing self-statements—assessing one's performance and making complimentary self-statements ("It worked; you did it" or "You can be pleased with the progress you're making").

A similar sequence for anger based on this model has been devised by Novaco (1975). Using Novaco's categories, self statements for the example of the child overreacting to corrective feedback might include:

Preparing for provocation
> If the teacher marks something wrong I can handle it.
> I know what to do if I get upset.
> Making a mistake is not so bad.

Impact on confrontation
> Keep calm.
> Think about the ones you got correct.
> It's silly to get angry about one problem.
> The teacher is really right to show me what I did wrong.
> Being corrected helps me learn.

Coping with arousal
> I'm beginning to breathe hard, relax.
> Stop and think about all the good work you did today.
> Try to keep cool.

Reflection on provocation
> a. *when conflict is unresolved:*
> It partly worked.

I can do better next time.
This is hard to do but I'll keep trying.
b. *when conflict is resolved or coping is successful.*
    I did a good job that time, I even smiled at the teacher.
    I can be a good student. The teacher likes me.

The third phase is the application phase, in which the child applies the above coping skills under various stressful conditions. Several techniques are used to facilitate skill application. Relaxation exercises are employed to reduce the child's emotional reactions and to aid in producing coping self statements. Through imagery, the child is instructed to place himself in a stressful situation:

Imagine that you are in class and you just finished taking a spelling test. You are saying things to yourself that will help you prepare for the teacher correcting your paper, such as, "I can handle it if I have made a mistake; I will not get angry." Now, the teacher has corrected your paper, you got two wrong. You are telling yourself to keep calm. You notice that you are feeling hot and are breathing heavily but you are telling yourself to control these feelings. You remind yourself that even though you got two wrong you did get eight correct. The teacher tells you that you did a better job on this spelling test. You say, "thank you," and congratulate yourself for controlling yourself.

Note: The child may also be taken through a less successful resolution such as:

You tell yourself to keep cool but you feel hot and shaky inside. Then you notice tears running down your face and you put your head on your desk to continue crying. A few minutes later the teacher tells you that you did better on this test. You thank her and tell yourself that even though you weren't completely controlled at least you didn't have a tantrum or throw books. You will do better next time.

Role playing may also be used, providing for a more explicit demonstration of behaviors and, thus, greater opportunity for feedback and self-evaluation.

Controlling impulsive or aggressive behaviors is the focus of another form of verbal mediation. Referred to as self-instructional training (SIT) (Meichenbaum, 1977), the goals are: (1) to get the child to interrupt himself before performing some inappropriate behavior, and (2) to train the child to guide his behavior through "internal dialogue." To effect the first goal, instructional techniques include cueing the child that a problem situation exists and that he must stop and think out how he will proceed. Labeled "thought stopping" and initially used with adults, this procedure was devised to help the individual discontinue non-productive or self-defeating thought processes. For example, the individual who tends to engage in excessive self-denigrating thoughts might say "stop" out loud or to himself to terminate the thoughts, and then direct his thinking along a more productive path. In adapting thought stopping for children, environmental or physiological stimuli are identified that can be used as signals for the child to stop and employ prescribed thinking skills. For example, Palkes, Stewart, and Kahana (1968), in a program to train hyperactive boys to perform paper-and-pencil tasks, used large cue cards that included statements such as: "Before I start any of the tasks I am going to do, I am going to say: STOP!"

After interrupting himself, the child is expected to use internal mediators or to talk to himself in order to guide himself through the problem situation. Training for such "thought structuring" is exemplified by a sequence developed by Meichenbaum and Goodman (1971) where the intent is to show a child how to think through a difficult task.

1. An adult model performed a task while talking to himself out loud (cognitive modeling);
2. The child performed the same task under the direction of the model's instructions (overt, external guidance);
3. the child performed the task while instructing himself aloud (overt self-guidance);
4. The child whispered the instructions to himself as he went through the task (faded, overt self-guidance); and finally
5. The child performed the task while guiding his performance via private speech (covert self-instruction).   [Meichenbaum, 1977, p. 32]

The following is an example of the modeling situation:

Okay, what is it I have to do? You want me to copy the picture with the different lines. I have to go slow and be careful. Okay, draw the line down, down good; then to the right, that's it; now down some more and to the left. Good, I'm doing fine so far. Remember go slow. Now back up again. No, I was supposed to go down. That's okay. Just erase the line carefully.... Good. Even if I make an error I can go on slowly and carefully. Okay, I have to go down now. Finished. I did it.   [Meichenbaum & Goodman, 1971, p. 117]

In this example, impulsive second-grade children were being trained to use self-talk in order to monitor their behavior and respond more accurately. The problem situation was performance on various paper-and-pencil cognitive tasks such as the Porteus Maze Tests. As noted from the model, such training is designed to move the child gradually from copying the verbalization of the model, to making these statements out loud independently, to internalizing them finally in the form of thoughts. An important factor in this example is the provisions for failure. The trainer purposely encounters failure and demonstrates coping self statements. The ultimate goal is that, through repeated presentations, the child will be trained to use this thought pattern automatically when confronted with problem situations. This model subsequently has been modified so that, in addition to cognitive tasks, it has been used successfully for social skill instruction. An example is the Think Aloud Program (Camp, 1977), used to control aggressive behaviors in young boys. These procedures are presented in detail in Chapter 5 of this book.

Problem Solving

Children, as well as adults, are constantly confronted with conflict situations that, depending on how approached, may either be resolved with little difficulty or could be exacerbated. It appears that one critical factor is problem solving ability, since good problem solvers tend to evidence better social adjustment than those with limited skills in this area (Spivack & Shure, 1974). Goldfried & Goldfried (1975) provide a problem-solving method for adults consisting of: (1) general orientation, (2) problem definition and formation, (3) generation of alternatives, (4) decision making, and (5) verification. A variation of this model, involving determining the problem, alternative responses, the appropriate solution, and evaluation can be employed in developing decision making skills in children.

1. *Problem definition and formulation.* Before an individual can pursue the solution to a problem, he must be able to recognize that a problem exists (Meichenbaum, 1975). Helping a child to recognize a problem may be approached in various ways, for example, identifying and compiling problem situations encountered by a particular child or by children of a younger age group, or involving older children in listing their own problematic situations. The situations are discussed with the child in order to help him understand the nature of the problem and the related environmental and emotional factors. The trainer presents a situation of two friends going into a store where one child steals something; the other one is very upset. Through discussions and questions it is determined:

• The problem for the second child involves how to respond to this situation appropriately in order to avoid trouble for himself and how to structure his future relationship with the first child.
• The problem occurred in the company of someone who does something wrong.
• The accompanying physiological reactions included increased heart rate. sweating, quick breathing, and nervous movements translated into emotional states of fear and anger.

In the formulation stage, the trainer is helping the child to become aware of the problem and the special feelings and thoughts that these events produce. The goal is to help the child to develop a thinking style he may use to define problems independently. A series of questions may be used to help the child recognize aspects of the problem, e.g., (a) identifying feelings of being upset, (b) identifying when upset feelings started, (c) determining what happened to make him upset, and (d) determining what he wants to have happen instead of what did happen.

Trainer: You look upset, Ray.
Child: (Indicates he's not upset)
Trainer: Is that why you're not participating with your group in the listening center?
Child: (Indicates he doesn't enjoy the listening center)
Trainer: But you enjoyed those stories yesterday and today we're playing your favorite story.
Child: (Indicates that he is disappointed because he was to act as leader and show the book while listening but another child was doing it.)
Trainer: OK, so the problem is that you want to be leader, isn't it?
Child: (Yes.)
Trainer: You really want to listen to the story, don't you?
Child: (Yes.)

Once the child clearly understands what his problem is, he can begin to consider solutions.

2. *Determining alternatives.* In this step, the child is assisted in generating various alternative responses and the possible consequences to these solutions. For data collection, the child would list as many alternatives as possible, including those that might be undesirable. Alternatives for the example presented above might include:

• taking the book from the other child;
• asking the other child to let him be leader;
• telling the teacher she had promised him to be leader today;
• crying;
• saying nothing and not participating with the group; or
• saying nothing and participating with the group.

In a formal teaching situation, the list of responses may be depicted through simple stick pictures and displayed on a bulletin board or written on the chalkboard to help children remember the alternatives and their corresponding consequences (Spivack & Shure, 1974). Data analysis occurs when youngsters are required to review their suggested responses in terms of possible consequences, e.g., "If you told the teacher she promised to let you be leader today, what do you think will happen?" The consequences also may be listed in a manner similar to that for the alternatives.

For adolescents, an example of an instructional approach designed to train ability to predict consequences is the *Consequences Game* (McPhail, 1975) published by Developmental Learning Materials. The set includes 71 cards with humorous drawings that depict various environmental and social situations such as, "Someone ignores a call for help, because she thinks that the person calling may be drunk or fooling around," or "Someone always believes what people tell him." The youngster is then engaged in a discussion or similar activity to determine the effects this behavior would have on others, why he should avoid this act, and what to do instead.

3 .*Determining Solutions.* This decision making step involves matching the listed alternatives and consequences. Following the Spivack and Shure suggestions, the pictured behaviors could be coordinated so that the child sees that response X could possibly lead to consequence Y. For older children, words may be substituted for pictures. Also at this point, behaviors may be ordered so that children list the alternatives from most preferred to least preferred. Another consideration is the need to identify the exact way to carry out the most desirable alternative (Goldfried & Goldfried, 1975). Once the child has determined the most desirable way to resolve the situation, he should be assisted in trying it out. The behaviors may first be practiced through role playing. Behavior rehearsal is especially important if the actual problem situation is anxiety-provoking, and if the desired response consists of complex behaviors unfamiliar to the child. Depending on the nature of the problem and suggested solutions, the application sequence may entail:

- modeling of the suggested response—the trainer demonstrates how the responses should be made
- behavior rehearsal—the child acts out the desired behavior in a manner similar to that demonstrated by the trainer. Under role play conditions, a variety of responses may be considered and tried out in order to assess the relative effects.
- application in real-life conditions—the child tries the solution in the real situation. The trainer aids the child in assessing the results and in determining alternatives, if necessary. The child is encouraged to use problem solving strategies in his daily living.

4. *Evaluation.* The evaluation is conducted with the child in order to determine the effectiveness of the applied strategy. As with problem identification, the child may need guidance in deciding whether he accomplished what he wanted. If desired goals have not been met, the child is then helped to find other or additional ways to approach the situation.

The effective use of problem solving strategies is partly based on the child's ability to understand the nature of the problem, to be able to identify alternative responses, to think through various responses and their consequences, and to evaluate the alternatives in terms of desired ends. However, before embarking upon problem solving instruction incorporating the above steps, it should be noted that this model demands certain prerequisite abilities that may not exist in the repertoires of the learner, especially young children and children with special needs. Problem solving requires that the learner possess basic language skills, reasoning skills (ability to understand relationships, to identify realistic alternatives, and to anticipate consequences), ability to engage in sustained attention, and sufficient memory skills for learning to occur. In constructing a problem-solving training program for preschool inner city children, Spivack and Shure (1974) developed instructional activities for systematic teaching of preproblem solving skills, consisting of the following abilities and concepts:

1. Language—basic language skills involving the understanding and use of words such as and, not, or, is, same, different.
2. Emotions—labeling emotions, identifying emotions in others, and learning to cope with various feelings.
3. Situation analysis—recognizing that any situation consists of several factors that must be considered before acting.
4. Preferences—understanding that people have preferences and that they differ among individuals.
5. Causal relationships—understanding the relationship among events and the effect one may have on another's behavior.
6. Fairness—considering the rights of others.

Using game format, the authors provide for extensive instruction in the preliminary skills before engaging the child directly in problem solving strategies. A sample lesson for the prerequisite skill of using the words *or* and *is-not* follows:

Game 5: Or, Is-Not

"Today we are going to talk about the word OR. Am I pointing to Johnny OR (emphasize and pause) am I pointing to Jimmy?" Children reply. "Good, I am pointing to Jimmy."

"Am I pointing to Sally OR am I pointing to Susie?" Children reply. "Good, I am pointing to Sally." Have the children close their eyes and give them some pretty hats or trinkets. "Open your eyes. Who is NOT holding a hat? Raise your hand."

"Kevin, is Sally holding a hat?" Ask individual children who is and who is not holding a hat. If time permits let those who did not get a hat have a chance to hold one and repeat the game.
[P. 144]

The remainder of the script focuses on skills directly related to problem solving, i.e., identifying alternative solutions, anticipating consequences of specific acts, and matching the consequences to their respective solutions. During the training, the teacher conducts several sessions designed to help the child identify as many alternatives as possible to a problem situation. For example, "Robert is riding on the bicycle but Georgie wants to ride also. What can he do?" The teacher assists the children in listing solutions such as:

- asking Robert to let him ride;
- asking the teacher
- grabbing the bicycle from Robert; or
- giving Robert something to let him ride the bicycle.

The next set of sessions deal with identifying consequences for certain events. An act is presented such as Georgie pushing Robert off the bike and the children are guided in thinking out "what might happen next?" A list of consequences might include:

- Robert may cry;
- Robert may hit Georgie;
- Robert may tell the teacher; or
- Robert may get hurt.

The two previous skills are combined in the final series of lessons where a problem is presented and the child is prompted to think of a solution for the problem and immediately to identify the possible consequence to these actions. Values are not attached to the solutions suggested by the child, but it is hoped that he will be able to think through the various alternatives and choose the best course on his own. The authors stress that the program is not designed to teach children *what* to think but *how* to think in problem situations.

A somewhat different approach to developing problem solving skills is presented by Blackwood (1971). Whereas Spivack and Shure stress the identification of alternative, successful responses to problem situations, Blackwood emphasizes the importance of cueing oneself in order to avoid inappropriate responding. Instruction in Blackwood's model is designed to develop cognitive cueing skills through recognizing and defining the potential problem situation that, in turn, will set off a chain of thoughts involving the negative consequences of certain behaviors and the possible payoffs of more desired responses. For example, the child tempted to call a peer an unpleasant name may interrupt this train of thought, recognizing its potential for trouble, and say to himself such things as "What will happen if I call Tommy this name? He might tell the teacher and I will have to stay after school and miss the baseball game. If I am nice to Tommy, we can play this game together. It's really better to have Tommy as a friend than to have him angry at me." To help children engage in such thinking processes Blackwood suggests teaching them to answer four questions following some inappropriate behavior:

1. *What did you do wrong?* The child is required to describe precisely the problem behavior. If he refuses or says, "I don't know," then the teacher states it for him and requires the

child to repeat what she said. This is especially important for the young child and/or the child with learning problems. For example, one child who frequently abused other children was placed in time-out immediately after each incident. It was observed that this consequence was considerably more effective when the teacher required the child to say exactly what he had done, e.g., "I hit Carlos."

2. *What happens when you misbehave?* The consequences of the misdeed are described in the second question, e.g., "I have to stand in time-out because I hit Carlos." Blackwood suggests pointing out to children that misdeeds may be followed by positive consequences such as attention from peers, or fun, but that the long-term consequences of these behaviors may be costly. For example, the child who derives pleasure from impulsively hitting other children may find, over the long run, that this behavior results in peer rejection, punishment, and little opportunity to engage in highly-desired play activities such as group games.

3. *What should you do?* The child tells specifically what he might have done instead, e.g., "What's another way to get Carlos' attention?" or "How can you play nicely with Carlos?" Child's Response: "I could ask him to help me with the blocks or I should just talk to Carlos and show him my blocks, but not hit him." As with the previous questions, the trainer may have to give the child the answers to these questions and have him repeat them. (For the child evidencing difficulty in generating alternatives for his behavior, the trainer may wish to employ some of the strategies described above from the Spivack-Shure program.)

4. *What pays off good behavior?* The child is helped to identify the positive and negative consequences of the desired behavior. In the example of hitting another child, the child may identify consequences only according to the negatives, e.g., avoiding time-out or some other punishment. Blackwood suggests that the child also be helped to identify the positives, e.g., "Carlos will be my friend, other children will play with me, we will be able to get more work done and I will become a better student, etc." An additional consideration is to help the child recognize that some good behaviors such as studying may involve immediate discomfort, but the long-term consequences are highly rewarding.

The additional components of this approach include:

a. reinforcing consequences—every effort is made by the trainer to insure that the negative and positive consequences of the behavior occur as identified in the training sessions. Rewards for desired behaviors should materialize; for example, the child who has increased his studying behavior should be encouraged and rewarded, even if his efforts are less than perfect.

b. practice sessions—role playing may be used to help children practice alternative behaviors, following correct responses with rewards.

c. maintenance in the natural environment—under everyday circumstances, the trainer may initially cue the desired alternatives for the child, e.g., "What will you do when it's time to play with Carlos?" Over a period of time the trainer's reminders fade, and rewards are given on an intermittent rather than continuous basis.

For groups, Blackwood provides a modified version of this instruction which involves presenting the same four questions in relation to some problem behavior experienced by the group. The teacher initially provides the answers to the questions, leads a discussion in which children reproduce the points in their own words, and provides opportunities for practice in the positive alternatives. When real-life opportunities present themselves, the teacher provides verbal reminders and reinforcement. In a further variation, the teacher writes an essay in children's language that answers the four questions identified above. When a child misbehaves, demonstrating a need to learn the prescribed behavior, he is assigned to copy the essay exactly as written. The essay may have to be copied several times, depending on how often the misdeed occurs. Initially, the child is required to copy the essay as written, then to write from memory, translating the essay into his own words. Finally, if the behavior persists, the child is required to role play the behaviors and to verbalize out loud the desired answers. Through this procedure, it is intended that the thought processes presented in the essay will become self-cues which "act as commands or as warnings against misbehaviors" when similar conditions are encountered.

In employing cognitive models for social skill training, certain considerations and cautions have been identified by Meichenbaum (1977) as well as other authorities (Camp, 1978; Blackwood, 1971; Spivack & Shure, 1974). (1) Training should be presented in a relaxed rather than rigid manner, establishing rapport and individualizing according to the child's developmental and skill levels. For example, for very young children, play may be used as the point of initiating self-instructional training where the trainer talks his way through a skill game and assists the child to perform in a similar manner. In another example, older children may be less inclined to reveal their own self-statements or to verbalize outwardly. In such cases, the trainer may use tapes or scenarios of others in problem situations and have the child suggest what the fictional character might be thinking. For the child who has difficulty talking out loud during training, the trainer may monitor self-statements by periodically interrupting the child and asking what he is saying to himself. (2) Due to the heavy reliance on language and cognitive abilities, the child with language, cognitive, and attentional deficits may require extensive, systematic instruction before cognitive mediation procedures can be taught. Attention must be given to prerequisite skills, as identified in the discussion on problem solving strategies. After acquiring the basic skills, the child can be involved as a "collaborator" in determining the training procedures to be used. Through questioning, the trainer may get the child to identify, on his own, an effective self-training strategy rather than imposing one on him. The child's own language should be used when possible. (3) one major pitfall encountered in training children in self-talk is that the statements may become mechanical, in which case they are not controlling the maladaptive behavior. To counter this occurrence, it is suggested that training should be conducted so that it is impressed upon children that they are only to say what they mean. A serious learning climate should be established, possibly placing reinforcing contingencies on behaviors indicative of sincerity and appropriate self-statements. (4) Training can be enhanced by including modeling and behavioral rehearsal, relaxation, and imagery techniques. It appears that the opportunity to practice modeled cognitions is a critical factor and may determine the effectiveness of the training. (5) A final consideration is the quantity of instruction. The procedures outlined here are designed to be presented over an extended period of time, ideally on a daily basis. The trainer using cognitive approaches should be committed to regular instruction over a period of weeks. During and following training, monitoring should take place to make certain that the child's self-talk and overt actions are congruent and that the child appears to continue using internal mediators to direct appropriate responses.

AFFECTIVE BEHAVIOR

Teaching social skills related to affective behavior involves teaching the child to recognize and label emotions or feelings in himself and others and to find constructive means for expressing feelings in interpersonal situations. Most affective education programs begin with teaching the child to identify and label the emotions of others from various observable indicators, i.e., facial expression, body language, voice tone, and verbal content. Teaching the child to "read" emotions from facial expressions is probably the most important place to start. Developmental psychologists have pointed out the significance of facial expressions in early communication between mothers and infants. They consider the human face an important factor in social development, in that the face provides the most immediate and specific information about a person's emotional state. Another part of this task is teaching the child to connect emotions with preceding events in the environment so he understands that emotions do not occur randomly but have antecedents. A further task is acquainting the child with the range of possible human emotions and enabling him to make discriminations about them.

Some initial approaches to teaching children how to identify feelings would involve presenting various emotions in a variety of ways, asking the child to label and enact them. Sample activities may include:

1. Present pictures of faces from books or magazines to help the child learn to identify and label emotions. Have the child make up stories about why the people in the pictures are happy, sad, or otherwise.
2. Have the child draw faces reflecting emotions and tell stories explaining the emotions, or provide a scene for the child to relate to:
   Draw a face for someone who just had his money stolen.
   Draw a face for someone who just won a prize.
   Draw a face for someone who is being chased by a bully.
3. Have an adult model facial and bodily gestures and have children identify what emotions are involved.
4. Have children draw cards with names of emotions written on them and

role play emotions for each other to identify in a guessing game. A variation could ask for the child to role play the emotion with facial expressions, body language, or voice tone and words.

5. Have the children develop a vocabulary of feelings, making lists of synonyms for words describing feelings, using them to label pictures, for spelling words, as the basis for games. Pictures of faces might be displayed on a bulletin board labeled with a list of descriptive words.

Teaching the child to be aware of and label his own feelings may need to involve the adult initially in making inferences about the child's feeling states and providing information to call his attention to the cues he is giving out. "You are smiling, Mary. Are you feeling happy?" "You have a frown on your face, John. Can you tell me what you are feeling? What happened to make you feel that way?" The adult can also provide a model by identifying and labeling his own feelings, along with providing information to explain the feelings. Along with learning to identify his own feelings, the child can learn that others may have different feelings in the same situations. Some activities for teaching the child to label his own emotions are as follows:

1. Have the child draw his own face or role play how he would feel in different situations, for example:

   "Draw the face that shows how you would feel
   . . . if you fell in the mud with your new clothes on."
   . . . if your pet had not come home all day."
   . . . if opening presents on your birthday."

2. Provide an exercise using sentence completion, e.g., "For me, happiness is_____, accompanied by drawings. Have children compare notes on their answers in a discussion.

3. For negative emotions use a technique like the "Feeling Thermometer" (Rotheram, 1978) mentioned in Chapter 2, and the SUDS (Subjective Units of Discomfort Scale) concept. Using a drawing of a thermometer with a scale from 0 to 100, children may develop a hierarchy of low to high discomfort situations. For example, arriving late at school may create a SUDS of 30; having to present an oral report may be an 80; having to take a failing grade home may be regarded as 100. By generating discussion, and ranking a series of hypothetical problem situations, a child can learn that not all of his peers would regard a situation with the same degree of emotion. In discussing the ranking of problem situations, the physiological indicators of discomfort can also be identified, e.g., heart pounding, breath short, hands sweating, blushing; and a discrimination made between when these reactions signal anxiety, anger, or fear, and when they may merely indicate excitement. Beyond talking hypothetically about the SUDS level, the SUDS concept can be used to identify feelings in role plays and can be translated into the natural environment by using "SUDS" as a cue word, i.e., "What's your SUDS level?" to create awareness of negative affect and the need to exercise self control of behavior.

4. A somewhat similar approach is the "Boiling Point List" (Curwin and Curwin, 1974). This exercise is designed to provide awareness for the child of how he acts when angry and what produces the greatest anger. The procedures involve providing a list or having the students generate a list of anger-producing situations and rate each one on a one-to-five scale:

(1) I get extremely angry in this situation.
(2) I get mildly angry in this situation.
(3) I get irritated in this situation, but not very angry.
(4) This situation only slightly bothers me.
(5) This situation does not anger me at all.

Sample situations of the Boiling Point List include:
  (1) when someone tells on you,
  (2) when you try out for something and don't get it,
  (3) when your friends do something without you,
  (4) when you want to play with your friends but you have to go visiting with your family,
  (5) when someone borrows something of yours and breaks it,
  (6) when you want to do something and no one wants to do it with you,
  (7) when you are unjustly accused of something,
  (8) when you lose money,
  (9) when you do something good and no one notices,
  (10) when someone causes you to get in trouble. [Curwin & Curwin, 1974, pp. 35-37]

Some guidelines suggested by Fagen, Long, and Stevens (1975) are relevant to the task of teaching children to recognize and label their own feelings. For discussion related to emotions they suggest the following:

No individual should be pressured to respond or to divulge his feelings: Teacher or peers might question one another out of interest, but an explicit norm should be established for the "right to privacy" or the "right to pass."

It should be recognized that participation by pupils may be verbal, nonverbal, or vicarious: Students can be learning without saying or doing anything. The right to be silent, to listen, and to observe should be respected at all times. The watchful member is often learning more about emotions and acceptance of them (including his own) than is the rapid talker.

Practice with more personal and less anxiety-laden issues should be provided before taking up any directly personal or high-anxiety issues: For example, feelings about television, the weather, sports, etc., can be introduced before beginning to talk about feelings about parents, teacher, or other students. In this way, students can first learn that differences are acceptable, that retaliation or hurt is not a consequence of honest expression, and that feelings are not right or wrong.

The teacher should continually reiterate that feelings can be pleasant or unpleasant and enjoyable or painful, but he should emphasize that they are never bad or wrong: A clear distinction should be made between a person's right to own any and all feelings and his responsibility to place limits on acting on his feelings.

Feelings are most usefully introduced by focusing on some present event, experience, or issue: Questions introduced by: "How do you feel when . . .?" or "What thoughts or feelings do you have . . .?" or "When do you feel that way?" are preferable to questions in the past tense.   [P. 66]

Helping the child to find constructive ways to express feelings in interpersonal situations is complex because it involves not only the child's being able to identify his own feelings but the development of the ability to exercise control and selectivity over his responses. This latter task involves a three-way interaction between emotion, cognition, and motor activity. Social skills training aimed at teaching behavioral control of emotion is most effective if it develops awareness in the child of his feeling state in a situation, awareness of the cognitive evaluations he is making about the situation and about his feeling state, and a mastery of the range of behaviors he can engage in related to the situation. In helping the child made a distinction between his thoughts and feelings and his behavior, Fagen, Long, and Stevens (1975) suggest the following points that could be used as the basis for discussion:

1. All thoughts and feelings are OK and normal to have.
2. Thoughts and feelings can be private property; complete freedom is possible for thoughts and feelings.
3. All actions or behaviors are not OK; some are illegal, harmful to self or others, or against the rules.
4. Behaviors or actions cannot be private property; complete freedom is not possible for behavior.
5. Thoughts and feelings are different from behavior; you can think and feel things without needing to do them or without blaming yourself for having mean or "bad" ideas.   [P. 178]

Along with the task of learning to control one's own emotional responses, a related skill is that of learning to evoke positive responses in others. Studies have documented the reciprocal nature of the interaction between children and parents or children and teachers (e.g., Graubard, Rosenberg, & Miller, 1971). Teaching this skill can begin with having children identify the behaviors on the part of other people that make them feel happy and warm toward the person involved, then using those behaviors as the basis for role playing. Such a list might include, for example: smiling at others; greeting someone in a positive way; giving another person a compliment; saying something nice about someone to a third person; helping another person; or expressing appreciation. Fagen, Long, and Stevens (1975) present a series of questions that have the goal of teaching positive communication with others in situations that could otherwise result in negative interactions:

1. If someone did not agree with you, how would you want him to tell you? How could you tell someone that you don't agree with him, in a way that is not mean?
2. If someone did not like what you did, how would you want him to tell you? How could you tell someone that you don't like what he did, in a way that is not mean or hurtful?
3. If someone did not like what you said, how would you want him to tell you? How could you tell someone that you don't like what he said to you, in a way that is not mean?
4. If you were not sharing, how would you want someone to tell you? How could you tell someone that he is not sharing?
5. If you lost a game, what could someone say to make you feel better? What could you say to someone who has lost a game?
6. If you made a mistake, what could someone say to make you feel better? What could you say to someone who has made a mistake?
7. If you got into trouble, what could someone say to make you feel better? What could you say to someone who has gotten into trouble?

8. If someone were angry with you, how would you want him to tell you? What could you say to someone who has made you angry?
9. If you were afraid, what could someone say to make you feel better? What could you say to someone who is afraid?
10. If you were crying, what could someone say to make you feel better? What could you say to someone who is crying?   [P. 166]

Following the problem solving sequence presented earlier in the chapter, teaching specific positive alternative behaviors for dealing with problem situations can be carried out through presenting stories and discussions to identify hypothetical or actual situations that might result in negative emotions, specifying the problem behaviors that could follow, generating possible alternative responses, and discussing the advantages and disadvantages and potential outcomes of the different ways of behaving. For example:

Problem situation: James likes to get a rise out of other boys by making slurring remarks about their relatives. He walks up to Arthur and calls his mother a derogatory name. Arthur feels angry. What are some ways Arthur can respond? Arthur can
   1) hit James;
   2) reciprocate with comments about James' mother;
   3) complain to the teacher;
   4) get peers to help him retaliate;
   5) tell James that it makes him angry and ask him to stop;
   6) ignore James and walk away; or
   7) attempt to divert attention by changing the subject with a positive remark.

Alternative responses can be elicited from the children and listed, the possible consequences of each identified, and the responses ranked according to desirability. The responses that promise the most positive outcomes for Arthur can then be practiced through role playing.

In addition to the motoric production and practicing of alternative responses for problem situations, another element in self control of feelings is the cognitive activity surrounding the feelings. In the previous example, according to cognitive theory, Arthur's anger could be heightened and his ability to choose a constructive response impaired by his cognitive appraisal of the situation. An approach suggested by Knaus (1974) to help children understand that feelings come from thoughts is the "Happening-Thought-Feeling-Reaction Diagram" in which an event is written out on the board in diagram form. Using the problem event described above, the diagram would be, for example:

Happening +	Thought =	Feeling	Reaction
Arthur calls James' mother a name	It's terrible to have my mother called a name. . . . I can't stand it. . . . I have to get him for that. . . .	Strong anger (out of control)	James hits Arthur, fight results.

In order to demonstrate how different thoughts could lead to different feelings and actions, the same diagram can then be developed with alternative thoughts, feelings, and reactions generated by the children, for example:

Happening	+	Thought	=	Feeling	Reaction
Arthur calls James' mother a name		He doesn't even know my mother. . . . He wants me to get angry. . . . I don't have to do what he wants. . . .		Mild anger or annoyance	James ignores Arthur and walks away

Several additional techniques for helping children identify and alter negative and defeating cognitions were described in the previous section related to cognitive behavior.

Relaxation

Another set of procedures for controlling emotion involves the use of systematic relaxation as a means of altering negative feeling states and delaying the impulsive expression of negative emotion long enough to think of alternatives. Relaxation training has been widely used by behavior therapists as part of systematic desensitization procedures to assist phobic or anxious adult clients in confronting emotionally-charged and fear-producing situations. Relaxation is useful because the physiological state of relaxation is incompatible with fear, anger, and anxiety-provoking cognitions and feelings. Relaxation is incompatible also with aggressive motoric responses. Along with the teaching of relaxation, a procedure known as "conditioned relaxation training" or "cue-controlled relaxation" involves teaching the person to become relaxed in response to a self-produced cue word such as "relax" or "calm." The ability to become relaxed in anger or anxiety-producing interpersonal situations is a social skill that is being increasingly recognized as having relevance for children as well as adults. Children trained in relaxation possess a tool that can potentially enable them to decrease feelings of anxiety, fear, or anger in stressful social situations and substitute a constructive behavior for a less appropriate impulsive response to the problem situation.

Some general steps in teaching relaxation to children are as follows:

1. *Teach prerequisite skills.* Cautela and Groden (1978) have identified a set of readiness skills which may need to be assessed and taught prior to relaxation training. These involve being able to sit still in a chair for five seconds, maintaining eye contact for three seconds, imitation skills, and following directions.

2. *Set the stage.* Relaxation training should take place in a quiet, calm environment. Dim lights, soft music, and the absence of distracting loud

noise or visual stimuli will facilitate the atmosphere of relaxation. Children can be taught relaxation either sitting in comfortable chairs or lying on the floor on rugs or mats. Bean bag chairs lend themselves to relaxation. Cautela and Groden start with having the child sit in a chair with his head up and hands in his lap, identifying that as the "relaxing position." It is possible to build in stimulus control aspects by providing a special relaxation chair or thick rug in the home or classroom to which the child can remove himself and practice relaxation as an alternative to engaging in some problematic behavior. The voice tone of the adult is also important in relaxation training. Instructions should be given in a calm and even somewhat monotonous tone.

3. *Teach the concept of relaxation.* The most widely-used techniques for teaching the relaxation concept involve variations of those originally introduced by Jacobson (1938) in which relaxation is taught by alternately tensing and releasing various groups of muscles and becoming aware of the sensations of tension and relaxation. There are differences of opinion about whether tension should be presented to children along with relaxation, especially for hyperactive or highly tense children. In using contrasting tension and relaxation, most writers on the subject suggest a much shorter period of tension for children than for adults, not more than two to five seconds. Cautela and Groden suggest an alternative to tensing for children for whom the use of tension may be contraindicated. A statement like "relax your arm" is accompanied by a tactile approach such as stroking the child's arm. Another approach is having the child shake his hands and fingers while keeping his arms at his side. Continued shaking will lead to fatigue in the hands and arms and a feeling of relaxation when the shaking is discontinued. Several other aids can be used to help the child understand the concept of relaxation with or without the use of tension. One of these is modeling by the adult, who can demonstrate tension and relaxation in his own arms, for example, and let the child feel the difference. Another is the use of analogy and imagery. Concepts like wooden soldier or broomstick can convey stiffness and tension, while rag doll or melted ice cream can be equated with relaxation. Having the child imagine happy, restful scenes can also facilitate relaxation, and pictures of clouds, forests, or the sea can serve as aids for imagery. It can be suggested that the child may feel like floating on a cloud, on the lapping waves of a lake, or like walking in space. Developing the concept of relaxation through movement exercises is a useful approach with young children, who may easily be able to become limp rag dolls, melt to the floor, float like a feather, or drop like a heavy brick.

4. *Introduce relaxation in muscle groups.* Relaxation training for adults as developed by Bernstein and Borkovec (1973) takes the client through the following sequence related to different muscle groups:

1. The client's attention should be focused on the muscle group.
2. At a predetermined signal from the therapist, the muscle group is tensed.
3. Tension is maintained for a period of 5-7 seconds (this duration is shorter in the case of the feet).
4. At a predetermined cue, the muscle group is released.
5. The client's attention is maintained upon the muscle group as it relaxes.

The muscle groups include:

1. Dominant hand and forearm
2. Dominant biceps
3. Nondominant hand and forearm
4. Nondominant biceps
5. Forehead
6. Upper cheeks and nose
7. Lower cheeks and jaws
8. Neck and throat
9. Chest, shoulders, and upper back
10. Abdominal or stomach region
11. Dominant thigh
12. Dominant calf
13. Dominant foot
14. Nondominant thigh
15. Nondominant calf
16. Nondominant foot

Rather than progress through a series of muscle groups as with adults, the Cautela-Groden procedures focus the child's attention initially on his arms, hands, and legs along with breathing exercises. In relaxing the arms, the procedure is as follows:

ARMS

Demonstrate the position of holding your right arm out straight, making a fist, and tightening your whole arm from your hand to your shoulder. Ask the child to feel the parts that are tight (biceps, forearm, back of arm, elbow, above and below wrist and fingers). Ask the child to tighten his arm as you teach him to feel the tightness with his other hand. Use synonyms such as stiff or wooden-like. Next, tell him to gradually relax his arm back to the relaxing position. Repeat with the other arm. The child should gradually learn to tighten and relax his arm to the cue "Tighten your arm." It may be helpful to stroke his arm while it is in the relaxing position. Ask him to think of how those muscles feel as they begin to feel loose. Looseness can be tested by the "limp procedure." Lift his hand up and let it drop in his lap like a limp rag doll.

Criteria: Child can, upon request, tighten and relax each arm. The muscles should look tight and feel tight to the touch.

Problem: Often it is difficult for some children to make a fist and hold their arm out straight. This can be shaped by first holding your left arm under the child's elbow for support while having him push against your hand in an open palm fashion. Another way to shape a tight fist is to ask the child to tighten his outstretched hand around your index finger with his palm down.   [Cautela & Groden, 1978, p. 53]

The same process is followed with hands, making a fist and relaxing; and with legs, raising and tightening with toes bent back, then relaxing and bending the knee. The child is then taught to take a deep breath, hold it, and let go slowly while saying the word "relax" to himself. The process is repeated five times. The child is asked next to demonstrate relaxing arms and legs without tensing first. To aid in generalization, the child is taught to tense and relax in a standing position "like a tin soldier," to relax in a walking position, and relax in a prone position. The child who has mastered the above steps is then taught to tense and relax other muscle groups including forehead, eyes, smile muscles, lips, stomach muscles, nose, jaw muscles, back, chest, and muscles below the waist including thighs and buttocks. He is also taught alternative ways to relax the neck by moving the head backward and forward or sideways. The breathing exercise mentioned above is particularly important for cue-controlled relaxation. The ability to produce a physiologically-relaxed state upon exhaling and repeating a cue word such as "relax" is the principal aspect of relaxation training that might be regarded as a social skill when it can be used in troublesome interpersonal situations.

Relaxation instructions ("patter") have been written out and recorded for use in a rote fashion. There are, however, common elements that make it possible to improvise relaxation patter. Most relaxation talk includes: (1) Directions to tense and/or relax particular parts of the body. "First think about the muscles in your forehead. Let every muscle in your forehead relax. Relax, relax, the muscles in your forehead." (2) Directions to experience the feeling of relaxation, usually stated several ways. "See how soft and smooth your forehead feels. You can feel the tension going out of your forehead as you feel more and more relaxed. See how different and nice it feels to be relaxed." An area of debate involves the use of taped versus live training procedures. Taped procedures save time and can have considerable utility for the researcher who needs to have a standardized process. For the teacher or clinician working with children, the use of relaxation tapes can be a way to encourage the inexperienced person to get started without the need to become thoroughly familiar with relaxation "patter." Most research indicates, however, that tapes are less effective than live presentations for teaching relaxation. They proceed at a set pace and thus do not allow for assessment feedback about how the child is responding before moving to the next set of instructions.

5. *Practice.* Most relaxation programs suggest practice once or twice a day until skill at relaxing is achieved. Once the procedures are learned, relaxation tapes or records can be useful for inducing relaxation in practice sessions or in the absence of the original trainer.

A number of programs have incorporated relaxation as a self-control procedure along with other behavior change techniques. One of these is the Turtle program (Schneider and Robin, 1975). The Turtle technique involves a combination of coping behaviors that include (1) teaching the child to withdraw into an imaginary shell by pulling his arms and head in close to his body and closing his eyes when he feels threatened in a problem situation. "You can hide in your shell whenever you get that feeling inside you that tells you are angry. When you are in your shell, you can have a moment to rest and figure out what to do about it"; (2) teaching the child to relax his muscles while "doing turtle"; and (3) using problem solving techniques in which the child thinks through alternative courses of action for dealing with the problem and their various consequences. Children are also taught to discriminate when it is better to "do turtle," or to "stick their neck out" in a more assertive manner. This program illustrates a multielement approach to teaching self-control alternatives to impulsive striking out through the use of cues (i.e., "stop," "do turtle") along with relaxation to lessen negative emotions and provide a delay in response, thus allowing the child time to consider the other courses of action he had learned.

SOCIAL SKILLS GAMES

Presenting social skills instruction in the form of games can assist the instructor in a number of ways. For one, playing a structured game requires the exercise of various social skills. The game can become a vehicle for teaching such skills as taking turns, sharing materials, being a good winner or loser, teamwork, cooperation, attention to details, following rules, self-control, and various problem-solving skills. For another, games have considerable merit as a way to motivate children to participate, since games imply fun and an element of play rather than work. Using games may be particularly useful where social skills content can evoke anxieties and resistance. As pointed out by Gordon (1972), games simulate real life situations and provide a means of testing out real world events. At the same time, games create distance from real life and involve a suspension of the usual forms of evaluation. Games provide an opportunity for the child to learn the consequences of his actions without actually having to suffer them. In a game, mistakes and exposure of ignorance are more tolerated. Games usually encourage laughing and joking, which can be instrumental in relieving anxiety and facilitating involvement.

Games can be classified as paper-and-pencil, board games, role play games, or hybrid games that involve a combination of the others (Heitzmann, 1974). Some of the common elements for presenting social skills instruction in game format include: (1) an aspect of chance, such as drawing a card or spinning a wheel; (2) unknown aspects to be discovered by guessing;

(3) dramatic features, elements of surprise or novelty; (4) material presented in ways conveying humor or fun; (5) opportunities for active participation and a variety of kinds of activities or modes of response; (6) well-defined limits and rules; (7) clearly-understood goals or objectives to be reached involving the learning of specific concepts or skills; and (8) immediate feedback about the results of one's actions.

Almost any social skills content can be put into game format through very simple means, for example, picking a skill out of a hat to role play, or having teams take turns playing a form of charades in which a specific emotion, or coping strategy is pantomimed to be guessed by the other group. Game boards are more complex and limit the number of players, but at the same time they provide opportunities for considerable variety. Board games require a defined sequence of activities involving the order of player "turns" and the sequence of decisions or steps each player must make (Glazier, 1970). In a social skills board game, for example, players can move along the board according to a chance spin or roll of the dice, draw cards requiring the verbal or performance demonstration of a social behavior, and may land in a penalty box with a performance requirement in order to escape. Glazier presents the following list of materials as helpful for making one's own games:

Broad felt-tip markers
3" × 5" blank cards in various colors
5" × 8" blank cards in various colors
a die or dice
wooden blocks in assorted colors
wooden beads in assorted colors
play money
graph paper, up to one-inch grid
poster cardboard (for foldability, slit with razor and make tape hinge on reverse side)
water-base paints (Acrylic artist's colors will not smear like tempera or water-colors)
spinners
toy miniatures (tiny cars, doll furniture, etc.)
bold face typewriter
white oilcloth (for rollable gameboard)
transparent plastic film (for gameboard protection)
fruit juice can (for dice shaker)
pennies (for money), assorted coins or poker chips (for player tokens)
alarm clock (for timing intervals in a role-play simulation)
coin (to flip for a 50-50 probability)
small bell (to add drama to special announcements in a role-play simulation or to signal the
    end of a round)
stick-on labels (for name tags to identify players' role)
brightly colored baseball caps, toy badges, or colored ribbon armbands (to identify umpires
    or key players)   [Pp. 10,11]

A number of manufacturers are now marketing do-it-yourself game kits with blank boards, dice, spinners, markers, and other game equipment. (See Resource Materials list in Appendix.)

Role play games require the development of scenarios that are relevant and close to the child's reality, along with identification of roles to be assigned. Flowers (1975) stresses that the behaviors to be taught must be clearly defined. "The rule is generally that if you don't know what you want the client to be able to do he generally won't do it" (P. 171). Role playing techniques have been incorporated into a number of simulation games, described by Flowers as designed to teach a set of skills to a broad range of clients rather than focus on the problems of a single client. A summary developed by Flowers of simulation games and role playing exercises is presented in table 3.1. A more detailed discussion of role playing procedures is presented in an earlier part of this chapter.

A number of specific, mostly "hybrid," games have been devised for social skill instruction, and others could be adapted for that use. A social skills game for institutionalized adults originated by Quinsey and Varney (1977) could be modified for use with children. The game is played on a board marked with instructions, tasks, or directions to draw cards. The cards require answers to questions, present statements the player must identify as true or false, or give a situation for role playing, e.g., "Play a person who is being interviewed for a job as a janitor in a factory." A player rolls the dice and moves around the board, following instructions or drawing a card according to the space on which he lands. The other players decide as a group whether a player has carried out his task successfully, each task earning a given number of points. Players move successively through three levels as they gain points, or are placed in "jail" if they fail to make the required response. According to the authors, some of the positive values from the game are the group feedback about social behaviors, the non-threatening context, the need for close observation in order to award points which provides opportunities for learning, and the fact that everyone is involved continually either as a player or evaluator. Group members have little opportunity to withdraw or dominate as might happen in traditional group therapy. The staff structures the game to the needs of individual patients by the inclusion of cards that deal with relevant problems or information.

A game designed by Flowers (1975) to teach a specific social skill is the *Self-Confidence Game,* in which self confidence is defined as a student raising his hand to answer a question from the teacher in a classroom. Questions are made up by students from classroom material and placed in a question box. Teams of three students each are assigned on a random basis, and others are appointed to be moderator, blackboard scorer, hand-raising judge, score keepers, and timer. The game process is similar to a "College Quiz Bowl" format, in that questions are presented to the teams, the first

Table 3.1. Summary of Simulation Games and Role Playing Exercises

Type of Simulation	Type of Problem	Technique Reference	Research Reference
Psychodrama	Conflict Resolution	Moreno (1953)	Boies (1972)
Client Centered Active Listening	Low Self-Esteem	Pfeiffer and Jones (1970)	Truax and Mitchell (1971)
Assertion Training	Passive or Aggressive Behavior	Alberti and Emmons (1970)	see below
(a) Behavior Rehearsal		Casey (1973)	Lazarus (1966)
(b) Coaching			McFall and Marston (1970)
(c) Feedback			Flowers and Guerra (1974)
(d) Modeling			Melnick (1973)
Socialization Training	Low Social Skill Development	McFall and Lillesand (1971)	same
Job Interview Training	Unemployment	Rathus (1972)	Sarason (1968)
Barb	Low Impulse Control	Freedman (1972)	none
Management Game	Training Business Administration	Sarason and Ganzer (1969)	none
Life Career Game	High School Students Life Decisions	Prazak (1969)	same
Honesty Game	School Students Cheating	Kaufmann and Wagner (1972)	Boocock (1968)
Reducing Unwarranted Questions	School Children Gaining Maladaptive Teacher Attention	Uretsky (1973) / Varenhorst (1969) / Flowers (1972b)	same
Self-Confidence Game	Low Student Self-Confidence	Flowers (1975)	same
Fight Training	Fear of Verbal Fighting	Flowers and Marston (1972)	same
Group Warmup	Starting Group Process in Therapy or Training Groups	Bach and Bernhard (1971)	none
Marriage Communication Game	Marital Discord and Poor Partner Communication	Pfeiffer and Jones (1970)	none
Group Therapy Token Game	Unclear or Low Verbal Reinforcement and Punishment Levels, Low Self-Reinforcement Level	Flowers (1975)	Flowers, Booraem, Brown, and Harris (1974); Flowers, Booraem, and Seacat (1975)
Microteaching	Training Teaching or Counseling Skills	McAleese and Unwin (1973)	same
Personality Games	Decision Making	Harris (1971)	same

Source: Flowers, 1975.

person to raise his hand can attempt to answer and members of the oppposing team can raise their hands and answer a question that has been missed. The game is divided into three phases. In Phase One, those players who answer less than 10 percent of the questions are identified as the "low self-confidence" students. In Phase Two, the low self-confidence students are placed on teams together and only compete against each other. In Phase Three, the teams are again assigned on a random basis to determine whether the Phase Two treatment has resulted in increasing the child's hand raising in regular competition. Results obtained from studies with the game indicate significant increases in volunteering to answer questions and in correct answers in the game, as well as generalization to the regular classroom, improvement in grades, and increase in other forms of participation.

The game techniques developed by Gardner (1975) for use in psychotherapy with children lend themselves to the teaching of social skills, even though they were not devised for that purpose. *The Talking, Feeling, and Doing Game,* for example, involves a board, dice, playing pieces, cards which ask questions or give directions requiring verbal or motor responses, and reward chips that children receive for responding. The players move on the board according to the throw of the dice and land on squares instructing them to draw cards from one of three piles, related either to motor "doing" tasks, verbal expression of feelings, or more cognitive "talking" tasks. Because of the game's intended use in psychodynamically oriented psychotherapy, most of the cards are oriented toward eliciting feelings and materials related to areas of conflict. Some, however, present tasks relevant to social skills, for example: "You're standing in line to buy something, and a child pushes himself in front of you. Show what you would do." Some of the "feeling" cards could lend themselves to teaching the child to label his own feelings and those of others; i.e., "What's something you could say that would make a person feel good?" New cards could easily be devised with tasks involving verbal responses to indicate knowledge of a particular social behavior or brief scenarios that could be stimuli for role playing.

Another example of a social skills game is the commercially-marketed *Roll-a-Role Game* which presents a format for engaging participants in role playing. The equipment includes a large red and a large blue plastic cube with roles printed on each side of the cubes (e.g., elderly man, neighbor lady, single girl), a deck of "Talk Topics" cards, a "Where-It-Happens" chart, and a three-minute timer. Two players roll the cubes; the outcome determines their roles as well as the location for the role-played conversation. The locations, indicated by numbers on the cubes, include frontyard, hospital room, car, stranded in elevator, shopping center, in the park, telephone, airplane, laundromat, waiting room, and porch. A timekeeper draws a "Talk Topic" card and reads it, allows time for planning, and then sets the timer for three minutes, during which the players carry out a role play related to the topic on the card. The cards include such topics as:

RED is very shy and has no close friends. RED asks BLUE why this is true.
BLUE wants RED to have friendships and tries to build up his/her confidence. RED starts.
RED brags to BLUE that s/he has found a wallet and intends to keep it.
BLUE considers this immoral and tries to persuade RED to turn it in. RED starts.

The cards in the game are not specific to social skills or to children but, again, relevant cards could be made up and substituted. Since role playing is itself a social skill that needs to be learned if it is to be used in other social skill instruction, a game format such as this could be a useful vehicle for developing skill in role playing.

Some cautions about the use of games need to be presented. Social skills can be introduced or practiced in game format, but the connection between what is done for fun and its application to the real world needs to be made at some point. This could possibly be accomplished by a discussion after the game in which practical applications are identified or by references back to the game when a relevant problem arises. If the intent of the game is to provide practice in a specific skill, it is important to structure the game so each player has an opportunity to make the required response and cannot become a "winner" solely by chance; he can only win on the basis of his performance of the target behavior. The criteria for winning should relate to the concept or skills to be learned. Another caution relates to the need to minimize win-lose situations in social skills games, unless, perhaps, the target social skills are those encountered in competitive games, i.e., being able to win or lose with good sportsmanship and being able to cope with failure. If rewards are given during the game, they should ideally be given for participation rather than for winning or losing. Further, the game should be constructed so players are not "out" and then eliminated from the game without an opportunity to be rotated quickly back in to insure ongoing participation. Because much of the learning that takes place in games results from imitation of others' successful behavior, the composition of the group or the team needs to be structured so weak members are paired with stronger members.

SUMMARY

Teaching social skills involves many of the same procedures by which academic concepts are presented, i.e., the exposure of the child to a model for imitation, eliciting an imitative response, providing feedback about the correctness of the response, and structuring opportunities for practice. Motivational factors are also important in social skills instruction to insure the child's attention and willingness to participate. In addition to providing support and encouragement, the teacher or clinician can set the stage for social skills instruction in a way that enhances motivation through discussion, use of audio-visual material, attention to group composition, developmentally appropriate techniques, introducing rewards for participation, and the use of games and humor.

One method for teaching complex social behaviors is through the imitation of a model or social modeling. The social modeling process requires that the learner recognize the value of the behavior to be learned and is able to identify the specific responses that make up that behavior, that the behavior be modeled in a way that is attractive and understandable to the learner, that the learner be provided with opportunities to practice the behavior using various response modes, and that the learner receive feedback on his performance from others as well as through self-evaluative procedures. A behavior may be demonstrated but, if the child is unable to conceptualize the responses involved or does not recognize the importance of the behavior, social modeling is unlikely to occur. The trainer should also expect that initial efforts to produce novel behaviors may be awkward and unnatural with a need for continued practice and feedback.

The use of cognitions in teaching social skills focuses on efforts to structure thinking styles that are functional for directing social behaviors. One area of emphasis is the elimination of irrational, self-defeating, or faulty thought patterns, replacing them with more rational or productive ones. A second focus is the development of structured thought patterns to be used under certain conditions or for specific behaviors, i.e., Meichenbaum's stress inoculation training and self-instructional training. Problem solving procedures geared toward modifying the child's cognitions help the child to analyze social situations accurately and make decisions based on the possible alternatives and consequences. Although cognitive models vary, there are commonalities in that they all rely on language, implying some prerequisite skills on the part of the learner, and involve intensive instruction over an extended period of time.

Approaches to teaching social skills related to emotions involves the child's recognition and labeling of his own feelings and those of others, along with learning socially desirable ways to express his emotions. Activities for teaching about feelings also involve helping the child to recognize the differences in his emotional responses and those of others in similar situations, and developing some understanding about the role of his thinking processes in generating his feeling states. In teaching the child to express emotions in constructive ways, a problem solving approach can be applied in which the child identifies and role plays problem situations, alternative responses and outcomes, along with examining alternative thoughts and feelings that could be associated with the problem situation. Training the child in relaxation can provide him with another means of controlling negative emotion, since a relaxed state leads to a lessening of tension, anxiety, and anger. Learning to respond to relaxation cues with a state of relaxation may allow the child time to initiate constructive alternatives to impulsive emotional behavior.

Finally, the use of games as an instructional tool is particularly useful for providing motivation and introducing social skills teaching in a nonthreatening context. Social skills games can involve the use of a game board and equipment or modified commercially produced games as well as simple procedures devised by the teacher or therapist. Other games use role playing or simulation of realistic situations. Social skills games should deemphasize competition and provide sufficient opportunities for participation and practice in the skills to be learned.

Chapter 4

Generalization and Maintenance of Social Skills

Once social skills have been selected, assessed, and successfully taught, the remaining task is that of making sure the child can exhibit the skills when and where it is desirable for him to do so. The social behaviors need to be generalized from the instructional setting into other settings where they would be appropriate, and from one person or persons to others. They also need to be maintained over time. Stokes and Baer (1977), in their review of literature related to behavior generalization, point out that generalization does not automatically occur but needs to be planned and programmed as part of the training process. Some techniques described below as effective for generalization include (1) varying aspects of training, (2) training mediators, and (3) changing the contingencies of reinforcement.

ASPECTS OF TRAINING

The way in which social behaviors are taught appears to influence whether the new behaviors will occur in new settings beyond the training site and whether they will occur with persons other than the trainer. Two specific considerations related to ways in which training is carried out involve the settings for training and varying trainers.

Train in Different Settings

A frequent occurrence in behavior change programs is that newly acquired behaviors are maintained only within the setting where the child is instructed and do not naturally transfer to other settings. Thus, the child who learns greeting skills in the classroom may not express them elsewhere, unless specific steps are taken to develop such transfer. Ideally, social skill instruction should take place in the setting where the behavior is to occur. If, for example, the target behavior is increased participation in classroom discussions, then instruction in this behavior should take place in the classroom. Where this is not possible, the social skill trainer must program for transfer. Walker and Buckley (1974), in some extensive studies on generalization, suggest techniques for programming behavior change into the natural environment, one of which is labeled "equating stimulus conditions." It is considered that the more closely the training environment resembles the natural environment, the greater the likelihood that the child will transfer the newly acquired behaviors from the instructional to the noninstructional setting. Walker and Buckley used this technique to "equate" stimulus conditions from an experimental (special) classroom to the natural environment (regular) classroom with children who had been assigned to a special classroom for instruction in specific academic and social behaviors. Before returning the children to the regular classroom, the special class was modified by increasing workload and switching from tangible to social reinforcers in order to approximate regular classroom conditions more closely. An additional discussion of encouraging transfer through the "rule of identical elements" is provided in Chapter 9 of this book.

Another strategy for transfer of training from one setting to another is to provide for instruction in more than one setting. For example, the child receiving instructions in appropriate greeting skills in school should be provided with similar instruction in other situations such as home or on the playground in order to ensure that he will engage in this behavior under other appropriate conditions. An example of teaching a skill in multiple settings is provided by Murdock, Garcia, and Hardman (1977) in a study where retarded children were taught to articulate words. Each child was taught by one trainer in a small room, by a second trainer in the corner of a regular classroom, and by a third trainer in a learning center for individualized activities. Not only did the children learn to say the words in these settings consistently, but they also generalized the words to other settings where training had not been conducted. A significant aspect of this study was that the behaviors did not begin to generalize to other settings until they were taught in at least two settings.

While it may not be necessary to provide formal instruction in every setting or condition frequented by the child, procedures such as the following may be used to facilitate the transfer of these behaviors to other conditions:

- Set up role plays where the child demonstrates how he will perform this behavior in other settings. For example, "Let's act out how you will greet a guest who comes to your house."
- Establish reinforcing conditions for expressing the target behavior in

other settings. For instance, using the greeting example, specified individuals in other settings may prompt and reward the child for responses such as smiling, making eye contact, and saying hello upon an initial encounter.

• Assist the child in developing a personal recordkeeping system or diary wherein he records performing the target behavior in other settings, with incentives for his performance.

Related to generalization across settings is the need for the child to learn responses appropriate to a particular setting. While learning to generalize, the child must simultaneously learn to discriminate according to environmental stimulus conditions. For example, one uses different greetings to authority figures such as teachers, to peers, and to family members. Skills in learning to discriminate according to environmental conditions should be explicit in the instructional program.

When teaching for transfer, the social skills trainer should structure the procedures to ensure that the child's behavior is controlled by explicit aspects of the training, not incidental factors. For example, in a study with autistic children, Rincover and Koegel (1975) found that behaviors learned in instructional settings failed to transfer to a second setting because the children were responding to incidental stimuli such as the trainer's hand movements instead of his verbal commands. When these unintentional behaviors were introduced into the second setting, the children responded as they had under treatment conditions. An important consideration with this study is that, although the desired responses were produced, they were not under the control of the intended stimulus, the verbal command "touch your chin." These findings emphasize the importance of analyzing the social skill instruction situation in order to ensure that the child's behavior is being triggered by the appropriate social stimuli. A child, for example, may learn to make assertive responses only in the presence of a supportive peer group, or a child may depend on certain nonverbal behaviors such as eye contact from the teacher to signal behaviors such as making appropriate greetings. When removed from these conditions, the child may be less inclined to make assertive responses or appropriate greetings, even though the behaviors may be warranted by the situation.

In order to introduce a broader range of stimuli similar to real life conditions, the instructional setting should vary according to group constellation and size, allowing for different responses and environmental conditions. It appears that the most effective training conditions (i.e., individual or group) are dictated primarily by the behaviors to be learned, the child's skill level, and the conditions under which the child will have to perform the behavior under natural circumstances (Phillips, 1978). For example, the child learning to talk in class should receive instruction in large groups; on the other hand, the reverse may be necessary for the child being taught to engage in conversation with a peer. In the first example, however, it may be necessary to conduct training sessions which gradually move the child from individual to large group settings.

Another possible means of accomplishing generalization across settings is to provide opportunities for practice in different settings in the absence of the trainer. One program using this method is the "barb" approach developed by Kaufman and Wagner (1972) to teach adolescents positive ways to respond to anger-producing stimuli. The principal stimulus for response is the "barb," a remark intended to evoke a negative emotional reaction. Adolescents are taught to respond with eye contact, a pleasant facial expression, moderate tone of voice, and verbal responses which help avoid problems and possibly obtain positive consequences. Techniques for teaching these alternatives to temper tantrums or aggressive responses to barbs include rapport building, modeling, role playing, cueing, cue-fading, and intermittent reinforcement. After the initial training, the techniques include a planned program for generalization involving barbs delivered by a variety of persons in different places with token reinforcement for desired responses. The program for one youth was as follows:

1 & 2. Exploration, role playing, expectations, rapport building with several barbs delivered during private sessions: 1 week
   3. Training, cueing, immediate reinforcement; one barb per day, coordinator only, cue before barb, one token per behavioral requirement: 1 week
   4. Cue fading; 3 staff members delivering barbs: 2 weeks
   5. Stimulus generalization; all but three unit staff delivering barbs, temper control required during evening activity: 2 weeks
   6. Additional requirement and generalization; facial expression requirement, all unit staff delivering barbs: 2 weeks
   7. Fixed ratio reinforcement; all staff plus teachers delivering, all requirements met necessary to earn tokens: 3 weeks
   8. Further generalization; three barbs per day, seven tokens per barb, staff, students, administrators delivering barbs: 1 week
   9. Further fixed ratio; three barbs per day, must pass all to earn tokens: 3 weeks
  10. Rotating barb; five barbs per day, random barb earns tokens: 3 weeks
  11. "Intermittent" reinforcement, random programming: 14 weeks   [P. 87]

The program as outlined above demonstrates a number of generalization principles. It moves from practice with anticipated barbs delivered by one therapist in one setting to random barbs delivered by a gradually increasing number of adults and then peers in other settings. Barbs are initially preceded by cues, and then the cues are gradually eliminated. The schedule of reinforcement is changed from continuous immediate reinforcement, to a fixed schedule, and then to an intermittent schedule, the latter being that closest to the kind of recognition provided in the natural environment.

Train with Different People

Using more than one trainer is suggested in order to avoid the possibility that new behaviors will remain under the control of one trainer and will fail to generalize, as described earlier with the Rincover and Koegel (1975) study. Two trainers might alternate in training sessions, keeping conditions similar but requiring the child to respond to the social situation rather than the trainer. A study by Stokes, Baer, and Jackson (1974) illustrates this point. More than one trainer was used to teach institutionalized retarded children to greet others by hand waving. The first trainer, using prompting and shaping procedures, taught the child to make the greeting response. A second trainer was used when probes revealed no generalization or only transitory generalization to other staff members. The researchers found that generalization of the greeting response to staff not involved in the training was most effective when the child was taught by more than one trainer.

Other members of the child's environment such as teachers, parents and peers might be trained to instruct, prompt, and reinforce the desired social behaviors. The following guidelines for such instruction are adapted from Gelfand and Hartmann (1975):

1. Generally outline the instructional program.
2. Provide trainees with written description of instructional session, and invite them to observe your training.
3. Following observation, discuss procedures in detail.
4. If necessary, provide for additional observations.
5. Rehearse training session through role play where trainee provides instruction.
6. Observe trainee's instruction of child in social skills.
7. Provide corrective feedback either during or following session.
8. Provide taped recordings of your training sessions for the trainee to listen to and practice.

Walker and Buckley (1974) trained teachers in order to effect behavior generalization from the special class to the regular classroom. They found instructions in behavior modification procedures to be less effective than precise written descriptions, discussion of the procedures, and periodic classroom visits to provide direct assistance. An example of a maintenance strategy follows.

The teacher was given these instructions:

For a 2-month period, you as _____'s teacher, will be provided with the following materials. These materials were used by _____ in the experimental classroom and should be the instructional bases for language, reading, and spelling during this period.

I. Academic Materials. (materials varied for each subject)
   1. _____
   2. _____
   3. _____

II. Reinforcer System

You will be provided with 40 blue sheets to be used in recording points. Place a new sheet in the child's desk each day and save the record forms in a folder. _____ has already selected the items for which he would like to exchange his points. Each item requires an earned total of 100 points. It is possible for _____ to earn approximately one item per week.

III. Reinforcement Program for Social and Academic Behaviors

1. You are provided with a blue point record form which is divided into 50 squares: (1) 25 points for good academic production, (2) 25 points for good student behavior. A maximum of 24 points total can be earned by _____ in any single day.

2. Using a marking pen (felt), award points according to the following schedules:

(a) *Academics:* Check the child's academic work four times a day for correctness, neatness, completion within allotted time, etc. A good time to evaluate is toward the end of block activities such as math, reading, spelling, language, and so on. If his work is acceptable, satisfactory, or meets stated criteria, administer a maximum of three points per evaluation. Thus, for academics, a child could earn a maximum of 12 points per day. If his work is satisfactory, but barely so, you may want to administer no points for that evaluation.

(b) *Social Behavior:* For appropriate social behavior (Examples: paying attention, listening to and following instructions, completing assignments, good playground behavior, etc.) evaluate the child four times during the day, for example, at 10:15 a.m., 11:45 a.m., 1:30 p.m., and 3:00 p.m. If the child's behavior has been acceptable during the preceding time period, reinforce him with a maximum of 3 points per evaluation. Thus, a child could earn a total of 12 points during the day for appropriate social behavior. If his behavior has been satisfactory but not exemplary, 2 points or 1 point could be administered. If his behavior has not been satisfactory between 10:15 and 11:45, then no points would be awarded at the 11:45 evaluation.

3. *Social Reinforcement:* It is extremely important that you pair each administration of an earned point with some form of overt social reinforcement such as praise ("good work," "excellent," or "fine job"), approval, interest, attention, and/or affection. In this way, social reinforcement from you will come to have the same effect upon behavior as points. However, it is important that you do not verbally reprimand the child when points are withheld.

[Pp. 213-14]

Along with significant adults in the child's life, the peer group can be used to provide social skill training and maintenance. Stokes and Baer (1977) emphasize the advantages of training peers to help maintain behaviors since peers are generally found in both training and generalization settings. Children exercise considerable control over each other, and in many cases it becomes critical to enlist their involvement in the social skills instruction. Consider, for example, the child whose peers reward verbal and physical aggression, behaviors that may be incompatible with the social skills being taught. Walker and Buckley (1974) employed "peer reprogramming procedures" where the target child, upon making the desired responses, was able to earn a specified number of points to be exchanged for a reward for the entire class. The objective was to make it profitable for the peer group or other members of the child's environment to support and reward appropriate rather than inappropriate behaviors. In employing such a strategy the social skills trainer should make sure that:

• Reasonably attainable goals are established. Goals that initially are set too high may frustrate the child, giving him little incentive to try. As the child progresses, goals may be raised gradually.

• The target child does not become a victim, receiving punishment for inadequate responses as opposed to praise and encouragement for approximations.

• The peer group understands what the target behaviors are and exactly how to provide support and encouragement. Instruction sessions may be conducted, role playing the target behaviors and appropriate peer responses.

• Rewards to be earned are highly desired by the group and are programmed to be faded gradually once the behaviors appear to have stabilized and become maintained and are supported largely by social and other natural reinforcers.

TRAINING MEDIATORS

A promising approach to programming for generalization is that of developing cognitive mediators to assist the child in generalizing and maintaining appropriate behaviors in settings, times, and conditions beyond those explicitly involved in training. According to Bandura (1977a), response patterns can be represented in memory and retained in symbolic form primarily through imagery and verbalization. There are data indicating that behavior learned through observation is acquired and retained more effectively with mental and verbal rehearsal in addition to behavioral rehearsal. Although a number of questions have been raised (Franks & Wilson, 1978) related to the utility of cognitive strategies for generalization, Meichenbaum (1977), Stokes and Baer (1977), and others see the development of mediators as having considerable potential, particularly when they are deliberately programmed as strategies for generalization.

Language as a Mediator

Since most cognitive processes are verbal rather than visual, language is the mediator most often involved in training for generalization. Stokes and Baer (1977) point out that language serves as a common stimulus "to be carried from any training setting to any generalization setting that the child may ever enter'' (p. 361). A simple method for using language as a mediator is having the child state what he did or might do while engaging in a social behavior. For example, the child learning to exhibit appropriate behavior after winning a game might verbally list his responses as:

1. After my partner congratulates me I will say, "Thank you" and smile.
2. I will compliment him for playing a good game.
3. Then I will ask him if he wants to play another game.
4. If he says yes, I will let him go first.

The use of language as a mediator was demonstrated in a study conducted by Risley and Hart (1968) with preschool children. Food rewards were provided to the children for accurate reports of their use of play material. The authors viewed the self reports as having a generalizing effect on the child's play behavior, since behaviors for the subsequent day were altered to correspond with the previous verbal descriptions, suggesting that "saying" could be considered to control "doing."

Another example of language as a mediator was demonstrated by Clark, Caldwell, and Christian (1979) in a study using self reports to generalize conversation skills to other settings. Children who had been taught conversation skills in the classroom were directed to practice these skills during lunch period. Following lunch, the students indicated on a questionnaire whether they had made certain responses, e.g., "Did I ask a classmate about his/her mom, dad, brother, or sister?" The accuracy of these reports was ascertained through a videotape monitoring system that taped the children during lunch. Rewards were given for making the desired statements and truthfully reporting them. According to the authors, the combination of accurate self reports and delayed reinforcement was effective in maintaining conversational skills.

Self instruction and problem solving cognitive approaches are also potentially useful for behavior generalization. Since these procedures employ language to develop problem solving strategies, it is reasoned that the skills developed will be more lasting and more easily transferred to a variety of situations and behaviors. Meichenbaum (1977) presents evidence of the efficacy of self instructions for behavior generalization and durability when the training required overt rather than covert self instructions, and the training was conducted over more extensive periods of time. A variation of self instruction is the stress innoculation model (described earlier in Chapter 3) which Meichenbaum presents as a procedure explicitly developed for generalization training. In a review of self instruction research with children, Kendall (1978) concludes that treatment that stresses "metacognitive development" (i.e., awareness of one's thinking processes) is most likely to lead to generalization. Support for the facilitative effects of problem solving procedures in producing behavior maintenance and transfer is provided by Richards and Perri (in press) as cited by Franks and Wilson (1978). Using college students concerned about academic underachievement as subjects, the authors compared one treatment program that involved fading instructions in study skills and self-control procedures to a second program using the D'Zurilla and Goldfried problem solving model (See Chapter 3). A three-week evaluation revealed that maintenance of desired behaviors as evidenced by exam scores and grade point averages was greater for the problem solving than the fading group. Considering the brief time period for the follow-up evaluation, the relative sophistication of the subjects used in the study, and the cognitive nature of the behaviors being taught, the authors caution against loosely generalizing these results to other populations and behaviors. In Chapter 5 of this book, Bash and Camp provide anecdotal evidence of behavior generalization resulting from a combination of self instruction and problem solving methods. One other cognitive activity related to generalization of social skills, that of self-evaluation, is discussed elsewhere in this chapter as well as in Chapter 2.

Imagery as a Mediator

Visual imagery is another mediator that may be incorporated into the child's social training program, usually in combination with language. Bandura (1977a) points out, however, that visual imagery is particularly important when verbal skills are lacking. A common technique for the development of imagery is that of providing visual stimuli in the form of drawings, photographs, films, etc., and asking the child to close his eyes and imagine himself in the pictured situation. DeMille (1967), in a book of children's imagination games which provide practice in visualization, suggests the following means of facilitating visual imagery:

When you ask the child to imagine something going on in the yard at his school, he may say, "It's too far away. I can't see it." This problem can be handled step by step.

An easy visualization is to look at the room in which the game is being played, then close the eyes and see a mental image of it. If the child can do that, then ask him to remember or imagine how the next room looks.

Then another familiar room that is farther away—perhaps your garage, or a neighbor's or a relative's living room. After that, more and more distant places can be visualized, until the school yard—or the North Pole—is within easy reach. Do not be concerned about the vividness of the images. The child only has to say that he imagines or remembers how a place looks. The brightness, completeness, or constancy of the mental image is unimportant.   [P. 37]

Some procedures for developing imagery related to the teaching of social skills through covert rehearsal techniques are outlined in Chapter 3. The use of imagery for generalization of social skills would involve asking the child to imagine himself engaging in the target behavior under the familiar training situation, then introducing variations to be imagined, e.g., other persons, other places, and future times.

Expectations as Mediators

A further cognitive mediational variable related to generalization is that of expectations. Bandura (1977b) speaks of "efficacy expectations" as "the conviction that one can successfully execute the behavior required to produce the outcomes" (p. 103). He suggests that these expectations are generated through (1) "performance accomplishments"—awareness of one's actual successful performance; (2) "vicarious experience"—awareness of others' successful performance; (3) "verbal persuasion"—suggestions and exhortations from others or from oneself; and (4) reducing "emotional arousal"—the ability to apply various means of controlling emotions in stressful situations. Applying these dimensions to the generalization of social skills, the teacher or clinician can enhance the child's expectations of future success by training in actual skills, providing examples of successful models, suggesting through discussion and other verbal means how the learning of social behaviors will be helpful in the future, and engaging the child in various kinds of learning (e.g., relaxation) to develop feelings of competence in stressful interpersonal situations. Related to this can also be the establishment through role play, discussion, imagery, etc., of expectations about kinds of situations in which the social skills will be appropriate in the future.

CONTINGENCIES OF REINFORCEMENT

The maintenance of social behaviors once they have been taught is also referred to as resistance to extinction, durability, or generalization over time. The principal factor supporting maintenance of social skills over time is reinforcement and the contingencies of reinforcement operating in the settings where the social skills would be expressed. The learning of social skills is facilitated by reinforcement and feedback. For generalization to occur, the nature of reinforcement needs to be changed, and there are a number of ways in which this can take place. The sources of reinforcement can be changed, particularly from external to intrinsic sources of reward; the ways in which reinforcement is given can be changed; and the kinds of rewards provided can be changed.

Change the Source of Reinforcement

Rewards for social behaviors come primarily from persons in the external world or from intrinsic sources related to the satisfaction inherent in behaving in approved ways. If social skills to be taught are selected with attention to some of the criteria outlined in Chapter 1, especially the "relevance of behavior" rule, persons in the natural environment will respond in ways that keep the behaviors going. Social skills are, by definition, behaviors that will be reinforced by others. Such skills as positive approaches to others, conversations skills, problem solving skills, and ability to express emotion constructively are all behaviors to which others will generally respond positively. As Phillips (1978) points out, "social skills . . . imply reciprocity, interaction, and mutual reinforcement" (p. 8). Stokes and Baer (1977) speak of "behavioral traps," entry responses that expose the child to a community of natural reinforcers. For example, teaching an isolated child the skills to make friends will open up many new opportunities for positive experiences.

Although many social skills may, by their nature, evoke maintaining responses from the external environment, some planning and programming for generalization and maintenance through altered reinforcement may be necessary. It may be necessary at first, for example, to program a change in source of reinforcement from the teacher or therapist to persons in the child's larger environment. Enlisting the support of parents, peers, and other relevant persons in the child's environment is particularly necessary for transfer of the social behaviors taught in the school or clinic to his wider environment. In transferring reinforcement to the home or another setting, the social skills trainer will need to assess the parents' or others' ability to provide positive feedback. It may be sufficient to inform the parents or others that, for example, "Our social skill of the week is paying compliments. Please respond positively when John says something nice to you, even if he is not very smooth about it," or "John will bring home a feedback slip. Please mark a point on it whenever he makes a positive comment to someone." A program to transfer the source of reinforcement can involve reinforcement initially provided in the training setting based on behavior emitted there, reinforcement continued in the training setting given on a delayed basis from data provided by the home, then reinforcement transferred to the home based on behaviors expressed in the home. A program using delayed reinforcement was carried out by Jewett and Clark (1976), in which conversational skills were taught in preschool then practiced at home at the evening meal. Audio tapes were made of the mealtime conversation and scored the next day, with a snack provided at school as a reinforcer for children who had used the trained comments at home during the previous evening meal. Ultimately, the entire program was transferred to the home.

Many parents may easily be able to provide praise and other reinforcers, possibly initiating contingency contracts to maintain social behaviors. For parents without the skills to provide contingent reinforcement, numerous parent training programs and materials are available (for example Alvord, 1973; Becker, 1971; Cooper & Edge, 1978; Krumboltz & Krumboltz, 1972; Miller, 1975; Patterson, 1977; Patterson & Gullion, 1976; Smith & Smith, 1976), and it may be necessary for the practitioner to build parent training into the social skills training program. Along with parents, peers and siblings are potent sources of reinforcement. The use of peers to promote generalization is discussed in a previous section of this chapter as well as in Chapter 9.

An additional means of transferring the source of reinforcement from the therapist or teacher to others in the natural environment is providing the child himself with skills to elicit reinforcement, referred to by Stokes and Baer as "teaching the subject a means of recruiting, a natural community of reinforcement to maintain . . . generalization" (p. 354). Related to the ability to self reinforce (discussed below) and also to verbal mediators, the child needs to be able to recognize when he has done something praiseworthy and call others' attention to it in a way that will encourage their positive responses. Seymour and Stokes (1976) report a study in which adolescent girls in an institutional setting were trained through discussion and role playing how to "cue" staff to provide praise for their work improvement. In using this approach, there might be merit in developing cohorts in the environment who are willing to reward the child's positive remarks about himself, since this behavior has some risks of being misused or misunderstood by others.

A procedure that combines several elements (i.e., practice in other settings, teaching the child to elicit reinforcement, and transferring reinforcement to others) involves giving the child a card or feedback slip to carry after he has learned a skill. As he moves through the school or other environments, he is instructed to watch for opportunities to practice the target skill, then present the card to an available adult to mark confirmation that he performed the behavior satisfactorily. This technique is useful in a setting where the relevant adults can be informed in advance that, for example, children in Miss Jones' class are practicing giving compliments, will be carrying feedback slips, and that it would be helpful for the adult to mark the card and provide social reinforcement for a good attempt at a compliment. When the child returns to the teacher or therapist he can be asked to describe verbally each of the compliments he paid, and he can be reinforced again for the report.

Change in the Timing of Reinforcement

In the process of teaching new social behaviors, reinforcement needs to be provided immediately on a continuous basis for correct responses. Once behaviors are learned, persistence of behavior over time will occur most readily if the timing or schedule for reinforcement is "thinned" out to occasional reinforcement provided on an intermittent and unpredictable basis. Stokes and Baer (1977) suggest introducing noncontingent reinforcement, even "random or haphazard" delivery of reinforcement to assist in generalization, with the goal of establishing conditions in which the subject "cannot discriminate in which settings a response will be reinforced or not reinforced" (p. 358). The use of delayed reinforcement mentioned above, in addition to assisting in the generalization of behavior across settings and people and the transfer of sources of reinforcement from one set of persons to others, also assists in the thinning of reinforcement schedules. Related to thinning out of schedules is the fading technique used by Greenwood, Walker and Hops (1977) which involved the gradual removal of aspects of the behavioral program, i.e., recording, classroom rules, and chart of progress from an elementary school classroom. The resulting maintenance of appropriate behavior in the classroom was superior to that in classrooms where the program was terminated without a maintenance strategy. (For a detailed discussion of schedules of reinforcement, the reader is referred to other sources, e.g., Ferster, Culbertson, & Boren, 1975; Ferster and Perrott, 1968; Ferster and Skinner, 1957.)

Use of contingency contracts (Dardig and Heward, 1980; DeRisi and Butz, 1975; Homme et al., 1969; Kanfer, 1975) can be an aid to generalization and maintenance of social skills, since contracts provide a means by which rewards can be delayed and the source of reinforcement changed from one person to another. Further, the existence of a contract can serve as a reminder for children to engage in the target behaviors beyond the training setting. The contract can be made between the child and the trainer with rewards provided in the training setting for target behaviors to be carried out in another setting, or can be established between the parent and child with the trainer serving as negotiator for the target behaviors to be performed in the home. The contract can be verbal or written, formal or informal, but a written contract, signed and witnessed, may be taken more seriously by all participants. A contingency contract related to social skills should have the following components: (1) The social behavior clearly defined so all concerned can agree that it has occurred; (2) the performance criteria for the behavior, i.e., how much of the behavior has to occur to earn the payoff, and under what circumstances it should occur; (3) the reward to be provided when criteria are met and who provides the reward; and (4) a means of determining whether the reward has been earned.

Homme et al. (1969) provide some criteria for a successful contingency contract. The contract reward should be immediate at first; initial contracts should reward small steps; the contract should be fair; the terms of the contract should be clear; the contract should be honest, i.e., carried out immediately according to the specified terms; and the contract should be positive.

The following example of a social skills contingency contract is provided in Stephens (1978):

Teaching Strategy
Skill: The student makes positive statements when asked about himself.

Contingency Management

1. Present the task to the student in specific terms. When someone asks you to tell about yourself or about your work, think of some good things to say.

2. Define a consequence valued by the student which will be given following demonstration of the desired positive verbalization about himself.

3. State the contingency. If student says positive things when asked about himself, he will receive the agreed-upon desirable consequences.

4. Listen for the behavior to occur naturally, and reinforce it when it occurs according to established contingency. Or, set up a situation in which the behavior can occur. Give the student an activity at which he does well. Ask the student questions about himself and his work. If he responds to questions about himself or his work with positive statements, he will receive the established reward.

5. Example: Todd is a bright, well-behaved student in Mr. Downs' class. In spite of Todd's assets, Mr. Downs suspects that he has a poor "self-concept," because Todd, when asked about his work, usually makes some negative response such as "It's no good," or "I could have done better." He is critical not only of himself but of others as well, and he is quick to find fault with what other students do. Mr. Downs feels that possibly some of Todd's negative statements are perpetuated by the reactions they get when he "runs down" himself or his work. For example, somebody always responds by saying something like, "Oh no, Todd, it's *good.*" Mr. Downs sets up a conference with Todd and discusses with him his observations—that Todd has many good qualities and accomplishments, but that he continually looks for negative things to say about himself and others. He describes to Todd and rehearses with him some positive statements he would like him to make instead. He helps Todd understand the difference between "bragging" and being realistically proud of one's accomplishments and acknowledging them when asked.

Mr. Downs sets up a contract with Todd. For every positive statement Todd can make about himself or someone else when he is asked, Mr. Downs will give Todd two trading stamps. He will provide a bonus of five stamps if Todd can come and point out to him something good he or someone else has done which Mr. Downs is unaware of. Mr. Downs puts Todd in charge of a bulletin board labeled "Blowing Our Horn," on which are put positive observations about members of the class, which Todd and the others supply.

[P. 377]

A further advantage of the contingency contract is the potential for involving the child in setting his own rewards and criteria for reinforcement, thus moving the social behaviors closer to maintenance by self reinforcement.

Change the Nature of Reinforcement

Kinds of external reinforcement vary from social reinforcement (i.e., praise, smiles, positive attention, positive physical contact), to various forms of tangible reinforcers (such as food, toys, etc.), to generalized conditioned reinforcers (such as tokens or points that can stand for a wide variety of other reinforcing events). The work of Premack (1959) has established that almost any high-rate, presumably more preferred, activity can serve as a reinforcer for a low-rate, presumably less-preferred, activity. Since reinforcement is defined by its positive effect on behavior, effective reinforcers cannot always be predicted in advance. In Chapter 2, it was suggested that reinforcers as well as social skills be assessed to determine what kinds of rewards will encourage the child to engage in social skills training or perform the social behavior he has learned. The child who can progress from a need for immediate edible rewards, to a token exchange system, to behavior maintained by social rewards is considered to have become more highly socialized. If social skills instruction begins initially with tangible reinforcers, maintenance over time will be enhanced if the trainer moves toward the use of social reinforcement, since praise, smiles, and attention are potentially available in almost all settings. If social rewards do not initially serve as reinforcers, they can take on reinforcing value if they are paired with whatever is actually reinforcing to the child. Gelfand and Hartmann (1975) suggest exaggerating the praise and smiles at first so the child will attend to them, then gradually eliminating the artificial reinforcement, maintaining the behaviors on occasional praise or some other natural contingency.

Develop Self Reinforcement Skills

Although little research literature exists on self reinforcement, it appears to be one of the most promising means by which behaviors can be maintained over time. Bandura (1977a) regards self reinforcement, or the ability to regulate one's own behavior by self-produced consequences, as the highest level of development in the developmental hierarchy of incentives, and refers to self reward as a "generalizable skill in self regulation that can be used continually" (p. 144). The ability to self reinforce can be regarded as itself a social skill which has the following component parts: (a) The adopting of standards by which performance is to be evaluated; (b) monitoring one's own behavior; (c) evaluating one's performance according to the standards set; and (d) providing self reinforcement, based on the degree to which the behavior meets performance standards.

Standards for self reinforcement are developed either through being taught criteria or through observation of standards set by others. Polsgrove (1979) summarizes the following conclusions from the review of literature by Masters and Mokros (1974) on children's self-reinforcement processes:

1. Children may more readily adopt externally imposed than modeled standards for self-reward;
2. Children tend to select the self-reinforcement standards of more lenient social models;
3. When a model's imposed standards conflict with his modeled standards for self-reinforcement, children tend to adopt the more lenient standards;
4. In general, children more readily adopt the self-reinforcement standards of competent, powerful models but not necessarily that of nurturant models;
5. Children tend to imitate self-regulatory behavior of models whose performances are closer to their competence levels rather than those who show superior performances;
6. A model's praise may increase a child's imitation of self-controlling behavior.   [P. 123]

Self monitoring is discussed briefly in Chapter 2, with steps for self monitoring suggested by Kanfer (1975). One aspect of self monitoring is "correspondence training," teaching the child to make accurate reports about his previous verbal and nonverbal behavior. Correspondence training techniques generally involve teaching children to monitor their own behavior, comparing the child's report with data of an independent observer, and providing reinforcement to the child for accuracy of his data or his verbal reports. An unsuccessful study in self evaluation (Santogrossi, O'Leary, Romanczyk, & Kaufman, 1973) points out the need to train children to evaluate their own performance in a way that corresponds with others' objective evaluations before moving to self reinforcement. Several studies have built correspondence training into self evaluation programs. Wood and Flynn (1978) developed a self evaluation token system with delinquent youth in which external reinforcement for room cleanliness was transferred to a self reinforcement system. Accuracy of self evaluation was developed by giving two sets of points: one for room cleanliness and the other for the extent to which self evaluations agreed with those of an independent adult observer. After an 80 percent level of agreement was reached, the independent observation was discontinued, and accurate self evaluation was maintained by random spot checks. Bolstead and Johnson (1972) provided disruptive elementary school children with self-observation cards and instructed the students in recording their own behavior. At the end of each session, their data were matched against that of an observer, and fewer points were awarded if the self observation was inaccurate. Bolstead and Johnson (1972) make a case for the self monitoring procedures as being practical and inexpensive for the classroom teacher in that once the child has learned to monitor his own behavior, the self evaluation process can be maintained with only occasional checks by the teacher.

Like reinforcement delivered by external sources, self reinforcement can take a variety of forms. Self reward can range from self administered tokens or points, to self contracting for tangible items, to internalized rewards by means of positive self statements. The latter could be considered the ideal and an ultimate goal of social skills training. As mentioned earlier, contingency contracts can be useful vehicles for developing self reinforcement, since it is possible to increase the child's participation in the contracting procedure by gradual steps. Homme et al. (1969) provide the following stages for that process:

Level 1 - Manager-controlled system in which the manager determines the reinforcer and the task and delivers the reward.

Level 2 - Transitional step with partial control by student where student assumes joint control with the manager either over the amount of reinforcement or the amount of task.

Level 3 - Second transitional step in which manager and student share equally in determining both the reinforcer and the task.

Level 4 - Third transitional step in which the student assumes full control of either the task or reinforcer and shares joint responsibility with the manager for the other.

Level 5 - Student controlled contracting in which the student has assumed full control of determining both the amount of reinforcement and amount of task.

Children may need to be taught through specific procedures how to make positive self statements. Procedures for altering negative self statements are outlined in Chapter 3. The following strategy for the skill, "The student makes positive statements when asked about himself," is presented in Stephens (1978):

Teaching Strategy
Skill: The student makes positive statements when asked about himself.

Social Modeling
1. Identify a need for the behavior through a classroom discussion. Use stories, film strips or other aids where available. Bring up such points as the fact that everyone has good qualities and does some things well, even though no one is perfect. Have the class identify reasons why it's good to know about your own good qualities and recognize the things you do well. Have the class try to distinguish between behavior which could be considered "bragging" or inappropriately building oneself up at the expense of another, and behavior which involves appropriately saying positive things about oneself and what one has done. Generate with the class some positive sentences one might use to describe one's accomplishments. For example, "I like my picture." "That was a good hit I made." "I'm happy that I got 100 in spelling."

2. Identify specific behavior to be modeled. When someone asks you to tell about yourself or about something good you've done, try to think of something positive to say. (Stress that

one need not be perfect or do everything perfectly in order to find good things to say about oneself.)

3. Model the behavior for the class. Describe to the class some realistic positive traits you possess and skills you have. For contrast you might insert some negative comments and have students distinguish between the two.

4. Give each student an opportunity to practice. Make up a list of positive statements as prompts. Give each student a copy of the list. Go around the class and have each student find a statement which he could apply to himself and read it in response to a prompting question from the teacher. Go around the class again and have each student think of another statement which is not on the list. Provide prompts wherever necessary. Reward students who make appropriate responses.

5. Maintain through reinforcement the behavior of making positive statements about oneself or one's accomplishments.   [P. 374]

The progression of the child from self-administered tangible rewards to internalized rewards in the form of positive statements and thoughts can be programmed through shaping and fading procedures. Based on some of the limited research that exists in this area, the following steps are suggested for moving the child from self-provided, extrinsic rewards to self-administered, intrinsic rewards for appropriate social behaviors, with the understanding that movement from one part of the process to the next needs to be paced according to the success experienced at any one point:

1. Establish with the child the specific behavior to be rewarded and the criteria for reinforcement. Establish with the child the reward he will provide for himself, beginning with tangible rewards, if necessary, at whatever level is appropriate.

2. Initiate correspondence training, providing practice in self-monitoring with rewards for accuracy.

3. Initiate self reinforcement, providing verbal reinforcement from the trainer for both the social behaviors and the appropriate delivery of self reinforcement.

4. Have the child accompany self reinforcement with a verbal description of what he did to gain the reward. For example, have the child place a star on a chart at the end of a play period for target behaviors such as sharing or taking turns, then describe what he did to earn the star, giving himself an additional star for an accurate description.

5. Ask the child to think silently to himself what he did to earn the reward before he makes the statement.

6. Move to less frequent self-administered, tangible rewards and verbal descriptions, requiring the child to remember for a longer time what he did to earn the reward.

7. Discontinue the use of self-administered, tangible rewards but require verbal reports, reinforced by external praise.

8. Discontinue regular verbal reports but periodically use probes and reminders. "I saw you help Mary when she fell down. Did you congratulate yourself for doing something nice for someone else?"

Although theoretically social skills may be trained and generalized across settings and persons and maintained over time through alteration of contingencies ending with self reinforcement, realistically it may be necessary periodically to provide more training. Periodic booster sessions provide one way of providing for maintenance of behavior change (Hersen, 1979), although Franks and Wilson (1978) caution that booster sessions are most effective if they are timed to occur before a behavior has been allowed to deteriorate. Similarly, a teacher may need to present occasional abbreviated review lessons for previously learned social skills. Baer (1978) suggests that the concept of "savings" is relevant to the issue of generalization. Even though a behavior may be taught once and then require occasional reteaching for new settings or maintenance over time, the fact of the initial instruction will serve to decrease the time and effort required to provide additional teaching.

SUMMARY

Specific programming needs to be built into social skills instruction to assist in the generalization of the social behaviors to different settings and people and the maintenance of the behaviors over time. For newly learned skills to transfer from one setting to another, it is advisable to structure the training setting to resemble the real life environment as closely as possible. It is also helpful to use more than one setting in the training and more than one trainer. Involving people from the natural environment (e.g., parents and peers) in the training is particularly helpful for facilitating generalization.

The use of mediators in the form of language, imagery, self instruction, problem solving skills, and expectations can be a way to extend training into new environments, since these can be carried into any setting through the child's cognitive activities. Techniques for maintaining behaviors over time generally involve changes in the contingencies of reinforcement surrounding the social behaviors. Changes can be made in the sources of reinforcement from the trainer to someone in the natural environment, and in the timing of reinforcement from frequent predictable reinforcement to infrequent intermittent rewards. Contingency contracts are a useful way to change both the source and timing of reinforcement. The kinds of external reinforcement provided can also be changed from tangible rewards to more natural social reinforcement, and efforts can be made to develop the child's ability to monitor, evaluate, and provide his own internalized rewards for desirable social behavior. Even though behaviors can be programmed to generalize over time, persons, and settings, it may still be necessary to provide occasional reteaching to make sure that the child will continue to reap the positive benefits to be gained from learning social skills.

REFERENCES (Chapters 1-4)

Alberti, R.E. & Emmons, M.L. *Your perfect right.* San Luis Obispo, Calif.: Impact, 1970.

Allyon, T. & Azrin, N. *The token economy.* New York: Appleton-Century-Crofts, 1968.

Alkvord, J.R. *Home token economy: An incentives program for children and their parents.* Champaign, Ill.: Research Press, 1973.

Arkowitz, H.; Lichenstein, E.; McGovern, K.; Hines, P. The behavioral assessment of social competence in males, *Behavior Therapy, 6,* 1975, 3-13.

Ascher, L.M. & Phillips, D. "Guided behavior rehearsal," *Journal of Behavior Therapy & Experimental Psychiatry, 6* (3), 1975, 215-218.

Asher, S.R.; Singleton, L.C.; Tinsley, B.R.; & Hymel, S. A reliable sociometric measure for preschool children. *Developmental Psychology, 15* (4), 1979, 443-444.

Bach, G. & Bernhard, Y. *Aggression lab.* Dubuque, Iowa: Kendall/Hunt, 1971.

Baer, D.M. Remarks as discussant, Symposium on Research and Technological Consideration of Generalization and Maintenance Variables. American Psychological Association Convention, Montreal, September 1978.

Bandura, A. *Principles of behavior modification,* New York: Holt, Rinehart and Winston, 1969.

Bandura, A. *Aggression: A social learning analysis,* Englewood Cliffs, N.J. Prentice-Hall, 1973.

Bandura, A. *Social learning theory.* Englewood Cliffs, N.J.: Prentice-Hall, 1977a.

Bandura, A. Self-efficacy: Toward a unifying theory of behavioral change. *Psychological Review, 84* (2), 1977b, 191-215.

Beck, A. Cognitive therapy: Nature and relation to behavior therapy, Behavior Therapy, *1,* 1970, 184-200.

Beck, A. *Cognitive therapy and emotional disorders.* New York: International Universities Press, 1976.

Becker, W.C. *Parents are teachers.* Champaign, Ill.: Research Press, 1971.

Bellack, A.; Hersen, M.; & Turner, Samuel. Role-play tests for assessing social skills: Are they valid? *Behavior Therapy, 9,* 1978, 448-461.

Bernstein, D.A. & Borkovec, T.D. *Progressive relaxation training.* Champaign, Ill.: Research Press, 1973.

Bijou, S.W.; Peterson, R.F.; & Ault, M.H. A method to integrate descriptive and experimental field studies at the level of data and empirical concepts. *Journal of Applied Behavior Analysis, 1,* 1968; 175-191.

Blackwood, R.O. *Operant control of behavior: Elimination of misbehavior; motivation of children.* Akron, Ohio: Exordium Press, 1971.

Boies, K.G. Role playing as a behavior change technique: Review of the empirical literature. *Psychotherapy: Theory, Research and Practice, 9* (2), 1972, 185-192.

Bolstead, O.D. & Johnson, S.M. Self-regulation in the modification of disruptive classroom behavior, *Journal of Applied Behavior Analysis, 5,* 1972, 443-454.

Boocock, S.S. An experimental study of the learning effects of two games with simulated environments. In S.S. Boocock & E.O. Schild, (Eds.), *Simulation games in learning.* Beverly Hills, Calif.: Sage, 1968.

Bornstein, M.R.; Bellack, A.S.; & Hersen, M. Social-skills training for unassertive children: A multiple-baseline analysis. *Journal of Applied Behavior Analysis, 10,* 1977, 183-195.

Bowman, P.H.; DeHaan, R.F.; Kough, J.K. & Liddle, G.P. *Mobilizing community resources for youth.* Chicago: University of Chicago Press, 1956.

Calpin, J. & Kornblith, S. Training aggressive children in conflict resolution skills. Paper presented at Association for the Advancement of Behavior Therapy, Chicago, 1978.

Camp, B. Verbal mediation in young aggressive boys. *Journal of Abnormal Psychology, 86* (2), 1977, 145-153.

Camp, B. Cognitive-behavior therapy with children. Symposium, Second National Conference on Cognitive Therapy Research, New York, October 1978.

Cartledge, G. & Milburn, J.F. The case of teaching social skills in the classroom: A review. *Review of Educational Research, 1* (1), 1978, 133-156.

Casey, G.A. Behavioral rehearsal: Principles and procedure. *Psychotherapy: Theory, Research and Practice, 10* (4), 1973, 331-333.

Castaneda, A.; McCandless, B.R.; & Palermo, D.F. The children's form of the manifest anxiety scale. *Child Development, 27,* 1956, 317-326.

Cautela, J.R. & Groden, J. *Relaxation, a comprehensive manual for adults, children, and children with special needs.* Champaign, Ill.: Research Press, 1978.

Cautela, J.R. & Upper, D. The behavioral inventory battery: The use of self-report measures in behavioral analysis and therapy. In M. Hersen & A.S. Bellack (Eds.), *Behavioral Assessment: A Practical Handbook.* Elmsford, N.Y.: Pergamon Press, 1976.

Chittenden, G.E. An experimental study in measuring and modifying assertive behavior in young children. *Monographs of the Society for Research in Child Development, 7* (1, Serial No. 31), 1942.

Cianciolo, P.J. Children's literature can affect coping behavior. *Personnel and Guidance Journal, 43* (9), 1965, 897-903.

Clark, H.B.; Caldwell, C.P.; & Christian, W.P. Classroom training of conversational skills and remote programming for the practice of these skills in another setting. *Child Behavior Therapy, 1* (2), 1979.

Clement, P.W. & Richard, R.C. Identifying reinforcers for children: A children's reinforcement survey. In E.J. Mash & L.G. Terdal (Eds.), *Behavior therapy assessment,* New York: Springer Publishing, 1976.

Cobb, J.A. & Hops, H. Effects of academic survival skill training on low achieving first graders. *The Journal of Educational Research, 67,* 1973, 108-113.

Combs, M.L. & Slaby, D.A. Social skills training with children. In B.B. Lahey & A.E. Kazdin (Eds.), *Advances in Clinical Child Psychology,* Vol. I, New York: Plenum Press, 1977.

Cooper, J.O. *Measurement and analysis of behavioral techniques.* Columbus, Ohio: Charles E. Merrill, 1974.

Cooper, J.O. & Edge, D. *Parenting strategies and educational methods*. Columbus, Ohio: Charles E. Merrill, 1978.

Coopersmith, S. *The antecedents of self-esteem*. San Francisco: Freeman, 1967.

Corsini, R.J. *Roleplaying in psychotherapy: A manual*. Chicago: Aldine, 1966.

Csapo, M. Peer models reverse the "one bad apple spoils the barrel" theory. *Teaching Exceptional Children, 4*, 1972, 20-24.

Curwin, R.L. & Curwin, G. *Developing individual values in the classroom*. Palo Alto: Education Today Company, Inc., 1974.

Daley, M.F. The "reinforcement menu": Finding effective reinforcers. In E.J. Mash & L.G. Terdal (Eds.), *Behavior therapy assessment*. New York: Springer, 1976.

Dardig, J.C. & Heward, W.L. *Sign here: A contracting book for children and their parents*. Columbus, Ohio: Charles E. Merrill, 1980.

DeMille, R. *Put your mother on the ceiling*. New York: Walker, 1967.

DeRisi, W.J. & Butz, G. *Writing Behavioral contracts: A case simulation practice manual*. Champaign, Ill: Research Press, 1975.

Dinkmeyer, D. *Developing understanding of self and others* (DUSO Program). Circles Pines, Minn.: American Guidance Service, Inc., 1973.

Edleson, J.L. A behavioral roleplay test for assessing children's social skills: Testing booklet. Unpublished manual, University of Wisconsin-Madison, 1978.

Edleson, J.L. & Cole-Kelly, K. A behavioral roleplay test for assessing children's social skills: Scoring Manual. Unpublished manual, University of Wisconsin-Madison, 1978.

Edleson, J.L. & Rose, S.D. A behavioral roleplay test for assessing children's social skills. Paper presented at the annual convention of the Association for the Advancement of Behavior Therapy, Chicago, 1978.

Eisler, R.M. Behavioral assessment of social skills. In M. Hersen & A.A. Bellack (Eds.), *Behavioral assessment: A Practical Handbook*. Elmsford, N.Y.: Pergamon Press, 1976.

Ellis, A. *Reason and emotion in psychotherapy*. New York: Lyle Stuart Press, 1962.

Ellis, A. The basic clinical theory of rational-emotive therapy. In A. Ellis & R. Grieger (Eds.), *Handbook of rational-emotive therapy*. New York: Springer, 1977.

Erickson, E. *Childhood and society*. New York: Norton, 1963.

Evans, I. & Nelson, R. Assessment of child behavior problems. In A.R. Ciminero; K.S. Calhoun; & H.E. Adams (Eds.), *Handbook of Behavioral Assessment*. New York: Wiley, 1977.

Fagen, S.A.; Long, N.J.; & Stevens, D.J. *Teaching children self-control*. Columbus, Ohio: Charles E. Merrill, 1975.

Feldstein, G.E. Examination of test-retest reliability of the directive teaching instructional management system (DTIMS) social skill behavior rating scale. Masters thesis, Ohio State University, 1975.

Ferster, C.B.; Culbertson, S.; & Boren, M.C. *Behavior principles* (2nd ed.). Englewood Cliffs, N.J.: Prentice-Hall, 1975.

Ferster, C.B. & Perrott, M.C. *Behavior principles*. New York: Appleton-Century-Crofts, 1968.

Ferster, C.B. & Skinner, B.F. *Schedules of reinforcement*. New York: Appleton-Century-Crofts, 1957

Flowers, J.V. Behavior modification of cheating in an elementary school student: A brief note. *Behavior Therapy, 3*, 1972, 311-312.

Flowers, J.V. Modification of low self-confidence in elementary school children by reinforcement and modeling. Unpublished doctoral dissertation, University of Southern California, 1972.

Flowers, J.V. Simulation and role playing methods. In F.H. Kanfer & A.P. Goldstein (Eds.), *Helping People Change.* Elmsford, N.Y.: Pergamon Press, 1975.

Flowers, J.V.; Booraem, C.D.; & Seacat, G.F. The effect of positive and negative feedback on group member's sensitivity to the roles of other members in group therapy. *Psychotherapy: Theory, Research and Practice,* 1975.

Flowers, J.V.; Booraem, C.D.; Brown, T.R.; & Harris, D.E. An investigation of a technique for facilitating patient to patient interactions in group therapy. *Journal of Community Psychology, 2,* (1), 39-42.

Flowers, J.V. & Guerra, J. The use of client-coaching in assertion training with large groups. *Journal of Community Mental Health, 10,* 1974, 414-417.

Flowers, J.V. & Marston, A.R. Modification of low self confidence in elementary school children. *Journal of Education Research, 66* (1), 1972, 30-34.

Franks, C.M. & Wilson, T. *Annual review of behavior therapy: Theory & practice.* Vol. 6. New York: Brunner/Mazel, 1978.

Freedman, P.H. The effects of modeling, role playing and participation on behavior change. In B.A. Maher (Ed.), *Progress in experimental personality research.* Vol. 6. New York: Academic Press, 1972.

Gambrill, E.D. *Behavior modification.* San Francisco: Jossey-Bass, 1977.

Gardner, R.A. *Psychotherapeutic approaches to the resistant child.* New York: Jason Aronson, Inc., 1975

Gelfand, D.M. & Hartmann, D.P. *Child behavior analysis and therapy.* Elmsford, N.Y.: Pergamon Press, Inc., 1975.

Glazier, R. *How to design educational games.* Cambridge, Mass.: Abt Associates, 1970.

Goldberg, H.R. & Greenberger, B. *Getting it together.* Chicago: Science Research Associates, Inc., 1973.

Goldfried, M. & D'Zurilla, T. A behavioral-analytic model for assessing competence. In *Current Topics in Clinical and Community Psychology,* Volume 1. C.D. Spielberger (Ed.), New York: Academic Press, 1969.

Goldfried, M.R. & Goldfried, A.P. Cognitive change methods. In F.H. Kanfer & A.P. Goldstein (Eds.), *Helping people change.* Elmsford, N.Y.: Pergamon Press, 1975.

Goldstein, A.; Martens, J.; Hubben, J.; vanBelle, H.; Schaaf, W.; Wiersma, H.; & Goldhard, A. The use of modeling to increase independent behavior. *Behavior Research and Therapy, 11,* 1973, 31-42.

Goldstein, A.; Sherman, M.; Gershaw, N.J.; Sprafkin, R. & Glick, B. Training aggressive adolescents in prosocial behavior. *Journal of Youth and Adolescence, 7,* (1), 1978, 73-92.

Goldstein, A.P.; Sprafkin, R.P.; & Gershaw, N.J. *Skill training for community living: Applying structured learning therapy.* Elmsford, N.Y.: Pergamon Press, 1976.

Goldstein, H. Construction of a social learning curriculum. In E.L. Meyen; G.A. Vergason; & R.J. Whelan (Eds.), *Strategies for Teaching Exceptional Children.* Denver, Colo.: Love Publishing, 1972.

Goodwin, S.E. & Mahoney, M.J. Modification of aggression through modeling: An experimental probe. *Journal of Behavior Therapy and Experimental Psychiatry, 6,* 1975, 200-202.

Gordon, A.K. *Games for growth.* Chicago: Science Research Associates, 1972.

Gottman, J. Toward a definition of social isolation in children, *Child Development, 48,* 1977, 513-517.

Gottman, J.; Gonso, J.; & Rasmussen, B. Social interaction, social competence and friendship in children. *Child Development, 46,* 1975, 709-718.

Graubard, P.S.; Rosenberg, H.; & Miller, M.B. Student applications of behavior modification to teachers and environments or ecological approaches to social deviancy. In E.A. Ramp & B.L. Hopkins (Eds.), *A new direction for education: Behavior analysis 1971,* Vol. 1. Lawrence, Kans.: The University of Kansas, 1971.

Greenwood, C.; Walker, H.; & Hops, H. Issues in social interaction/withdrawal assessment. *Exceptional Children, 43* (8), 1977, 490-499.

Harris, R.J. Experimental games as tools for personality research. In P. McReynolds (Ed.), *Advances in psychological assessment,* Vol. II. Palo Alto, Calif.: Science and Behavior Books, 1971.

Heitzmann, W.R. *Educational games and simulations.* Washington, D.C.: National Education Association, 1974.

Henriques, M. Measures of social skills. *Head start test collection.* Princeton, N.J.: Educational Testing Service, 1977.

Hersen, M. Self Assessment of Fear. *Behavior Therapy, 4,* 1973, 241-257.

Hersen, M. Limitations and problems in the clinical application of behavioral techniques in psychiatric settings. *Behavior Therapy, 10* (1), 1979, 65-80.

Hersen, M. & Barlow, D.H. *Single case experimental designs: Strategies for studying behavior change.* Elmsford, N.Y.: Pergamon Press, 1976.

Hewett, F. *The emotionally disturbed child in the classroom.* Boston: Allyn and Bacon, 1968.

Homme, L.; Csanyi, A.P.; Gonzales, M.A.; & Rechs, J.R. *How to use contingency contracting in the classroom.* Champaign, Ill.: Research Press, 1969.

Hops, H. & Cobb, J.A. Survival behaviors in the educational setting: Their implications for research and intervention. In L.A. Hammerlynk, L.C. Handy; & E.J. Mash, (Eds.), *Behavior Change.* Champaign, Ill.: Research Press, 1973, 193-208.

Hops, H. & Cobb, J.A. Initial investigations into academic survival skill training, direct instruction and first grade achievement, *Journal of Educational Psychology, 66,* 1974, 548-553.

Hymel, S. and Asher, S. Assessment and training of isolated children's social skills. National Institute of Child Health and Human Development (NIH), Bethesda, Md., March, 1977.

Inhelder, B. & Piaget, J. *The early growth of logic in the child, classification and seriation.* New York: Harper and Row, 1964.

Izard, C.E. *Human emotions.* New York: Plenum Press, 1977.

Jacobson, E. *Progressive relaxation.* Chicago: University of Chicago Press, 1938.

Jewett, J.F. & Clark, H.B. Training preschoolers to use appropriate dinner time conversation: An analysis of generalization from school to home. Presented at the Association for the Advancement of Behavior Therapy, New York, December, 1976.

Kagan, J. & Moss, H.A. *Birth to maturity.* New York: Wiley, 1962.

Kanfer, F.H. Self-management methods. In F.H. Kanfer & A.P. Goldstein (Eds.), *Helping People Change.* Elmsford, N.Y.: Pergamon Press, 1975.

Kaufman, L.M. & Wagner, B.R. Barb: A systematic treatment technology for temper control disorders. *Behavior Therapy, 3,* 1972, 84-90.

Kendall, P.C. Self-instructions with children: An analysis of the inconsistent evidence for treatment generalization. Paper presented at the Association for the Advancement of Behavior Therapy Convention, Chicago, November, 1978.

Kent, R.N.; & Foster, S.L. Direct observational procedures: Methological issues in naturalistic settings. In A.R. Ciminero; K.S. Calhoun; & H.E. Adams (Eds.), *Handbook of behavioral assessment.* New York: Wiley, 1977.

Knaus, W.J. *Rational emotive education*. New York: Institute for Rational Living, 1974.

Kohlberg, L. Stage and sequence: The cognitive-developmental approach to socialization. In D.A. Goslin (Ed.), *Handbook of socialization theory and research*. Chicago: Rand McNally, 1969.

Krathwohl, D.; Bloom, B. & Masia, B. *Taxonomy of educational objectives*. New York: David McKay, 1956.

Krumboltz, J.D. & Krumboltz, H.B. *Changing children's behavior*. Englewood Cliffs, N.J.: Prentice-Hall, 1972.

Lambert, N.M., Windmiller, M., Cole, L., & Figueroa, R. AAMD Adaptive Behavior Scale: Public School Version (1974 Revision). Washington, D.C.: American Association on Mental Deficiency, 1974.

Lazarus, A.A. Behavior rehearsal *vs.* non-directive therapy *vs.* advice in effecting behavior change. *Behavior Research and Therapy, 4,* 1966, 209-212.

Libet, J., & Lewinsohn, P.M. The concept of social skill with special references to the behavior of depressed persons. *Journal of Consulting and Clinical Psychology, 40,* 1973, 304-312.

Mager, R. *Goal analysis*. Belmont, Calif.: Fearon, 1972.

Mager, R.G. and Pipe, P. *Analyzing performance problems*. Belmont, Calif.: Fearon, 1970.

Mann, R.A. Assessment of behavioral excesses in children. In M. Hersen & A.A. Bellack(Eds.), *Behavioral assessment: A practical handbook*. Elmsford, N.Y.: Pergamon Press, 1976.

Mash, E.J. & Terdal, L.G. (Eds.) *Behavior therapy assessment*. New York: Springer, 1976.

Masters, J.C. & Mokros, J.R. Self-reinforcement processes in children. In H. Reese (Ed.), *Advances in child development and behavior,* Vol. 9, New York: Academic Press, 1974.

Marlatt, G.A. & Perry, M.A. Modeling methods. In F.H. Kanfer & A.P. Goldstein (Eds.), *Helping people change*. Elmsford, N.Y.: Pergamon Press, 1975.

Mayleas, P. *Rewedded bliss*. New York: Basic Books, 1977.

McAleese, W.R. Unwin, D. A bibliography of microteaching. *Programmed learning and educational technology, 10*(1), 1973, 40-54.

McFall, R.M. & Lillesand, D.B. Behavior rehearsal with modeling and coaching in assertion training. *Journal of Abnormal Psychology, 77,* 1971, 313-323.

McFall, R.M. & Marston, A.R. An experimental investigation of behavior rehearsal in assertive training. *Journal of Abnormal Psychology, 76,* 1970, 295-303.

McPhail, P. *Consequences*. Niles, Ill. : Developmental Learning Materials, 1975.

Meichenbaum, D. Self instructional methods. In F. Kanfer & A.P. Goldstein (Eds.), *Helping people change: A textbook of methods*. Elmsford, N.Y.: Pergamon Press, 1975.

Meichenbaum, D. A cognitive behavior modification approach to assessment. In M. Hersen and A.S. Bellack (Eds.), *Behavioral assessment: A practical handbook*. Elmsford, N.Y.: Pergamon Press, 1976.

Meichenbaum, D. *Cognitive-behavior modification: An integrative approach*. New York: Plenum Press, 1977.

Meichenbaum, D. & Goodman, J. Training impulsive children to talk to themselves: A means of developing self-control. *Journal of Abnormal Psychology, 77,* 1971, 115-126.

Melnick, J.A. Comparison of replication techniques in the modification of minimal dating behavior. *Journal of Abnormal Psychology, 81,* (1), 1973, 51-59.

Milburn, J.F. Special education and regular class teacher attitudes regarding social behaviors of children: steps toward the development of a social skills curriculum. Unpublished doctoral dissertation, the Ohio State University, 1974.

Miller, D.C. *Handbook of Research Design and Social Measurement.* New York: David McKay, 1977.

Miller, W.H. *Systematic parent training: procedures, cases and issues.* Champaign, Ill.: Research Press, 1975.

Moore, S. & Updegraff, R. Sociometric status of preschool children related to age, sex, nurturance-giving and dependency. *Child Development, 35,* 1964, 519-524.

Moreno, J.L. *Who shall survive?* New York: Beacon House, 1953.

Moyer, J. & Dardig, J. Practical task analysis for special educators. *Teaching Exceptional Children, 11* (1), 1978, 16-18.

Murdock, J.Y.; Garcia, E.E.; & Hardman, M.L. Generalizing articulation training with trainable mentally retarded subjects. *Journal of Applied Behavior Analysis, 10,* (4), 1977, 717-733.

Nay, W. Analogue measures. In A.R. Ciminero; K.S. Calhoun; & H.E. Adams (Eds.), *Handbook of behavioral assessment.* New York: Wiley, 1977.

Northrup, J., Wood, R., & Clark, H.B. Social Skill Development in Children: Application of Individual and Group Training. Invited workshop. Association for Behavior Analysis, Fifth Annual convention: Dearborn, Mich., June 1979.

Novaco, R. *Anger control: The development and evaluation of an experimental treatment.* Lexington, Mass.: Lexington Books, 1975.

O'Conner, R.D. Relative efficacy of modeling, shaping and combined procedures for modification of social withdrawal. In C.M. Franks & G.T. Wilson (Eds.),˙ *Behavior therapy and practice.* New York: Brunner/Mazel, 1973.

Oden, S. & Asher, S.R. Coaching children in social skills for friendship making. *Child Development, 48,* 1977, 495-506.

The Ohio State University Research Foundation. Adaptive behavior scale development. Department HEW Social and Rehabilitation Services. Bureau of Education for Handicapped Grant #G007604686, 1979.

Palkes, H.; Stewart, M.; & Kahana, B. Porteus maze performance after training in self-directed verbal commands. *Child Development, 39,* 1968, 817-826.

Patterson, G.R. *Families: Applications of social learning to family life.* (Rev. ed.) Champaign, Ill.: Research Press, 1977.

Patterson, G.R. & Gullion, M.E. *Living with children: New methods for parents and teachers.* (Rev. ed.) Champaign, Ill.: Research Press, 1976.

Pfeiffer, J.W. & Jones, J.E. *A handbook of structured experiences for human relations training.* Iowa City, Iowa: University Associates Press, 1970.

Phillips, E. *The social skills basis of psychopathology: Alternatives to abnormal psychology.* New York: Grune & Stratton, 1978.

Piaget, J. *The moral judgment of the child.* New York: Free Press, 1965.

Polsgrove, L. Self-control: Methods for child training. *Behavior Disorders, 4,* 1979, 116-130.

Prazak, J.A. Learning job-seeking interview skills. In J.D. Krumboltz and C.E. Thorsen (Eds.), *Behavioral Counseling: Cases and Techniques.* New York: Holt, Rinehart and Winston, 1969.

Premack, D. Toward empirical behavior laws, part 1: Positive reinforcement. *Psychological Review, 66,* 1959, 219-233.

Premack, D. Reinforcement theory. In D. Levine (Ed.), *Nebraska symposium on motivation.* Lincoln, Neb.: University Press, 1965.

Quay, H.C. & Peterson, D.R. Manual for the behavior problem checklist. Children's Research Center, University of Illinois, Champaign, Ill., 1967.

Quinsey, V.L. & Varney, G.W. Social skills game: A general method for the modeling and practice of adaptive behaviors, *Behavior Therapy, 8,* 1977, 279-281.

Rathus, S.A. An experimental investigation of assertive training in a group setting. *Journal of Behavior Therapy and Experimental Psychiatry, 3,* 1972, 81-86.

Rathus, S.A. A 30-item schedule for assessing assertive behavior. *Behavior Therapy, 4,* 1973, 398-406.

Richards, C.S. & Perri, M.D. Do self-control treatments last? An evaluation of behavioral problem solving and faded counselor contact as treatment maintenance strategies. *Journal of Counseling Psychology,* in press.

Rie, E.D. & Friedman, D.P. *A survey of behavior rating scales for children.* Columbus, Ohio: Office of Program Evaluation and Research. Division of Mental Health, Ohio Department of Mental Health and Mental Retardation, 1978.

Rincover, A. & Koegel, R.L. Setting generality and stimulus control in autistic children. *Journal of Applied Behavior Analysis, 8,* 1975, 235-246.

Risley, T.R. & Hart, B. Developing correspondence between the nonverbal and verbal behavior of preschool children. *Journal of Applied Behavior Analysis, 1,* 1968, 267-295.

Roff, M.; Sells, S.B.; & Golden, M. *Social adjustment and personality development in children.* Minneapolis: University of Minnesota Press, 1972.

Rogers-Warren, A. & Baer, D.M. Correspondence between saying and doing: Teaching children to share and praise. *Journal of Applied Behavior Analysis, 9* (1976), 335-354.

Roistacher, R.C. A micro-economic model of sociometric choice, *Sociometry, 37* (2), 1974, 219-238.

Rose, S.D. *Treating children in groups.* San Francisco: Jossey-Bass, 1972.

Rosenberg, M. Society and the adolescent self-image. Princeton, N.J.: Princeton University Press, 1965.

Rosenhan, D. & White, G.M. Observation and rehearsal as determinants of prosocial behavior. *Journal of Personality and Social Psychology, 5,* 1967, 424-431.

Rotheram, M.J. Social skills training programs in elementary and high school classrooms. Paper presented at Seventh Annual Behavior Therapy Assn. Conference, Houston, Texas, April 1978.

Santogrossi, D.A.; O'Leary, K.D.; Romanczyk, R.G.; & Kaufman, K.F. Self evaluation by adolescents in a psychiatric hospital school token program. *Journal of Applied Behavior Analysis, 6,* 1973, 277-287.

Sarason, I.G. Verbal learning, modeling and juvenile delinquency, *American Psychologist, 23,* 1968, 253-266.

Sarason, I.G. & Ganzer, V.J. Developing appropriate social behaviors of juvenile delinquents. In V.D. Krumboltz and C.E. Thorsen (Eds.), *Behavioral counseling: Cases and techniques.* New York: Holt, Rinehart and Winston, 1969.

Sarason, S.B.; Davidson, K.F.; Lighthall, F.F.; Wate, R.R.; Ruebush, B.K. *Anxiety in elementary school children.* New York: Wiley, 1960.

Schneider, M. & Robin, A. The turtle technique: A method for the self-control of impulse behavior. Unpublished manuscript, State University of New York at Stony Brook, 1975.

Seymour, F.W. & Stokes, T.F. Self-recording in training girls to increase work and evoke staff praise in an institution for offenders. *Journal of Applied Behavior Analysis, 9,* 1976, 41-54.

Shaftel, F.R. & Shaftel, G. *Role-playing for social values: Decision-making in the social studies,* Englewood Cliffs, N.J.: Prentice-Hall, 1967.

Sheppard, W.C.; Shank, S.B.; & Wilson, D. *How to be a good teacher: Training social behavior in young children.* Champaign, Ill.: Research Press, 1972.

Smith, J.M. & Smith, D.E.P. *Child management: A program for parents and teachers.* Champaign, Ill.: Research Press, 1976.

Spielberger, C.D. Manual for the state-trait anxiety inventory for children. Palo Alto, Calif. Consulting Psychologist Press, 1973.

Spivack, G.; Platt, J.J.; & Shure, M. *The problem-solving approach to adjustment.* San Francisco: Jossey-Bass, 1976.

Spivack, G., & Shure, M.B. *Social adjustment of young children: A cognitive approach to solving real-life problems.* San Francisco: Jossey-Bass, 1974.

Spivack, G. & Spotts, J. *Devereux child behavior (DCB) rating scale.* Devon, Pa.: Devereux Foundation, 1966.

Spivack, G.; Spotts, J.; & Haimes, P. *Devereux adolescent behavior rating scale.* Devon, Pa.: Devereux Foundation, 1966.

Spivack, G. & Swift, M. *Devereux elementary school behavior rating scale.* Devon, Pa.: Devereux Foundation, 1967.

Staub, E. *Positive social behavior and morality: Volume I, socialization and development.* New York: Academic Press, 1978.

Staub, E. *Positive social behavior and morality: Volume 2, socialization and development.* New York: Academic Press, 1979.

Stephens, T.M. *Directive teaching of children with learning and behavioral handicaps.* (2nd ed.) Columbus, Ohio: Charles E. Merrill, 1976.

Stephens, T.M. *Teaching skills to children with learning and behavior disorders.* Columbus, Ohio: Charles E. Merrill, 1977.

Stephens, T.M. *Social skills in the classroom.* Columbus, Ohio: Cedars Press, 1978.

Stokes, T.F. & Baer, D.M. An implicit technology of generalization. *Journal of Applied Behavior Analysis, 10* (2), 1977, 349-367.

Stokes, T.F.; Baer, D.M. & Jackson, R.L. Programming the generalization of a greeting response in four retarded children. *Journal of Applied Behavior Analysis, 7,* 1974, 599-610.

Trower, P.; Bryant, B.; & Argyle, M. *Social Skills and Mental Health.* Pittsburgh: University of Pittsburgh Press, 1978.

Truax, C.B. & Mitchell, K.N. Research on certain therapist interpersonal skills in relation to process and outcome. In A.E. Bergin and S.L. Garfield (Eds.), *Handbook of psychotherapy and behavior change.* New York: Wiley, 1971.

Turnbull, A.; Strickland, B.; & Brantley, J. *Developing and implementing individualized education programs.* Columbus, Ohio: Charles E. Merrill, 1978.

Tyler, R.W. *Basic principles of curriculum and instruction.* Chicago: University of Chicago Press, 1949.

Uretsky, M. The management game: An experiment in reality, *Simulation and Games, 4* (2), 1973, 221-240.

Varenhorst, B.B. Learning the consequences of life's decisions. In J.D. Krumboltz and C.E. Thorsen (Eds.), *Behavioral counseling: Cases and techniques.* New York: Holt, Rinehart and Winston, 1969

Waber, B. *Ira sleeps over.* New York: Scholastic Book Services, 1972.

Wahler, R.G. Setting generality: Some specific and general effects of child behavior therapy. *Journal of Applied Behavior Analysis, 2,* 1969, 239-246.

Walk, R.D. Self ratings of fear in a fear-invoking situation. *Journal of Abnormal and Social Psychology, 22,* 1956, 171-178.

Walker, H. *Problem behavior identification checklist.* Los Angeles: Western Psychological Services, 1970.

Walker, H.M. & Buckley, N.K. *Token reinforcement techniques.* Eugene, Oreg.: E-B Press, 1974.

Walker, H.M. & Hops, H. Increasing academic achievement by reinforcing direct academic performance and/or facilitative nonacademic responses. *Journal of Educational Psychology, 68,* 1976, 218-225.

Wilson, G.T. Cognitive behavior therapy: Paradigm shift or passing phase? In J.P. Foreyt & D.P. Rathjen (Eds.), *Cognitive Behavior Therapy.* New York: Plenum Press, 1978.

Winnett, R.A. & Winkler, R.C. Current behavior modification in the classroom: Be still, be quiet, be docile. *Journal of Applied Behavior Analysis, 5,* 1972, 499-504.

Wolf, M.M. Social validity: The case for subjective measurement or how applied behavior analysis is finding its heart. *Journal of Applied Behavior Analysis, 11* (2), 1978, 203-214.

Wolpe, J. *The practice of behavior therapy.* Elmsford, N.Y.: Pergamon Press, 1969.

Wood, M. *Developmental therapy.* Baltimore: University Park Press, 1975.

Wood, R. & Flynn, J.M. A self-evaluation token system *vs.* an external evaluation token system alone in a residential setting with predelinquent youth. *Journal of Applied Behavior Analysis, 11*(4), 1978, 503-512.

Wood, R. & Michelson, L. Children's Assertive Behavior Scales. Unpublished manuscript, 1978.

Zimmerman, B.J. & Pike, E.O. Effects of modeling and reinforcement on the acquisition and generalization of question-asking behavior. *Child Development, 43,* 1972, 892-907.

Part II:
Teaching Social Skills To Special Populations

Introduction to Part II

The five chapters in Part Two demonstrate ways in which the process of selecting social skills, assessing the child's level of performance, teaching the needed skills, and developing strategies for maintenance and transfer can be applied to a variety of populations. Programs are suggested for children at different age levels, preschool and primary, elementary school age, and adolescence; and at different levels of functioning, normal as well as handicapped. The chapter by Sapon-Shevin is aimed at normal preschool children in the early processes of socialization; Wehman and Schleien define procedures for the severely handicapped child, or even adult. Although the program outlined by Bash and Camp was originally developed in research with impulsive and aggressive boys, these authors now see their program as having potential for many learning situations as well as a help to children with a variety of behavior problems. The actual target population in the article included here is the teacher who will be using their procedures. Oden's techniques for teaching social skills to the "socially isolated" child are designed not only for the withdrawn child, but the child who may be rejected by peers for a variety of reasons related to social skill deficits. The skill-deficient adolescent population for whom Goldstein's Structured-Learning approaches are to be applied includes those who are labeled aggressive, withdrawn, immature, and so forth, with a particular emphasis on the aggressive youth as having the greatest social impact and, thus, the greatest need for intervention.

In the selection of social skills for teaching, there is a need to select skills that are relevant to the child according to a number of different criteria, one of the most salient being the selection of skills that will be reinforced by others in the environment and, thus, maintained over time. There is a common set of such behaviors identified by the authors of the chapters oriented to the younger or lower functioning child, i.e., those skills which combine to make up the class of behaviors called "cooperation," clearly an important area for young and severely handicapped children if they are to develop the ability to interact appropriately with their peers. Wehman and Schleien demonstrate the importance for the severely impaired child of providing basic skills around which to structure interaction, in this case, games and other motor activities which could serve to put the child in proximity to others and enable him to relate to them in the context of the activity. In her approach to teaching cooperation to the young child, Sapon-Shevin similarly stresses the value of games and provides a number of games that require certain kinds of interaction defined as facilitating cooperation, i.e., talking nicely, sharing and taking turns, including others, and gentle physical contact. Oden presents techniques for the teaching of behaviors that will serve to enhance peer acceptance and, thus, serve to either prevent or remedy the problem of social isolation. The concepts she deals with are those of participation, cooperation, communication, and validation or support, i.e., giving attention and help. For the population addressed by Bash and Camp, the goal is to reduce impulsivity and increase the child's repertoire of alternative responses. Among the specific skills described are problem solving through self-guiding speech, self evaluation, recognition of emotions, and the concept of fairness. Goldstein et al. provide an inventory of 50 social skills appropriate to the adolescent. The categories include dealing with feelings, alternatives to aggression, dealing with stress, and planning skills. Their techniques also provide opportunities for the youth participating in the program to identify for themselves the skills relevant to their own lives, a provision particularly necessary for the adolescent population.

Procedures for assessing social skill deficits are suggested by several contributors. Wehman and Schleien use a task analysis approach to assessment, outlining in detail the sequence of steps involved so the subcomponents of the skill can be identified, the child's ability assessed, and instruction begun at the point of deficit. Oden suggests various approaches to assessing the child to determine the nature of peer relationships, making use of several informants—the peers, the adults, and the child—as well as differing methods —sociometrics, interview, and observation—and several contexts. Goldstein's assessment procedures involve the use of a skill checklist to identify deficiencies, using checklist profiles as a guide for structuring group composition based on common needs for training in particular skills.

The methods used by the contributors in Part Two show both diversity and similarities, suggesting some of the ways in which the same approaches can be used with different populations and, also, some of the ways in which teaching needs to be tailored to the child's level of functioning. The explicit set of teaching instructions in the task analysis approach of Wehman and Schleien provides a step-by-step individualized program using verbal instruction, physical guidance, modeling, and reinforcement to teach the motor behaviors that can become the vehicle for social interaction. Although the systematic and detailed approach suggested in this chapter is especially necessary for the severely handicapped population, the ability to analyze learning tasks in this form could add to the effectiveness of any teaching effort. The use of games and children's literature proposed by Sapon-Shevin to teach cooperation to groups of young children is combined with discussion and application of the concepts to other classroom activities. The games and books presented in her chapter can be particularly useful for introducing a variety of kinds of social skills teaching methods.

Oden presents a "coaching" procedure designed to be used with individual children in which the adult provides verbal instruction to a child prior to a play session. Following the coaching session on concepts related to positive peer interaction, the child has an opportunity to practice in an actual play situation with a peer, then engages with the instructor in a review of the concepts following the play period. Oden's procedures primarily involve verbal instructions, prompting, and feedback. The Oden chapter provides a coaching scenario which can serve as a model for teaching a variety of concepts. Bash and Camp also present specific scripts demonstrating how the teacher can provide a model through his or her own thinking-out-loud problem solving processes. The principal emphasis of the Bash and Camp article is the need for the teacher to understand and master the problem solving sequences first in order to be an effective model. The Structured Learning approach of Goldstein et al., as presented here, is structured primarily for use with a group. It makes use of four components —modeling, role playing, feedback, and training for transfer. Models are provided through audio tapes, video tapes, or films.

Programming for maintenance of skills over time and transfer to settings outside the training situation are accomplished in several different ways. The play skills taught by Wehman and Schleien's methods to the severely handicapped, the games suggested by Sapon-Shevin, and the cooperative interactions developed in the Oden program can be said to be those which, by their nature, open up the child to the "natural community of reinforcers." Children who master the abilities to share, take turns, talk pleasantly, and help other children will certainly be reinforced by other children as well as by adults. The cognitive skills in the Bash and Camp program, particularly the self evaluation procedures and problem solving strategies constitute metacognitions or awareness of cognitive activities, the kind of process highly likely to promote generalization. Goldstein et al. suggest a variety of procedures for transfer of social skills from the training to real life settings, including the structuring of the training setting so it resembles the actual life situation, teaching self evaluation and self reinforcement skills, homework assignments in which the skills are practiced outside the training setting, and programming parents and peers to provide reinforcement.

There are adequate data presented to establish the value of the teaching procedures presented in Part Two. Wehman and Schleien and Sapon-Shevin cite a variety of studies supporting the kinds of procedures suggested for their populations. Camp and Bash have successfully applied the Think-

Aloud procedures in several empirical studies, as have Oden with coaching procedures and Goldstein with Structured Learning. The diversity of approaches presented in Part Two, all with evidence of successful application, suggests something of the breadth of methods available for teaching social skills.

Chapter 5

Teacher Training in the Think Aloud Classroom Program *

Mary Ann S. Bash and Bonnie W. Camp

Think Aloud is a program designed to increase cognitive and social problem solving skills in elementary school children. It was originally proposed as a method of improving self control in young aggressive boys through reducing impulsivity, increasing the repertory of alternative responses in frustrating situations, and providing skills for successful problem solving. In developing the curriculum and procedures used in the program, the authors leaned heavily on the work of Meichenbaum (Meichenbaum and Goodman (1971), and Shure and Spivack (1974a).

Previous work with aggressive boys (Camp, 1977; Camp, Zimet, Van Doorninck, & Dahlem, 1977) had demonstrated that they differed from normal boys not only in behavior but in cognitive skills as well. Despite good verbal intelligence, the aggressive boys of ten failed to use their verbal skills to think through complex problems. As a result, they reacted impulsively and failed to perform as adequately as might otherwise be expected. It seemed that both their behavior problems and their poor performance on cognitive tests might be improved if they could learn to slow down and use their good verbal skills to guide their behavior.

Several previous studies suggested that this might be accomplished most effectively if they were first trained to think out loud. Meichenbaum and

*Portions of the materials and scripts included in this chapter were developed through the support of a Research Scientist Award No. MK 2047-356 from the National Institutes of Mental Health and Grant No. NEG-00-3-002 from the National Institute of Education. Funds from the Piton Foundation supported preliminary development of the classroom program. Most of the teacher and student anecdotes derive from the implementation of Think Aloud procedures in the Denver Public Schools under the Cognitive Problem Solving Program funded by Title IV-C from the Colorado Department of Education.

143

Goodman (1971), for example, demonstrated that training in self-guiding speech could assist children in special classes to improve behavior and cognitive test performance. Other research (Hetherington & McIntyre, 1975) suggested that children were unlikely to transfer self-guiding speech into self discipline unless they witnessed someone else modeling this behavior. In addition, the work of Spivack and Shure (1974) suggested that learning to think of alternative solutions to a problem might be essential for achieving improvement in social behavior.

These features were combined into the Think Aloud program (Camp & Bash, 1978b) and were applied to both cognitive and social problems. In early trials with the program, resource room teachers had daily half hour sessions with one or two children for a period of eight weeks. Children who participated were first and second grade boys identified as having significant aggressive behavior problems. Evaluation of progress achieved with the program indicated significant improvement in cognitive ability and in prosocial behavior (Camp, Blom, Hebert, Van Doorninck, 1977).

Early in the development of Think Aloud we recognized that aggressive boys were not the only ones with limited problem solving skills. Spivack and Shure (1974) had noted that inability to think of alternatives was often encountered in youngsters with many types of behavioral problems. Additionally, ability to think of many alternative solutions to problems has been used in measures of creativity (Torrance, 1966) and cited as critical to successful problem solving discussions (Maier, 1963).

Both successes and failures with aggressive boys led us to consider the potential value of expanding this program for use in a regular classroom. For the greatest effect, children needed to apply Think Aloud skills in the "real life" situation of the classroom. Early attempts were made to enlist classroom teachers' assistance. They were willing to complement the resource room program but did not understand what to do. Clearly, we needed a training program for teachers if we wanted them to reinforce problem solving skills in the classroom. Moreover, a classroom program would make the training available to a broader range of children, many of whom might have borderline deficiencies easily amenable to a small boost.

The focus of the remainder of this chapter will be on describing our experience with this classroom program, the obstacles encountered in teaching the program to teachers, and our solutions to these problems.

DESIGNING THE CLASSROOM PROGRAM

Two major problems confronted us from the outset. One concerned the development of materials and procedures which could be used in a group setting to elicit self-guiding speech in dealing with both cognitive and social problems. The second problem concerned how to teach teachers to model verbalization of their own cognitive behavior and to let children develop their own solutions.

The first problem required development of both technique and materials. The core of the Think Aloud program is use of self-guiding speech in problem solving. Overt practice is required before this verbalization is faded to a covert level. How does one get young children to verbalize aloud in this fashion? In the resource room program, we used the "copy cat" game to elicit attention to the teacher's language and gestures as she modeled a task. A similar procedure could be used with groups resulting in unison repetition of standard answers. The copy cat game poses many obvious problems, including the fact that children often repeat mindlessly without thinking about what they are saying. Many educators would look with horror on the situation where 30 children in a classroom are all talking at once, particularly when they are saying different things as they work on a task. We had, however, seen effective use of individual verbalization in small groups at the Exemplary Center for Reading Instruction in Salt Lake City and thought it worth trying.

There was still the problem of finding appropriate materials so that every child in the classroom could participate. The final program drew on a wide variety of materials and procedures to elicit verbalization of plans, alternatives, coping with errors, conceptual shifts, and memory. Each task selected met three criteria: (1) it is amenable to several strategies, (2) it is solvable by means available to the student, and (3) the goal is personally engaging. The problems include increasingly complex tasks such as coloring, finding similarities and differences, mazes, classification, perceptual puzzles, and matrices.

Finally, we decided to try a teacher training program which lasted one month. This involved one or two preparatory sessions in which modeling was practiced, followed by daily lessons in the classroom during which the trainer and classroom teacher alternated days as teacher and observer.

Description of the Program

Using the lead of Meichenbaum and Goodman (1971), the initial phase of the program concentrates on developing an organized approach to problem solving. This approach is applied primarily to cognitive problems, and consists of four questions: (1) What is my problem? or, What am I supposed to do?; (2) How can I do it? or, What is my plan?; (3) Am I using my plan?; and (4) How did I do? The students learn to ask themselves these questions to organize their approach to an assignment. They ask and answer the first two questions before they begin their work.

Their answer to the first question ("What is my problem?") guides them to focus on the specific task. In answering the second question ("How can I do it?") the students, as a group, brainstorm a myriad of alternative plans for solving the problem. This repertory of choices provides students second or third chances to be successful on an assignment if the plan they first choose is ineffective. These alternative strategies might increase the time students spend on-task if, indeed, they follow through with the proposed strategies. To increase the likelihood of follow-through, Think Aloud teaches students to address the third question "Am I using my plan?" to themselves several times while they work on their task. This question enables students to increase self control as they change or correct plans on the basis of their performance. Answers to this question might take any of the following directions: (1) Yes, because I'm doing what I planned and it's working; (2) Yes, because I'm doing what I planned, but there must be a better way to get the job done so I'll change my plan; (3) No, because I forgot to do what I planned so I'll start again; or (4) No, because I forgot what I planned, but what I'm doing is working so I'll use this new plan. The students would, in fact, articulate the details of the plan they were and/or were not following instead of verbalizing the general comments described above.

After the work is done, the students direct the fourth question to themselves: "How did I do?" Self evaluation might be based on a combination of several criteria: completing the task, effort, efficiency, following the plan, neatness, accuracy, on-task behavior, how they feel about their work. Self evaluation answers have taken all of the following forms: (1) I did everything you told me to, and I did it quickly and quietly; (2) I was good at following my plan; (3) I was terrific at thinking out loud; (4) I was not good at staying in my seat, but I got my work done; (5) I couldn't figure out the puzzle, but I kept trying; (6) I'm proud because I found a better way than we planned. This self evaluation precedes teacher assessment and is the means for reducing teacher-student conflict when a teacher might otherwise criticize or overestimate a student's performance by assessing only the final product.

Students learn the four organizational questions effortlessly, but learning to answer the questions is a major hurdle. Young children are introduced to the self instruction questions by playing "copy cat" on a simple coloring task. Answering the questions on a different task, such as a puzzle, they typically verbalize the plan, "I'll color slowly and carefully and stay inside the lines," that they learned on the coloring problem. It takes several lessons for young children to discover that different tasks require different answers to the four self instruction questions.

Cognitive tasks of increasing difficulty are introduced to students by teacher modeling. The teacher verbalizes an appropriate plan and the obstacles which interfere with the plan. Following the teacher's model, the students practice self instruction technique on a different example of the task.

Presented here are two scripts for modeling self instruction. Note that for both tasks (1) the problem is stated, (2) alternative plans are proposed, (3) coping with an error is modeled, (4) the use of the proposed plan is monitored, and (5) the teacher evaluates his or her performance.

Day 2 Think Aloud Introduction and Practice*
> Materials: Large cue pictures which remind children of the four self-instruction questions [fig. 5.1]
> coloring shapes worksheets [fig. 5.2]
> crayons
> clipboard

Review first 2 questions, and add next 2.

Think out loud on coloring shapes.

Teacher: [*Show shape papers.*] You are all very good at coloring. Let's practice thinking out loud while we color. [*Point to fattest-bordered circle.*] Our problem is to color this shape the best we can without going outside the lines. Your problem is to be copy cats and copy just what I *say* and *do.* What is your problem? [*Point to cue picture-1.*] Good.

Teacher: [*Give children and yourself the paper of shapes to be colored. Select the circle with a fat border first.*] We each have a paper with some shapes on it. The problem is to color this shape the best we can without going outside the lines. Pick a colored pencil and I'll pick one.

Teacher: Let's learn to think out loud to help us do this paper. Remember you must copy what I *say* and *do.* Let's try it.

Teacher: [*Holding crayon in air. (The questions and answers are all to be copied by the children.)*]

> Q. What is my problem?

> A. I am supposed to color this circle without going outside the lines.

> Q. How can I do it?

> A. I'll go slowly. I'll be careful. I'll outline the circle first. Then I can go faster in the middle. OK, here I go. [*Begin coloring.*]

> [*Note: Children may become so intent on coloring that they fail to copy. Remind them as often as necessary:* Where are my copy cats?]

Teacher: Q. Am I using my plan?
> A. Yes. I'm making a frame around the outside. I'm going slowly. Now I can go faster in the middle. [*Cross line boundary.*] Ooops, I went too fast. I went outside the line. That's O.K. I'll be more careful. I'll go slower. There I did it.

---

*From Mary Ann Bash, *Think Aloud Classroom Resource Manual,* grades 1-2, Denver Public Schools, 1978. Used with permission of the author.

Fig. 5.1. "What is my problem?"

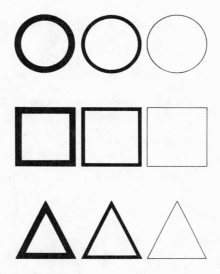

Fig.5.2. Coloring shapes worksheet.

Q. How did I do?

A. I tried hard. I went slowly. I usually stayed inside the lines. That makes me feel good.

Teacher: Good, you were good copy cats. And I learned something. Is it a good idea to color fast?

Children: _____

Teacher: *[Ask classroom teacher to model thinking out loud on a different shape while the kids copy. Then have a child or two think out loud on different shapes while others copy him.]*

Alternative plans for the coloring task might have included using only one crayon so coloring doesn't take too long, or using the side of the crayon instead of the point, or pressing softly to shade the shape lightly.

MAZES*

Materials: Bear cue pictures
          Trails A & B
          Picture mazes (Fido, Red Riding Hood, Puddle)
From: *Activity Fun,* A Whitman Book, Western Publishing Company, Inc., Racine, Wisconsin

*From Bonnie W, Camp & Mary Ann S. Bash, *Think Aloud Group Manual,* November 1975, ERIC EDS No. 142024. Used with permission of the authors.

Teacher: I have a new problem for us today. We are going to make trails. What is a trail?

Children: _____

Teacher: Yes, it is like a small road where motorcycles can go or where people can hike. *[Show Trail A, see Fig. 5.3 for sample trails A and B.]* The problem is to draw a trail from #1 to #2 to #3 to #4 and so on without lifting your pencil from the paper. I'll try the first one. You be copy cats.

Teacher: *[Looking at task but before picking up pencil.]*
Q. OK. What is my problem?

  A. I need to draw a trail to each number in order—like 1,2,3,4—without lifting my pencil from the paper.

Teacher: Q. How can I do it?

  A. Before I draw a line, I'll find the next number I have to go to. That's how thinking out loud will help me. I *could* go fast *but* I might make a mistake, so I'll go slow.

Teacher: Here I go. *[Pick up pencil.]* Here's #1—that's where I start. Now my plan—I'll find #2. Good, here it is *[hold finger on #2 and draw line to it]*. #3—Yep. Good, I'm going slow and I'm planning ahead. *[While looking for #4 lift pencil off of paper. If children don't catch you, say:]* Oops. I'm supposed to keep my pencil on the paper. That's kind of hard. I better remind myself—keep my pencil on the paper. *[Holding pencil on paper]* OK, now where do I go? I'm at #3 so I better find #4. Yep. *[From #4 go directly to #6 without planning. When recognize error, feign anger and slam pencil on desk.]* I did it wrong. I didn't plan ahead. I can't even do this. *[Pout, in manner typical of the students, then calm yourself.]* Well I just went too fast. I knew I'd make a mistake if I went too fast. If I slow down I can do all right. *[Place pencil back at #4.]*

  Q. Am I using my plan?

  A. Yes, I'm looking ahead. There's #5—that's where I need to go. I feel better now—I'm doing a good job. After 5 comes 6. Good. And that's how we do this trail. I'll let you have a turn now.

Teacher: Q. How did I do?

  A. I got kind of mad, but then I slowed down. I did better when I planned ahead. I wasn't very good at keeping my pencil on the paper.

Teacher: You try making a trail. *[Hand children another short trail but turn paper over after brief exposure. Point to cue picture #1 if necessary to initiate verbalizations. If children want to silently verbalize while paper is overturned, that should be sufficient. When mazes become harder, overt verbalizations will be required.]*

Children: _____

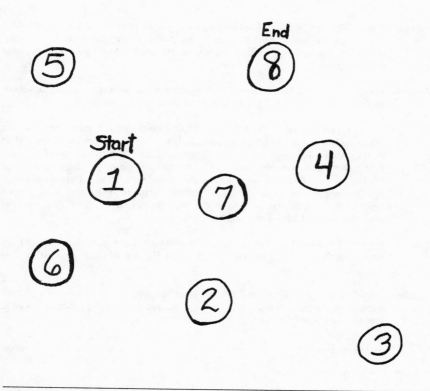

Fig. 5.3. Sample trails A and B.

Teacher: *[When they finish the sample, hand children Trail B with numbers 1 through 15.]* Here's a problem with more numbers. What plan will help you do this problem?

Children: _____

Teacher: Is it a good idea to go fast on this problem?

Children: _____

Teacher: *[After self evaluation, hand children Fido Maze.]* Now I have a different problem for you. This time I want you to draw a trail, but the numbers won't tell you where to go. I'll give you a picture of a dog. His name is Fido. He is trying to get across the street without being hit by a car. He wants you to find a trail across the street for him. *[Provide no reminders of thinking out loud. See if children talk spontaneously. Place pencil on table beside paper.]*

Children: _____

Teacher: *[Show Little Red Riding Hood Maze.]* Now it's my turn. What's my problem? I want to get Little Red Riding Hood to her grandmother's house without getting trapped by the wolf and without stepping on any plants. And I can't lift my pencil from the paper.

Teacher: How can I do it? I have a new plan. I will look ahead with my eyes and fingers to find the best trail for her. I'll have to go slow so I don't get caught.

Teacher: 1. This is one way she could go. *[Trace with finger into wolf trap plus along branches off of it.]* Nope, this way I'll get trapped. 2. *[Eye trace south route from Red Riding Hood.]* Am I using my plan? Yes, I'm planning ahead. I can go this way. *[Set pencil to paper.]* Go slowly because I can't step on any plants. *[Slowly finger trace backwards from house.]* I have to get to the house, right? Good. I can go this way. *[Cut through tree leaf in haste.]* Oh, I knew that would happen if I went fast. Now I made a mistake and I was doing so good at planning ahead. *[Calm self.]* I'll just have to be more careful. Now I'm doing better.

Teacher: How did I do? I was good at planning ahead with my finger and eyes. I learned I can plan from the beginning or from the end. But I've got to remind myself to slow down.

Teacher: *[Hand children Puddle Maze.]* You are supposed to get Martha to school without stepping in any puddles and without lifting your pencils from the paper. Is it a good idea to plan ahead from the beginning or the end?

Children: _____

Teacher: *[Turn papers over and wait for thinking out loud.]*

Children: _____

Teacher: *[At end of task]* What new plan can help us on these problems?

Children: _____

Teacher: Is it a good idea to plan ahead with your finger and eyes when you do a trail?

Children: _____

Teacher: Why?

Children: _____

> [Note: *Picture mazes from any children's activity book could be substituted in this activity.]*

Alternative plans for a maze might include planning a short distance and making the path, or tracing with the eraser end of the pencil to leave a hint of a trail, or tracing with two fingers simultaneously from the start and the end and meeting them in the middle.

Following the teacher-modeled task, the students attempt a different example of the problem while instructing themselves through the four problem solving questions.

Chart 1 summarizes the organized approach used on cognitive tasks.

Chart 1

Problem Solving Approach to Cognitive Tasks

Step 1 Identify the problem or assignment.
Step 2 Propose several alternative plans for solving problem or assignment.

Begin Work

Step 3 Monitor use of plan: change, correct, or stay with plan.
Step 4 Self evaluate performance in terms of effort, success, behavior, feelings.

Soon after children have become thoroughly familiar with thinking out loud by asking and appropriately answering the self instruction questions, interpersonal problems are introduced. Interpersonal problems are conflicts which arise between students and teachers, parents, siblings, or other students.

Most of Think Aloud's interpersonal problem solving instruction derives from Myrna Shure and George Spivack's (1974a) work with preschool and kindergarten children. In their year-long programs for young children, Shure and Spivack use commercial pictures and games to teach concepts such as "and/or," "same/different," "not." Where possible, Think Aloud introduces concepts such as "same/different" on cognitive tasks early in the program. Other Shure and Spivack lessons were shortened or combined for use with primary school children. As a result, Think Aloud includes nine interpersonal lessons dealing with (1) identifying and sharing emotions (i.e., How does the child in this picture probably feel?), (2) recognizing physical causality (i.e., What are lots of different reasons why she might have fallen off her bike?), (3) recognizing emotional causality (i.e., What are lots of different reasons why David might be mad?), (4) What might happen next? (i.e., What might happen next if you sit on a broken fence?), (5) Is it a good idea or not a good idea? (i.e., Is it a good idea to call a person a name?), and (6) Problem solving (i.e., What are lots of different things Danny could say or do to get a chance to play with the kite?).

The four-step cognitive problem solving approach plus this preliminary instruction in consequential thinking prepare students to begin developing a repertory of alternative solutions for dealing with interpersonal problem situations. Then they must learn to evaluate each alternative solution. Here, we found the Shure and Spivack kindergarten program needed expanding to provide children with more explicit concepts for evaluating the outcomes of interpersonal problems. Whereas Shure and Spivack rely primarily on "Is it a good idea?", Think Aloud carries this further and articulates four specific criteria to use in judging if a solution is a good idea: (1) is it safe? (2) is it fair? (3) how does it make you and others feel? and (4) does it solve the problem? Even primary school children are cognizant of safety needs, so little instruction is required on this criterion, though it must be highlighted as an important dimension of problem solving.

Because "fairness" appears to be such an important concept for children, an entire lesson was designed to provoke discussion around this issue. To teach standards of justice, we developed verbal situations to accompany line drawings of situations which provoke frustration. The script which follows is the Think Aloud lesson which introduces the concept of fairness. Frequently, students disagree on the fair solution, and this interaction among students introduces the reality that fairness is not a clear-cut issue and that conditions affect the observer's perception of what is fair.

Fig. 5.4. Fairness #1.

SOCIAL #7 — Fairness*
[Use mounted Fairness pictures and Dragon & Wolf puppets.]

Teacher: Today we are going to talk about fairness. Let's look at this picture. *[Show figure 5.4 —Fairness #1, bike.*

Teacher: This girl took Teresa's bike away from her. Was that a fair thing for her to do?

---

*From Bonnie W. Camp & Mary Ann Bash, *Think Aloud Group Manual,* Revised 1978, University of Colorado Medical Center, C250, Denver, Colorado 80262. Used with permission of the authors.

Children: _____

Teacher: Why not?

Children: _____

Teacher: What is the problem? What does the girl want to do?

Children: _____

Teacher: What could she *say* or *do* that would be fair so she can ride the bike?

Children: _____

Teacher: Why would that be fair?

Children: _____

Teacher: How does Teresa feel, *(least verbal child)*?

Child: _____

Teacher: Is that fair?

Child: _____

Teacher: Let's pretend that *[one child's name]* has Wally *[hand wolf puppet to less demanding child. This action will no doubt provoke a spontaneous social situation that should be dealt with.]* And I have Dilly. You have this toy that Dilly wants. So Dilly grabs it. *[Use Dilly to grab at Wally.]* Is that fair?

Children: _____

Teacher: Why not?

Children: _____

Teacher: What does Dilly want?

Children: _____

Teacher: *[Hand Dilly to noninvolved child.]*
Tell Dilly something he could *do* or *say* to Wally that would be fair.

Child: _____

Teacher: *[Put puppets away.]* Let's look at another picture. *[Show figure 5.5—Fairness #2, boy and girl coloring.]* Pretend that Peter and Lisa are coloring. Peter has a box of five crayons, but no red crayon. Lisa has only three crayons, including a red one. Pretend that Peter wants the red crayon. Is it fair for him to take it away from Lisa?

Children: _____

Fig. 5.5. Fairness #2.

Teacher: [If "no" is given] _____, what does Peter want?

Child: _____

Teacher: What would be a fair thing he could *do* or *say*?

Children: _____

Teacher: [Show figure 5.6—Fairness #3, father giving money to girl.] Father says, "Sally, since you were my helper today, I want to give you some money to buy that record you've been wanting" Is that a fair thing for father to say?

Fig. 5.6. Fairness #3.

Children: _____

Teacher: *[If "yes"]* Why? *[If child says it is not fair, ask* Why? *and* What would be a fair thing for him to say or do?]

Children: _____

Teacher: How does Sally feel when father gives her the money?

Children: _____

Teacher: How does father feel when he makes Sally *(happy)?*

Children: _____

Teacher: *[Show figure 5.7—Fairness #4, big girl with popsicle.]*

Fig. 5.7. Fairness #4.

The big girl has the last popsicle. Her little sister ran to tell mother. Mother says to the big girl, "Let her have the popsicle *because* she is little." Is that a fair thing for mother to say? *[If children are still distracted by presence of puppets, address them through puppets to answer the question. i.e.,* Wally, is that a fair thing for mother to say?]

Children: _____

Teacher: *[If "no"]* Why not?

Children: _____

Teacher: What would be a fair thing for mother to say?

Children: _____

Teacher: [Show figure 5.8—Fairness #5, boy on swinging rope. Point to boy swinging on rope.]

Fig. 5.8. Fairness #5.

"I'm going to keep swinging all afternoon." Is that a fair thing for Brian to say?

Children: _____

Teacher: How does his friend feel?

Children: _____

Teacher: What is something different Brian could say or do that would be fair?

Children: _____

Teacher: How would his friend feel if Brian [repeat one child's response]?

Children: _____

Teacher: Let's look at the last picture. [Show figure 5.9—Fairness #6, boys playing baseball.]

Fig. 5.9. Fairness #6.

These 3 boys were playing baseball and broke Mr. Blake's window. Only Jim got caught. Is it fair for Mr. Blake to punish Jim?

Children: _____

Teacher: *[If "no"]* What would be fair?
[If "yes"] Why is it fair for him to punish Jim?

Children: _____

Teacher: How does Mr. Blake feel?

Children: _____

Teacher: He might feel *[repeat child's response]*. Why?

Children: _____

A different criterion for evaluating if a solution is a good idea or not is to attend to how it makes you and others feel. For example, if a selfish action is committed and other people feel left out or disappointed, students are asked to think of a different solution which would make everyone feel happy.

Finally, a problem solution is judged in terms of effectiveness. If a student wants a toy another child has, ignoring the child is probably not a good idea because it will not solve the problem. However, asking to play with the child probably is a good idea because the student's desire will be satisfied.

The student's understanding of these evaluation criteria is tested when the teacher states the problem "I need a pencil." She proceeds to grab a pencil from a student and claims the solution is a good idea because it solved the problem. Consistently, Think Aloud students counter the teacher by explaining that grabbing was not a good idea because it was not really safe, it was not fair, and it made the victim angry. The students make the discovery that effectiveness cannot stand by itself as an evaluation criterion. It must be judged in light of the three other criteria—safety, fairness, and feelings. Once the criteria for evaluating outcomes are established, we post in our classrooms cue cards to remind the children of the criteria (see figure 5.10).

Fig. 5.10. Evaluation Criteria.

This interpersonal instruction sequence establishes the readiness skills in language and consequential thinking to prepare students to understand responsible behavior. At this point, students require extensive practice in interpersonal problem solving through verbal situations and through role playing before they consistently engage in responsible behavior in their own lives. Chart 2 summarizes the organized approach used with social tasks.

Chart 2

Interpersonal Problem Solving Instruction

Step 1   Identify emotions

Step 2   Physical causality

Step 3   Emotional causality   } Consequential thinking

Step 4   What might happen next?

Step 5   Is it a good idea?

Safety

Fairness   } Evaluation of
                  possible conflict
How it makes people feel   solutions

Effectiveness

Step 6   PRACTICE verbal situations and role playing

Step 7   Application to real life conflict or conflict resolution.

TEACHING TEACHERS
HOW TO THINK ALOUD

Despite teachers' enthusiasm for Think Aloud concepts, we quickly found that few were able to use the technique in spontaneous classroom situations. Part of the problem seemed to arise from the fact that implementation of Teach Aloud procedures requires some adjustment of philosophies regarding classroom management.

To promote self control through Think Aloud, a teacher must be able to accept two classroom management philosophies: (1) a noisy classroom may be the product of constructive activity, and (2) students are capable of responding to most questions if given enough time to organize their thoughts.

The first management principle in Think Aloud initially shocks students, teachers, principals, and parents. Think Aloud students are retaught to verbalize what goes on in their minds while they work productively. At the outset of the program, they resist thinking out loud because they have been instilled with the idea from teachers, principals, and parents that they must be quiet to be good workers. We have no evidence that the students will not achieve equally in a quiet classroom but our observations on language development and self control encourage us to pursue the thinking-out-loud philosophy.

On one occasion, second graders were productively verbalizing as they attempted to organize twelve pictures into a logical matrix. Every student was in his seat and a few students were explaining to their neighbors their rationale for categorizing a few of the pictures. There were no obvious disruptive behaviors and the Think Aloud trainer did not hear any off-task conversation. But when the assistant principal walked into the room he ad-monished the class: "I want everyone of you to be quiet. There is no reason for all this noise. You know what your work is. Get it done quietly." The powerful effect of self instruction was blotted from the lesson.

The second classroom management procedure is most difficult to use consistently. Teachers are uncomfortable when they pose a question and it is not answered immediately. So they rephrase the question or provide the answer. Thus, the students have escaped responsibility for doing their own thinking. Think Aloud requires teachers to increase the amount of time be-tween asking a question and repeating it or rephrasing it, so students have enough time to organize their thoughts. This "wait time" may cause unner-ving pauses; but students will accept responsibility for thinking, planning, and accepting consequences of their behavior when they must verbalize answers to school and behavior related questions.

Even if they accepted the philosophy behind Think Aloud, teachers often simply did not know how to implement it. We heard teachers phrase give-away questions so students could mimic an answer. We watched teachers dictate solutions, which was less time consuming (and less effective) than in-volving the students in problem solving. And most disappointing to us, teachers continued giving or revising directions of modeling when students encountered difficulty with the task.

We tried several strategies to increase teachers' internalization of the Think Aloud technique. First we wrote more detailed scripts for teachers to practice. Each script was a perfect model of integration of Think Aloud elements. When teacher performance failed to improve, we thought we might be providing too many crutches for teachers. Therefore, our second strategy was to reduce the amount of modeling the Think Aloud staff pro-vided teachers. Whereas the formal curriculum was originally taught alter-nately by a teacher-in-training and a Think Aloud specialist, we cut back to a maximum of two specialist lessons a week. Still, the results were disap-pointing. Even increasing the number of inservice hours failed to elicit the result we sought.

Then we realized that, perhaps, some teachers were unable to see more than one way to solve a problem. Generating multiple solutions was a behavior we were trying to develop in students and, yet, some teachers had not mastered the skill. The evidence was clear that many of our teachers needed instruction and practice in this basic aspect of problem solving before they could develop enough proficiency to instruct others.

In addition to lacking skill in thinking of alternative strategies, teachers frequently failed to give adequate directions or neglected to model ways of surmounting obstacles that might block the way to task completion.

These experiences led us to develop a teacher training program which begins with exercises in the three problem solving skills which trouble teachers the most: (1) emphasizing process, not end product; (2) generating and accepting alternatives equally; and (3) predicting obstacles. Teachers usually assess students' performance based on their end products: the completed workbook page, the typed composition, the varnished table. Think Aloud teachers are asked to put more emphasis on the thinking process which leads to the end product. To practice recognizing "process," teachers complete modified Chinese tangrams (Puzzle Grams No. 6042, Ideal School Supply Company, Oak Lawn, Illinois 60453) which provide five geometric shapes (two small triangles, a large triangle, a square, and a parallelogram) which can be arranged to form many different figures. The thinking process is emphasized by having the teachers verbalize the task strategies they use to help them organize the pieces into the prescribed shape. They are stopped before they have time to finish the tangram, and successful strategies are reviewed. The end product is not evaluated.

A different "process" exercise gives teachers practice in asking questions for information. Again, the exercise focuses on "process" instead of end product. In this task, teachers are allowed 20 questions to help them determine what an object is. Each question must be phrased so that it can receive a "yes" or "no" response. Most important, when the teachers ask questions, they must tell why they asked that question or how they can use the information from the question. Twenty questions rarely provide enough information to determine the use for the plastic items pictured below:

Fig. 5.11.

The second problem solving behavior — generating and accepting alternatives equally — is developed through an "elaborative thinking" exercise. Teachers in Think Aloud training work together to think of all the different reasons why Lucy Anchor, a retired millionnaire, might not want to take a Caribbean cruise. No condition of reality versus fantasy is prescribed. The teachers are encouraged to accept each idea as a "different" idea without indicating a preference. This neutral response by the teacher will be important during classroom instruction.

Finally, teachers practice another element of effective problem solving — predicting obstacles. One exercise teachers practice to develop this skill is to write the part of a story which connects its beginning to the prescribed end. The teachers are instructed to write about several "means" used to reach the "end" of the story and to change means which might be blocked by obstacles. The obstacles might derive from traits of the story's characters or they might be external to the characters. This ability to develop several ways to overcome obstacles on the way to a goal is described by Platt and Spivack (1975) as means-ends thinking. Another exercise requires teachers to predict the obstacles which will prevent their students from completing a task successfully. They test their predictions by giving the task to their students.

Once teachers have developed some skill in the preliminary exercises, the training program moves toward helping them incorporate these skills into mastery of the Think Aloud teaching methodology. They still need a great deal of practice which comes largely from presenting Think Aloud's problem content to children.

At this point, many teachers still find it difficult to (1) model the thinking "process," (2) withhold judgment of students' performance until students have evaluated themselves, and (3) teach emotions.

Teachers are so practiced at giving directions that they often misunderstand the difference between giving directions and modeling. The following examples will illustrate the distinction that is critical to Think Aloud teaching proficiency.

Task 1:   Primary reading worksheet on alphabetizing first letters only.

a	Does boy
b	come before
c	or after cat?
d	
	before/after

e	Does house
f	come before
g	or after go?
h	
	before/after

Fig.5.12. Reading worksheet

Often this type of task prompts a teacher to give directions such as: "On this worksheet, you must circle the word before or after to answer the questions. Use the letters along the side of the paper to help you remember the order of the alphabet. If the word comes before the other word, circle 'before.' If the word comes after the other word, circle 'after.'"

In the Think Aloud program, however, modeling might take the following form: *"What is my problem?* I have to figure out if a word comes before or after another and to circle the word 'before' or 'after' to show the answer. *How can I do it?* First I'll write the letters next to each other the way I'm used to: a b c d. Then I'll write the words next to the letters. Before means first so, if the word comes first, I'll circle 'before.' The question is about the word 'boy.' I'll underline 'boy' to help me remember it is the important word."

Task 2:   Math task of coloring only triangles among many shapes to find a hidden picture.

Again, the teacher who directs rather than models may say: "On this paper you are to color only the triangles. When all the triangles are colored you will see a hidden picture."

The teacher who models her thinking might say: *"What is my problem?* I have to color only the triangles to find a hidden picture. *How can I do it?* First I will put a triangle at the top of my page to help me remember just to color triangles. Then I will count the sides of each shape to be sure it is a triangle. I see some places on the paper where two triangles come next to each other and share a side. I had better make a plan that will help me remember to count the same side for both of the triangles." This last plan illustrates how predicting obstacles can be incorporated into modeling to reduce the risk of student failure because of unforeseen obstacles.

Intrusion of evaluative responses too early in the problem solving procedure is one of the hardest habits for teachers to change. Praise is important reinforcement for most students when it is well timed and task specific. However, when the goal of a lesson is to engage many students in discussion, it is imperative that the teacher accept each response without evaluation. When the teacher says to one student "That's a good idea" during discussion, other students commonly respond, "My idea isn't as good as his," "He took my idea," or "That's just what I was going to say." If the goal is to encourage responses from many students or to encourage students to judge the quality of their own responses, the teacher should reinforce the fact of contributing rather than assessing a value on the contribution. An appropriate teacher response might be, "You are coming up with lots of different ideas. Who can add a third idea?"

Withholding judgment of a student's performance offers another opportunity for increasing the student's self discipline and for contributing to a positive classroom climate. When a student has practiced self evaluation, he learns to evaluate his performance fairly. Gradually, he can own up to off-task behavior and can plan more appropriate activity. This skill of students to evaluate themselves gives teachers a way of avoiding confrontation when students are not performing up to the teacher's expectations. When a student works on a paper haphazardly or participates disruptively in a group activity, for example, the teacher may ask the student to monitor his use of his plan more carefully or to reassess his plan. If the student is able to plan a more appropriate behavior, he will be more committed to following the plan than if the teacher dictates the behavior in a reprimand. In the case where the student is not yet capable of appropriate self evaluation, the teacher must continue to serve as a model.

The third difficult aspect of Think Aloud for teachers to internalize is teaching emotions. Young children typically recognize and have the verbal labels for only a few emotions: happy, glad, sad, bad, and mad. To increase the breadth of their understanding, Think Aloud defines a wide range of emotions, provides the verbal labels, and encourages students to describe occasions when they felt the emotion.

Whereas teachers frequently use or elicit from children words to describe how a character in a story might feel, they rarely define the feeling in words. Nor do they stress how the feeling causes us to react to others or how we might reduce a negative feeling or intensify a positive one. We have developed a sequence for teaching an emotion which includes a definition, examples of emotional responses, and strategies for altering the emotion.

STEPS IN TEACHING AN EMOTION
1. Identify need for recognizing a particular emotion.
2. Show facial expression which characterizes emotion.
3. Label emotion for students.
4. Define emotion.
5. Provide personal example.
6. Restate definition.
7. Show picture. What might have provoked the emotion?
8. Show different picture. What might have provoked the emotion?
9. What's something the person could say or do to lessen or to intensify the emotion.
10. Follow up by using the emotion label during class or by identifying the emotion in literature.

We have used this sequence to teach anxiety, pride, disappointment, jealousy, confidence, and embarrassment. Following is the Think Aloud anxiety script.

20-minute lesson

Object:	Introducing the "feeling" — anxious, nervous, worried.
Rationale:	Anxiety is a common feeling children experience. However, many times they are unable to talk about this feeling because they lack the necessary language. Children also need to know what they can do to help themselves feel better when they are feeling anxious.
Student Objectives:	The children will be able to identify people showing feelings of anxiety; suggest causes for feeling this way; and identify ways of reducing "anxious" feelings.
Materials:	Pictures from:

AWARE, Activities for Social Development by Phyllis Elardo & Mark Cooper, Menlo Park, California: Addison-Wesley Publishing Company: 1977, pages 42 and 86.

Understanding Our Feelings study prints, Instructo Corporation, Paoli, PA 19301: woman chewing on kleenex

Moods and Emotions teaching pictures, David C. Cook Publishing Co., 850 N. Grover Avenue, Elgin, Illinois 60120: picture #7 and story from guide pg. 16 "All Alone."

Word cards for anxious, nervous, worried.

Follow-Up: *Moving Day* by Tobi Tobias, Knopf, 1976.

Teacher: [show anxiety picture — page 42] All of these children feel the same way. Are they smiling?

Children: _____

Teacher: How do you think these children feel?

Children: _____

Teacher: Here's a word to describe how these children feel. [Show word card—anxious.] These children feel anxious. How do these children feel?

Children: _____

Teacher: When we feel anxious, we usually are worried about what might happen to us in the future. Today I felt anxious because I didn't know if my car was going to start this morning. Thumbs up if you have ever felt anxious. Thumbs down if you don't know if you have ever felt anxious.

Children: _____

Teacher: We can use other words to describe this feeling of not knowing what might happen in the future. The other words are nervous and worried. *[Show word cards.]* Sometimes the word anxious can also mean excited. *[Give examples.]* I am anxious to go to the movies or I am anxious to finish my work so I can go to the art center. But today, we are only going to talk about anxious as meaning nervous or worried about what might happen to us in the future.

[Show Understanding our Feelings picture.] How does this woman probably feel?

Children: _____

Teacher: Yes, this woman might feel anxious *[nervous, worried]*. What's one thing that might make her feel anxious.

Children: _____

Teacher: That's one idea. *[Repeat idea.]* Or, she might feel anxious because...

Children: _____

Teacher: That's a different idea. *[Encourage children to make complete statements using because. If children have difficulty thinking of ideas, ask them if their mother has ever looked like this and what caused her to look worried or anxious.]*

Children: _____

Teacher: *[Show boy picture from AWARE, page 86.]* This boy is at school. How do you think he feels?

Children: _____

Teacher: He might feel anxious because...

Children: _____

Teacher: That's one idea of what might make this boy feel anxious. Let's think of lots of different ideas. *[If children have difficulty in suggesting ideas, ask* "How many of you have ever felt anxious when you had to read out loud in front of the class?"*]*

Children: _____

Teacher: *[Accept 3 or 4 different ideas.]* Let's listen to a story about a girl named Cindy. *[Read story—"All Alone" from Moods and Emotions Guide, page 16. In the first sentence substitute the word "nervous" for "afraid":* "Cindy was nervous." *End story after* "Maybe something dreadful had happened."*]*

(Show Moods and Emotions picture #7—Cindy.)

Teacher: This is Cindy. How does Cindy Feel?

Children: _____

Teacher: Why does Cindy feel anxious?

Children: _____

Teacher: What does feeling anxious mean?

Children: _____

Teacher: Our problem is to think of lots of different things Cindy could say or do so she doesn't feel so anxious. Let me hear you think out loud.

Children: _____

Teacher: That's one idea. *[List ideas on board.]* What are some different ideas? *[Continue in this manner until children have exhausted their supply of ideas. Add your own ideas to stimulate student responses when necessary.]*

Children: _____

Teacher: *[Guide children to self evaluate their work.]*

Children: _____

Follow-up: *[Read story "Moving Day." Half way through story ask how the girl is feeling and why she is feeling that way. Continue story to its end. Discuss ways the little girl handled her anxious feelings. What did she do? What did she say?]*

GENERALIZATION OF THINK ALOUD SKILLS

The success of Think Aloud has been assessed both formally through testing and informally through observation and reported anecdotes. Because the classroom program is both newer and more difficult to evaluate than the individual program, most evaluation to date has been on students with aggressive behavior problems working in a one-to-one or two-to-one situation.

With the basic individual program, the most consistent differences from control populations have been registered on cognitive test performance where Think Aloud graduates have surpassed all types of controls (Camp, Blom, et al, 1977; Camp, in press). Prosocial behavior in the classroom has increased more among Think Aloud graduates than untreated controls (Camp, Blom, et al, 1977) and equivalent to that of children in a self-esteem training program (Camp, in press). Aggressive behavior problems have also decreased significantly, but no more than in control populations (Camp, Blom, et al, 1977; Camp, in press). One study with learning disabled children (Watson & Hall, 1977) has also reported significant improvement in both achievement and behavior following Think Aloud training as compared to other types of training.

Formal evaluation of the classroom program to date is consistent with results of the individual program. In the earliest version which did not contain lessons in social problem solving, children exposed to Think Aloud registered significantly more improvement in cognitive test performance than unexposed children (Camp & Bash, 1978a). Participants in the classroom version which includes the social problem solving lessons have also demonstrated significant increases in nonaggressive solutions on the Preschool Interpersonal Problem Solving Test of Shure and Spivack (1974b).

Informal observations by trainers and teacher reports have produced a rich volume of anecdotes which reflect unique responses from students and teachers as a result of Think Aloud instruction. The first level at which this appears is often during actual Think Aloud lessons. For example, one aspect of the interpersonal problem solving training is to teach students to identify other people's feelings and to empathize with others. Even first graders readily apply these social skills to ease their teacher's frustration and embarrassment.

When one Think Aloud teacher became very discouraged because she could not complete a geometric puzzle, several students quickly offered help: "Don't worry, Miss Allen, we'll help you do it." "Why don't you find the pieces that go in the corner before you work on the middle." In another first grade, the teacher raised her hand for the trainer to help her when she was unsure of herself in teaching a Think Aloud lesson. The students identified with her discomfort and said, "Mrs. Riley, you're a student too. You're learning how to think aloud with us."

Empathy for other students was also observed during a Think Aloud lesson in a second grade classroom. During the lesson, felt-backed pictures would not adhere to a felt board while the teacher and students worked to classify the pictures. The last student to work at the felt board evaluated himself: "How did I do? Terrible because I kept knocking the pictures off the board. But I'm sure I know how the pictures go together if I could think of a different plan for making them stay on the board." However, one mainstreamed learning disabled student refused to let Kenneth downplay his own effort: "You really did a good job because you kept trying even when you felt mad when the pictures kept falling off. You ought to feel proud."

Think Aloud's self instruction questions teach students to monitor the use of their plans and develop an understanding that making mistakes is part of the problem solving process. Jack, a sixth grader, dashed to the teacher for a second paper any time he made a mistake. During Think Aloud training he began spontaneously to verbalize a change in plan to prevent errors and to eliminate the need for fresh paper.

A second level in generalizing Think Aloud skills occurs when the teacher restructures a typical school situation into a problem solving lesson in which students assume some responsibility for planning a solution. Lining up for gym is one of the first situations in which teachers commonly apply Think Aloud. Prior to Think Aloud training, teachers often call children by table or by row to line up for gym. After exposure to Think Aloud, several teachers have reported approaching this issue in the following manner. "My problem is to get children to the gym quickly and safely without disturbing other classes. How can I do it? I could call each child by name but that would take too long. What are some other plans which would help me solve my problem?"

Another common school problem develops on Halloween when some children lack costumes for the annual Halloween parade. Typically, children without costumes are jeered at by costumed students. In one second grade Think Aloud classroom, the teacher prevented the taunting by identifying a class problem and its corresponding solution: to design costumes for any student without one. The costumed students enthusiastically helped create innovative garb which eliminated the potential for heckling.

Before Think Aloud training, teachers often took on student problems as their own. For example, a student who bothered other students was told how to get along with others. Or when money was stolen, teachers employed new procedures for storing money. In both cases the teacher attempted to solve the problem, but the problem persisted. Some teachers have used Think Aloud to engage the class in looking together for the cause of the behavior. In one class discussion, it was determined that the student pest might be seeking friends or attention by bothering peers. The Think Aloud teacher set up the following puppet situation to help the student pest find more appropriate ways of getting attention: Peter wants people to talk to him and to be his friends. What are different things for Peter to do or say to get people to pay attention to him? The class suggested many solutions which they would accept as motions of friendship. The unidentified pest listened attentively and came to school the next day with a toy he was willing to share.

In another classroom, it was decided that the thief might be stealing money in order to buy something. The teacher set up a role-play situation to reduce the need for stealing money: Rita wants to give her sister a birthday present but she does not have any money. What are different things she could do or say so she can get a present for her sister? The children verbalized alternative solutions as to how Rita could make or get a present for her sister. The stealing in the classroom was not repeated.

One goal of Think Aloud is to teach students to evaluate their own work spontaneously. For them to develop this spontaneity, the teacher must first model self evaluation and then structure situations wherein the students practice such self evaluation. One first grade teacher modeled self evaluation for the problem of getting children to the gym quickly and safely. "How did I do? My plan to call children by the month of their birthday didn't work because some students weren't sure of their birth date. When I changed my plan to call children by colors of the clothes they were wearing, all children knew when to line up and all children listened for directions. That plan worked and I feel good."

A student in the class had a chance to practice evaluating his performance later in the day. Mark was talking when he was supposed to be completing math seat work and was required to self evaluate when the period ended. "How did I do? I was messing around so I didn't do my paper, but I know how to do the problems. I might as well stay in from recess and do it." The student was angry for having to stay inside, but he was mad at himself as the offender not at the teacher as a punisher.

Finally, when teachers present a lesson in the style of Think Aloud they talk less. As students gain proficiency at identifying problems, generating plans, and monitoring their adherence to plans, teachers make fewer repetitions of task directions and fewer task reminders. A teacher was awed when her second graders produced their best art projects after thinking out loud. A student explained the miracle: "This time we really knew what our problem was." This time the students had been required to articulate the problem statement rather than simply hearing the teacher rephrase it for them.

Evidence of the third level of generalization comes from anecdotes about children using Think Aloud skills independently, without prompting. Students frequently report their own think aloud triumphs. A first grader chattered quietly at her seat as she completed a music task. Her assignment was to listen to melodies and to circle an arrow which indicated the direction the tune took. When she finished, she beamed and proudly reported to her teacher how thinking out loud helped her do her work. She reviewed for the class each of the answers she gave to the four Think Aloud questions.

Another first grader who was assigned to a resource room for disruptive behavior reported to her teacher that she knew she was behaving better because "Ralph* whispers in my ear to be quiet and raise my hand whenever I forget my plan."

In one case, a mother recounted how her second grader improved the climate at home. When the family's five year old was unresponsive to traditional toilet training, the second grader suggested posting Ralph's questions on the bathroom wall. The problem solver proceeded to instruct the

---

*Ralph is the name children have given the bear who illustrates the four self-instruction questions. All Think Aloud students have a copy of Ralph and his questions at their desks.

younger child to think out loud. The plan worked and the story's ending was a happy one.

Teachers love to report occasions when students have relieved them from intervening in potential conflict situations. During reading seatwork, one boy was wandering aimlessly around the room. The teacher heard a student admonish the boy: "You better use a different plan to get your work done before the teacher catches you."

Another second grade teacher overheard the following dialogue between two students during an art lesson:

Alex: This stitchery is boring!
Ellen: What's wrong with it?
Alex: It's too hard.
Ellen: You planned your own thing. Maybe you need a new plan. What's a different idea?

The same teacher was excited by the empathy and attention to feelings which Ruth expressed in the following hall scene:

Mark to Susan: I don't like you. Nobody likes you!
Ruth to Mark: Does that make her feel good?
Mark: It's true.
Ruth: Yes, but there's something better you could say. You didn't have to make her feel bad.

Finally, students actively seek opportunities to recognize problem situations and to plan solutions. Planning even begins to appear in students' creative writing. The examples which follow were written by first grade Think Aloud students.

SAM'S SLED

Nip ran up the hill and the sled is there. Nip got on the sled and the sled moved. I can't get off the sled. The milkman is down there. I hope Nip can get off the sled. Sam has a plan. I think this will work if I can get this over here. Here is a sled. I hope this will work. Yes, it worked. I am glad.

RALPH AND THE BERD HOUS

One day Ralph dsidide too bild a berd hous. But he had a polbem. He did not know WHAT! too do beacas he did not have the rite aqupment. But THENE! he had a ideea. How can I do it. He sied if I only had a rooler. "I cood do it."

The end.

Think Aloud instruction can also occur outside the classroom. For example, while monitoring the lunchroom, a Think Aloud teacher restructured a problem situation so that the students took responsibility for resolving the dilemma. The school had designated a Captain's Table to recognize students who cleaned their plates, showed good manners, and talked softly. The monitor was pleased to find a table of six fifth graders who each merited a seat at the Captain's Table. However, he told the girls it was too hard for him to pick just one representative. He asked the girls to help him. The girls agreed that feelings might be hurt if only one of them were chosen, so they planned that each girl could sit at the Captain's Table one day of the week and they wrote out a schedule. But the dilemma had two parts. A roster had to be signed for the week. The girls identified two plans: sign all the names or pick a group name. The girls chose to sign the roster, "The Six Angels."

Teachers might be immortalized by the words "Walk, don't run!" The Think Aloud skill of requiring students to plan alternate ways of behaving has helped more than one teacher avoid such immortality. One Think Aloud teacher asked her sixth grader who was running up the stairs, "What's a different way you could go up the stairs?" John answered that he could walk up, and did so. The next day, both John and the teacher saw another boy bounding up the steps. This time, John said to the other boy, "What's a different way to go up the stairs?" The other boy responded to John by walking up the stairs.

COMPARISON WITH OTHER PROGRAMS

Many teachers have encountered a number of programs designed to improve their management of interpersonal conflict among students. They have often asked for explanations regarding the differences between Think Aloud and these other programs. In this context, the work of Glasser (1969), Gordon (1970), and Kohlberg (see Mattox, 1974, and Galbraith & Jones, 1976) have come up most often. In this section, we would like to review each of these briefly and to contrast them with the Think Aloud program.

Kohlberg has been concerned with describing and classifying the reasons children give for what they do. He has grouped these into six stages which he believes reflect moral development: Stage I—primary motivation is to avoid punishment; Stage II—motivation is primarily What's in it for me?; Stage III—a desire to please or conform emerges; Stage IV—emphasis is placed on social order; Stage V—stresses the rights of the individual; Stage VI—conscience and self-chosen principles determine decisions. Kohlberg has been interested in trying to facilitate growth from one stage to another through group discussion of moral dilemmas.

An example of a moral dilemma which may be used in such discussion is as follows:

JOE'S MORAL DILEMMA

Joe is a fourteen-year-old boy who wanted to go to camp very much. His father promised him he could go if he saved up the money for it himself. So Joe worked hard at his paper route and saved up the $40 it cost to go to camp and a little more besides. But just before camp was going to start, his father changed his mind. Some of his friends decided to go on a special fishing trip, and Joe's father was short of the money it would cost. So he told Joe to give hime the money he had saved up from the paper route. Joe didn't want to give up going to camp, so he thought of refusing to give his father the money.

[Fenton, 1976, pp. 189-90].

Teachers may be prepared for these discussions by general training in discussion skills which may consist of discussions and modeling of taking an "open, nonjudgmental attitude" and preparing "what if" and "probe" questions to keep the discussion going. Because the discussion focuses on what we would call the final evaluation stage, it presupposes an understanding of cause and effect. Acceptance and internalization of higher moral stage solutions are expected to occur without explicit instruction, presumably through the power of peer models.

In the Think Aloud program, no formal stages have been posited. However, we have accepted Shure and Spivack's notion that children need to have an understanding of cause and effect before they can consider the question of what someone should do. In addition, Think Aloud discussions emphasize the idea derived from Shure and Spivack (1974a), Maier (1963), and others that immediate evaluation of solutions often curbs development of alternatives. Kohlberg's discussions of moral dilemmas could easily be included as one part of the Think Aloud program, particularly for children who have already developed skill in problem analysis or an understanding of cause and effect. Story dilemmas are already included in the Think Aloud program as the "Fairness" lesson presented earlier. Plans for a program in upper grades include the use of moral dilemmas such as Kohlberg's beginning in early lessons.

However, Think Aloud is a much broader program than can be covered in the discussion of moral dilemmas alone. At this stage in the development of the Think Aloud program, training for teachers involves, in particular, a more far-reaching development of skill in taking a nonjudgmental attitude and promoting discussions which stimulate multiple student contributions. Discussion of moral dilemmas can, like most of the Think Aloud program, be used in a preventive sense as well as in analyzing on-the-spot problems.

The other two programs are designed primarily to assist teachers in developing skill in resolving conflicts as they arise. Gordon's (1975) film, *Teacher Effectiveness Training in the Classroom,* starts with the premise that resolution of conflicts is impaired by faulty communication. Teacher Effectiveness Training is designed to improve communication skills of teachers through what Gordon describes as a "no lose" method of communication. This method attempts to cut the flow of resentment which interferes with resolution or problem solving. Elements of this method which are discussed in his film include: (1) establishing problem ownership;

(2) active listening characterized by giving feedback and listening for feelings; (3) use of "I" messages; (4) identifying roadblocks to communication (directing, threatening, moralizing, advising, lecturing, judging, praising, name calling, interpreting, reassuring, probing, withdrawing, sarcasm); and (5) practice in the "no lose" method.

Gordon's use of the "no lose" method of communication in a conflict situation shares much in common with Think Aloud and includes the following steps: (1) defining the problem in terms of needs, (2) generating possible solutions, (3) evaluating and testing the various solutions, (4) deciding on mutually acceptable solutions, (5) implementing the solution, and (6) evaluating the solution. Gordon's approach and Think Aloud both emphasize defining the problem, but Think Aloud does not restrict definition to "needs." On the other hand, Think Aloud does not deal only with conflict as it arises; rather, much of the Think Aloud program is preventive. The two methods are similar in emphasis on generating many possible solutions and evaluating and testing them. Think Aloud goes beyond Gordon's program, however, in helping children to develop a repertoire of alternatives, to think in terms of alternatives, and to understand concepts of cause. On the other hand, development of good communication has not been dealt with as completely and systematically in Think Aloud training as in the Gordon program. The Gordon program tends to be more immediately applicable to the problems teachers have in dealing with children, while Think Aloud requires building a good deal of background skill before its tenets are readily applicable.

In general, however, the Gordon training in communication would seem to be an excellent background for teacher development of the type of attitudes and discussion skills needed by both the Think Aloud program and for developing the nonjudgmental attitudes proposed by Kohlberg.

Like Gordon's Teacher Effectiveness Training, Glasser's use of reality therapy in the school situation is directed primarily toward providing teachers with a method of dealing with situational crises. Glasser proposes eight steps toward dealing effectively with interpersonal problem situations. These are: (1) make friends, be personal; (2) deal with the present, ask "What are you doing now?"; (3) deal with behavior (not feelings), ask "Is it helping?"; (4) make a plan to do better; (5) get a commitment; (6) do not accept excuses; (7) do not punish, but do not interfere with reasonable consequences; (8) never give up. This approach can be applied in counseling students, classes, teachers, and parents to achieve appropriate resolution of problem situations. Teacher training involves instruction in Glasser's background psychological theory of motivation, needs, and desirable goals in human growth. For example, Glasser suggests that people are "ill" because they act irresponsibly, and treatment needs to be directed toward helping them act more responsibly. Camp would say that behavior is likely to persist in being maladaptive if the person does not have alternative methods of coping with different situations. The two positions are not in conflict but put emphasis on different aspects of behavior. Glasser's approach can also be applied in a preventive fashion, though it has not been presented primarily for this purpose.

Glasser's first three steps can be viewed as setting the stage for problem solving and defining the problem. It begins directly with discussion and involves no modeling of cognitions. Altogether, the eight steps outlined by Glasser are much broader and far-reaching than the Think Aloud program. However, Think Aloud could be viewed as concentrating primarily on Glasser's Step 4—Make a plan. The advantage of Think Aloud in this stage is that it provides children with a method of developing alternatives to their usual behavior and builds an understanding of cause and effect. Although it may be argued that a more haphazard approach may accomplish the same thing. Think Aloud may help develop planning skills and evaluating skills more rapidly, thereby shortcutting some of the negative consequences which may have to be experienced otherwise. In addition, the emphasis on modeling in the Think Aloud program has some theoretical advantage in assisting with internalization of verbal regulation of behavior. Again, the amount of discussion contained in the Glasser program and the way in which it is carried out, probably, in the long run, achieve results similar to Think Aloud. Glasser's Steps 5 through 8 go well beyond the Think Aloud program and involve suggestions regarding direct management of problem situations, especially those which occur repeatedly despite plans and commitments.

Viewing all of these approaches together, it is conceivable that a very powerful curriculum for teacher training could be developed using all four. For example, one could envision training teachers by beginning with Gordon's communication skills, followed by the preliminary problem solving exercises which introduce the Think Aloud technique. This could be followed by training in the Think Aloud program with inclusion of Kohlberg's moral dilemmas toward the end of the program for younger children or early in the program for older children. Finally, all of the preceding could easily be incorporated into an overall management approach based on Glasser's eight steps.

REFERENCES

Camp, B.W. Verbal mediation in young aggressive boys. *Journal of Abnormal Psychology, 86,* 1977, 145-153.

Camp, B.W. Two psychoeducational training programs for aggressive boys. In C. Whalen & B. Henker (Eds.), *Hyperactive children: The social ecology of identification and treatment.* Academic Press, 1979, in press.

Camp, B.W. & Bash, M.A. The classroom "Think Aloud" program. Paper presented at the American Psychological Association Convention, Toronto, Canada, August 1978a.

Camp, B.W. & Bash, M.A. Think Aloud: Group Manual (Revised). Denver, Colo. University of Colorado Medical School, November 1978b.

Camp, B.W.; Blom, G.E.; Hebert, F.; & Van Doorninck, W.J. "Think Aloud": A program for developing self-control in young aggressive boys. *Journal of Abnormal Child Psychology, 5,* 1977, 157-169.

Camp, B.W.; Zimet, S.G.; Van Doornink, W.J.; & Dahlem, N.W. Verbal abilities in young aggressive boys. *Journal of Educational Psychology, 69,* 1977, 129-135.

Fenton, E. Moral education: The research findings. *Social Education, 40,* 1976, 189-193.

Galbraith, R.E. & Jones, T.M. *Moral reasoning: A teaching handbook for adapting Kohlberg to the classroom.* Anoka, Minn.: Greenhaven Press, 1976.

Glasser, W. *Schools without failure.* New York: Harper & Row, 1969.

Gordon, T. *Parent effectiveness training.* New York: Peter H. Wyden, 1970.

Gordon, T. *Teacher effectiveness training.* Hollywood, Calif. Media Five Film Distributors, 1975.

Hetherington, E.M. & McIntyre, C.W. Developmental Psychology. *Annual Review of Psychology, 26,* 1975, 97-136.

Maier, N.R.F. *Problem-solving discussions and conferences.* San Francisco: McGraw-Hill, 1963.

Mattox, B.A. *Getting it together: Dilemmas for the classroom.* La Mesa, Calif. Pennant Educational Materials, 1974.

Meichenbaum, D. Theoretical and treatment implications of developmental research on verbal control of behavior. *Psychologie Canadienne/Canadian Psychological Review, 16,* 1975, 22-27.

Meichenbaum, D., & Goodman, J. Training impulsive children to talk to themselves: A means of developing self-control. *Journal of Abnormal Psychology, 77,* 1971, 115-126.

Platt, J.J. & Spivack, G. *Manual for the means-ends problem solving procedure (MEPS): A measure of interpersonal cognitive problem solving skill.* Philadelphia: Department of Mental Health Sciences, Hahnemann Community Mental Health/Mental Retardation Center, 1975.

Shure, M.B. & Spivack, G. *A mental health program for kindergarten children: A cognitive approach to solving interpersonal problems.* Philadelphia: Department of Mental Health Sciences, Hahnemann Community Mental Health/Mental Retardation Center, 1974a.

Shure, M.B. & Spivack, G. *Preschool interpersonal problem solving (PIPS) test: Manual.* Philadelphia: Department of Mental Health Sciences, Hahnemann Community Mental Health/Mental Retardation Center, 1974b.

Spivack, G. & Shure, M.B. *Social adjustment of young children: A cognitive approach to solving real-life problems.* San Francisco: Jossey-Bass, 1974.

Torrance, P. *Torrance tests of creative thinking.* Columbus, Ohio: Ginn, 1966.

Watson, D.L. & Hall, D.L. Self-control of hyperactivity. La Mesa, Calif.: Pupil Services Division, La Mesa-Spring Valley School District, 1977.

Chapter 6

A Child's Social Isolation: Origins, Prevention, Intervention

Sherri Oden

Every child experiences social isolation from peers at varied times and places throughout development. The experience of social isolation is not only unavoidable, it is constructive to the child's development. Time to one-self allows for the pursuit of interests which enhance unique qualities of the child's personality and intellect; the exploration of the subjective view of the self; the search for insight into values and goals; and the view of reality from a distance, perhaps toward fantasy, but ultimately toward greater objectivity. The ability to tolerate time alone, even when not especially desirable, is critical for the development of discipline in work and other endeavors. Furthormore, in some situations, the child's ability to separate from peer group pressure or abusive action is critical to the preservation of self confidence, individual values, and even physical well being. Peer groups, as well as individual children, thus, may elect to be isolated given certain circumstances.

Alternatively, social inclusion with peers provides the child with resources for development: participation in new activities and interests and exposure to differing values and perspectives. In the context of peer interaction, children learn to coordinate their actions effectively and to communicate, compete, and cooperate; in time, conceptions of morality and justice are realized. Continuity in relationships such as friendships engenders the child's appreciation of another's uniqueness and furthers the development of reciprocity and attachment, concern, and responsibility.

Considering the apparent importance of peers in children's development, it is unfortunate that research on the topic has been meager. The available evidence is also quite limited since the research designs most often employed require statistical analyses which are correlational, thus making causal interpretations tenuous, if not unwarranted. Experimental research methods can also present considerable ethical problems unless it is likely that children can benefit from a given study or, at least, are unlikely to be negatively affected. Nevertheless, sufficient evidence exists to begin to sketch a picture of the child's social experience.

Overall, the evidence indicates that children who are well accepted by peers, compared to those who are not, also exhibit greater social knowledge, more complex social reasoning, and more positive social behavior in peer interactions (see reviews by Asher, Oden & Gottman, 1977; Hartup, 1970; 1977). Investigations are ongoing, but it is well known that there are children who remain socially unaccepted or isolated across a variety of peer groups and circumstances and over a considerable period of time. It is often believed that a child will simply "outgrow" isolation or rejection from peers or that he or she has some unique ability or talent which precludes inclusion, at least for a time. Meanwhile, compared to other children, these children are likely to become increasingly excluded from positive or friendly interactions and relationships with peers and, thereby, they are excluded from important social learning. Ultimately, due to reputational factors and limitation in social ability, the child's experiences with peers may be constrained to a cyclical pattern of peer rejection or isolation. A few longitudinal studies have found that social isolation or problematic peer relationships in childhood are predictors of social and emotional adjustment problems in young adulthood (e.g., Cowen, Pederson, Babigian, Izzo & Trost 1973; Kohn & Clausen 1955; Roff 1961; Roff, Sells & Golden 1972). Furthermore, some evidence indicates that a low level of peer acceptance is likely to be an enduring condition by the time a child is nine or ten years old (Ladd 1979; Oden & Asher 1977).

CHILDREN WHO LACK PEER ACCEPTANCE

Children who are quite isolated or rejected are frequently easy to identify: the child who nearly always plays alone; the child who is last to be selected for games; the child no one wants to sit next to on the bus; the child who erupts with a physical attack on a classmate; or, the child who seems to undermine or sabotage nearly every activity. Identifying children who are usually found on the periphery of social interaction or in the middle of a fight is not overly difficult. However, these children, along with other children who lack peer acceptance, do not share an equivalent profile, but rather an equivalent problem.

Conceptions of Peer Status

In both formal and informal discussions of children's peer relationships, parents and professionals utilize a motley of terms or concepts to sort out how children act, feel, and think about each other as they interact. While there is some correspondence between the language of the educators, parents, counselors, and researchers on this topic, there is also confusion. An agreed upon set of concepts is important for identifying children whose social development or circumstances precludes their peer acceptance. Furthermore, concepts are needed which further our understanding of children's peer relationships by providing language to describe what is known, can be observed, and will provide a basis for discussion and investigation. Currently, terms lack definition, are arbitrarily employed, and serve only to roughly approximate a child's peer status and social ability.

A brief review of the range of concepts and terms frequently used to identify and discuss children who lack peer acceptance may serve to further illustrate the problem. (For a more extensive presentation, see Gronlund, 1959.) Children whose peer relationships are viewed as essentially positive have been frequently referred to as popular, well liked, liked, or accepted. In contrast, children whose relationships with peers are negative in some way or in many circumstances have been typically referred to as unpopular, disliked, rejected, or unaccepted. Children who lack interaction and relationships with peers have been referred to as socially isolated, shy, withdrawn, or neglected. In comparison to simply relating or interacting with peers across various circumstances, participation in activity with particular peers over time may result in mutual positive feelings. These children then seek out interaction with each other and may be regarded as acquaintances, friends, and close or best friends. In contrast, a child who is not accepted or received as a friend by peers in these situations may be referred to as a deviate, a loner, withdrawn, or autonomous. And these are just the more common terms! Of course, children themselves have a vocabulary they use to describe their actions, feelings, and thoughts about each other ranging from the positive to the negative pole on the continuum of peer acceptability. When we eavesdrop on children's conversations, we hear terms such as "neat," "nice," "friendly," "fun," "cool," "smart," and contrarily, "mean," "weird," "bully," "dumbbell," "icky," and the lingo continues with variations on the same themes throughout adolescence and into adulthood.

Many terms used by parents and professionals to refer to children's state or status in various peer relationships specify a range from negative to positive in dimension, whereas other concepts include some interpretation of the cause or origin of the child's peer status. Researchers often utilize terms that are arbitrary conveniences or constructs under examination in the search for a better understanding and prediction of children's peer social status. Terms such as social isolation or peer acceptance are also typically used to refer to some particular measurement of peer status (e.g., low frequency of peer interaction, average peer ratings). These terms do not necessarily explain or predict anything about a particular child, but do provide language labels for discussion of general patterns in peer relationships. For the purposes of this chapter, children who infrequently interact with peers and children who are not well accepted when they do interact with peers will both be referred to as socially isolated or lacking in peer acceptance or friendships.

Origins of Social Isolation

The origins of social isolation versus acceptance would seem to begin with the child's experience in previous peer contexts and in relationships in the family context. Only a few studies have investigated the contributions of the family. The evidence has indicated a relationship between a positive attachment with a parent and positive peer relations (e.g., Leiberman, 1976).

More extensive research has focused on the child in peer contexts. Studies have revealed that personal status characteristics (e.g., physical attractiveness) and social competence are origins of a child's acceptance in peer contexts.

SOCIAL SKILLS AND PEER CONTEXT A child's social competence can be evaluated according to his or her knowledge of what is appropriate and effective for various situations, contexts, and relationships and also how skillful the child is in applying that knowledge. For example, in a recent study (Ladd & Oden, 1979), we individually interviewed elementary school age children to determine their knowledge about what kinds of actions would be helpful to a peer in need of help in a peer group context (e.g., being teased by a group of peers), and then, immediately after, the peer group departs from the scene and the two children are alone (i.e., peer dyad context). Children were shown cartoons depicting the teasing scene or incident and other social situations with a child in need of help. The specific kinds of actions suggested by the children differed according to the theme of the cartoon scene. For example, more instructive strategies (e.g., "Show him how to do it.") were frequently suggested to help a child with a schoolwork problem in contrast to the teasing incident where "order-command" strategies ("I'd tell them: 'Stop it'.") were very frequent. A child, thus, learns to apply social action according to the specific features of various situations and environments. This study also revealed that it is important for children to pay attention to the overall structure of the social context, that is, group versus dyad. Console-comfort strategies (e.g., "I'd say: 'It's not so bad'.") were very rarely recommended by children as ways to help a peer when other children were watching, or being negative, or rejecting to the child, but were highly recommended when alone with the child who was sad or upset, i.e., in the dyadic context. In this study, children with low peer acceptance appeared to be less aware of peer values and norms. They suggested strategies which their peers would probably consider to be unhelpful or inappropriate.

Similarly, a child's social ability can be examined in the context of specific group and dyadic relationships in the school or classroom and the neighborhood community. A child's peer status can be assessed by determining how many children accept the child or participate in activities with the child in group and dyadic contexts. At the same time, the continuity or endurance and quality (e.g., positive approach, friendliness, reciprocity) of these relationships should be considered. The child's playmates in a group and in close friendships provide different contexts for social learning. Finally, across ongoing and new situations, contexts, and relationships, does the child have essential social abilities? Several reviews provide guidelines for identifying basic social abilities in the child's social development (e.g., Asher et al., 1977; Gottman, Gonzo & Rasmussen, 1975; Hartup, 1979; Selman, 1976; Spivack & Shure, 1974; Turiel, 1978).

It is unclear to what extent or how frequently social ability determines the beginnings of the process or sequence of social acceptance or unacceptance from peers. Social skill training studies with children who lack peer acceptance and friends have found increases in peer acceptance of these children after the children receive social skill instruction (Ladd, 1979; Oden & Asher, 1977). These findings suggest a causal relationship between social skills and peer acceptance. Other data indicate a correlation between peer acceptance and social knowledge (e.g., how to make a new friend; how to help a peer) (Gottman et al., 1975; Ladd & Oden, 1979) and sociability in behavior (e.g., positive approach to peers) (Hartup, Glazer & Charlesworth, 1967).

Alternatively, some evidence indicates that, in many cases, a lack of overall social competence may be the result of being unaccepted due to personal status characteristics, such as being of a different race from others in the peer context (Singleton & Asher, 1977), having an unusual or strange sounding name (McDavid & Harari, 1966) or being physically unattractive (Dion & Berscheid, 1974). Some of these children may lack social skills, but others may simply lack the opportunities to participate in a given social context.

Another major origin of social isolation includes factors such as going to schools where the contexts in which the children interact present constraints for peer interaction and social relationship development, including certain types of curriculum structure (Hallinan, 1976), activities (Charlesworth & Hartup, 1967; Hallinan & Tuma, 1978), or degree of population mobility (Roistacher, 1974). While some children lack skills which are likely to be critical to positive peer relating (such as sharing or taking turns), many children simply lack skills which are critical to certain social situations or contexts. Thus, in understanding the origins of peer acceptance and isolation, it is important to appreciate that there is a relationship between social situations and social behavior. Since children have diverse social experiences, they vary in their social skills and in their lack of social skills. If a school context does not provide a diversity of social experiences, the likelihood that a child's lack of specific social skills may result in social isolation in present or future social contexts is, thereby, increased. For example, one child might be quite unskilled in participating in group discussion or a group game (O'Connor, 1969), whereas another child might have difficulty knowing how to initiate interaction with a peer (Gottman et al., 1975) or handle conflicts with peers (Johnston et al., 1977). A child who lacks social skills for group participation may be well accepted in a classroom without many group discussions, but may be more likely to become socially isolated or lack peer acceptance in future experiences in which effective participation in discussion will be essential.

In summary, a child who lacks social skills may or may not lack peer acceptance or friends, depending on the social situations which frequently occur or are inherent in the social context of the classroom, neighborhood, or community in which the child interacts.

PERSONAL STATUS CHARACTERISTICS As indicated previously, a lack of social skills may also occur because of limited social opportunities for participation with peers in past or present contexts due to the structure of the context or to status attributed to specific personal characteristics (e.g., race, sex, age, etc.). In addition to lack of social acceptance between children of the opposite sex, different races, and ethnic origins, children who are considered deficient in learning ability (Bryan, 1977), mentally retarded (Goodman, Gottlieb & Harrison, 1972), or physically handicapped (Richardson et al., 1961) have also been found to lack acceptance in many peer group contexts. Among children who lack peer acceptance in the classroom, however, many children may be socially skilled. Other experiences in the home, neighborhood, or in a specific peer group may be quite sufficient to these children's social skill development even though they are isolated in some peer contexts. These children may or may not lack critical social skills, but their opportunities for social development tend to remain limited.

Studies by DeVries and Edwards (1974) and others have demonstrated activities in the classroom context which enhance positive peer interaction with children of different races and between boys and girls. However, when the cultural context or the family supports the view that some characteristics are appropriate bases for exclusion, interventions in schools will have limited effects. It may be assumed that social isolation and rejection is the problem of individual children or that some minority groups are rejected or isolated because they lack essential knowledge and skills; if these children were more socially skilled, they would be included and accepted by peers.

However, when the social environment is not responsive to changes in behavior, teaching a child social skills is severely limited in its long-term effects. Many a parent and teacher has witnessed a child who tries to join a group or make a friend and is met with exclusionary tactics from peers. Often, children who are unaccepted by peers never really have a chance to become otherwise. For example, in one kindergarten classroom we visited, a child asked if she could join the play activity of two classmates. One of the children demanded an entrance requirement, "Well, okay if you can spell 'New York'." The child responded by writing a few letters she knew on a sheet of paper and was told by the young gatekeeper, "No, that's wrong! Now you can't play with us!"

Evidence indicates that simply providing common territory and activities does not automatically result in children's mutual acceptance (Blaney et al., 1977). Yet, appealing to children's goodwill by providing platitudes is also short-sighted. Examination of the "hidden curriculum" which includes the social behaviors enhanced by the teacher and the curriculum (e.g., Cartledge & Milburn, 1978) is needed to evaluate the contributions of the academic curriculum to children's social interaction. Children may overcome stereotyping by learning social skills for communication and problem solving. Where teachers, schools, and communities decide to support greater peer interaction between children of diverse characteristics (such as race or ethnic origin, religion, sex, age, and physical and mental abilities), children who do not often interact are more likely to benefit from increased opportunities to know each other better. In such cases, although it has been found that close friendships do not often result, more positive attitudes and interactions have been observed (Singleton & Asher 1979).

In summary, a child's acceptance by peers for peer interaction and friendships does not directly correspond to his or her social knowledge and skill; rather, a child's relative acceptance and isolation in a peer group appears to be related to three factors: social knowledge, skill in applying the knowledge, and personal status characteristics. While it seems that some social actions are quite important in any peer context, some social actions are considered more appropriate or inappropriate, effective or ineffective according to the context. There is, thus, no easy formula to utilize in identifying those children who lack acceptance from peers. However, examination of the contexts in which peers interact as well as evaluation of children's peer status in various situations and contexts appears to be a beginning toward prevention and intervention of problematic peer relationships.

ASSESSMENT OF PEER RELATIONSHIPS

These are key questions prior to intervention: Are a child's social difficulties considerably outside the realm of the problems in which other children are engaged? Are the peer relationships in a given classroom or group constructive for both individual and group development? Although there is a general understanding of the factors which contribute to children's peer status, parents and professionals often do not have a firm ground upon which to make decisions about whether or not to intervene to enhance children's social competence or peer status.

Following from the previous discussions on the peer context, an assessment of children's peer relationships should include a focus on the context in which they occur. The child may first be evaluated as a social being, that is, across a variety of contexts, such as the home, classroom, playground, or neighborhood. The child may then be evaluated by specifically focusing on the group context. Does the child have knowledge and skill in relating to peers in groups, e.g., participating in games or activities with appropriate cooperation, competition, and awareness of the norms and conventions of the peer group? (See Turiel, 1978, for further discussion.) In a peer group which has continuity, does the child contribute as a member of that group and play a role in constructing the group's rules, activities, and agenda? Finally, is the child able to relate in a dyadic context (with another child)? The dyadic context is potentially a friendship relationship context in which individual children have been observed to create their own structure and in which they can explore similarities and differences, provide mutual reinforcement and feedback, resolve conflicts, and seek to sustain the relationship over time (Gottman & Parkhurst, in press). Similarly, we can assess a group or classroom in terms of its cohesiveness at a dyadic level. For example, are there friendships and best friendships which emerge and sustain within groups? According to Hallinan and Tuma (1978) "... both open and traditional classroom settings have some characteristics that promote children's friendships as well as others that interfere with the development of these relationships" (p. 281).

Three major perspectives provide resources for the teacher, parent, or counselor for gathering information about children's social skills, and group and dyadic relationships: the peer perspective, the adult perspective, and the child's perspective. Three corresponding methods often used by researchers and other professionals are available for gaining insight into each of these perspectives: sociometric methods, observational procedures, and interview techniques. In the remainder of this section, each of these methods will be briefly described as they most typically have been used, followed by a description of the kinds of information which they provide about children's peer relationships. Finally, readings will be recommended which provide a range of specific methods, further description, and guidelines for learning how to apply the methods.

Sociometric Methods

The sociometric method is applied to gain understanding of how children, as individuals and as a group, feel about or perceive each other. Two basic types of methods have been used by researchers and professionals including the limited choice or nomination method originally devised by Moreno (1934), and the roster and rating questionnaire in which each child makes a judgment about every other child on some dimension or issue of interest. These two methods tend to provide results which are highly correlated (Oden & Asher, 1977).

The nomination method is typically used to gather information about children's friendships and best friendships and is probably best suited to these purposes since children are not likely to be friends with everyone in the classroom. Children may be asked to list the names of friends, e.g., three, five, or no limit. A list from which to circle the names of friends is helpful as children may need instruction in spelling a friend's name. These methods were used by numerous researchers and have been described by Gronlund (1959) and more recently by Gottman et al. (1975) and Oden and Asher (1977). Hallinan and Tuma (1978) gave children in the upper elementary grades a list of their classmates and asked them to indicate whether they regarded each child as a best friend, a friend, or someone they knew but who was not a friend. This method allows for some differentiation between friend and best friend and clarifies which children are not friends. Presumably, a child could also be asked to note those children whom they would be interested in getting to know, which would provide some guidelines for activity arrangements. While collecting sociometric data, children often tell us that they hope we will do something to get some different kids in activities in the classroom so they could make more friends.

With data from the nomination sociometric method, a couple of measures may be derived including simply the total number of nominations a child gives and receives from classmates; and these can be summed across various peer groups to see how they view the child, e.g., children of the opposite sex, children of a different age (in mixed-age classrooms), or of a different race or ethnic origin. These data also allow for an assessment of reciprocity, that is, how many children's choices were, in fact, reciprocated by the children who chose them? This measure of reciprocity also allows for a picture of the cliques which exist in a classroom and how open these children are to friends outside that group. In general, reciprocity as measured by this method in which children have limited choice results in a large number of children without reciprocal scores (e.g., Hallinan 1976). The method introduced by Hallinan and Tuma (1978), if used to establish reciprocity, would seem likely to provide a more accurate spread of reciprocity scores for children in a classroom. A child's total friendships (reciprocated, nominated, or received by a child from classmates) provides some indication of his or her status as a friend in dyadic relationships. Children without any nominations from classmates should be a focus of some concern to a teacher or parent, especially in the upper elementary grades where the stability of peer groups is more established. Teachers might also assess how well a group activity functions to enhance dyadic relationships by noting which children choose each other and what additional situations they share, such as the reading groups (e.g., Hallinan & Tuma, 1978). The classroom as a whole can be assessed since classrooms in which a small number of children have most of the nominations tend also to have more isolates (Schmuck, 1963), and this tendency indicates either that some characteristics of children (particular skills or other attributes) are receiving too much emphasis or that some activities are structured such that only the most skilled gain attention and interaction with all peers. For assessment of children's dyadic relationships among preschoolers, Asher, Singleton, Tinsley, and Hymel (1979), McCandless and Marshall (1957), and others have used children's photographs (from a class photograph or individual photographs) and asked the children to point out their friends or best friends.

The roster and rating sociometric method requires each child to rate or make a judgment about each classmate. This method may be employed with older children by using a questionnaire in which every child's name appears and each child privately responds to each name according to some criterion (e.g., "How much do you like to play with this child in school?") and marks a point on a scale. Younger children have been found to respond well to scales with two or three points, especially if pictures are used to indicate variations of smiling faces (e.g., Asher et al., 1979; Oden & Asher, 1977). The advantages of the roster and rating method are the same as indicated by the Hallinan and Tuma procedure, that is, every child makes a judgment about every other child, thus providing a more complete picture of the child's social relationships and providing data which is not susceptible to memory problems. The roster and rating technique also is useful for asking about broader issues than friendship where considerable selectivity is expected from children. Thus sociometric rating scale methods have also focused on questions such as: "How much do you like to work with this child in school?"

The data from the sociometric rating scale can be used to compute average ratings assigned to peers by a given child and received from peers for a given child. Averages can also be computed for groups within the classroom and for the classroom as a whole. Establishing an average score for a classroom can be helpful in determining if some children appear to be considerably far from the average. It is important to consider that some children receive very low scores from most children and some high scores from a few children which raises their average. In contrast, other children with the same average receive somewhat higher but low scores from all classmates. A child who receives low scores from everyone will be easily determined by the sociometric rating scale. It is also helpful, once again, to look at the classroom distribution of scores. In some classrooms, the majority of children receive highly similar scores except for a couple of popular and isolated children. In contrast, another classroom may have a small number of children who receive high scores and the rest of the classroom receives considerably lower scores. Finally, other classrooms will have a considerable spread in scores. Reciprocity scores may also be derived from rating scale data (see Roistacher, 1974). Finally, the sociometric methods must be administered with care to ensure privacy and confidentiality of results so that an individual child is not stigmatized.

In summary, the sociometric method provides information about how peers see each other. This allows us to understand that children may value different kinds of behavior and characteristics than we would have expected. The sociometric method may be the best place to start to understand children's peer relationships, to know what to observe and what questions to pursue further.

Observing Children

Observing can be useful informally as well as more systematically. Through observation of children in different situations, at different times, and over a period of time, a teacher or parent can determine which social skills are important for social interaction and relationship building in the classroom, or in other groups, or in the dyadic context. From observation, it can be determined how much time and enthusiasm a given setting, activity, or section of the classroom tends to foster. We can determine which activities result in endless conflicts and struggles versus those activities in which children learn to coordinate activities with others, and those activities which result in exclusiveness from a given peer group versus openness to new members. If alert, we can observe the processes by which a child tries to join a group and the responses he or she tends to receive. We can witness friendships developing and the conflicts which ensue and must be resolved. We can spot the child who "hovers" on the periphery (e.g., Gottman, 1977) and the children who are frequently in a fight or struggle (e.g., Johnston, et al., 1977).

What to observe for more systematic assessment can be determined from a sociometric technique, or from talking with teachers, parents, or other children. If it is feasible, continuous recording observations are also a beginning in which many situations and children are observed throughout the day, and the behaviors of children are written down as completely as possible. Often, a teacher's assistant or coteacher is helpful here. Another alternative is to set aside a time when the children know the teacher should not be continually interrupted. After reviewing the initial transcripts, the teacher or parent can determine what the focus of the systematic observations should be, depending on what is observed. Let's say that a teacher finds that some children constantly interrupt and disrupt the activities, or a child is never included in an activity successfully. This situation would be considered an "event" and could be counted for the number of times or for the durations of time it occurred. Or, the range of social behaviors, positive and negative, which were included in the event could be noted. The frequency of the behaviors might also provide some clues for positive behaviors to encourage and chart to see if they increase over time. Sometimes setting up an activity and observing it ensures that the types of behaviors of interest will be more fully observed. Among the many types of observational methods available, the continuous account, event sampling, and the behavior frequency methods are quite informative. A teacher most likely will want to assess every child as well as groups of children. Thus, to evaluate the activity and identify the peer groups and dyads within the classroom, children can be observed in terms of who is present and for how long in a given activity. For observing individuals and determining their activities and skills, the observer can make up a random list of the children and spot-check for a few seconds what each child is doing, then go to the next child and so on; or, observe a given child for a longer period of time and then go to the next and so on. Another procedure allows the observers to scan the entire group for a few seconds and mark behavior on a few dimensions, such as positive socializing versus playing alone. Many of these procedures take considerable practice and, yet, much can be learned from simply trying to master them. An essential skill is learning to describe children's behavior according to their actions rather than according to the observer's impressions of their unobservable feelings or personality characteristics (e.g., "He yelled out loud," rather than "He was disgusted," and "He did not answer," rather than "He is shy."). To determine one's objectivity and the validity of the types of behaviors being assessed, another person should sometimes observe independently but along with the observer, and their results should be compared. Several reviews of the observational procedures are available and provide examples, explanations, and instructions for application (Gardner, 1974; Rowen, 1973; Sackett, 1978; Wright, 1960).

From observing children often, we can learn some of the social skills of most children at a given developmental level or age. Thus, we have some guidelines for what to focus on with children who lack these skills. Furthermore, we may find that a given child is quite skilled but is not welcomed due to the types of activities in the classroom or the attitudes in peer group cliques which have developed. When children are socially isolated but are socially skilled, the intervention should be at the level of program intervention so that more opportunities are created in which more children can get to know each other.

Interview Approaches

Studies in which children have been individually interviewed about their peer relationships indicate that children vary considerably in their understanding of peer norms, values, and roles for appropriate action in a given social situation (Gottman, et al., 1975; Ladd & Oden, 1979). There are many interview formats available from research and clinical or counseling work with children (see Yarrow, 1960, for a review) from which teachers and parents may select whatever questions and types of questioning processes seem appropriate to their role and relationship with the child or children. In general, a conversational or informal style seems appropriate, even for research purposes. The major concern is to try to gain an understanding of how the child perceives a given situation or idea, or problem, and the kinds of language the child uses in constructing and expressing his conceptualization. Piaget's clinical interview technique is surely the most outstanding example of asking children questions and using probes to discover their ways of approaching problems (Piaget, 1928).

In discussions with a child, a teacher or parent may discover the child's understanding of reasons why he or she may be accepted or rejected by peers in various circumstances; the child's attitude and feelings toward peers; the child's perception of how he or she is perceived by peers; and finally, the child's ability to devise plans for action to make a friend or alter peer relationships.

In summary, a variety of methods are available for teachers, parents, and counselors which provide useful examples of how to learn more about children's viewpoints and their behavior toward each other as individuals and as a group. A more informed picture of children's peer relationships is a necessary beginning toward making decisions about focus for preventive programs and for intervention on the behalf of individual children or selected groups.

METHODS OF PREVENTION AND INTERVENTION

Several educational models have been described and applied to prevent social adjustment problems of children in school settings. The models of curricula or specially designed programs differ in the kinds of experiences they provide for children: activities which allow full participation of children who have diverse skills or abilities (e.g., Blaney et al., 1977); pairing a child of less mature social skills with younger children (Hartup, 1978); design of activities to enhance group cooperation (DeVries & Edwards, 1974); problem solving activities and instruction for individual children or small groups of children (Cowen, 1977; Spivack & Shure, 1974). Throughout this discussion, it has been proposed that changes in the various peer contexts can aid individual children and peer groups in developing positive peer relationships. Methods of assessment have been reviewed which provide information for selecting the social skills and peer contexts to focus on when developing prevention and intervention programs. The following section will focus on methods of social skill instruction.

Social Skill Instruction

Although the evidence is unclear, at this point, on how an individual child who lacks peer acceptance or friendships arrives at his or her given status, some studies have demonstrated that such a child can benefit from further socialization, i.e., from verbal instruction and behavioral "rehearsal" (Ladd, 1979; Oden & Asher, 1977) and from modeling (O'Connor, 1969). These procedures are based largely on Bandura's (1972) theory of how humans learn in social settings. Parents and other adults in a child's early experience frequently provide the child with considerable modeling, verbal instruction, prompting, and feedback as children learn to join a peer group at the sandbox, settle a fight during a game in the backyard, or share or take turns in the classroom. It may be that some children receive less social skill instruction or that they were not able to use this information adequately when it was provided. Other children may have lacked the opportunities to try new behaviors with peers or may have received insufficient feedback during play experiences.

Oden and Asher (1977) found that providing instruction in social skills was helpful even for third- and fourth-grade children. In their study, 11 classrooms of children were asked to respond to two sociometric techniques: a roster and rating scale questionnaire and a friendship nomination method. Children who were the lowest rated and received just one or no-friend nominations were selected for participation in the study. The purpose of the study was to assess the effects of "coaching" children in social skills as a method of teaching socially isolated children social knowledge and skills for making gains in peer acceptance and friendships.

The coaching method included three components during each of five sessions: verbal instruction was given individually to each child by an adult, followed immediately with an opportunity to practice while playing with another child who was randomly selected from the class and was moderately well accepted by classmates and, finally, an individual postplay review session was conducted with the same adult. The content of the instruction consisted of social skill concepts and examples which were proposed to the child as ideas for how to make a game fun or enjoyable to play with another person: (1) participating in a game or activity, (2) cooperating (e.g., taking turns and sharing materials, (3) communicating (e.g., talking and listening), and (4) validating or supporting (e.g., giving attention or help).

Three experimental conditions were included in the study: coaching, peer pairing, and control. Each condition or "group" was formed by randomly selecting one of the three lowest rated children from each classroom for each condition, resulting in 11 children in each group. Children in each condition were provided with six play sessions over a four-week period. [No instruction was given for the first sessions.] They played with a different classmate each time. Six different games (e.g., Dominoes, Blockhead, picture drawing) were used. In the peer pairing condition, each isolated child was paired with the same peer partners and played the same games as in the coaching condition, but these children received no coaching instruction or postplay review. A control condition was included to examine the possible prestige effects of simply being taken out of the classroom by the experimenter along with more-liked peers to play games. The control children were, therefore, taken out of the classroom with the same peer partners as in the other conditions, but they played solitary games and did not interact.

The sociometric measures were again administered to the 11 classrooms approximately ten days after the experimental period had ended. The results were that children in the coaching condition had significantly increased on the sociometric measure of acceptance for playing with peers, but not for working with peers. Although some children made gains in friendships, the gains were not statistically significant. In contrast, children in the peer pairing group declined on all measures, and children in the control group remained unchanged. A follow-up assessment was made approximately one year later to determine the endurance of these initial increases in peer acceptance for playing with peers. Of the 33 children in the original sample of isolated children, 22 remained in the district one year later and were distributed among 11 different classrooms with eight from the coaching group, seven from the peer pairing group, and seven from the control group. The coached children had continued to improve with an average score that was only somewhat below the classroom average. The peer pairing group also made some gains, recovering from their previous initial loss of peer status, and the control group made no significant gains. The results demonstrate the lasting effects of verbal coaching along with practice in peer interaction and feedback or review.

A recent study by Ladd (1979) found corroborative evidence with third-graders who were found to be low in peer acceptance on the sociometric measure of playing with peers and also low in frequency of specific social skills in a natural play context. The skills included asking positive questions, leading or offering useful suggestions, and being helpful to another. Three conditions were used in this study: verbal social skill training, attention control, and no treatment control. In the group whch received skill training, pairs of children were given verbal instruction from an adult along with immediate guided rehearsal during a game. Gradually, across the eight sessions, this guidance was withdrawn and the child was individually asked to evaluate his or her own behavior. In the latter sessions, two additional peers were included. The children in this study received more specific verbal social skill training for a more limited specific set of skills than in the Oden and Asher study; they were given more direct guidance and feedback with respect to their behavior in practicing the skills. They gradually practiced and critiqued their own behavior independently. The second condition was an attention control group which was included to assess the attentional effects of receiving instruction from an adult; these children received instruction and practice in how to play games according to the rules. Finally, a control group was included which did not participate in any instruction or activity in the study. The results were that both the verbal skill training group and the attention control group made initial gains in peer acceptance and general social behavior, while only the skill training group made gains in two of the specific behaviors in which they had received instruction. The control group did not change. Furthermore, at follow-up one month later, the control group remained unchanged, and the attention control group returned to the level of peer acceptance and social behavior prior to the study. In contrast, the skill training group continued to improve by making further gains in peer acceptance, general positive social behavior, and specific social skills. These two studies together comprise the most consistent evidence for the merits of verbal instruction with children. Some studies have found promising results with younger children (e.g., Chittenden, 1942; Zahavi & Asher, 1978) and others with older children (e.g., LaGreca & Mesibov, 1979).

The following section will present a discussion of the "coaching" social skill procedures, examples based on the script used in the Oden and Asher study, and suggestions for adapting the procedure for use by teachers and parents.

Coaching Social Skills

Coaching (as used in the Oden and Asher study) includes the *instruction* of concepts or rules, the opportunity for *practicing* or *rehearsing* related behavior, and *feedback* on the new learning. Coaching may be thought of as the provision of a conceptual framework which provides a model for behavior and a social context in which behavior may be modeled, shaped, and responded to with feedback. The "coach" also tends to elicit positive attention and motivation. Coaching should be built around the context of an opportunity for rehearsal or practice. Without potentially stressful evaluation, learning is further enhanced from the coaching instruction and feedback. Many of the creative arts experiences and children's games are particularly appropriate contexts for social learning. As previously discussed, the teacher or parent should evaluate, however, whether the properties or requirements of activities allow a child to participate and experience a range of behaviors. Many games, for example, exclude children due to the requirements; or the requirements exclude the very behaviors to be encouraged; or negative behaviors are encouraged. In the instruction and feedback components of coaching, the teacher or parent provides information through language labels or concepts which refer to types of behavior to be kept in memory by the child for use when appropriate.

The child is first instructed in social concepts (e.g., cooperation) by an adult who encourages the child to suggest specific behavioral examples and adds examples when a child does not provide any. Throughout, the "coach" repeats and reviews the concepts and gives feedback on how well the child understands their applicability. More general social reality concepts may be included, such as taking into consideration the perspectives or viewpoints of others and considering the consequences of various behaviors on all persons involved. Spivack and Shure (1974) have demonstrated the effectiveness of instruction in additional problem solving and social reasoning skills.

GUIDELINES FOR PLANNING INSTRUCTION In research and consultant work, we have found that even a well-engineered plan or script can fall flat if delivered to children in lecture style. To achieve an effective communication process between adult and child, the teacher or parent has to have the selected social skill concepts and specific examples for each concept well in mind. The teacher or parent should also avoid the role of judge or disciplinarian, if possible, and strive to assume the role of a guide who is a supportive and knowledgeable adult in how to make friends and get along with others. In social skill instruction sessions, the child's task is to develop skill as a "cognizer," planner, and evaluator of his or her social experiences.

The following is a list of guidelines for preparing for social skill instruction with a child or a peer group.

1. *Select a content focus.* From one or more of the assessments described in previous sections of this paper, select the social skill or skills to be instructed (e.g., cooperation).
2. *Organize the content.* The content should be organized in a consistent fashion. The particular language used to refer to the social skills depends on the developmental level of the children. With younger children, use simpler language and more concrete examples, and some props may help (e.g., puppets, cartoons). With older children, the language used to refer to the social skills can be organized from more abstract and general concepts to ones with more specific behavioral referents or examples (e.g., cooperation—sharing, taking turns).

3. *Prepare for the instruction session.* Thoroughly review what will be said to the child or children ahead of each session. A script may help, but it should be memorized so that it can be presented or delivered in a fluid and conversational manner. A list of social skill examples should be handy for reference during the session. The list may be extended to include the children's appropriate examples given during the session. Focus on one or two social skill concepts may be sufficient for a given session.

4. *Presentation skills.* The skills which are important are basic instructional skills for teaching any content to children. These include knowing how to maintain the children's attention and interest by a positive, well-paced approach and by responding positively and constructively (e.g., "Right," "Okay," "That's one idea, but how about . . . .") to the children's responses. At the same time, basic skills in behavior management (e.g., setting limits for acting-out behavior, see Ginott 1972) are important to ensure that the social skill instruction will not be undermined.

5. *Select activities and participants for peer interaction.* The social skill instruction may be built around normal activities in the classroom (e.g., prior to an art activity), or may include introduction of a new activity or game which the teacher or parent believes has a high likelihood of being a positive experience. (Highly competitive games should be avoided at first.) The selection of particular children who will participate should also be considered (e.g., a friend, several children who rarely interact), or children may wish to select their own playmates or work partners. However, the pairing of two long-standing enemies is not a good peer context in which to try out new behaviors! Finally, social skill instruction may be integrated into a related curricula activity (e.g., reading children's literature, see Moss & Oden 1976).

6. *Prepare for postplay feedback and review.* Feedback should be positive and constructive, and aimed at helping the child to make the associations between language conceptions of social skills and his or her behavioral enactment of these skills. The feedback and review prompts as well as the directions of the teacher or parent may be quite similar to the instructional style often used by a sports coach or a theatrical director (see Strauss 1966). For example, a given child may initiate some action (e.g., offering to share materials) which would be one step in the right direction toward learning cooperation, but off course a bit (e.g., taking up too much space on the art table), and then the child should receive some corrective direction. The child's positive examples and reasoning about a social skill and its application should be confirmed (e.g., "That's right!") and the negative or inappropriate examples should be redirected (e.g., "No, that's not an example of cooperation, but how about taking turns? Is that an example of cooperation?").

The following describes the coaching social skills procedure used in Oden and Asher (1977).

The coach (experimenter) began instruction prior to the second play session for each child. The experimenter instructed the child in a separate space out of view from the play session room and the classroom. The child was first asked how he or she liked the game played the first time and why it was or was not enjoyable. The coach then said, "I have some ideas I'd like to discuss with you about what makes it fun to play a game with another person."

The child received instruction for five to seven minutes on these concepts: *participation* (e.g., getting started, paying attention); *cooperation* (e.g., taking turns, sharing materials); *communication* (e.g., talking with the other person, listening); and *validation-support,* referred to as friendly, fun, and nice (e.g., looking at the other person, giving a smile, offering help or encouragement).

In the first two or three sessions, the coach instructed each of the general concepts separately and in order. In each session, the same key steps were to be followed in sequence for each concept:

Step 1: Suggest concept (e.g., cooperation).
Step 2. Probe child's knowledge of concept and request examples.
Step 3. Repeat and rephrase child's examples which are appropriate to the concept, and disconfirm and redirect the examples which are not appropriate.
Step 4: Probe child's understanding of counter or opposite concepts and examples.
Step 5: Repeat and rephrase child's examples and clarify that these are or are not counter examples of the concept.
Step 6: Probe child's understanding and reasoning of different social consequences of the social behavioral examples and the counter examples for each concept, from the perspective of both the child and the other child or person with whom the child interacts during a game.
Step 7: Check to see if the child remembers one or two examples for each concept. Review each concept and suggest examples which were not mentioned or remembered.
Step 8: Suggest or instruct that the child try some of the instructed "ideas" in the play session to follow immediately.
Step 9: Inform child of the postplay review session which will take place later, and explain that the ideas will be discussed to determine how useful they are for playing with another child.

The following are the social skill concepts and the list of examples.

Participation: get involved;
get started;
pay attention to the game or activity;
try to do your best.
Cooperation: take turns;
share the game or materials;
make a suggestion if we have a problem with the game;
give an alternative if we disagree about the rules.

Communication: talk with the other person;
                    say things about the game or yourself;
                    ask a question about the game;
                    ask a question about the person;
                    listen when the other person talks;
                    look at the other person to see how he's doing.
Friendly-Fun-Nice: give some attention to the other person;
                    say something nice when the other person does well;
                    give a smile sometimes;
                    have fun in the game;
                    offer some help or suggestions;
                    give some encouragement.

The following is an excerpt from the script used to coach the concept of co-operation and some of the typical responses given by children to the coach, quoted from Oden and Asher (1977, p. 500):

Coach: Okay, I have some ideas about what makes a game fun to play with another person. There's a couple of things that are important to do. You should *cooperate* with the other person. Do you know what cooperation is? Can you tell me in your words?

Child: Ahh . . . sharing.

Coach: Yes, sharing. Okay, let's say you and I are playing the game you played last time. What was it again?

Child: Drawing a picture.

Coach: Okay, tell me, then, what would be an example of sharing when playing the picture drawing game?

Child: I'd let you use some pens, too.

Coach: Right. You would share the pens with me. That's an example of cooperation. Now let's say you and I are doing the picture drawing game, can you also give me an example of what would *not* be cooperating?

Child: Taking all the pens.

Coach: Would taking all the pens make the game fun to play?

Child: No!

Coach: So, you wouldn't take all the pens. Instead, you'd *cooperate* by *sharing* them with me. Can you think of some more examples of cooperation? *[The coach waited for a response.]* Okay, how about taking turns. . . Let's say you and I. . . [etc.]. Okay, I'd like you to try out some of these ideas when you play *[name of new game]* with *[other child]*. Let's go and get *[other child]* and after you play I'll talk to you again for a minute or so and you can tell me if these things seem to be good ideas for having fun at a game with someone.

In the 3-5 minute postplay review, the coach asked the child, "Did you get a chance to try out some of the ideas we talked about?" *[The coach waited for a response.]* "Do you think that *[other child]* liked playing the game with you? Let's see, did you *participate,* that is, did you get started," etc.

The child was then escorted back to the classroom and asked if he or she would like to try out another game next time and talk again with the coach about what makes a game fun to play. All children agreed each time.

In the third through fifth coaching sessions, the coaching was geared to the individual child in that only those concepts which the child did not appear to understand and/or remember were coached and reviewed. When the child mastered all the concepts, the coach focused the instruction on classroom play activities and games using the same key steps as outlined earlier: "What are some of the games or activities you could play in the classroom with the other kids? Okay, so what would be an example of *[e.g., participation]* while you were playing *[name of a game]* in the classroom with another child? Okay, maybe you could try out some of these ideas in the classroom during games or activities with other kids. See how they work there too."

In these latter sessions, the coach asked the child if he or she had a chance to try out some of the ideas in the classroom during a game or play activity and how well the ideas seemed to work for making the activity fun or enjoyable for him- or herself and other children.

During the last session, children were thanked for their help in trying out some ideas about what makes a game fun to play with another child.

In applying social skill instruction, it is important not to call undue attention to a child or children. Otherwise, the child may be stigmatized by peers or not feel positive about himself or herself or the instruction. A teacher or parent should plan for full participation of classmates or playmates in the various peer interaction activities provided in the social skill instruction procedure. Every child should also have an opportunity to participate in some discussions with the adult as was done in the social skill instruction sessions.

The feasibility of these social skill instruction procedures may present many practical problems for teachers and parents. In schools, the aid of a coteacher, assistant, counselor, or parent may be especially helpful. Modified versions of the social skill instruction can also be integrated into existing activities or curricula. The generalization of children's social learning may also be increased by alterations in the curriculum or activities of a given setting.

SUMMARY AND CONCLUSION

Children experience social isolation and inclusion from peers throughout development. Some children, however, are quite isolated or unaccepted by peers for interaction and friendship for considerable periods of time. There are numerous and diverse origins of social isolation including a child's personal status characteristics (e.g., physical appearance). Researchers are investigating the problem of the origins and processes of inclusion and isolation among children in various peer group contexts (e.g., group, dyad) and various settings (school, neighborhood). At the same time, children who are isolated have limited opportunities for social growth. Teaching social knowledge and skills may be helpful to these children, especially in a supportive context in which children can interact in a variety of activities. For selecting social learning objectives, assessment methods are available including the sociometric technique, observational methods, and interview procedures. Finally, prevention and intervention methods have been demonstrated. It was recommended that teachers and parents adapt a given procedure according to their children's peer context.

In conclusion, social isolation in childhood is a subject which requires more extensive study, especially given the social issues in schools today (such as the integration of children of diverse characteristics and backgrounds). The subject of social isolation and inclusion may seem to be overly delicate, private, or inappropriate for a major focus in education. Teachers and other professionals often comment that they do not have sufficient knowledge and skill to be helpful when children experience problematic peer relationships. Considering the importance of relationships with peers through a person's development, the social problems of children will require further study.

REFERENCES

Asher, S.R.; Oden, S.L.; & Gottman, J.M. "Children's friendships in school settings." In L.G. Katz (Ed.), *Current topics in early childhood education,* Vol. 1. Norwood, N.J.: Ablex, 1977.

Asher, S.R.; Singleton, L.C.; Tinsley, B.R.; & Hymel, S. A reliable sociometric measure for preschool children. *Developmental Psychology, 15,* 1979, 443-444.

Bandura, A. "Modeling theory: Some traditions, trends, and disputes." In R. Park (Ed.), *Recent trends in social learning theory.* Academic Press, New York: 1972.

Blaney, N.T.; Stephan, C.; Rosenfield, D.; Aronson, E.; & Sikes, J. Interdependence in the classroom; a field study. *Journal of Educational Psychology, 69,* 1977, 121-128.

Bryan, T.H. Peer popularity of learning disabled children: A replication. *Journal of Learning Disabilities, 9,* 1977, 307-311.

Cartledge, G.; & Milburn, J.F. The case for teaching social skills in the classroom: A review. *Review of Educational Research, 48,* 1978, 133-156.

Charlesworth, R.; & Hartup, W.W. Positive social reinforcement in the nursery school peer group. *Child Development, 38,* 1967, 993-1002.

Chittenden, G.F. An experimental study in measuring and modifying assertive behavior in young children. *Monographs of the Society for Research in Child Development,* 1, 7, 1942.

Cowen, E.L. Baby steps toward primary prevention. *American Journal of Community Psychology,* 1, 5, 1977.

Cowen, E.L.; Pederson, A.; Babigian, H.; Izzo, L.D.; & Trost, M.A. Long-term follow-up of early detected vulnerable children. *Journal of Consulting and Clinical Psychology, 41,* 1973, 438-446.

DeVries, D.L.; & Edwards, K.J. Student teams and learning games: Their effects on cross race and cross sex interaction. *Journal of Educational Psychology, 66,* 1974, 741-749.

Dion, K.K. & Berscheid, E. Physical attractiveness and peer acceptance among children. *Sociometry, 37,* 1974, 1-12.

Gardner, W.I. *Children with learning and behavior problems.* Boston: Allyn & Bacon, 1974.

Ginott, H.G. *Teacher and child.* New York: Avon Books, 1972.

Goodman, H.; Gottlieb, J.; & Harrison, R.H. Social acceptance of EMRs integrated into a nongraded elementary school. *American Journal of Mental Deficiency, 76,* 1972, 412-417.

Gottman, J.M. Toward a definition of social isolation in children. *Child Development, 48,* 1977, 513-517.

Gottman, J.M.; Gonso, J.; & Rasmussen, B. Social interaction, social competence, and friendship in children. *Child Development, 46,* 1975, 709-718.

Gottman, J.M.; & Parkhurst, J.T. A development theory of friendship and acquaintanceship processes. In W.A. Collins (Ed.), *Minnesota Symposium on Child Psychology.* Lawrence Erlbaum Assoc., in press.

Gronlund, N.E. *Sociometry in the classroom.* New York: Harper, 1959.

Hallinan, M.T. Friendship patterns in open and traditional classrooms. *Sociology in Education, 49,* 1976, 254-265.

Hallinan, M.T.; & Tuma, N.B. Classroom effects on change in children's friendships. *Sociology of Education, 51,* 1978, 270-282.

Hartup, W.W. Peer interaction and social organization. In P. Mussen (Ed.), *Carmichael's manual of child psychology,* Vol. 2. New York: Wiley, 1970.

Hartup, W.W. "Children and their friends." In H. McGurk (Ed.), *Child Social Development.* London: Methuen, 1978.

Hartup, W.W. "Peer relations and the growth of social competence." In M.W. Kent & J.E. Rolf (Eds.), *The primary prevention of psychopathology. Vol. 3. Promoting Social Competence and Coping in Children.* Hanover, N.H.: University Press of New England, 1979.

Hartup, W.W.; Glazer, J.A.; & Charlesworth, R. Peer reinforcement and sociometric status. *Child Development, 38,* 1967, 1017-1024.

Johnston, A.; Deluca, D.; Murtaugh, K.; & Diener, E. Validation of a laboratory play measure of child aggression. *Child Development, 48,* 1977, 324-327.

Kohn, M.L.; & Clausen, J.A. Social isolation and schizophrenia. *American Sociological Review, 20,* 1955, 265-273.

Ladd, G.W. "Social skills and peer acceptance: Effects of a social learning method for training verbal social skills." A paper presented at the biennial meeting of the Society for Research in Child Development, San Francisco, 1979.

Ladd, G.W.; & Oden, S. The relationship between peer acceptance and children's ideas about helpfulness. *Child Development, 50,* 1979, 402-408.

LaGreca, A.M., & Mesibov, G.B. "Social skills intervention with learning disabled children." Paper presented at the annual meeting of the Midwestern Psychological Association, Chicago, 1979.

Leiberman, A.F. "The social competence of preschool children: Its relation to quality of attachment and to amount of exposure to peers in different preschool settings." Unpublished doctoral dissertation, Johns Hopkins University, 1976.

McCandless, B.R.; & Marshall, H.R. A picture sociometric technique for preschool children and its relation to teacher judgments of friendship. *Child Development, 28,* 1957, 139-148.

McDavid, J.W.; & Harari, H. Stereotyping of names and popularity in grade-school children. *Child Development, 37,* 1966, 453-459.

Moreno, J.L. *Who shall survive? A new approach to the problem of human interrelations.* Washington, D.C.: Neurosis and Mental Disease Publishing, 1934.

Moss, J.; & Oden, S. "Children's books: A resource for reading and social development." Unpublished manuscript, University of Rochester, 1976.

O'Connor, R.D. Modification of social withdrawal through symbolic modeling.

Journal of Applied Behavior Analysis, 2, 1969, 15-22.

Oden, S.; Asher, S.R. Coaching children in social skills for friendship making. *Child Development, 48,* 1977, 495-506.

Piaget, J. *The language and thought of the child.* London: Humanities Press, 1926.

Piaget, J. *Judgment and reasoning in the child.* New York: Harcourt, Brace, 1928.

Richardson, S.A.; Goodman, N.; Hastorf, A.H.; & Dornbusch, S.A. Cultural uniformity in reaction to physical disabilities. *American Sociological Review, 26,* 1961, 241-247.

Roff, M. Childhood social interaction and young adult bad conduct. *Journal of Abnormal and Social Psychology, 63,* 1961, 333-337.

Roff, M.; Sells, B.; & Golden, M.M. *Social adjustment and personality development in children.* Minneapolis: University of Minnesota Press, 1972.

Roistacher, R.C. A microeconomic model of sociometric choice. *Sociometry, 37,* 1974, 219-238.

Rowen, B. *The children we see: An observational approach to child study.* New York: Holt, Rinehart and Winston, 1973.

Sackett, G.P. *Observing behavior,* Vol. 2. Baltimore: University Park Press, 1978.

Schmuck, R.A. Some relationships of peer liking patterns in the classroom to pupil attitudes and achievement. *School Review, 71,* 1963, 337-359.

Selman, R.L. "Toward a structural analysis of developing interpersonal relations concepts: Research with normal and disturbed preadolescent boys." In A.D. Pick (Ed.), *Minnesota Symposium on Child Psychology,* Vol. 10, 1976.

Singleton, L.C., & Asher, S.R. Peer preferences and social interaction among third-grade children in an integrated school district. *Journal of Educational Psychology, 69,* 1977, 330-336.

Singleton, L.C., & Asher, S.R. Social integration and children's peer preferences: An investigation of developmental and cohort differences. *Child Development,* 1979, in press.

Spivack, G., & Shure, M.B. *Social adjustment of young children.* San Francisco: Jossey-Boss, 1974.

Strauss, A. "Coaching." In B.J. Biddle & E.J. Thomas (Eds), *Role theory: Concepts and research.* New York: Wiley, 1966.

Turiel, E. "The development of concepts of social structure: Social convention. In J. Glick & K. Alison Clarke (Eds.), *The Development of Social Understanding.* New York: Gardner Press, 1978.

Wright, H.F. "Observational child study." In Paul H. Mussen (Ed.), *Handbook of research methods in child development.* New York: Wiley, 1960.

Yarrow, L.J. "Interviewing Children." In Paul H. Mussen (Ed.), *Handbook of research methods in child development.* New York: Wiley, 1960.

Zahavi, S.L.; & Asher, S.R. The effect of verbal instructions on preschool children's aggressive behavior. *Journal of School Psychology, 16,* 1978, 146-153.

Chapter 7

Severely Handicapped Children: Social Skills Development Through Leisure Skills Programming

Paul Wehman and Stuart Schleien

The purpose of this chapter is to discuss assessment techniques, instructional procedures, and intervention strategies in leisure skills programming that can be utilized to facilitate social skill development in severely handicapped children. Individualized programs in four recreational program areas (Toy Play, Games, Hobbies, Sports) are also presented in the latter part of the chapter to assist in the acquisition of leisure and social skills. The material presented in this chapter provides the basis for the systematic programming of social development in severely handicapped children. The task analyses presented are not meant to be comprehensive, but, instead, are representative of group-oriented leisure skills which severely handicapped children can master through systematic instruction.

A RATIONALE FOR LEISURE EDUCATION

Abundance of Leisure Time

All too often, severely handicapped persons have not developed the necessary skills to use their free time creatively or constructively. They will participate in an educational program for a small part of their day and have nothing to do during its remainder. Unoccupied time must cease to be the dominant quality of the child's life style. Constructive activities can be offered to the individual to fill this void. The development of nonwork, nonschool related skills must be encouraged and systematically programmed to resolve the critical problem of free time. The child's use of leisure time and his attitude toward recreation may determine the degree of success he will experience through the educational efforts. Constructive use of free time has become a vital aspect of healthy and normal living, especially in these times when leisure time has become increasingly available for all people. For severely handicapped persons, learning leisure-time activities can facilitate the development of interpersonal relationships and social skills.

Means of Teaching Social, Cognitive, and Motor Skills

The development of leisure skills in severely handicapped children will enhance social, cognitive, and gross/fine motor skill development. Involvement in recreational activities offers some of the most effective means for children to acquire and develop these skills.

Social skill development is facilitated through group play. Children who fail to develop the necessary skills to engage in play are considered handicapped. The development of cooperative play behavior and participation in leisure activities will lead to making friends, getting along with others, learning to share, compete, cooperate, take turns, and a generally more satisfactory social adjustment. An adequate social adjustment is required for successful daily living, including time on the job, in the community, and with friends and family.

Recreation is also a vehicle by which gross and fine motor skills are developed. Inactivity usually results in poor eye-hand coordination, cardiovascular endurance, agility, dynamic and static balance, manual dexterity, and muscular strength. Because physical development is essential for a healthy body and self-concept, it is critical that severely handicapped children be given every opportunity to experience play and develop physically.

Constructive play also contributes to cognitive development. During play and creative activity, individuals will communicate with each other and learn concepts related to language, arithmetic, and other forms of learning that foster academic capabilities. Even for the nonverbal individual, vast amounts of facial and bodily communications are facilitated during play, helping to develop cognitive abilities and broadening the range of knowledge and personal involvement of participants.

Systematic Instruction Required for Appropriate Leisure Activity

Without systematic instruction in leisure skills programming, severely handicapped children will not learn the skills necessary to play appropriately. At times, even after the child has acquired the skill, without systematic instructional strategies (e.g., external positive reinforcement), he may never maintain, generalize, or self-initiate the skill into other environments. Besides emphasizing the provision of activities that build on the present capabilities of the youth and prevent further disability, systematic instruction must be provided to foster engagement in appropriate leisure activity. Instruction of this sort may include assessing the leisure skill competencies of the individual, careful selection of materials and skills for instruction, and implementation techniques or specific training methods to assist in the acquisition, maintenance, and generalization of the skills.

Reduction of Inappropriate Social Behaviors

Severely handicapped children (e.g., autistic) often engage in seemingly inappropriate, unacceptable social behavior. Children who are constructively using their leisure time do not exhibit the behaviors (i.e., body rocking, head banging, violent actions, social withdrawal) typically characteristic of these individuals. Research has clearly indicated that there is an inverse relationship between acquisition of play skills and self-stimulated/abusive behavior. Recreational activity of a social nature provides opportunities through which the participant can learn to adjust to the social demands of society.

Acceptance in Community and Reduction of Institutionalization

One of the major goals of any recreation program for severely handicapped persons is to contribute to the individual's ability to function independently in the community. By fostering the child's capability for independent living (e.g., transportation, self-help skills), the need for institutionalization is significantly reduced. Unfortunately, many of these individuals are isolated from peers and the community in general because of untidy appearance, nonacceptable social behavior, and negative attitudes of community members. It is nearly impossible for them to develop any social relationships, and they are typically excluded from normal contacts. Every recreational experience has a contribution to make in social skill development and community living. One of the more effective ways to reduce the attitudinal barriers prevalent within the mainstream of community living is for handicapped children to play with normal peers, allowing all to notice the similarities, not the differences, between them when they play.

PLAY SKILL VARIABLES FOR INITIAL ASSESSMENT

Once a commitment to leisure education has been made, teachers and other practitioners are faced with the following question: Which leisure skills should be selected for instruction? With the large number of leisure skills (games, toys to manipulate, sports, hobbies) available, and the recreation skill deficits characteristic of most severely handicapped children, assessment of these individuals' leisure skill strengths and weaknesses is a process critical to efficient instruction.

Initial assessment will help determine which skills the participant can perform independently and which skills require verbal, gestural, or physical assistance. Unfortunately, we are not aware of any published or unpublished social-leisure skill inventories or criterion-referenced curriculum guides which are sensitive to the unique needs and problems of moderately and severely handicapped persons. Although work is underway in this area (e.g., Wehman, 1979), at this point, it is necessary to use leisure skill inventories designed for higher-functioning individuals or recreation activity guides with activities or skills that have not been task analyzed. In the absence of a comprehensive curriculum guide, the variables listed below highlight important leisure skill areas for functional assessment.

Proficiency of Leisure Skill: Task Analytic Assessment

Although there are a number of areas which can be assessed in a recreation environment, an initial consideration must be: *Does the individual know how to interact with the materials?* Stated another way, when given leisure skill materials, can the participant use them appropriately? If not, then systematic instruction is required.

What is required for evaluating leisure skill proficiency is task analytic assessment (Knapczyk, 1975). An instructional objective must be written for a given material. The objective should reflect the specific skill which the teacher wants the child to learn. An example of a task analytic assessment for playing with a spinning top is provided in table 7.1. This table contains an instructional objective, a task analysis for playing with a top, and the verbal cue provided during the assessment. The recording form indicates that for the first five days of assessment (baseline) the child performed a total of three, three, two, four, and four steps independently. This indicates that instruction should begin at step three in the task analysis.

Table 7.1. Task Analytic Assessment for Playing with a Top

	M	T	W	Th	F
1. S approaches top	+	+	+	+	+
2. S places hands on top	+	+	+	+	+
3. S finds handle of top	+	+	−	+	+
4. S pushes handle down on top once	−	−	−	+	+
5. S brings handle up	−	−	−	−	−
6. S brings handle down on top twice	−	−	−	−	−
7. S brings handle up each time	−	−	−	−	−
8. S brings handle down on top three times	−	−	−	−	−
9. S brings handle up each time	−	−	−	−	−
10. S brings handle down on top four times	−	−	−	−	−
11. S brings handle up each time	−	−	−	−	−
12. S brings handle down on top five times	−	−	−	−	−
13. S brings handle up each time	−	−	−	−	−
14. S stops top from spinning	−	−	−	−	−
15. S puts top away	−	−	−	−	−

There are multiple advantages of this type of observational assessment. First, the information collected about the child on this particular play skill helps the teacher to pinpoint the exact point where instruction should begin. In this way, the child does not receive instruction on skills in which he is already proficient. Secondly, this facilitates step-by-step individualized instruction for children with complex learning problems. Evaluation of the child's proficiency with different toys over an extended period of time will also be more objective, precise, and less subject to teacher bias.

Duration of Activity

As suggested by the findings of Reid, Willis, Jarman, and Brown (1978), if the individual has some degree of proficiency with leisure materials, then the instructional variable of interest may be the duration or length of time the participant engages in activity. This is assessed by recording the length of time devoted to different activities. Since this may be an extremely time-consuming measure to use with several individuals, the teacher may elect to observe only half the participants one day and the other half the next. Another option would be to record activity involvement only twice a week instead of daily.

The length of independent leisure activity is particularly important to assess because of its relevance to most home situations where parents cannot constantly occupy time with their handicapped child. A frequently-heard request from many parents is to teach the child to play independently, thereby relieving the family of continual supervision. A careful assessment of the child's duration of leisure activity before instruction will help the teacher and parents set realistic independent leisure goals for the child. Figure 7.1 presents a sample data collection sheet.

Leisure Skill Object	Minutes/Seconds Engaged with Object	Type of Action
1. Waterpaints		
2. Record player		
3. Plants		
4. Goldfish		
5. Ball		
6. Magazine		
7. Box of Cracker-Jack		
8. Lincoln Logs		
9. Viewfinder		
10. Pinball machine		

Fig. 7.1. Initial object assessment.

Appropriate Versus Inappropriate Object Manipulation

Another assessment issue faced by teachers and researchers is differentiating between appropriate actions with objects versus actions which would not be considered appropriate. Several play studies have failed to address this issue (Burney, Russell & Shores, 1977; Favell & Cannon, 1977; Wehman, 1977). Inappropriate play actions have typically been considered those behaviors which are harmful or destructive to the child, peers, or materials. However, many profoundly retarded and autistic children will exhibit high rates of repetitive self stimulated behavior with toys (e.g., banging, pounding, slamming) that are not necessarily harmful or destructive, yet, still inappropriate. Furthermore, the problem is compounded since, with certain objects, banging or slamming actions may be inappropriate. Many children will do unusual things with toys which *might* be considered appropriate by other observers (Goetz & Baer, 1973).

Hence, teachers are faced with how to assess the qualitative nature of object manipulation. There are several ways of coping with this difficulty. The first one involves using two or three observers periodically, and having these observers rate the appropriateness of the action. Objective judging provides a check and balance system for the teacher. A second method of assessing appropriateness of object manipulation is to identify the principle actions which a nonhandicapped child of comparable mental age might carry out with each object (Fredericks et al. 1978). These actions may serve as guidelines.

Identifying a number of fine-motor categories for object manipulation is yet another means of coding the qualitative nature of responses. This requires generating a fine-motor classification system which observers can use as a basis for recording actions. Tilton and Ottinger (1964) provided nine categories; these are self explanatory and were identified after extensive observational analysis of normal, trainable retarded, and autistic children:

1. Repetitive Manual Manipulation
2. Oral Contacts
3. Pounding
4. Throwing
5. Pushing or Pulling
6. Personalized Toy Use
7. Manipulation of Movable Parts
8. Separation of Parts of Toys
9. Combinational Uses of Toys

Leisure Preference Evaluation

Assessing favorite leisure activities is an important step in initiating a recreation program. The goal in this process is to identify which, if any, activities are preferred by the participant. This is a fairly easy task. By employing duration assessment, the amount of minutes/seconds spent with each leisure material can be recorded. This observation and recording should take place for at least a week.

A second means of assessing leisure preference is through presenting a small number of different materials and determining the amount of time before the participant responds. This is referred to as a *latency* measure of behavior. McCall (1974) has used latency as a measure of length of time which elapsed before infants acted on a variety of objects, each possessing different stimulus attributes such as configural complexity or sound potential. Through measuring passage of time until a response, teachers may be able to evaluate the relative attractiveness of and preferences for certain materials with severely handicapped individuals.

Frequency of Interactions

For many severely handicapped children, an important instructional goal is to initiate and sustain more frequent interactions with peers. A relatively common occurrence may be the presence of several handicapped children all playing in isolation from each other during free play (Fredericks et al., 1978). When this happens, the potential benefits of social interaction are not accrued.

One way of assessing social interaction is a simple count of the number of times one child (1) initiates an interaction, (2) receives an interaction, and (3) terminates interaction. Duration assessment may be used to measure the length of the interaction between peers and also between the child and adults in the room.

A second means of gathering more information on social interactions is the coding of specific types of interactions. Carney and her associates (1977) have detailed the following social interactions skills:

Social Interaction

A. Receives Interaction
   1. Receives hug
   2. Returns smile
   3. Gives object to other who has requested it
   4. Returns a greeting
   5. "Receives" cooperative play
   6. Answers questions
   7. Recognizes peers, teachers by name
   8. Shows approval
   9. Discriminates appropriate time, place, situation before receiving

B. Initiates Interaction
   1. Greets another person
   2. Requests objects from another person
   3. Initiates cooperative play
   4. Seeks approval
   5. Seeks affiliation with familiar person
   6. Helps one who has difficulty manipulating environment
   7. Initiates conversation

C. Sustaining Interactions
   1. Attends to on-going cooperative activity
   2. Sustains conversation

D. Terminates Interactions
   1. Terminates cooperative play activity
   2. Terminates conversation

This sequence provides an important step toward detailing the specific skills which teachers should be attempting to elicit in delayed children. In addition to providing sequence, these skills may be task analyzed and the child's proficiency on selected behaviors assessed. These four categories of interaction can be employed to code the qualitative nature of the interaction (Hamre-Nietupski & Williams, 1977).

Direction of Interaction

Analyzing to whom interactions are directed may also be helpful in assessing which individuals in the play environment are reinforcing to the child. As Beveridge and his colleagues (1978) observed, child-teacher interactions occur more frequently than child-child interactions, especially with severely delayed children. Structured intervention by an adult is usually required to increase child-child interactions (Shores, Hester & Strain, 1976).

When making home visits and observing the child playing with siblings or with neighborhood children, the direction of interactions should be assessed. This should be done not only with handicapped children, but also with nonhandicapped peers. This type of behavioral analysis can be revealing since most nonhandicapped children do not include handicapped children in play unless prompted and reinforced by adults (e.g., Apolloni & Cooke, 1978).

In conducting a behavioral assessment of social interactions, the checklist below might be utilized as a means of coding a number of interactions:

	Initiated Interaction	Received Interaction
Robert		
Wendy		
Martha		
James		

This form, however, would not allow for analyzing the direction of interactions. The checklist below would facilitate assessing which peers or adults the child interacted with:

	Robert	Wendy	Martha	James	Teacher
Robert	x				
Wendy		x			
Martha			x		
James				x	

Free Play Assessment

In some cases, there may be little interest or time to collect the specific types of information which have been discussed above. Some teachers may want to consider using a simpler method of assessing the level of free play at which the child is functioning (Wehman & Merchant, 1978).

The strategy makes use of Parten's (1932) developmental sequence:

Autistic-Unoccupied-Independent-Observing-Attempt-Associative-Cooperative Interaction

With this strategy, the teacher clearly defines the types of behaviors which are characteristic of the different developmental levels of play. For example, in the autistic play stage, characteristic behaviors might include not touching or physically acting on any play materials during free play periods, or nonfunctional repetitive actions for long periods of time. Independent play might be considered as any appropriate play behaviors that were exhibited alone or away from other peers. Cooperative or social play would be another skill level in the basic developmental sequence and would include such skills as physical or verbal interaction with other peers and teachers (Fredericks et al., 1978).

This assessment strategy is convenient and economical in terms of time expended; it can allow for ease in collecting fairly accurate information provided the categories are clearly defined and, therefore, easy to discriminate. This type of behavioral assessment does not, however, capture many of the collateral skills which are clearly associated with play skill development such as fine-motor skills, changes in emotionality, and social behavior.

Programming for Cooperative Play: State of the Art

There have been several studies reported with the severely handicapped which purport to develop cooperative play. While these will be briefly reviewed, it should become readily apparent that these efforts fall far short of the sustained cooperative play which early childhood researchers such as Parten and Newhall (1943), Gesell (1940), and more recently Barnes (1971), have studied.

Whitman and his associates (1970) trained ball-rolling skills between two severely retarded children. Extensive physical guidance and modeling were required before the children performed the skill under the trainer's verbal cues. Generalization was achieved through the phasing in of two other peers and having them enter into the ball rolling game.

A similar study, but with a greater emphasis on comparing the effects of a higher-functioning peer model versus an adult model, has also been carried out with an extremely withdrawn, profoundly retarded boy (Morris &

Dolker, 1974). Ball rolling was also the skill being trained. Results indicated that no significant differences were found between models, and that extensive behavior shaping, e.g. physical guidance, was required in addition to modeling for the behavior to develop.

Somewhat contradictory results were found in another program which included TMR students (Knapczyk & Peterson, 1975). In this study, nonretarded, older children were integrated into the playroom with the TMR children and encouraged to interact through cooperative play. It was discovered that substantially increased rates of cooperative play occurred with the normal models. This was empirically evaluated in a reversal design with the results that, contingent on the removal of these models, cooperative play levels decreased to baseline levels.

A second study carried out by the same investigators was equally revealing. Introduction of nonretarded preschool children of equivalent mental ages but younger chronological ages (three- and four-year olds) led to few changes in cooperative play levels of the same TMR students. Knapczyk and Peterson (1975) interpret these findings as an indication that competence in models when viewed by less competent observers influences the likelihood of behavior being imitated.

A recent study illustrates the potential of arranging the environment in such a way as to promote playful activity (Strain, 1975). In this program, eight severely retarded preschoolers listened while the teacher read stories to them; each child was then given an opportunity to pretend he or she was one of the characters in the story. Immediately after story-telling time was over, the children were encouraged to engage in cooperative play. Evaluation through a reversal design revealed that socio-dramatic story-telling increased the frequency of cooperative play responses.

Imitation has proven to be an effective means of training severely retarded children and adolescents in cooperative play skills. This is further supported in the often cited study by Paloutzian and his colleagues (1971). Imitation training was given to ten severely and profoundly retarded children. With the development of generalized imitation skills, cooperative play behaviors were acquired. Children were trained through modeling to pull peers in wagons, engage in cooperative ball games, and share play materials.

This general strategy of extensive modeling and direct intervention has also been carried out with severely handicapped adolescents and adults (Wehman, 1976). Workshop clients were shaped into different cooperative play experiences by adult trainers with the use of physical guidance.

One of the most comprehensive efforts at analyzing the instructional components of social interaction training can be found in the excellent work by Williams and his associates (Williams, 1975) with TMR students. These workers analyzed social interaction into four components:

- initiates interaction
- receives interaction
- sustains interaction
- terminates interaction

Peer functioning level, task availability, and training across environmental settings are major points considered by these programmers when arranging an appropriate environment for social interaction to occur. Several task analyses for leisure time programs (e.g. use of a Viewmaster, playing "Old Maid") are also presented. What makes this research unique is the explicit instructional direction given for carrying out the program. Also, supportive data is given for each program that was completed by the student.

There are numerous strategies through which the goal of cooperative play and social interaction between two or more peers can be attained. Some of these include:

1. A child can be paired with an adult trainer and trained in different play situations.
2. A child can be paired with a higher functioning, although still retarded, peer who engages in appropriate play (Morris and Dolker, 1974).
3. A child can be paired with a nonretarded peer who engages in appropriate play.
4. Two equivalent (low functioning) peers can be paired and trained by one or more adult trainers (Wehman, 1976).
5. A group of severely handicapped children can be integrated with nonretarded peers (Knapczyk and Peterson, 1975).
6. Any of the previous combinations can be used and different types of reinforcement given, i.e., points, edibles, or praise for instances of cooperative play.
7. Environmental arrangements preceding the onset of play sessions may be manipulated through toy selection, room size, or background music.

These different strategies have yet to be exhaustively examined by programmers or researchers. It is frequently believed by many teachers and recreation professionals that the severely handicapped do not and will not socially interact or play cooperatively. It should be emphasized that verbal language is not required for cooperative play; nonverbal language can be a most efficient means of communication for the severely handicapped, provided training is given. Toys and play materials are excellent vehicles for communication between peers as well as between student and teacher. Many of the institutionalized severely retarded have no desire or reason to communicate after years in a dismal and apathetic ward environment. Stimulating and attractive play materials that are associated with positively reinforcing play sessions can alter this limited incentive to communicate.

LEISURE CURRICULUM
FACILITATING SOCIAL INTERACTION

The balance of this chapter will provide selected individualized programs designed for severely handicapped children. These programs have been adopted from our work on leisure skill curriculum development. We have selected for discussion leisure skills that facilitate social interaction. The skills depicted are representative of the four program areas and are chronologically age appropriate for the preschool (0-6 years) and school aged (7-15 years) child.

Toy Play

Leisure skills falling into this activity grouping are a basic form of recreation/leisure participation. These skills involve interaction with an inanimate object by the participants. The toy and the other player are the focus of each individual's attention. Usually, no rules exist during toy play activity and, therefore, the individuals may design their own activity for use with the toy. With two or more persons, objects are selected to stimulate parallel or cooperative activity, to allow the individuals to express themselves creatively, and to exercise acquired abilities in each phase of development.

PRESCHOOL Matchbox cars are a favorite with preschoolers. These are miniature cars, trucks, and motorcycles with wheels that turn, several with opening doors and hoods. These car models are inexpensive and relatively sturdy. By allowing the players to race their cars, an activity requiring cooperation, social skill development could be significantly enhanced. Besides the enjoyment from racing the cars, participants will gain an interest in collecting and trading them (see fig. 7.2).

SCHOOL AGED A frisbee is a saucer-shaped disc with a radius of 10 to 12 inches. The frisbee has a rounded outer edge which is grooved and curves under for easy grasping. The frisbee could be tossed back and forth in a game, requiring each player to throw and catch it. A frisbee game is an excellent means to teach the participant to share, take turns, listen to others, and cooperate. Several players can participate simultaneously (see fig. 7.3).

Games

Games are recreational activities which involve definite rules allowing for simple to high-functioning levels of participation. They may or may not involve the manipulation of objects or toys. A game may involve cooopera-

NAME OF ACTIVITY: Race Matchbox Cars

Instructional Objective: Given a matchbox car and a second participant with a matchbox car, the participant will race the cars by pushing them forward 24".

Materials: Two matchbox cars

Verbal Cue: "Lucy, race your car."

Task Analysis	Correction Procedures / Activity Guidelines / Special Adaptations
1. Bend knees, lowering rear to ground, assuming squatting position. 2. Extend dominant arm downward toward matchbox car, palm faced down. 3. Lower dominant arm until palm makes contact with top (roof) of matchbox car. 4. Curl fingers around one side of matchbox car. 5. Wrap thumb around other side of matchbox car. 6. Apply inward pressure between thumb and fingers to grasp car firmly. 7. Bend elbow, raising car off ground. 8. Position matchbox car 6" from and parallel with second participant's car (both cars facing forward). 9. On verbal command "Go!", extend elbow outward, applying downward and forward pressure onto car with hand, pushing car forward. 10. When elbow is fully extended, extend fingers and thumb, releasing car, causing car to "race" with second car. 11. Race car 6". 12. Race car 12". 13. Race car 24".	1. Teacher gives verbal cue to participant; if participant responds correctly, teacher provides reinforcement immediately. 2. If participant does not respond correctly, then teacher repeats verbal cue and models correct response. 3. If participant still does not respond correctly, then teacher repeats verbal cue and physically guides participant through correct response. 4. This instructional sequence is repeated several times in each training session with participant. 5. The teacher may need to explain the meaning of the action verbs "go" and "stop" before the race begins. Subsequently, the participant will be able to follow the commands independently. 6. Electric race car and track sets are available which would require a minimum of motor activity to move cars around the track. 7. Weights attached to the bottoms of matchbox cars will keep the participant from throwing the car rather than rolling it.

Fig. 7.2. "Race matchbox cars" activity.

NAME OF ACTIVITY: Catch Frisbee

Instructional Objective: Given a frisbee thrown by another person, the participant will catch the frisbee from 5' away.

Materials: Frisbee

Verbal Cue: "Katy, catch the frisbee."

Task Analysis	Correction Procedures / Activity Guidelines / Special Adaptations
1. Stand 5' away from and facing other player, feet parallel and 6" apart. 2. Extend both arms outward toward other person, palms faced outward, fingers extended. 3. Follow path of frisbee through air. 4. As frisbee approaches, position palms directly parallel with frisbee. 5. When frisbee makes contact with palms, curl fingers inward toward palms until they are resting on top of frisbee, thumbs resting on underside of frisbee. 6. Apply inward pressure between fingers and thumbs to grasp frisbee firmly, catching frisbee.	1. Teacher gives verbal cue to participant; if participant responds correctly, teacher provides reinforcement immediately. 2. If participant does not respond correctly, then teacher repeats verbal cue and models correct response. 3. If participant still does not respond correctly, then teacher repeats verbal cue and physically guides participant through correct response. 4. This instructional sequence is repeated several times in each training session with participant. 5. Participant may practice catching the frisbee when it is slid across the floor to her; with proficiency, begin throwing frisbee through the air from a short distance, gradually increasing the distance from which it is thrown. 6. Some persons may find it easier to catch a larger frisbee, others may find a smaller frisbee easier to catch. Frisbees come in several sizes and weights and should be selected according to individual preference and skill level. 7. Initially, Nerf frisbee could be used to prevent injury and to make it easier to catch.

Fig. 7.3. "Catch frisbee" activity.

tion/competition of participants, and usually involves more than one person. The players must learn to take turns and abide by the rules. The concepts of winning and losing are introduced. However, games are the purest form of recreation in that they are played because the participants enjoy that particular game and appreciate each other's presence, with pleasure being the primary motivating factor. This activity category could include board and table games, social (get acquainted) games, gross motor games, musical/rhythmical games, and card games.

PRESCHOOL London Bridge is a musical game that has been a favorite with children for years. The game is played in a group with two youngsters joining hands and holding them high above their heads to represent a bridge. The other players march around in a circle and underneath the bridge simultaneously with their singing of the song "London Bridge is Falling Down." When the words "My Fair Lady" are sung, the bridge falls on a player. That person then joins the two players to enlarge the bridge. The children will acquire the ability to follow game procedures, work together in forming the bridge and will enjoy singing this popular tune together (see fig. 7.4).

SCHOOL AGED As a chronologically age-appropriate active game for school aged children and older, musical chairs facilitates social development, as all players must march together and attempt to sit in a chair at the same time. Music is played and the children walk in a circle around the chairs (one less chair than number of players) until the music stops. When the music does stop, all players try to sit in the chairs. One person is left standing, and a chair is removed. Players do not have to be eliminated, but could remain seated without removing a chair. Players will learn to cooperate and gain an understanding of win and lose (see fig. 7.5).

Community Activity/Hobbies

Activities and hobbies carried out in the community have potential for contributing to the development of life-long leisure skills. An individual may pursue a community activity or hobby as a youngster and continue to excel in and use those skills with increasing degrees of sophistication throughout his/her lifetime. Participation in community activities and hobbies tends to be less active than in either sports or other physical games and may include such activities as playing a musical instrument in a home rhythm band and a wide variety of arts and crafts activities. Participation in a community activity or hobby is usually of a noncompetitive nature, without the concepts of win and lose. While we would hope that an interest in many of the different leisure skills would certainly develop throughout a person's life-

NAME OF ACTIVITY: London Bridge

Instructional Objective: Given knowledge of the London Bridge song, the participant will sing and continue to walk under the bridge until the bridge falls.

Materials: Five or More Players

Verbal Cue: "Betsy, walk under the bridge."

Task Analysis	Correction Procedures / Activity Guidelines / Special Adaptations
To Build Bridge: 1. Stand facing other player. 2. Keeping arms extended, raise arms upward and outward until palms meet with other player's hands. 3. Interlock hands with other player by curling fingers through spaces of other player's fingers until participant's fingers touch back of other player's hands. 4. Maintain above stance allowing players to pass under bridge until bridge falls down catching one player. **To Catch Player:** 5. Keeping hands clasped with other player, lower arms concurrently as one player is passing directly under bridge, until arms are surrounding caught player at waist. 6. Rock caught player by swaying arms first to one side and then to the other side of caught player's body. 7. Release hand grips by extending fingers and lowering arms toward body to make bridge fall. 8. Caught players become part of bridge until all players have been caught.	1. Teacher gives verbal cue to participant; if participant responds correctly, teacher provides reinforcement immediately. 2. If participant does not respond correctly, then teacher repeats verbal cue and models correct response. 3. If participant still does not respond correctly, then teacher repeats verbal cue and physically guides participant through correct response. 4. This instructional sequence is repeated several times in each training session with participant. 5. This musical game is an excellent facilitator of social skill development as all players must work cooperatively to form bridge. 6. To make game more realistic for participants, the name of the bridge could be changed from London Bridge to another name of a bridge in the player's hometown (e.g., in New York: Brooklyn Bridge). 7. Players unfamiliar with game could be paired with more competent individuals to form bridge. 8. Players should be encouraged to sing along after they have learned the motions of the game. Participants physically unable to play could be singers, therefore, all may be participating in one way or another. 9. Players forming bridge should be encouraged to be gentle when catching a player, making sure not to hit a player's head as the bridge falls.

Fig. 7.4. "London Bridge" activity.

NAME OF ACTIVITY: Musical Chairs

Instructional Objective: Given several participants and one less chair, arranged in a circle with backs of chairs toward inside of circle, and a source of music that can be turned on and off, participants will walk around the chairs to the music, sitting down in a chair when the music stops.

Materials: Record player, record, 5 (or more) participants, 1 less chair than number of players.

Verbal Cue: "Sara, play musical chairs."

Task Analysis	Correction Procedures / Activity Guidelines / Special Adaptations
1. Listen for music to begin. 2. Walk around chairs in clockwise direction as music plays. 3. Sit in closest chair as soon as music stops. 4. Participant who is unable to find vacant chair must leave circle. 5. Remove chair from circle. 6. Continue to play until one participant (winner) is remaining.	1. Teacher gives verbal cue to participant; if participant responds correctly, teacher provides reinforcement immediately. 2. If participant does not respond correctly, then teacher repeats verbal cue and models correct response. 3. If participant still does not respond correctly, then teacher repeats verbal cue and physically guides participant through correct response. 4. This instructional sequence is repeated several times in each training session with participant. 5. Game may be played by non-ambulatory persons by merely outlining areas on floor with tape that participants move to when music stops. 6. A cassette tape player may be used allowing a participant to stop and start the music by merely pressing a button on the deck. 7. Players who have left the game should be encouraged to cheer or otherwise stay involved so as to maintain interest in the game. A player who is "out" can control the music or could remain seated without removing a chair so as not to be eliminated. 8. Players should be encouraged to march with their knees raised high to avoid running around the chairs.

Fig. 7.5. "Musical chairs" activity.

time, the skills in this activity area are typically most enduring for the individual.

PRESCHOOL The ringing of an approaching ice cream truck is one of the most welcomed sounds a child will hear outdoors. The process of buying ice cream from a vendor requires the participant to wait his turn, learn to communicate and interact with others, receive an item from the ice cream man, pay for it, and possibly share it with a friend. All these component skills facilitate social development in some manner and, therefore, are important social skills. Throughout the child's lifetime, he will be expected to take turns, wait in lines, purchase goods, and request assistance from others. Buying ice cream could be an enjoyable way to acquire essential social and daily living skills of relating and responding to others. This activity could be part of a leisure walk program (see fig. 7.6).

SCHOOL AGED Foosball is a table game that cannot be played without actions in which two or more players participate. A minimum of two players is required, thereby arranging a social interaction. The foosball men are moved by manipulation of levers extending from the table, and the game is played like soccer with a goal on each side of the board. In addition to the entertaining aspect of this table game, foosball provides a means to learn the concepts of winning and losing, taking turns, working together, and following rules (see fig. 7.7).

Sports

The distinction between sports and games is often characterized by a time line. Although activities falling in both categories employ a definite set of rules, sports tend to contain greater sophistication in the rules and equipment used, with greater emphasis placed on the competitive aspects of the activity. An individual's leisure skill repertoire should include both individual and team sports requiring various degrees of social and motor coordination. Severely handicapped children are becoming more active in sports nationwide as can be observed by the increased interest in special Olympics and wheelchair sports and games.

PRESCHOOL A see-saw is a piece of recreational equipment found in playgrounds and school yards across the nation. It requires the cooperation of two individuals to raise and lower their ends of the board simultaneously. Participants take turns raising their side of the see-saw off the ground. Several games could be played on the see-saw, as the participants must work cooperatively to gain success. If one player does not cooperate, success will

NAME OF ACTIVITY: Buy Ice Cream from Ice Cream Truck

Instructional Objective: Given an ice cream truck, the participant will purchase ice cream from the vendor.

Materials: Ice cream truck, money

Verbal Cue: "Claudette, buy some ice cream."

Task Analysis	Correction Procedures / Activity Guidelines / Special Adaptations
1. Walk to ice cream truck, holding money in dominant hand using palmar grasp. 2. Stand opposite vendor's window. 3. When asked, name or point to desired ice cream item. 4. Release money onto counter by extending fingers. 5. Grasp ice cream with dominant hand using palmar grasp. 6. Wait for change if appropriate. 7. Walk away from ice cream truck and consume ice cream.	1. Teacher gives verbal cue to participant; if participant responds correctly, teacher provides reinforcement immediately. 2. If participant does not respond correctly, then teacher repeats verbal cue and models correct response. 3. If participant still does not respond correctly, then teacher repeats verbal cue and physically guides participant through correct response. 4. This instructional sequence is repeated several times in each training session with participant. 5. This activity could be simulated in the classroom using a large piece of cardboard as the ice cream truck, and a bell. Pictures of various ice cream items could be painted on the cardboard. Have participants walk up to the window (cut a section out of cardboard) and purchase ice cream using poker chips. A quantity of ice cream cones could be bought and hidden behind the cardboard, so that each participant is reinforced with ice cream during the practice session. 6. The teacher could contact the local ice cream vendor and request a special trip to the playground for the benefit of participants. Perhaps this could become a weekly summer treat for them. 7. Participants will probably learn very quickly to associate the sound of the bell with the approaching ice cream truck.

Fig. 7.6. "Buy ice cream" activity.

NAME OF ACTIVITY: Play Foosball

Instructional Objective: Given a foosball table and another player, the participant will manipulate his two rows of playing men to hit the ball into his opponent's goal to score one point (first player to score 7 points wins the game).

Materials: Foosball table

Verbal Cue: "Tom, play foosball."

Task Analysis	Correction Procedures / Activity Guidelines / Special Adaptations
1. Stand facing levers on side of foosball table. 2. Grasp levers with both hands using palmar grasp. 3. Follow path of ball across table. 4. Position one row of playing men directly in path of ball by either extending or bending at either elbow, pushing or pulling appropriate lever to move row of men laterally across table. 5. When ball makes contact with playing man and has been stopped, quickly rotate either wrist counterclockwise to turn appropriate lever, causing playing man to make contact with ball, hitting ball forward toward opponent's goal. 6. Opponent attempts to block ball. 7. Hit ball into goal, scoring one point. 8. Continue playing until one player scores 7 points to win the game.	1. Teacher gives verbal cue to participant; if participant responds correctly, teacher provides reinforcement immediately. 2. If participant does not respond correctly, then teacher repeats verbal cue and models correct response. 3. If participant still does not respond correctly, then teacher repeats verbal cue and physically guides participant through correct response. 4. This instructional sequence is repeated several times in each training session with participant. 5. Levers can be built up using adhesive tape or sponge to provide a better gripping surface for participant. 6. For participants in wheelchairs, the table can be lowered to a comfortable level and the levers can be elongated by attaching wooden dowels to them. 7. A participant having use of only one hand can still play foosball by using one hand to alternately manipulate the two rows of playing men. 8. Initially, a heavier ball of the same size as the foosball can be used to slow down the pace of the game, making it easier for participants to move the ball around the table. 9. Since all four levers extend outward on both sides of the table, with proficiency, four players can play: two players manipulating two levers on each side of the table.

Fig. 7.7. "Play foosball" activity.

NAME OF ACTIVITY: See-Saw Play

Instructional Objective: Given an 8′ see-saw, the participant will raise and lower the see-saw while sitting on it with another player, 3 consecutive times.

Materials: See-saw

Verbal Cue: "Lisa, ride the see-saw."

Task Analysis	Correction Procedures / Activity Guidelines / Special Adaptations
1. Stand facing left side of see-saw, feet parallel and 6″ apart. 2. Bend knee of right leg, lifting foot over seat of see-saw. 3. Lower rear to see-saw. 4. Lower right foot to ground. 5. Extend arms outward toward handles of see-saw, palms faced down. 6. Lower arms until palms make contact with handle. 7. Curl fingers around handle. 8. Wrap thumbs around opposite side of handle. 9. Apply inward pressure between thumbs and fingers to grasp handle firmly. 10. Extend knees, pushing off from feet, raising see-saw into air. 11. As see-saw descends, lower feet onto ground, bending knees as see-saw touches ground. 12. Go up and down on the see-saw 2nd time. 12. Go up and down on see-saw 3rd time.	1. Teacher gives verbal cue to participant; if participant responds correctly, teacher provides reinforcement immediately. 2. If participant does not respond correctly, then teacher repeats verbal cue and models correct response. 3. If participant still does not respond correctly, then teacher repeats verbal cue and physically guides participant through correct response. 4. This instructional sequence is repeated several times in each training session with participant. 5. If it is believed that the participant cannot hold onto the handle and remain seated when lifted into the air on the see-saw, the teacher may initially sit on the see-saw with the participant. In this way, the danger of participant falling off is diminished and the range of motion is still experienced. 6. Before a conventional playground see-saw is used, a miniature one should be practiced on. A Gym-Dandy space rocker works the same way except that the participants are not raised into the air and the danger of falling to the ground is reduced. This space rocker seats 3 persons (1 in the center), and is an excellent means for participants to learn appropriate see-saw body movements.

Fig. 7.8. "See-saw play" activity.

NAME OF ACTIVITY: Underhand Serve

Instructional Objective: Given a volleyball and a net, the participant will serve the ball over the net in an underhanded fashion from 10' away.

Materials: Volleyball, net

Verbal Cue: "Jessica, serve the ball."

Task Analysis	Correction Procedures / Activity Guidelines / Special Adaptations
1. Stand directly behind ball, feet parallel and 6″ apart.	1. Teacher gives verbal cue to participant; if participant responds correctly, teacher provides reinforcement immediately.
2. Bend knees, lowering rear toward ground.	
3. Extend arms outward toward opposite sides of ball, palms faced inward.	2. If participant does not respond correctly, then teacher repeats verbal cue and models correct response.
4. Move arms inward at shoulders until palms make contact with sides of ball.	3. If participant still does not respond correctly, then teacher repeats verbal cue and physically guides participant through correct response.
5. Apply inward pressure between hands to grasp ball firmly.	
6. Bend elbows, bringing ball to chest.	4. This instructional sequence is repeated several times in each training session with participant.
7. Extend knees, raising body to upright position.	
8. Walk to back right corner of court behind end line and stand facing net 10' away.	5. The underhand serve may be performed with a closed fist or with an open hand (hitting ball with heel of palm). The ball will usually travel further when a fist is used.
9. Rotate both wrists counter-clockwise so that dominant hand is resting on top of ball and nondominant hand is supporting ball on the bottom.	6. Initially, the participant should serve the ball a short distance from the net to assure success. As players progress, continue moving them further back until they are serving from the end line (right corner).
10. Extend fingers of dominant hand releasing ball onto palm of nondominant hand.	
11. Extend elbow of nondominant arm, moving ball outward to front of body.	7. To improve eye-hand coordination and make the task easier, the participant may practice the serving motion with a balloon instead of the standard volleyball. The balloon may not get hit over the net, but it is a good way to practice the proper underhand motion. Also, the balloon is easier to hold in the nondominant hand while hitting with the other hand.
12. Curl fingers of dominant hand inward to palm, making a fist.	
13. Extend elbow of dominant arm, bringing fist downward to side of body.	
14. Quickly bend elbow, raising fist upward and outward to lower half of ball.	
15. Extend elbow, continuing to raise fist upward against ball, hitting it forward, serving ball 2'.	
16. Serve ball 4'.	
17. Serve ball 6'.	
18. Serve ball 8'.	
19. Serve ball 10' over net.	

Fig. 7.9. "Underhand serve" activity.

not be reached. Children learn to trust each other and take turns (see fig. 7.8).

SCHOOL AGED Volleyball is a team sport with six to nine players per team. The object is to hit the ball over the net to the opposing team's side without allowing it to hit the ground. This net game is an excellent facilitator of social skill development since each player is dependent on his teammates to get the ball over the net to the opposite side. Players are required to rotate to the left every time their team wins a serve. In this way, all players get a chance to play each position including the serving position so each player serves in turn. This not-too-strenuous sport facilitates teamwork, cooperative skills, and the reciprocal exchange of positive social behaviors. Volleyball is an excellent way to give a large group a chance to play at the same time (see fig. 7.9)

SUMMARY

The purpose of this chapter has been to discuss the implementation and development of social skills in severely handicapped children. With appropriate assessment techniques, skill selection, instructional strategies and skill adaptations, severely handicapped children will learn to play cooperatively and, as a consequence, develop socially.

A section of this chapter described several types of leisure skill competency areas which can be assessed in severely handicapped children. These included the *proficiency* with which toys, objects, or materials were engaged; the *length* of self-initiated action; materials *preference* by clients; and frequency and direction of social *interactions*.

When these assessment and intervention strategies are used in conjunction with logically sequenced recreation curriculum and instructional technology, the application of the systematic instruction process to leisure skill development is complete.

The latter part of the chapter presented a series of recreational programs that have been task analyzed and specially adapted for implementation with severely handicapped preschoolers and school aged children. The ultimate goal of any recreational program is for the special population individual to develop an age-appropriate leisure skill repertoire in order to use his leisure time constructively and to acquire the necessary social skills that facilitate daily independent living within the community, home, or agency. We have attempted to describe such a program to accomplish this goal.

REFERENCES

Apolloni, T. & Cooke, T. Integrated programming at the infant, toddler, and preschool levels. In M. Guarlanick (Ed.), *Early intervention and the integration of handicapped and nonhandicapped children.* Baltimore: University Park Press, 1978.

Barnes, K. Preschool play, Norms: A replication, *Developmental Psychology 5,* 1971, 99-103.

Beveridge, M.; Spencer, J.; & Miller, P. Language and social behavior in severely educationally subnormal children. *British Journal of Social and Clinical Psychology, 17(1),* 1978, 75-83.

Burney, J.; Russell, B.; & Shores, R. Developing social responses in two profoundly retarded children. *AAESPH Review, 2(2),* 1977, 53-63.

Carney, I,; Clobuciar, A.; Corley, E.; Wilcox, B.; Bigler, J.; Fleisler, L.; Pany, D.; & Turner, P. Social interaction in severely handicapped students. In *The severely and profoundly handicapped child.* Springfield, Ill.: State Department of Education, 1977.

Favell, J. & Cannon, P.R. Evaluation of entertainment materials for severely retarded persons. *American Journal of Mental Deficiency, 81 (4),* 1977, 357-361.

Fredericks, H.D.; Baldwin, V.; Grove, D.; Moore, W.; Riggs, C.; & Lyons, B. Integrating the moderately and severely handicapped preschool child into a normal day care setting. In M. Guarlanick (Ed.), *Early intervention and the integration of handicapped and nonhandicapped children.* Baltimore: University Park Press, 1978.

Gesell, A. *First five years of life,* New York: Harper, 1940.

Goetz, E. & Baer, D. Social control of form diversity and the emergence of new forms in children's blockbuilding. *Journal of Applied Behavior Analysis, 6,* 1973, 209-217.

Hamre-Nietupski, S. & Williams, W.W. Implementation of selected sex education and social skills programs with severely handicapped students. *Education and Training of the Mentally Retarded, 12(4),* 1977, 364-372.

Knapczyk, D. Task analytic assessment of severe learning problems. *Education and Training of the Mentally Retarded, 16,* 1975, 24-27.

Knapczyk, D. & Peterson, N. Task analytic assessment of severe learning problems. *Education of Mentally Retarded, 10,* 1975, 74-77

McCall, R. Exploratory manipulation and play in the human infant. Monograph of Society for Research on Child Development. Chicago, Ill.: University of Chicago Press, 1974.

Morris, R. & Dolker, M. Developing cooperative play in socially withdrawn retarded children. *Mental Retardation, 12(6), 1974,* 24-27.

Paloutzian, R.; Hasazi, J.; Streifel, J.; & Edgard, C.L. Promotion of positive social interactions in severely retarded young children. *American Journal of Mental Deficiency, 75,* 1971, 519-524.

Parten, M.B. Social play among school children. *Journal of Abnormal Psychology, 28,* 1932, 136-147.

Parten, M. & Newhall, S.M. Social behavior of preschool children. In Barker, R.; Kounin, J.; & Wright, H. (Eds.), *Child Behavior and Development.* New York: McGraw-Hill, 1943.

Reid, D.; Willis, B.; Jarman, P.; & Brown, K. Increasing leisure activity of physically disabled retarded persons through modifying resource availability. *AAESPH Review, 3(2),* 1978, 78-93.

Strain, P. Increasing social play of severely retarded preschoolers through social dramatic activities. *Mentally Retarded, 13,* 1975, 7-9.

Shores, R.; Hester, P.; Strain, P.S. The effects of amount and type of teacher-child interaction on child-child interaction during free play. *Psychology in the Schools, 13,* 1976, 171-175.

Tilton J. & Ottinger, D. Comparison of toy play behavior of autistic, retarded and normal children. *Psychological Reports, 15,* 1964, 967-975.

Wehman, P. A leisure time activities curriculum for the developmentally disabled. *Education and Training of the Mentally Retarded, 11,* 1976, 309-313.

Wehman, P. Research on leisure time and the severely developmentally disabled. *Rehabilitation Literature, 38(4),* 1977a, 98-105.

Wehman, P. Toward a recreation curriculum for developmentally disabled persons. In P. Wehman (Ed.), *Recreation programming for developmentally disabled persons.* Baltimore: University Park Press, 1979.

Wehman, P. & Marchant, J. Improving free play skills of severely retarded children. *American Journal of Occupational Therapy, 32(2),* 1978, 100-104.

Whitman, T.; Mercurio, J. & Caponigir, V. Development of social responses in severely retarded children. *Journal of Applied Behavioral Responses, 3,* 1970, 133-138.

Williams, W. Procedures of task analysis as related to developing instructional programs for the severely handicapped. In L. Brown; T. Craivner; W. Williams & R. York (Eds.), *Madison alternatives to zero exclusions: A book readings.* Madison, Wis.: Madison Public Schools, 1975.

Chapter 8

Teaching Cooperation in Early Childhood Settings

Mara Sapon-Shevin

The area of teaching social skills to young children has only recently begun to receive the attention it warrants. There have been major impediments to the recognition that young children's social behavior can be established systematically. First is the assumption by followers of Piaget that the young child is incapable of interpersonal communication because he lacks the ability to take the role of the other child. For example, Flavell (1963) writes that the preoperational child, who is primarily egocentric, "repeatedly demonstrates a relative inability to take the role of the other person, that is, to see his own viewpoint as one of many possible and to try to coordinate it with these others" (p. 156). He goes on to state "The young child is...the unwitting center of his universe. Only his own point of view, *his* schemas, *his* perceptions, etc. can really figure in his various activities, since he is unaware that others see things differently, i.e., that there are points of view of which his is only one" (p. 274). This assumption has, to many, implied that systematic teaching of interpersonal social skills to young children represents a fruitless endeavor.

A second major impediment has been the global way in which early childhood curriculum goals and objectives are stated.

Goals are vague: "educating the whole child," "providing for emotional and social growth," "developing a feeling of self worth," "providing the child-oriented curriculum" and "developing creativity and independence" are phrases often cited by early children educators as objectives for preschool, day care, or nursery school programs. Although these are all important educational goals, they do not clarify the instructional tasks ahead for the teacher (Lillie, 1975, p. 21).

229

Even when social learning milestones are elaborated more fully, these descriptions are often viewed as checklists for achievement (i.e., the teacher marks off those children who have attained a specific level or criterion) as opposed to being viewed as teaching goals or objectives for which the teacher accepts the responsibility. Although some early childhood guides list the social skills which children are expected to master; i.e., "The child participates in group activities without dominating the group" (Broman, 1978, p. 242); "the child is willing to help others; the child interacts with a number of different children each day"; the provision of specific strategies for reaching these goals is less common.

Fortunately, these impediments are being removed. The "egocentric child" concept has been effectively challenged recently (Cairns, 1979). Garvey and Hogan (1973) conducted studies which showed that children in the age range 3½ to 5 spend considerable time in social interaction and much of that interaction involves talking. Yarrow and Waxler (1977) conducted a study on prosocial behaviors in very young children, particularly in response to the discomfort or pain expressed by someone else in the environment. They report:

While in the youngest children others' crying tended to elicit contagious crying as well as amusement, crying began to decrease, and as it waned, it was replaced by serious or worried attending. Around one year most of the youngest cohort first showed comfort to a person crying or in pain by patting, hugging, or presenting an object. Among 1½ and 2 years old comforting was sometimes sophisticated and elaborate, e.g., fixing the hurt by trying to put a Band-aid on, covering mother with a blanket when she is resting, trying to locate the source of the difficulty. Children also began to express concern verbally, and sometimes gave suggestions about how to deal with the problem. Such precocity on the part of the very young gives one pause. The capabilities for compassion, for various kinds of reaching out to others in a giving sense are viable and effective responses early in life. How such behaviors develop and change in the process of socialization in various cultures and subcultures are issues to which science has addressed little investigation. [P. 79]

Cross-cultural studies further support the hypothesis that even very young children are capable of empathic responses to other individuals. Borke (1973) studied children in both America and China and found that "Chinese and American children by 3 to 3.5 years of age were able to differentiate easily between social situations which evoke happy and unhappy responses in other people. These results... provide further evidence that the capacity for social sensitivity and empathic awareness develops at a very early age" (p. 107).

The crumbling of previously-accepted notions of fixed developmental stages has been accompanied by growing data to support the crucial role played by teachers and by the general social environment in establishing and maintaining social behaviors in children. Smith, Neisworth, and Greer (1978) state: "Teachers are all too quick to assume that a child's inappropriate behaviors must be the result of problems at home or due to immaturity. Teachers need to realize that these behaviors are, at least partially, a consequence of their own actions'' (p. 84).

Much of the early work which focused on children's social behavior concerned itself with the factors that generate and maintain aggressive behavior in children. Bandura and Walters (1963) pointed out the need for a close examination of aggression and its relation to the environment. Subsequent experimentation confirmed the notion that it was, indeed, possible to shape aggressive behavior in children. In an experiment by Walters and Brown (1963), the following hypothesis was tested: ''Children rewarded for hitting responses in an impersonal play situation subsequently show more interpersonal physical aggression than children who have not been rewarded'' (p. 564). An experiment was carried out in which seven-year old boys played with a toy doll that dispensed marbles and lit up when punched. In subsequent game-playing activity, these boys showed more physical aggression than those who had not experienced the training session.

A study by Wahler (1967) addressed the possibilities of strengthening and weakening different kinds of play behavior (aggressive play, solitary play, cooperative play) through the use of contingent peer attention. This study confirmed the notion that social behavior could be brought under the control of the social environment; and, more important, the other children in the classroom situation represented part of the social environment and could, therefore, be seen to be controlling properties of children's social behavior.

A study by Allen and his colleagues (1965) established that social reinforcement (in this case, teacher praise and attention) could bring about prominent changes in the social behavior of an ''isolated'' nursery school child. In this study, the teacher presented systematic attention to the child whenever she interacted with other children. This was followed by a marked increase in the amount of time this child spent interacting with other children.

In a further attempt to assess relevant aspects of the environment, particularly in terms of their potential for providing the occasion for different types of social behavior, Quilitch and Risley (1973) undertook a study in which the role of different kinds of toys in affecting social behavior was assessed. This experiment established that: ''The type of toys given to children within a free-play setting had a pronounced and dramatic effect on their social play and the amount of time spent playing cooperatively with each other'' (p. 577). Quilitch and Risley concluded their study with the following recommendations:

Schools and child-care centers can now take charge to maximize children's opportunity to practice social and cooperative play behaviors. This social training, traditionally left to chance, could be planned so that all children have the maximum possible opportunity to develop their social skills. . . . Play materials that set the occasion for aggressive play, verbal behavior, sharing behavior or competition might be used with groups of children suffering certain behavioral play deficits. . . . Thus, the study of the effects of toys upon children's social behaviors allows the applied psychologist to create developmental or therapeutic play environments that promote social behaviors previously found amenable only to individual remediation programs. [Pp. 577-78]

The Quilitch and Risley article is important in that it identifies activities (such as games and toys) as part of the environment which can affect social behaviors.

The studies quoted above established experimentally the possibility of shaping certain social behaviors in children through systematic reinforcement procedures. Various programs have been developed to assist the parent, teacher, or therapist in applying these principles to the socialization of young children in natural settings (Becker, 1971; Patterson & Gullion, 1976; Sheppard, Shank & Wilson, 1972).

TEACHING COOPERATION

Although there are clearly numerous areas in social development that could benefit from systematic analysis and subsequent teaching programs, this chapter will focus on two sets of teaching procedures, i.e., the use of games and literature, to assist in the establishment of cooperative social interaction in young children. The focus on cooperation is perceived as significant, as the absence of such positive social interaction is a common problem for teachers of young children. Both those children who engage primarily in "isolate" play and those whose social interaction is characterized by aggressive and/or competitive features present important targets for the systematic establishment of a broad range of social skills loosely labeled as "cooperation."

Problems of aggression often confront teachers of young children in educational settings, and considerable research attention has been focused on the origins and control of aggressive behavior. Many common assumptions about aggression center on its innateness as a biological trait, including the Freudian notion that aggression inevitably dominates over personal and communal activity. Lorenz (1966) contends that aggression represents an instinctive biological disposition.

Recent research, however, has questioned some of these underlying assumptions and has provided information which describes aggression in ways more compatible with the development of systematic strategies for decreasing aggressive behavior and with teaching more socially desirable responses to conflict situations. Sears and his associates (1953) and Eron and his associates (1963) report positive correlations between the amount of physical punishment a child receives at home and the amount of aggressive behavior children display in school. In other words, children who are themselves punished tend to punish other children. Caldwell (1978), in an article entitled "Aggression and Hostility in Young Children," reviews relevant research in the area and makes the following suggestions: (1) Physical punishment of aggression is not the answer; (2) ignoring aggression in children is not the answer; and (3) nonpermissiveness in our attitudes toward aggression may be as important as punishment for aggressiveness. These suggestions are supported by Sears, Maccoby, and Levin (1957) who state:

"...the way for parents to produce a nonaggressive child is to make abundantly clear that aggression is frowned upon, and to stop aggression when it occurs, but to avoid punishing the child for his aggression." [P. 766]

Recent observations made by educators of nursery and day care settings in China have also cast doubt on the presumption that aggression in young children is inevitable and to be expected. Kessen (1976) reports in *Childhood in China:*

The children were generally docile and conforming, displaying little of the restlessness, rough and tumble play, grabbing of property, or the pushing and striking of peers that are common in American homes and nursery schools.   [P. 56]

Sidel (1976) reports a similar observation:

What is so amazing, of course, in walking the streets of Peking or Shanghai, or visiting a commune or urban neighborhood, is that we never saw aggression among the children. No doubt it exists, but we never witnessed it.   [P. 114]

And Greene (1962) shares his experience:

I have spent a lot of time watching children playing on the streets—little tots all on their own. ...They never fight! *Why* don't they? They never snatch—never 'That's mine!'...They not only never fight, but they *never* cry. The only child I have heard crying was one who was physically hurt.   [P. 54]

In analyzing these findings, and contrasting them with a much higher rate of aggressive behaviors found among Kibbutz-raised children in Israel, Sidel (1976) comments:

Part of the reason for this difference might stem from acceptance on the part of those who live in the Kibbutz of Freudian psychology and of aggression as a natural component of man, possibly one which is better acted out than repressed. The Chinese, of course, do not study Freud and those who are aware of his teachings do not believe they are relevant to their setting. That the Chinese do not believe that aggression is necessarily inevitable seems evident.   [P. 168]

The psychoanalytic approach to aggression control has been that of catharsis or purging of aggressive activity. Many still advise that children and adults need to express their anger and hostility openly in order to remain psychologically "healthy" (Caldwell, 1978). Others however, consider this position highly questionable. Berkowitz (1973) after reviewing the literature on controlling aggression in children concludes:

He [the child] should not be encouraged to attack someone to express his hostility in the hope that he will drain some hypothetical energy reservoir. The catharsis notion is an outmoded theoretical conception lacking adequate empirical support which also has potentially dangerous social implications. Violence ultimately produces more violence.   [P. 135]

Other studies have also indicated that exposure to aggression may stimulate and increase aggression rather than reduce it (Cohen, 1976).

Environmental Structure

What, then, can teachers do to decrease aggression and promote positive social interactions? A look at the practices of nursery and day care settings in China provides some valuable insights into the role of environmental expectations and structure in developing cooperation. Many observers of the Chinese nurseries commented that "the gentleness and control of the children bear resemblance to the gentleness and control of their teachers" (Kessen, 1976, p. 70). Aggressive behavior in children was dealt with by what the teacher described as "gentle persuasion." An interesting contrast between American and Chinese nurseries was the relative lack of toys in the Chinese schools. The American visitors who questioned the sparse furnishings were told that the lack of toys was by design—specifically to *promote* sharing and cooperation. This position clearly contrasts with standard advice to provide plenty of toys so children will not squabble over them. Similarly, Chinese children wear jackets which button up the back, again requiring the help and interaction of other children. When children fell and hurt themselves on the playground, the Chinese children were encouraged by their teachers to give immediate aid and solace. Children identified as "naughty" were given responsibility for teaching "slower" children in order to channel what was perceived by the Chinese teachers as an excess of energy or activity. The Chinese children also engaged in specific role play of appropriate social behaviors; they presented musical-dance numbers in which some of our common assumptions about young children are violated:

Clearly very young children *are* capable of prolonged periods of cooperative, mutually-supportive activity.

Cooperative Games

Cooperation is not simply a "mind set" or an inclination. Rather, there are very specific skills and strategies that children need to be taught in order to cooperate successfully. These skills include: listening to one another, coordinating their movements and energies with other children, and engaging in those social behaviors that will facilitate and prolong interaction with those other children involved in the play situation. In other words, children need repertoires that will keep other children interacting with them rather than driving other children away.

Although there are numerous such "facilitative" skills that could be identified, for the purposes of elaboration here, four specific such behaviors can be identified as teaching objectives for social interaction:

1. Talking nicely to classmates: calling classmates only by names they like, noticing and commenting on classmates' strengths rather than weaknesses.
2. Sharing and taking turns.
3. Including children who have been left out; opening one's games or activities to others, finding a part for another child to play.
4. Touching other children gently; helping other children who have fallen down or who are experiencing difficulty.

One strategy for establishing cooperative behaviors is through the use of games, especially those that stress cooperation rather than competition. As discussed in chapter 3, games are a way of providing children with "fun"; games represent activities chosen because of their appeal to children and/or their general acceptance as a standard part of early childhood programming. Games, however, can be examined as ways of structuring the environment for a brief period of time according to very specific "rules." During the game, children can be observed to engage in specific social interactions—touching each other in various ways, repeating set words or phrases, choosing and/or excluding other children, and so forth.

Competitive situations are those in which children work against one another, thus producing losers as well as winners, and often many losers and only one winner. In cooperative situations, the obstacle to be overcome is not another player, but rather the inherent difficulty of the task itself or some external obstacle, such as time. For example, two children attempting to build a tall tower of 12 blocks are confronting the obstacles of gravity and balance; if they succeed, they have triumphed over these obstacles rather than over each other.

Since not all games are of equal value in teaching appropriate social skills, teachers who are seeking consistency in the models they present to children and in the behaviors in which children engage during school-time will want to seek out games that will help strengthen, rather than contradict, the establishment of certain social behaviors. Many teachers already have extensive repertoires of cooperative activities, but may not refer to them as "games." To many people, a game must be, by definition, a competitive activity in which there are winners and losers. Even children become socialized at a very young age to consider only certain kinds of activities to be "games." A seven-year old, after watching a group of four-year olds play a cooperative game, exclaimed to this author: "Hey, that's not fair, that's an everybody wins game; somebody's gotta lose." For this reason, early childhood educational settings represent ideal locations for teaching children that "fun" does not have to mean one winner only, and that "winning" need not necessarily be the desirable or only objective of an activity.

The following game activities have been identified as ones that structure positive social interaction between children, with particular reference to the four key areas outlined earlier: talking nicely, sharing, including or involving others, and gentle physical contact. Each game is described with its components, and the social behaviors inherent in them. The games all fit into one or more of the categories, although there is considerable overlap and crossover between the games.

Including Others/Sharing

Cooperative Tale [Arnold, 1972]
   One player starts a story and each player adds a little piece to the story, moving around the circle.

Because [Arnold, 1972]
   The first player describes an event, the second player must give a reason for the occurrence of that event, and the third player must give a probable effect of that event such as: "The toast burned"; "Because the toaster was too hot"; "So everyone had charcoal for breakfast."

   Social Behaviors: Listening to others; taking turns; coordinating one's efforts with those of other children;

   Notes/Suggestions: These games require the systematic inclusion of many children. Children less able may be given prompts or help by the adult or by other children, but may still participate in the activity.

Cooperative Shapes, Numbers, or Letters [Orlick, 1978]
   Groups of children are asked to use their bodies to form various shapes (circle, square) letters or numbers.

Social Behaviors: Gentle physical contact; inclusion; problem solving.

Notes/Suggestions: In order for this activity to be successful, children must find a way to decide collectively how to form the shape/letter *and* how to use all of the children. This can be seen as a crucial antecedent to subsequent discussions of "What part can you find for Johnny to play?" or "How can Susie be part of this game?"

Musical Laps [Harrison, 1976]

This is a cooperative version of Musical Chairs. The whole group forms a circle all facing in one direction, close together, each with hands on the waist of the person ahead. When the music starts, everyone begins to walk forward. When the music stops, everyone sits down in the lap of the child to the rear. If the whole group succeeds in sitting in laps without falling to the floor, the *group* wins. If children fall down, gravity wins. Works best with more than ten children about the same size.

Non-Elimination Musical Chairs [Orlick, 1978]

The object is to keep everyone in the game even though chairs are systematically removed. As in the competitive version, music is played, and more and more chairs are removed each time the music stops. In this game, though, more children have to sit together to keep everyone in the game.

Social Behaviors: Gentle physical contact; sharing inclusion; group problem solving.

Notes/Suggestions: These two games are unique in that they represent crucially different alternatives to traditional musical chairs in which pushing, shoving, and grabbling lead to success. In Musical Laps, the obstacle is gravity; this game is ideal because it rarely works the first time, as children tend to stand too far apart. When everyone falls down the group must then engage in problem-solving, i.e. "What can we try to make it work?" Young children playing this game have been observed engaging in elaborate planning and hypothesis-testing. When the group finally succeeds, there is general rejoicing. An additional positive feature of this game is the fact that when the group collapses, it cannot be identified as "Billy's fault" but, because many children fall, is usually seen as a failure of the group.

In Non-Elimination Musical Chairs, rather than the pushing and exclusionary tactics of traditional Musical Chairs, children must find ways to make room for more and more children. The verbal behavior heard during this game is generally of the form — "come sit on/with me" or "Make room for Johnny."

This game represents an ideal starting point for exploring issues of "limited resources" with children; rather than confirming the "each child must have his own material" notion, teachers can explore ways in which children can find creative alternatives to exclusion. For example, on the playground, if more than two children want to use the see-saw, what ways could that be done? (For example, two children on each end; two children counting, while two see-saw then switching places, etc.)

Barnyard [Harrison, 1976]

People stand in a large circle, choose six animals (less for a group smaller than 20) and count off by animals. Then, with everyone's eyes closed, each person finds all the others of his or her kind by constantly calling the animal sounds, "Baa-a-a," "Meow, meow," etc. When two of the same animals come across each other, they hold hands and find others until they are all together. It is a very funny game.
Note: The idea is not to finish first, but merely to find your own kind.

Social Behaviors: Gentle touching; inclusion; listening.

Notes/Suggestions: This game can be used as a way of structuring interaction between *specific* children. For example, by naming Billy and Sam (who don't generally interact) both "Horses," the adult insures that the two boys will "find each other" and become a part of the same group. Animals can also be assigned in such a way as to pair an out-going active child (who can be predicted to participate freely) with a withdrawn or quiet child who seldom participates, thus insuring the involvement of *both* children.

Magic Carpet [Orlick, 1978]

A group of about seven children take turns giving each other magic carpet rides on a gym mat. With kindergarten children, the middle person's "ride" can consist of getting "jiggled" around in one spot, which they all seem to enjoy. In some cases, the "carpet" is pulled steadily to the other side of the gym, with the middle person lying, sitting, or crouching on the mat. The rider can choose the riding position and can control the speed ("slower," "faster," "just right"). In the beginning, a rotation for taking turns could be suggested or it can occur spontaneously, depending on the group.

Big Turtle [Orlick, 1978]

A group of about seven or eight children get on their hands and knees under a large "turtle shell" and try to make the turtle move in one direction. A gym mat works fine as a shell; use your imagination for other materials, such as a large sheet of cardboard or plastic, or a blanket, tarpaulin, or mattress.

Big Snake [Orlick, 1978]

The children start by stretching out on their stomachs and holding the ankles of the person in front of them to make a two-people snake that slithers across the floor on its belly. They soon connect up for a four-people snake, an eight-people snake, and so on, until the child group is one Big Snake. At various lengths, the children like to see if they can turn the whole snake over on his back without coming apart. The snake can also go over "mountains" through "holes" or up "trees," or may curl up and go to sleep. It takes a coordinated snake to do these last two feats.

Social Behaviors: Taking turns; coordinating movements; following requests; sharing limited materials; communicating and taking cues from other children; gentle physical contact.

Notes/Suggestions: These three activities are all ones in which children must work together to accomplish a given task. They also involve situations which attempt to include a varying number of children and to use the bodies/energies of all of the children.

After children have successfully played these games, teachers can refer back to them as examples when situations arise which require the cooperation and/or collaboration of numerous children. "Remember how you all worked together to make the big turtle move in the same direction?" Each of these games also presents a situation in which the direction to move must give way to the wishes of others for this activity to succeed. This fact can be used as a discussion starter for an exploration of:

1) Who decided what to do?
2) How could you tell that person what *you* wanted to do?
3) Could you decide together? If not, how did you take turns deciding?
4) How did you feel about being the one to decide about going along with the others' idea?

Helping Others

Frozen Bean Bag [Orlick, 1978]
(Help Your Friends)

This is an active game of helping. All the children begin by moving around the area at their own pace, each balancing a bean bag on his head. The leader can change the action or pace by asking the children to try to skip, hop, go backwards, go slower, go faster, etc. If the bean bag falls off a child's head, he or she is frozen. Another child must then pick up the bean bag and place it back on the frozen player's head to free him, without losing his own bean bag. The object of the game is to help your friends by keeping them unfrozen. At the end of the game the children can be asked how many times they were helped or helped others. If desired, a quick count of helping acts can be taken.

Social Behaviors: Being attentive to and finding those who need help; providing assistance; gentle physical contact; insuring the continued participation of all children.

Notes/Suggestions: This game serves as an introduction to several crucial concepts:
a. How can one tell when someone needs help?
b. What are some ways of helping?
c. How does one respond *after* he has been helped?

Following this game, the teacher might introduce role play situations in which one child is working or playing at some activity and somehow gets "stuck"; children can then brainstorm ways of helping that child continue, i.e., help him find his missing puzzle piece, help him carry over a stool so he can reach the top of his building, etc.

Hot or Cold [Arnold, 1972]

An object is hidden while one player, chosen to be "it" is not in the room. He is then brought back and asked to find it. Other players tell him when he is "hot" or "cold" depending on whether he is approaching or going away from the place where the object is hidden. When the player has found the object, he then takes his turn at hiding it and joins the rest in directing the next player. This game can also be played by having children clap (loudly for "near," or softer for "far") to guide another child to a hidden object.

Social Behaviors: Following directions, giving directions accurately.

Notes/Suggestions: Unlike many activities that involve an "it" player, in this game all of the individuals are engaged in a facilitative activity for that "it" player, i.e., they are all working directly for his/her success. Games of this type represent the epitome in cooperation: the success of the individual and the success of the group are not only compatible, but one is the function of the other. All of the players are working for the success of one child.

Gentle Physical Contact

Knots [Harrison, 1976]

Everyone closes eyes and moves together, each child taking a different child's hand in each of his or her hands. When each child has two hands, then all open their eyes and try to untangle themselves without dropping hands. The group must work together to get out the knots. It leads to very amusing situations because, although the group may end up in one big circle, most of the time there will be a knot or two in the circle, and even two or more circles, either intertwined or separate.

Mile of Yarn [Orlick, 1978]

This is an interesting way to "knit" young children together. One child starts with a bright ball of thick yarn (or a strip of material), wraps the end of the yarn around her waist, and passes the ball to another child. He wraps it around his waist, and passes it to another child, and so on. Once the whole group has been intertwined in yarn, the whole process is reversed. The last player begins to rewind the ball, passes it to the next child, and so on until the fully wound ball reaches the first child.

Touch Blue [Harrison, 1976]

The leader announces, "Everyone touch blue!" (or another color, object, etc.). Participants must touch something on another person. "Touch a sandal!" or "Touch a bracelet!" ensures physical contact. There are endless variations, such as "Touch a knee with your left thumb!"

Ha Ha [Harrison, 1976]

Lots of floor space needed, or a lawn under a warm sun. Someone lies down and the next child lies down putting his or her head on the stomach of the first child. The third child puts his or her head on the stomach of the second child, and so on. Then the first child says HA! Second child HA HA! Third child HA HA HA! and so on, increasing the number of HA's. The laughter is infectious.

Social Behaviors: Group problem solving; gentle physical contact.

Notes/Suggestions: Many children have experienced few opportunities to engage in activities in which they touch other children in gentle, nonaggressive ways. While gentle physical contact is not in and of itself a sufficient antecedent for cooperation, it does establish relationships between children which are more likely to lead to continuing physical proximity and social interaction. Adults use these games to introduce the ideas of making people feel better by touching them. Children who observe that another child looks sad or is crying can be encouraged to offer hugs, touching, and other physical contact, *already* a part of their repertoire from the game situation. For many children for whom touching is not encouraged at home, particularly boys, games provide a safe, structured way of insuring contact.

Talking Nicely

Make Me Laugh

Participants get in a circle. In turn, each child turns to the child on his/her left and attempts to say or do something which will make that child smile or laugh. This can be done by saying something funny or complimentary to the other child, by making a funny face or by any other means suggested by the teacher.

Social Behaviors: Saying nice things to someone; problem solving.

Notes/Suggestions: This activity is useful because it represents a systematic effort to teach children how to work at making each other happy. Many children already possess elaborate rituals for making other children (especially specific other children) miserable. This activity can also be viewed as a link to the procedures described by Spivack and Shure (1974) relative to problem solving around the question "How could he make Billy happy?"

Introductory Name Game [Prutzman et al., 1977]

Have children sit in a circle to foster group feeling and to allow everyone to see and pay attention to the child speaking. Ask a simple, interesting question. "What is your favorite dessert?" or "What is a game you enjoy?" or "What is your favorite soup?" Go around the circle and have everyone say his or her name and answer the questions. Children can then be asked what they remember about each child, i.e. "What is Billy's favorite toy?" Participation should be voluntary. Some children may choose not to answer the question.

The Affirmation Interview [Prutzman et al., 1977]

An activity for a large group where one child is interviewed and given special attention in front of the whole group. The questions should be simple, nonthreatening, and interesting enough to hold the attention of those listening. Some examples are:

1. What is your favorite sandwich?
2. What place would you like to visit?
3. What is something you enjoy doing? on Saturday morning? after school?
4. What good movie have you seen lately?

The interviewer should look directly at the child being interviewed, and ask questions that seem appropriate to that child. The interviewer should be very positive, praising the interviewee as much as possible. Also, only one or two children should be interviewed in one time block so that everyone is able to enjoy an equal amount of attention from those listening.

Social Behaviors: Asking and answering questions; listening to others; taking turns.

Notes/Suggestions: These activities can be easily adapted to the age and maturity levels of the children involved. They represent systematic ways for teaching children to "make conversation" and to say nice things about each other.

All of the preceding activities represent systematic ways for structuring positive social interactions between children, using games as a starting point. Because young children are likely to respond positively to the suggestion "Let's play a game!", teachers can use these opportunities to have children interact in cooperative (and perhaps novel) ways. The fact of playing a game that incorporates cooperative behaviors such as including others or sharing may not, however, insure that children will generalize those behaviors into other situations. The teacher will need to follow the games with other activities that help the child to develop an awareness of the process in which he was engaging and ways in which the game behaviors apply to other parts of his life. The teacher may want to conduct discussions after the game, asking children to remember what happened, why the game turned out well or poorly, what could have been improved, and pointing out the specific positive behaviors that occurred. The children can also be helped to identify other situations where those behaviors are appropriate, for example, following the *Frozen Bean Bag* game with a discussion of ways we help others at school, at home, on the playground, etc. Helping others could then be used as a theme over a period of one to two weeks during which "helping others" projects could be generated. The teacher can use the games as a basis for problem solving and role playing similar real-life situations, i.e., "We have fifteen children and only ten packages of crayons, what can we do?"or "Mary and Elaine are playing hospital, and Karen wants to join them—what part could she have?" Having children engage in cooperative play activities can help teachers to establish a consistency in their classroom regarding *what* solutions are considered acceptable and *how* these solutions can be reached.

Teachers should exercise caution in the games they select to play with young children, as a careful analysis reveals that many games provide the occasion for social interactions that are considered undesirable in other (nongame) settings and that often contradict the social behavior likely to be proposed by a teacher at other times in the school day. For example, "Simon Says," although ostensibly a game to teach listening and discrimination skills, when examined from a viewpoint of what actually happens during the game, also provides the opportunity for one child to cause other children's elimination from the game through attempts to mislead or trick. Teachers who have worked hard to establish positive social relationships among children in their classrooms may find a need to look critically at the games.

In a previous study (Sapon-Shevin, 1976) this author examined several hundred children's games in terms of the social behaviors initiated by the games and found many that provided the occasion for the display of a wide range of social behaviors generally considered undesirable. For example:

1. *Taunting/teasing:* Children are required to call another player a name or to repeat in chant-like fashion some mocking refrain (Examples: *Lame Wolf, King of the Castle*).
2. *Grabbing or snatching in scarcity situations:* A situation is presented in which there are more children than there are objects (chairs, clubs, etc.) and children who are able to secure one may remain in the game while other children are eliminated (Examples: *Musical Chairs, Steal the Bacon*).
3. *Monopolizing or excluding other children:* A situation is organized such that some children are in control (of a ball or a situation) and use their energy to keep other children from participating (Examples: *Keep Away* or circle games in which children try to keep other children from breaking through the circle).
4. *Physical force:* Situations in which children are asked to hit another player with a ball, pull another player across a line, slap another child with one's own hands or with a ruler, or push another child out of the circle (Examples: *Spud, Tag Ball, King of the Castle*).

Inasmuch as such game behaviors can be viewed as incompatible with the establishment of the desirable social skills identified earlier, teachers must carefully analyze the behavioral components of the games they select.

Children's Literature

Another potential source for teaching children cooperative skills is the use of children's books. Because most children enjoy story time and because many early childhood educators already include a story in their daily activities, the use of children's books in this regard can be easily incorporated into many ongoing programs.

Streibel (1977) reviewed recent children's books in an effort to see how these books handled the time of conflict resolution and to explore the potential of using children's books to teach alternatives to "fighting." She presents the following goals and guidelines for analyzing and evaluating young children's books:

Problem solving/Conflict resolution—The goal of peace education is teaching children methods of creative problem solving. The following questions were used to facilitate evaluation of the books in this category:

(a) Who, if anyone, accepts responsibility for finding a solution to the problem/conflict?

(b) How are fears of rejection/failure or needs to save face resolved?

(c) Is the problem solved? How do you know it is solved? What are the implied standards for a "successful" solution?

(d) Is the solution "realistic"? (Could the same behaviors in "real life" lead to similar resolutions?)

(e) Is the solution a direct consequence of someone's actions, or does it occur by chance or by magic? Does the story imply that actions have consequences, or that things happen regardless of any plan or problem solving approach?

(f) What is the role of adults in the story? What does this teach about children's abilities to solve problems, what does it teach about adult problem solving? Are children encouraged to depend on adults or authority figures for solutions to conflicts?

(g) Are there patterns along age, sex, ethnic lines in passivity-activity, leadership, decision making, or power in dealing with conflict.

(h) What is the role of aggression or violence (either physical or verbal)?

(i) What is the role of cooperation or competition?

(j) Is any decision making *process* shown? Does this process include exploring alternatives, or is only one solution presented? Are consequences of actions visualized before the solution is enacted? Are any standards presented for evaluating the best alternative?

(k) Are everyone's needs taken into account in the solution?   [Pp. 2-3]

These broad questions can serve as the basis for adults to evaluate the potential of various books for teaching cooperation to young children, and the following selected books can be used as the starting point for teaching.

The book *Two Good Friends* by Judy Dalton provides an excellent example of a book that could be used as part of a teaching unit on cooperation. Bear and Duck are very good friends, but they are very different: Duck is a meticulous housekeeper whose house is always clean and neat, but he often has no food in the house; Bear, however, is an excellent cook, and his house is always full of good things to eat, but he is a terrible housekeeper and his house is always very dirty. After some initial difficulties in reconciling their differences, they reach a perfect solution in which Duck cleans Bear's house for him and Bear bakes delicious things for Duck to eat.

Teachers might read the story aloud to children and then have them discuss the following:

1. What was Duck good at?

2. What was Bear good at?

3. What wasn't Duck good at?

4. What wasn't Bear good at?

5. How did Duck and Bear feel about each other's weaknesses? (anger, frustration)

6. What did they decide to do?

As a follow-up activity, teachers might then have children identify one or two things they were good at and one or two things they were not good at. (While children may be asked to help identify other children's strengths, it is highly preferable for children to identify only their *own* weaknesses.) The teacher can then ask students to try out the solution in the book by finding someone they can help with something and someone who can help them. For example, if Mary identifies herself as good at jumping rope and singing and not very good at remembering her library book, and Billy identifies himself as good at remembering things but not good at jumping rope, the children can be encouraged to engage in some exchanging of skills. Such exchanges, of course, need not be limited to two children; it is hoped they will involve children interacting with several other children. Children can be encouraged to explore solutions which involve both helping people learn how to do things better themselves *and* doing things for people, and teachers can explore with children the implications of each.

Once this helping/cooperation model has been established, the teacher can attempt to face out such structure until the children are able independently to seek the help of other children and offer to help in areas of difficulty. Teachers can do this by following a sequence such as the following:

1. If Billy needs help with something, teacher offers her help and also verbally identifies another child who might be able to help. ("I bet next time Karen could help with that.")

2. The next time Billy needs help, the teacher either encourages Karen to go help him ("Karen, I bet you could help Billy with that.") or encourages Billy to seek out Karen's help ("I wonder if Karen might be able to help you with that.").

3. The next time a similar situation arises, the teacher steps even further into the background, perhaps by saying to the class, "Billy's having trouble with 'x.' What do you suppose you could all do about it?" and by encouraging other children to do the matching, i.e., "Steve, why don't you help Billy find someone who can help him."

After each of these stages, the teacher should praise all of the participants, not just the helper. The teacher must be sure to model that admitting that one doesn't know or can't do something and asking for help are appropriate and expected behaviors. He or she can do this both by praising the child who asks for help appropriately, i.e., "Billy had a problem, but he sure found a good way to get help," and by modeling asking behavior him/herself, "I'm having a lot of trouble moving this desk—who could help me?" Following such a progression should allow the teacher to structure cooperative interactions systematically *and* to gradually withdraw her/himself as the exclusive source of help and information.

Another book suggested by Streibel (1977) can also form the beginning of an exercise in cooperation. *That's Mine,* by Elizabeth Winthrop, is the story of a boy and a girl who are playing with blocks. At first they are extremely competitive and verbally abusive, which leads to a fight in which both of their structures tumble to the ground. When they realize that they can work together, they are able to build something even more elaborate and exciting than they could alone. This book can be read to children, and discussion can focus on the advantages of cooperation: "How did the children feel about each other when they were building separate buildings?" "What happened when both children wanted the same block?" "What made the children decide to work together?" "What kind of a building were they able to make together?"

Discussion can then proceed to an elaboration of activities best accomplished cooperatively. A follow-up book, *Some Things You Just Can't Do By Yourself* (Schiff & Becky, 1973) can be shared with the children. This very brief book details things "you can't do by yourself," i.e., hug, play checkers, play hide and seek, shake hands, ride in a wagon, kiss, etc. It ends by asking children to generate some additional things that can't be done alone. Children could be asked to draw or cut out pictures of other activities, and a book of cooperative activities might be assembled.

After this activity, the teacher may wish to select some of the cooperative games previously identified, particularly those that involve active sharing, to play with the children as further reinforcement of the notion of cooperation. Teachers may also wish to maintain an ever-alert posture toward instances of cooperation in their own classrooms and to reward such behavior, for example, by allowing the children involved to record their cooperation by dictating or drawing in the class book of cooperative activities.

Several of the other books Streibel (1977) suggests for using with young children include: *Swimmy,* by Leo Lionni, in which a band of little fish decide to swim together to avoid being eaten by bigger fish; and *I Can't Said the Ant,* by Polly Cameron, in which a tiny ant, with the help of many friends with different talents, solves a difficult dilemma.

The potential for using children's books to model cooperation is an exciting one, worthy of future exploration by educators who work with young children.

SUMMARY

This chapter has focused on two major strategies for establishing appropriate social skills in young children, with particular emphasis on cooperation and conflict resolution. The research reviewed has supported the notion that "stopping aggression" is not enough, children need to be taught specific repertoires for dealing with those situations of conflict and stress that invariably present themselves in social environments. Although it is ultimately desirable that children be able to articulate the reasons for various social behaviors, children can be taught to display those behaviors at an age when their limited verbal skills would not lend themselves to such articulation. Thus it is not necessary to wait until a child can explain "why we apologize when we hurt someone" or "why it's nice to share with people" before we can teach them to apologize and share. It is appropriate with this age group to engage in teaching activities which specify, directly, the social behaviors which are to be displayed, e.g., patting the person on your left, saying something nice to someone in the circle. The use of children's games and children's books has been proposed because of their potential for establishing socially appropriate behavior and because game time and story time are already a part of most early childhood curricula. Early childhood educational environments provide ideal settings for such instruction because (1) there is already a high priority placed on social behavior in such environments, and (2) young children, because of their limited school and social experience, can more easily acquire new repertoires of social behavior.

REFERENCES

Allen, K.E.; Hart, B.M.; Buell, J.S.; Harris, F.R.; and Wolf, M.M. Effects of social reinforcement on isolate behavior of a nursery school child. In L.P. Ullman and L. Krasner (Eds.), *Case studies in behavior modification.* New York: Holt, Rinehart and Winston, 1965.

Arnold, A. *Children's games.* New York: World Publishing, Times Mirror, 1972.

Bandura, A. and Walters, R.H. *Social learning and personality development.* New York Holt, 1963.

Becker, W.C. *Parents are teachers.* Champaign, Ill.: Research Press, 1971.

Berkowitz, L. Control of aggression. In B.Caldwell and H. Ricciuti (Eds.), Review of child development research, Vol. III. Chicago: University of Chicago Press, 1973.

Borke, H. The development of empathy in chinese and american children between three and six years of age: A cross-cultural study. *Developmental Psychology, 9,* 1973, 102-108.

Broman, B.L. *The early years in childhood education.* Chicago: Rand McNally College Publishing, 1978.

Cairns, Robert B. *Social development: The origins and plasticity of interchanges.* San Francisco: W.H. Freeman, 1979.

Caldwell, B.M. Aggression and hostility in young children. In C. Torriero (Ed.), *Readings in early childhood education.* Guilford, Conn.: Dushkin, 1978.

Cameron, Polly. *I can't said the ant.* East Rutherford, N.J.: Coward McCann Georgian, 1961.

Cohen, S. *Social and personality development in childhood.* New York: Macmillan, 1976.

Dalton, Judy, *Two good friends.* New York: Crown, 1974.

Eron, L.D.; Walder, L.O.; Toigo, R.; & Lefkowitz, M.M. Social class parental punishment for aggression and child aggression. *Child Development, 34,* 1963, 849-867.

Flavell, John N. *The developmental psychology of Jean Piaget.* New York: Van Nostrand Reinhold, 1963.

Garvey, C. and Hogan R. Social speech and social interaction: Egocentrism revisited. *Child Development, 44,* 1973, 562-568.

Greene, F. *China.* New York: Ballantine Books, 1962.

Harrison, M. *For the fun of it: Selected cooperative games for children and adults.* Philadelphia: Nonviolence and Children. Friends Peace Committee, 1976.

Kessen, W. Childhood in china. New Haven: Yale University Press, 1976.

Lillie, D.L. *Early childhood education: An individualized approach to developmental instruction.* Chicago: Science Research Association, 1975.

Lionni, Leo. *Swimmy.* Westminster, Md.: Partheon, 1963.

Lorenz, K. *On Aggression.* New York: Harcourt, Brace and World, 1966.

Orlick, T. *The Cooperative Sports and Games Book: Challenge Without Competition.* New York: Pantheon Books, 1978.

Patterson, A.R. and Gullion, M.E. *Living with Children: New Methods for Parents and Teachers.* (Rev. ed.) Champaign, Ill.: Research Press, 1976.

Prutzman, P.; Burger, M.L.; Bodenhamer, G.; and Stern, L. *The friendly classroom for a small planet: Handbook of the children's creative response to conflict program.* New York: Quaker Project on Community Conflict, 1977.

Quilitch, H. and Risley, T.R. The effects of play materials on social play. *Journal of Applied Behavior Analysis, 6,* 1973, 573-578.

Sapon-Shevin, M. Formal group contingencies and games as the occasions for social interactions between children. Unpublished doctoral dissertation, University of Rochester, 1976.

Schiff, Naomi and Sarah Becky. *Some things you just can't do by yourself.* Stanford, Calif.: New Seed Press, 1973.

Sears, R.R.; Maccoby, E.E.; and Levin, H. *Patterns of child rearing.* Evanston, Ind.: Row, Peterson, 1957.

Sears, R.R.; Whiting, J.W.M.; Nowlis, V.; and Sears, P.S. Some child-rearing ante-
cedents of aggression and dependency in young children. *Genetic Psychological
Monographs, 47,* 1953, 135-234.
Sheppard, W.C.; Shank, S.B.; and Wilson, D. *How to be a good teacher: Training
social behavior in young children.* Champaign, Ill.: Research Press, 1972.
Sidel, R. *Women and child care in China: A firsthand report.* New York: Penguin
Books, 1976.
Smith, R.N.; Neisworth, J.T.; and Greer, J.G. *Evaluating educational environ-
ments.* Columbus, Ohio: Charles E. Merrill, 1978.
Spivack, G. and Shure, M.B. *Social adjustment of young children: A cognitive ap-
proach to solving real-life problems.* San Francisco: Jossey-Bass, 1974.
Streibel, B. *Conflict resolution in children's literature.* Madison, Wis.: Center for
Conflict Resolution, 1977.
Wahler, R.G. Child-child interactions in free field settings: Some experimental analy-
ses. *Journal of Experimental Child Psychology, 5,* 1967, 278-293.
Walters, R.H. and Brown, M. Studies of reinforcement of aggression III: Transfer
of responses to an interpersonal situation, *Child Development, 34,* 1963, 563-
571.
Winthrop, Elizabeth. *That's mine.* New York: Holiday, 1977.
Yarrow, M.R. and Waxler, C.Z. The emergence and functions of prosocial behaviors in young children. In *Readings in child development and relationships.* (2nd
ed.) Smart, R.C. and Smart, M.S., Eds. New York: Macmillan, 1977.

Chapter 9

The Adolescent: Social Skills Training Through Structured Learning

Arnold P. Goldstein, Robert P. Sprafkin, N. Jane Gershaw, and Paul Klein

Structured Learning, a skills training approach developed for use with certain adolescent and other skill-deficient populations, is the focus of the present chapter. We will present, in some depth, the nature of our target adolescent populations—who they are, how they are optimally identified and classified and how they have been dealt with in treatment and skill remediation efforts in the past. Structured Learning will then be presented in detail. Its history, specific procedures, target skills, and research evaluation outcomes will each be described. In all, our effort will be to familiarize the reader with the substance of this approach, highlight its strength and weaknesses and, in doing so, hopefully encourage both its further application and continued research examination.

THE SOCIAL SKILL DEFICIENT ADOLESCENT

A number of diverse attempts have been undertaken to develop classification systems which adequately describe children and adolescents exhibiting behavior disorders. Prior to 1966, 24 such systems had been proposed (Group for the Advancement of Psychiatry, 1966). Unfortunately, most were essentially lacking in evidence of sufficient reliability, as well as evidence that the system related meaningfully to decisions about the types of remedial treatment best recommended. The Group's own classification sys-

249

tem made some beginning strides at dealing with these chronic deficiencies. But a truly useful system of classifying behavior disorders, perhaps of technological necessity, awaited the development of multivariate statistical techniques. By means of such techniques, investigators in recent years have been able to bring together and simultaneously draw upon very diverse types of information on a broad range of behaviorally disordered adolescents. In this regard, Quay, Peterson, and their colleagues have used observational behavior ratings by teachers, parents, clinic staff, and correctional workers; case history materials, the responses of adolescents themselves to personality testing, and other types of information—all obtained from and about adolescents in public schools, child guidance clinics, institutions for delinquents, and mental hospitals. In the research of these investigators, as well as several others (Achenbach, 1966; Achenbach and Edelbrock, 1978; Hewitt and Jenkins, 1946; Patterson and Anderson, 1964; Peterson, Quay and Tiffany, 1961; Ross, Lacey and Parton, 1965), a three-category classification pattern has consistently emerged. The three patterns—aggression, withdrawal, and immaturity—account for the vast majority of behaviors typically included under the term "behavior disorders."

Aggression

Quay (1966) comments:

Almost without exception multivariate statistical studies of problem behaviors . . . reveal the presence of a pattern involving aggressive behavior, both verbal and physical, associated with poor interpersonal relationships with both adults and peers. This pattern has received a variety of labels: e.g., unsocialized aggressive (Hewitt and Jenkins, 1946); conduct problem (Peterson et al, 1961; Quay and Quay, 1965); aggressive (Patterson and Anderson, 1964); unsocialized psychopath (Quay, 1964); psychopathic delinquency (Patterson, Quay, and Cameron, 1959); antisocial aggressiveness and sadistic aggressiveness (Dreger, Lewis, Rich, Miller, Reid, Overlade, Taffel and Flemming, 1964); and externalizing (Achenbach, 1966).   [P. 9]

This classification reflects such specific behaviors as fighting, disruptiveness, destructiveness, profanity, irritability, quarrelsomeness, defiance of authority, irresponsibility, high levels of attention-seeking behavior, and low levels of guilt feelings. In Quay's research, youngsters in this category typically answer affirmatively to such questionnaire items as:

I do what I want to whether anybody likes it or not.

The only way to settle anything is to lick the guy.

If you don't have enough to live on, it's OK to steal.

It's dumb to trust other people.

I'm too tough a guy to get along with most kids.

Quay (1966, pp. 10-11) observes that the essence of this pattern is an active antisocial aggressiveness almost inevitably resulting in conflict with parents, peers, and social institutions. Children and adolescents extreme on this pattern seem likely to be in such difficulty as to be involved in the courts and institutions for delinquents.

Withdrawal

Numerous researchers have also consistently identified a behavior disorder pattern characterized by withdrawal and variously labeled overinhibited (Hewitt and Jenkins, 1946); personality problem (Peterson, et al., 1961), disturbed neurotic (Quay, 1964), internalizing (Achenbach, 1966), and withdrawn (Patterson and Anderson, 1964; Ross, Lacey and Parton, 1965). Quay (1966) describes this pattern further:

These behaviors, attitudes, and feelings clearly involve a different pattern of social interaction than do those comprising conduct disorder; they generally imply withdrawal instead of attack. In marked contrast to the characteristics of conduct disorder are such traits as feelings of distress, fear, anxiety, physical complaints, and open and expressed unhappiness. It is within this pattern that the child who is clinically labeled as an anxiety neurotic or as phobic will be found. (P. 11)

In addition, as the relevant studies demonstrate, the behavior disorder pattern characterized centrally by withdrawal is also marked by depression, feelings of inferiority, self-consciousness, shyness, anxiety, hypersensitivity, seclusiveness, and timidity.

Immaturity

As is true of aggression and withdrawal, immaturity has frequently emerged as a third prominent class of adolescent behavior disorder. It has been identified as such in samples of adolescents studied in public schools, child guidance clinics, and institutions for delinquents. Behaviors forming a significant component of the immaturity pattern include short attention span, clumsiness, preference for younger playmates, passivity, daydreaming, and incompetence. As Quay notes, this pattern represents a persistence of behaviors which were largely age-appropriate earlier in the youngster's development, but which have become inappropriate in view of the chronological age of the adolescent and of society's expectations of him.

Quay's (1966) reflections on the three patterns of behavior disorders are most relevant to our skill deficiency focus. He comments:

The characteristics of the three . . . patterns may all be said to be clearly maladaptive either from the social or individual viewpoint. Extremes of such behaviors are at variance with either the expectations of self, parents, or educational and other social institutions. . . . Each of the previous patterns also involves interpersonal alienation with peers, attack in the case of conduct disorders, withdrawal in the case of personality disorder, or lack of engagement in the case of immaturity.   [Pp. 13-14]

To describe the aggressive, withdrawn, or immature adolescent as we have done above, is to focus on what each youngster is and does. But it will be profitable from a skill deficiency viewpoint to examine correspondingly what each such youngster is not, and does not do. Thus, the aggressive adolescent is not only often proficient in fighting, disruptiveness, destructiveness, and similar anti-social skills; he is also deficient in such prosocial skills as self-control, negotiating, asking permission, avoiding trouble with others, understanding feelings of others, and dealing with someone else's anger. The withdrawn youngster, in an analogous manner, lacks proficiency in such prosocial skills as having a conversation, joining in, dealing with fear, decision making, dealing with being left out, responding to persuasion, and dealing with contradictory messages, as well as skills relevant to expressing or receiving apologies, complaints, or instructions. The parallel skill deficiency pattern for the immature adolescent typically involves a lack of competence in sharing, responding to teasing, responding to failure, dealing with group pressure, goal setting, and concentration. The illustrative prosocial skills we have enumerated here are a brief sampling of the skill training targets which form the major focus of Structured Learning.

DEVELOPMENTAL HURDLES

We have proposed that behavior disordered youngsters are primarily of three types, and that each may be described not only in terms of the presence of a repertoire of dysfunctional and often antisocial behaviors, but also in terms of the absence of a repertoire of prosocial or developmentally appropriate behaviors. It is our belief that a treatment oriented toward the explicit teaching of prosocial skills can function as an optimal treatment approach for such adolescents. Desirable, functional skills missing from their behavioral repertoires can, we propose, be taught successfully. However, it is not only the aggressive, withdrawn, or immature youngster with whom we are concerned. Many other adolescents (those less likely to come to the attention of school, clinic, or institution personnel) are, we feel, appropriate potential targets for skill training efforts. Manster (1977), in his book, *Adolescent Development and the Life Tasks,* describes very well the sequence of life tasks which all adolescents must successfully master. In school, at work, in the community, and with peers, family, authority figures, the developing adolescent meets, must cope with and master a wide and increasingly more complex series of personal and interpersonal life tasks. These tasks are many and varied. In the realm of love, sex, and peer relationships, the skills demanded may include social skills (e.g., having a conversation, listening, joining in), skills for dealing with feelings (e.g., dealing with fear, expressing affection, understanding the feelings of others), and skills useful for dealing with stress (e.g., dealing with embarrassment, preparing for a stressful conversation, responding to failure). School related tasks demand proficiency at yet other skills. Certainly primary here are planning skills (e.g., goal setting, gathering information, decision making). School settings also require daily success at tasks involving both peers (e.g., dealing with group pressure) and authority figures (e.g., following instructions). The work setting similarly is multifaceted in its task demands and, hence, in its requisite skills—again involving planning and stress management competencies in particular. For many youngsters, whether in school, at work, or elsewhere, the skill demands placed upon them frequently involve the ability to deal satisfactorily with aggression—either their own or someone else's. In these instances, skills to be mastered include self-control, negotiating, and dealing with group pressure.

The developmental sequences we have hinted at here are rarely smooth, and efforts at aiding their progression appear to be a worthy goal. It is in this sense, therefore, that the clinically "normal" adolescent experiencing the need for assistance over certain developmental hurdles is also a potential target trainee for the skill training approach which forms the substance of this chapter.

TREATMENT APPROACHES

We now wish to turn to an examination of the diverse treatment approaches in use for skill deficient adolescents. In doing so, we will place heaviest emphasis upon efforts to remediate the aggressive youngster. We will not slight the withdrawn, the immature, or the normal adolescent. Techniques applied to these latter youngsters, and the effectiveness of these techniques, will, indeed, be examined. But in terms of its impact on society, altering the overt behavior of aggressive adolescents and reorienting such behavior in more prosocial directions are goals of prime importance—and, thus, clearly deserving of our special attention.

A Prescriptive Viewpoint: What Works for Whom?

A number of diverse approaches exist for the training, treatment, and rehabilitation of aggressive, withdrawn, immature, and other seriously skill deficient youngsters. These include such putatively correctional, rehabilitative procedures as incarceration and probation; an array of traditional types of individual and group psychotherapy; several less psychodynamic group-oriented approaches, such as use of positive peer culture or guided group interaction procedures; a series of newer behavioral techniques, mostly centering around efforts to alter overt maladaptive or antisocial behavior by the management of reinforcement contingencies; and, very recently, certain psychoeducational therapies in which the treatment goal is usually to increase the adolescent's proficiency in prosocial skills and, by implication, decrease his reliance on antisocial behaviors. Each of these approaches has its proponents and opponents. For each there are testimonials, critics, and, in some instances, research supporting its value.

Our own view regarding these several correctional, rehabilitative, counseling, psychotherapeutic, behavioral, and psychoeducational procedures is prescriptive. By this we mean that none of them may be viewed as "good" or "bad" or "effective" or "ineffective" in any absolute sense. Let us, for example, consider the recent history of psychotherapy. In the 1950s, when research on the effectiveness of psychotherapy was just beginning, investigators asked "Does treatment A work?" or "Is treatment A better than treatment B?" But answers to such questions, even when positive, proved next to useless. Little or no information was provided by answers to such global questions either about how to improve the effectiveness of the particular treatment (since it was studied as a whole, with no attention to its separate components), or how to use the research findings to help any individual person (because only group effects were studied).

In response to such shortcomings, and the companion awareness that none of our treatments can yet be sufficiently powerful to help all or almost all types of people, clinicians and researchers have come more and more to ask a new, more differential type of outcome question: "Which type of patient, meeting with which type of therapist, for which type of treatment, will yield which outcome?" This customized, differential, or prescriptive view of the helping enterprise leads to avoiding the assignment of all types of patients to any given treatment; to acknowledging that a given psychotherapist or counselor may be therapeutic for one type of patient, but may be unhelpful or even psychonoxious for another; to steps which counteract the patient uniformity myth, the therapist uniformity myth, and the treatment uniformity myth. Mostly, this view leads to positive efforts to match patients, therapists, and treatments so that the likelihood of a beneficial outcome is maximized. We and others have elaborated this prescriptive viewpoint in considerable detail elsewhere (Goldstein & Stein, 1976; Goldstein, 1978).

In 1974, Martinson published an article titled "What Works?", a review of diverse efforts to alter the deviant behavior of juvenile offenders. Research on the treatments and correctional efforts examined by Martinson focused upon a large number of rather diverse intervention procedures. His conclusion was unequivocal: "With few and isolated exceptions, the rehabilitative efforts that have been reported so far have had no appreciable effect on recidivism" (p. 25). This singularly negative conclusion, however, has been effectively shown by Palmer (1976) to rest on Martinson's reliance upon what we called the "one-true-light-assumption" (Goldstein & Stein, 1976). This assumption, the antithesis of a prescriptive viewpoint, holds that specific treatments are sufficiently powerful to override substantial individual differences and aid heterogeneous groups of patients. Research in all fields of psychotherapy has shown the one true light assumption to be erroneous (Goldstein & Stein, 1976; Goldstein, 1978), and Palmer (1976) has shown it to be especially in error with regard to aggressive and delinquent adolescents. Palmer returned to the data which Martinson had examined and from which he drew his "nothing works" conclusion. In each of literally dozens of the studies thus reexamined by Palmer, there were homogeneous subsamples of adolescents for whom the given treatments under study did work. Martinson's error was to be unresponsive to the fact that when homogeneous subsamples are combined to form a heterogeneously composed full sample, positive, negative, and no-change treatment outcome effects of different subsamples will cancel one another out and make the full sample appear no different in average change than an untreated control group. But, to repeat, when smaller, more homogeneous subsamples are examined separately, many treatments work. Our task, then, is not to continue the futile pursuit of the one true light, the one treatment that works for all; but, instead, to discern which treatments administered by which treaters work for whom, and for whom they do not.*

Incarceration

It is one thing to espouse a prescriptive clinical strategy regarding the treatment of disturbed and disturbing adolescents, but quite another to implement such a strategy. Our state of prescriptive knowledge is primitive. Most investigators and correctional practitioners, for example, view incarceration as the least desirable alternative treatment for juvenile offenders. "Locking them up" as a correctional treatment is seen as often leading to more and not less eventual antisocial behavior. Yet, in almost every instance, holders of this essentially anti-incarceration viewpoint simultaneously acknowledge,

---

*The reader involved in elementary or secondary education will find the reasoning we have put forth here to be familiar, in that what we have described as a growing orientation toward prescriptiveness in the practice and investigation of psychotherapy parallels quite directly a very similar movement in the field of education. The work of Cronbach and Snow (1977) on aptitude treatment interactions, Hunt's (1971) behavior-person-environment matching model, and Klausmeier, Rossmiller & Saily's (1977) individually guided education are but three of several emerging examples in recent years of growing attention in educational theory and practice to a prescriptive intervention strategy.

directly or by implication, that there is likely a yet-to-be specified subsample of offenders, probably chiefly characterized by a high prior rate of recidivism, for whom incarceration may well be the optimal intervention (Achenbach, 1974; Bailey, 1966; Empey, 1969; Kassenbaum, Ward & Wilner, 1972; McClintock, 1961; Robinson & Smith, 1976).

Probation

Probation, too, has its champions as a differentially offered treatment. Evidence exists that probation may be an appropriate intervention for adolescent offenders who are neurotic (Empey, 1969); who display some reasonable level of prosocial behavior (Garrity, 1956) or social maturity (Sealy & Banks, 1971); or who are, in interpersonal (I-level) maturity terminology, Cultural Conformists (California Youth Authority, 1967). In differential contrast, however, probation may well be a considerably less than optimal prescription when the youth is nonneurotic (Empey, 1969); manipulative (Garrity, 1956); or low in social maturity (Sealy & Banks, 1971).

Individual Psychotherapy

A clearly analogous differential position may be taken regarding the appropriateness of other treatment interventions for disturbed and disturbing adolescents. Depending on which type of youngster is involved, a given treatment may or may not be prescriptively appropriate. Individual psychotherapy, for example, has been shown to be effective with highly anxious adolescents (Adams, 1962); the socially withdrawn adolescents (Stein & Bogin, 1978; those displaying, at most, a moderate level of psychopathic behavior (Carney, 1966; Craft, Stephenson & Granger, 1964); and youngsters, displaying a set of characteristics summarized by Adams (1961) as "amenable." More blatantly psychopathic youngsters, low anxious youngsters, or those "nonamenable" in Adam's (1961) terms are appropriately viewed as prescriptively poor candidates for individual psychotherapy interventions. Thus, we see once again that depending on which type of youngster is involved, a given treatment may or may not be prescriptively appropriate.

Group Approaches

Many group approaches have been developed in attempts to aid aggressive, withdrawn, or immature adolescents. Some of the more popular have been activity group therapy (Slavson, 1964), guided group interaction (McCorkle, Elias & Bixby, 1958), and positive peer culture (Vorrath & Bendtro, 1974). Research evidence demonstrates that such approaches are, indeed, useful for older, more sociable and person-oriented adolescents (Knight, 1969), for those who tend to be confrontation-accepting (Warren, 1972), and the more neurotic-conflicted (Harrison & Mueller, 1964), or acting-out neurotic (California Youth Authority, 1967). Youngsters who are younger, less sociable, or more delinquent (Knight, 1969), who are confrontation-avoiding (Warren, 1972), or psychopathic (Craft, 1964) apparently are less likely to benefit from group interventions.

Behavior Modification

In recent years, a host of therapeutic procedures have been developed and proffered under the rubric, "behavior modification." While withdrawn (O'Connor, 1972) and immature (Stumphauser, 1972) youngsters have been the recipients of some behavioral treatment efforts, much of it has focused upon the aggressive, oppositional, or delinquent adolescent (Bernal, Duryea, Pruett, & Burns, 1968; Braukmann & Fixsen, 1975; Drabman, 1973; Patterson & Reid, 1973; Sumphauser, 1972; Wahler, 1969). As Braukmann & Fixsen (1975) note, the more effective of these behavior modification programs typically include (1) a teaching component (e.g., modeling, shaping) designed to add the desired behavior to the adolescent's repertoire; (2) an incentive component (e.g., token economy, behavioral contract) to motivate him; and (3) the actual delivery of reinforcement contingent upon performance of the desired behavior. Literally dozens of specific techniques incorporating one or more of these components have been developed. Even though behavior modification has been the focus of much more experimental scrutiny than any other orientation, a very great deal of evaluative research is still to be done before the effectiveness of such interventions is firmly established. We would add to their admonition by proposing that the outcomes of such research are much more likely to be positive if the treatments thus considered are conceived, implemented, and evaluated prescriptively.

Summary

This very brief prescriptive view of the array of interventions currently in use for adolescents—incarceration, probation, individual and group psychotherapy, other group approaches, and a number of behavior modification efforts—all converge on the same conclusion. Bailey (1966), Martinson (1974), Vinter & Janowitz (1959), Kassenbaum, Ward & Wilner (1972) and others who have similarly reviewed the (especially aggressive) adolescent research literature and concluded, in essence, that "nothing works" are, in our view, simply wrong. In considering relevant research literature they have succumbed to the joint influence of the one-true-light assumption and the patient uniformity myth. It is not correct that "nothing works." It is correct that almost everything works, but, in each instance, only for certain youngsters. To be sure, our prescriptive sophistication for the treatment of adolescents is at a mere beginning. The relatively few adolescent characteristics we were able to point to in connection with each treatment considered above clearly shows the very rudimentary level of prescriptive matching now possible. But it is, indeed, a beginning. Our task, therefore, is to develop and continuously refine an array of treatment offerings, and to engage in the types of prescriptive research which enables us to make even better matches of treaters, youngsters, and treatment approaches. How such research is optimally planned, executed, and evaluated has been considered by us elsewhere (Goldstein & Stein, 1976; Goldstein, 1978), and the interested reader is referred to these sources. The remainder of this chapter is devoted to a presentation of one prescriptive approach, Structured Learning. It is a psychoeducational intervention, designed specifically to enhance the prosocial, interpersonal, stress management, and planning skills of the aggressive, withdrawn, immature, and "normal" but developmentally lagging adolescent—all of whom are, by our definition, skill deficient.

WHAT IS STRUCTURED LEARNING*

Structured Learning consists of four components—modeling, role playing, feedback, and transfer training—each of which is a well-established behavior change procedure. *Modeling* refers to providing small groups of trainees with a demonstration of the skill behaviors we wish youngsters to learn. If the skill to be learned were negotiating, we would present youngsters with a number of vivid, live, audio taped, video taped, or filmed displays (geared to maximize attention and motivation to learn) of adolescents who use the skill effectively. In the display, the skill of negotiating would be broken down into a series of behavioral steps which make up negotiation, and each example presented or modeled would illustrate the use of these behavioral steps. Thus, trainees would see and hear the models negotiating successfully in a variety of relevant settings: at home, at school, and with peer groups.

Once the modeling display has been presented, the next step in learning the skill is role playing. *Role playing* is behavioral rehearsal or practice for eventual real-life use of the skill. To use our example of the skill of negotia-

---

*A further examination of the background and content of this approach appears in Goldstein, Sprafkin, Gershaw and Klein (1979). This source also contains a detailed presentation of the Structured Learning skills taught to adolescents and the forms (Checklist, Grouping Chart, Homework, etc.) used in selecting and grouping trainees, as well as recording their skill acquisition progress.

tion, individuals in the group are asked to think about times in their own lives when they would benefit from using the skill they have just seen modeled or demonstrated. In turn, each youth is given the opportunity to practice using the skill (i.e., the steps which make up the skill) as he or she might eventually use it in real life. This role playing is accomplished with the aid of other group members, as well as the trainers, who simulate the real-life situation. The teenager who wishes to practice negotiation with a friend regarding where to go after school might role play the scene with another group member who acts out the part of the friend.

Feedback, the third component in Structured Learning, refers to providing the youngster with an evaluation of the role-played rehearsal. Following each role play, group members and trainers provide the role player with praise (and sometimes material rewards) as his/her behavior becomes more and more like that of the model. During this part of the group session, adolescents are given corrective instruction which will enable them to continue to improve their skill use.

The last element in Structured Learning is *transfer of training.* This refers to a variety of procedures used to encourage transfer of the newly learned behaviors from the training setting to the real-life situation. Homework assignments, use of real or imaginary props and procedures to make role playing realistic, and rerole playing a scene even after it is learned well (i.e., overlearning) are some of the several transfer enhancing procedures which are part of Structured Learning. Several additional means of potential usefulness for increasing transfer of training are described in detail in Goldstein and Kanfer (1979). In a real sense, transfer of training is the most important, and often most difficult aspect of Structured Learning. If the newly learned behavior does not carry over to the real-life environment, then a lasting and meaningful change in the youngster's behavior is extremely unlikely to occur.

ORGANIZING THE STRUCTURED LEARNING GROUP

Selecting Participants

Each Structured Learning group should consist of trainees who are clearly deficient in whatever skills are going to be taught. If possible, trainees should also be grouped according to the degree of their deficiency in the given skill. Trainees can be selected who are all deficient on certain common groups of skills, as assessed by the Structured Learning Skill Checklist. Defining which skills to work on are the *behavioral objectives* for the trainees in the class. The optimal size group for effective Structured Learning sessions consists of five to eight trainees plus two trainers.* The trainees selected for a Structured Learning group need not be from the same class or even the same grade. However, since behavioral rehearsal or role playing in the group is most beneficial when it is as realistic as possible, it is often useful to include trainees whose social worlds (family, school, peer groups) have some important elements of similarity. In this way, when a participant is asked to role play a part, this can be done in a reasonably accurate fashion.

There are times when it will not be possible to group trainees according to shared skill deficits. Instead, the trainer may want to group according to naturally occurring units, such as school classes, residential cottages, etc. If the trainer decides to use naturally occurring units, the group members will probably reflect some range of skill strengths and weaknesses. In this case, it will be helpful to fill out a Skill Checklist for each trainee in order to obtain a group profile. Starting skills should be those in which many of the group members show a deficiency. In such a potentially divergent group, it is likely that one or two members will be proficient in the use of whatever skill might be taught on a given day. In that case, these more skillful youngsters can be used in helper roles, such as co-actors or providers of useful feedback.

Number, Length, and Spacing of Sessions

The Structured Learning modeling displays and associated procedures typically constitute a training program which can be broken into segments matching part or all of the semesters of the school or training setting. It is most desirable that training occur at a rate of one or two times per week. Spacing is crucial. Most trainees in skill training or other programs learn well in the training setting. However, most fail to transfer this learning to where it counts—at home, in school, with friends, in the community. In order to provide ample opportunity for trainees to try out in real life what they have learned in the training setting, there must be ample time and opportunity for skill use between sessions.

Typically, each training session should focus on learning one skill. As such, it should include one sequence of modeling, several role plays, feedback, and assignment of homework. Each session should be scheduled for

---

*We recognize that most classes in school settings are much larger than is desirable for a Structured Learning class. Often it is possible for two or more teachers to combine their classes for a period or two and have one teacher take the larger group while a smaller group of five to eight students participates in Structured Learning. Other means for organizing Structured Learning groups in regular classes are described in Goldstein, Sprafkin, Gershaw, and Klein (1979).

one hour in length. Session length should be determined by a number of factors, such as attention span, impulsivity, verbal ability, etc. If most trainees in a given group show particularly brief attention span, the session can be as brief as twenty minutes. In such cases, more frequent sessions are advisable. Sessions longer than an hour are possible for trainees whose capacity for sustained attention is greater. Since Structured Learning is intensive, we recommend that sessions not last beyond one-and-a-half hours, as learning efficiency tends to diminish beyond that length of time.

Trainer Preparation

The role playing and feedback activities which make up most of each Structured Learning session are a series of "action-reaction" sequences in which effective skill behaviors are first rehearsed (role play) and then critiqued (feedback). As such, the trainer must both lead and observe. We have found that one trainer is hard pressed to do both of these tasks well at the same time; thus, we recommend strongly that each session be led by a team of two trainers.

Two types of trainer skills appear necessary for successful Structured Learning leadership. The first might best be described as General Trainer Skills—i.e., those skills requisite for success in almost any training or teaching effort. These include:

1. oral communication and listening skills;
2. flexibility and capacity for resourcefulness;
3. enthusiasm;
4. ability to work under pressure;
5. interpersonal sensitivity; and
6. broad knowledge of human behavior, adolescent development, etc.

The second type of requisite skills are Specific Trainer Skills—i.e., those germane to Structured Learning in particular. These include:

1. knowledge of Structured Learning—its background, procedures, and goals;
2. ability to orient both trainees and supporting staff to Structured Learning;
3. ability to initiate and sustain role playing;
4. ability to present material in concrete, behavioral form;
5. ability to deal with management problems effectively; and
6. sensitivity in providing corrective feedback.

For both trainer selection and development purposes, potential trainers should first participate, in the role of trainees, in a series of Structured Learning sessions. These sessions are led by two experienced trainers. After this experience, beginning trainers can then co-lead a series of sessions with an experienced trainer. In this way, trainers can be given several opportunities to practice what they have seen and, also, receive feedback regarding their performance. In effect, we recommend the use of the Structured Learning procedures of modeling, role playing, and feedback as the method of choice for training Structured Learning techniques appropriately.

THE STRUCTURED LEARNING SESSIONS

The Setting

One major principle for encouraging transfer from the classroom or clinical situation to the real-life setting is the rule of identical elements. This rule states that the more similar or identical the two settings—i.e., the greater number of physical and interpersonal qualities shared by them—the greater the transfer from one setting to the other. We urge that Structured Learning be conducted in the same general setting as the real-life environment of most participating youngsters, and that the training setting be furnished to resemble or simulate as much as possible the likely application settings. In a typical classroom, one can accomplish this, in part, through the creative use of available furniture and supplies. Should a couch be needed for a particular role play, several chairs can be pushed together to simulate the couch. Should a television set be an important part of a role play, a box, a chair, or a drawing on the chalkboard can, in imagination, approximate the real object. If actual props are available (for example an actual TV set, store counter, living room furniture) they should certainly be used in the role play scenes.

A horseshoe seating arrangement is one good example of how furniture might be arranged in the training room. Participating trainees sit at desks or tables so that some writing space is provided. Role playing takes place in the front of the room. Behind and to the side of one of the role players is a chalkboard displaying the behavioral steps which make up the skill being worked with at that time. In this way, the role player can glance up at the steps during the role play. If film strips or other visual modeling displays are used, the screen should be easily visible to all.

Premeeting Preparation of Trainees

Preparation of trainees individually may be helpful prior to the first meeting of the Structured Learning class. This orientation or structuring should be tailored to the individual needs and maturity level of each trainee. It should be designed to provide each group member with heightened motivation to attend and participate in the group, as well as to provide the trainee with accurate expectations of what the activities of the group will be like.

Methods of trainee preparation might include:

1. Mentioning what the purposes of the group will be, as they relate to the specific skill deficits of the youngsters; for example, the trainer might say, "Remember when you got into a fight with Billy, and you wound up restricted for a week? Well, in this class you'll be able to learn how to stay out of that kind of trouble so you don't get restricted."
2. Mentioning briefly and generally what procedures will be used. The trainee must have an accurate picture of what to expect and not feel as if he/she has been tricked. The trainer might say, "In order to learn to handle (these kinds of) situations better, we're going to see and hear some examples of how different kids do it well, and then actually take turns trying some of these ways right here. Then we'll let you know how you did, and you'll have a chance to practice them on your own."
3. Mentioning the benefits to be gained from participation, stating that the group will help the trainee work on particular relevant issues such as getting along in school, at home, and with peers.
4. Mentioning the tangible or token (e.g., points, credits, etc.) rewards which trainees will receive for participation.
5. Using the trainer-trainee relationship to promote cooperation; for example, the trainer might ask the youngster to "Give it a try. I think you'll get something out of it."
6. Presenting the Structured Learning class as a new part of the curriculum in which the trainee is expected to participate. Along with the message of expected participation, trainees should also understand that the group is not compulsory and that confidentiality will be respected. A verbal commitment from the youngster to "give it a try" is useful at this point.
7. Mentioning the particular skills that the youngster is likely to identify as his/her major felt deficiency, and how progress might be made in working on such skills.

The Opening Session

The opening session is designed to create trainee interest in the group as well as to educate the group regarding the procedures of Structured Learning. The trainers open the session by first introducing themselves and having each trainee do likewise. A brief familiarization period or warm-up follows, with the goal of helping trainees to become comfortable interacting with the trainers and with one another in the group. Content for this initial phase should be interesting as well as nonthreatening. Next, trainers introduce the Structured Learning program by providing trainees with a brief description of what skill training is about. Typically, this introduction covers such topics as the importance of interpersonal skills for effective and satisfying living, examples of skills which will be taught, and how these skills can be useful to trainees in their everyday lives. It is often helpful to expand upon this discussion of everyday skill use, so as to emphasize the importance of the undertaking and its personal relevance to the participants. The specific training procedures (modeling, role playing, etc.) are then described at a level which the group can easily understand.

New trainers should note that, although this overview is intended to acquaint trainees with Structured Learning procedures, frequently trainees will not grasp the concepts described until they actually get involved in the training process. Because of this, we do not advise trainers to spend a great deal of time describing the procedures. Instead, we recommend that trainers describe procedures briefly, as introduction, with the expectation that trainees will actually experience and understand the training process more fully once they have actually started.

Modeling

As the first step, the trainer describes the skill to be taught and hands out cards (SKILL CARDS) on which the name of the skill and its behavioral steps are printed. The first live modeling display of the skill is then enacted. Trainees are told to watch and listen closely to the way the actors in each vignette portray the behavioral steps. The skills taught by Structured Learning are listed in figure 9.1.

Modeling displays should begin with a narrator setting the scene and stating the name of the skill and the behavioral steps that make up that skill. The trainers then portray a series of vignettes in which each behavioral step is clearly enacted in sequence. Content in the vignettes should be varied and relevant to the lives of the trainees. We have described in detail elsewhere (see Goldstein, Sprafkin, & Gershaw, 1976) those characteristics of modeling displays which usually enhance or diminish the degree of learning that occurs. Model characteristics are also discussed in chapter 3 of the present volume.

Examples of Structured Learning skills for adolescents, and the behavioral steps which constitute each skill, include:

Starting a Conversation:
1. Greet the other person.
2. Make small talk.
3. Decide if the other person is listening.
4. Bring up the main topic.
Giving Instructions:
1. Decide what needs to be done.
2. Think about the different people who could do it and choose one.

3. Ask that person to do what you want done.
4. Ask other person if he or she understands what to do.
5. Change or repeat your instructions if necessary.

Understanding the Feelings of Others:
1. Watch the other person.
2. Listen to what the person is saying.
3. Figure out what the other person might be feeling.
4. Think about ways to show you understand what he or she is feeling.
5. Decide on the best way and do it.

Negotiation:
1. Decide if you and the other person are having a difference of opinion.
2. Tell the other person what you think about the problem.
3. Ask the other person what he or she thinks about the problem.
4. Listen openly to his or her answer.
5. Think about why the other person might feel this way.
6. Suggest a compromise.

Role Playing

The trainer should direct discussion following the modeling display toward helping trainees relate the modeled skill use to their own lives. The trainer invites comments on the behavioral steps and how these steps might be useful in the real-life situations which trainees encounter. Focus should be placed on dealing with specific current and future skill use by trainees, rather than only general issues involving the skill.

It is important to remember that role playing Structured Learning is viewed as behavioral rehearsal or practice for future use of the skill. As such, trainers should be aware that role playing of past events which have little relevance for future situations is of limited value to trainees. However, discussion of past events involving skill use can be relevant in stimulating trainees to think of times when a similar situation might occur in the future. In such a case, the hypothetical future situation rather than the past event would be selected for role playing.

Once a trainee has described a situation in his/her own life in which skill usage might be helpful, that trainee is designated the main actor. He or she chooses a second trainee (co-actor) to play the role of the significant other person (e.g., mother, peer, etc.) in his or her life who is relevant to the skill problem. The trainee should be urged to pick as a co-actor someone who resembles the real-life person in as many ways as possible. The trainer then elicits any additional information from the main actor needed to set the stage for role playing; for example, a description of the physical setting, a description of the events immediately preceding the role play, a description of the co-actor's mood or manner.

Group I.   Beginning Social Skills
           1. Listening
           2. Starting a conversation
           3. Having a conversation
           4. Asking a question
           5. Saying thank you
           6. Introducing yourself
           7. Introducing other people
           8. Giving a compliment

Group II. Advanced Social Skills
            9. Asking for help
           10. Joining in
           11. Giving instructions
           12. Following instructions
           13. Apologizing
           14. Convincing others

Group III. Skills for Dealing with Feelings
           15. Knowing your feelings
           16. Expressing your feelings
           17. Understanding the feelings of others
           18. Dealing with someone else's anger
           19. Expressing affection
           20. Dealing with fear
           21. Rewarding yourself

Fig. 9.1. Structured learning skills for adolescents.

Group IV. Skill Alternative to Aggression
           22. Asking permission
           23. Sharing something
           24. Helping others
           25. Negotiating
           26. Using self-control
           27. Standing up for your rights
           28. Responding to teasing
           29. Avoiding trouble with others
           30. Keeping out of fights
Group V. Skills for Dealing with Stress
           31. Making a complaint
           32. Answering a complaint
           33. Sportsmanship after the game
           34. Dealing with embarrassment
           35. Dealing with being left out
           36. Standing up for a friend
           37. Responding to persuasion
           38. Responding to failure
           39. Dealing with contradictory messages
           40. Dealing with an accusation
           41. Getting ready for a difficult conversation
           42. Dealing with group pressure
Group VI. Planning Skills
           43. Deciding on something to do
           44. Deciding what caused a problem
           45. Setting a goal
           46. Deciding on your abilities
           47. Gathering information
           48. Arranging problems by importance
           49. Making a decision
           50. Concentrating on a task.

Fig. 9.1. (continued)

It is crucial that the main actor seek to enact the behavioral steps which have been modeled. The trainer should go over each step as it applies to the role-play situation prior to any actual role playing being started, thus aiding the main actor in making a successful role play effort. The main actor is told to refer to the skill card on which the behavioral steps are printed. As noted previously, the behavioral steps should also be written on a chalkboard visible to the main actor during role playing. Before the role playing begins, the trainer should remind all of the participants of their roles: the main actor should be told to follow the behavioral steps; the co-actor, to stay in the role of the other person; and the observers, to watch carefully for the enactment of the behavioral steps. For the first several role plays, it is helpful for the trainer to coach the observers as to what kinds of cues to observe, e.g., posture, tone of voice, content of speech, etc. This also provides an opportunity to set a positive example for feedback from the observers.

Next, the trainer instructs the role players to begin. It is the trainer's main responsibility, at this point, to provide the main actor with whatever help or coaching he/she needs in order to keep the role playing going according to the behavioral steps. The trainer urges trainees who "break role" and begin to explain or make comments to get back into role and explain later. If the role play is clearly going astray from the behavioral steps, the trainer may stop the scene, provide needed instruction, and begin again. One trainer should be positioned near the chalkboard and point to each behavioral step, in turn, as the role play unfolds, thus helping the main actor (as well as the other trainees) to follow each step in order.

The role playing should be continued until all trainees have had an opportunity to participate (in either role) and preferably until all have had a chance to be the main actor. Sometimes this will require two or three sessions for a given skill. We again suggest that each session begin with two or three modeling vignettes for a skill, even if the skill is not new to the group. It is important to note that while the framework (behavioral steps) of each role play in the series remains the same, the actual content can and should change from role play to role play. It is the problem as it actually occurs, or could occur, in each youngster's real-life environment that should be the content of the given role play. When completed, each trainee will, thus, be better armed to act appropriately in a real situation requiring skill use in his/her own life.

There are a few further procedural matters relevant to role playing which will serve to increase its effectiveness. Role reversal is often a useful role play procedure. A trainee role playing a skill may, on occasion, have a difficult time perceiving his/her co-actor's viewpoint, and vice versa. Having them exchange roles and resume the role playing can be most helpful in this regard. The trainer can assume the co-actor role, in an effort to expose youngsters to the handling of types of reactions not otherwise role played during the session. For example, it may be crucial to have a difficult adult role realistically portrayed in the role play. It is here that trainer flexibility and creativity will certainly be called upon. This may be particularly helpful when dealing with less verbal or more hesitant trainees.

Feedback

A brief feedback period should follow each role play. This helps the main actor to find out how well he/she followed or departed from the behavioral steps, to explore the psychological impact of his/her enactment on the co-actor, and to provide encouragement to try out the role play behaviors in real life. To implement this process, the trainer should ask the main actor to wait until he/she has heard anyone's comments before talking. The trainer then asks the co-actor about his/her reactions first. Next the trainer asks the observers to comment on the behavioral steps and other relevant aspects of the role play. The trainers should comment in particular on how well the behavioral steps were followed, and provide social reinforcement (praise, approval, encouragement) for close following. To be most effective with the use of reinforcement, trainers should follow the guidelines listed below.

Guidelines for Positive Reinforcement
1. Provide reinforcement at the earliest appropriate opportunity after role plays which follow the behavioral steps.
2. Always provide reinforcement to the co-actor for being helpful, cooperative, etc.
3. Provide reinforcement only after role plays which follow the behavioral steps.
4. Vary the specific content of the reinforcements offered, i.e., praise particular aspects of the performance, such as tone of voice, posture, phrasing, etc.
5. Provide enough role playing activity for each group member to have sufficient opportunity to be reinforced.
6. Provide reinforcement in an amount consistent with the quality of the given role play.
7. Provide no reinforcement when the role play departs significantly from the behavioral steps (except for "trying" in the first session or two).
8. Provide reinforcement for an individual student's improvement over his/her previous performance.

After the main actor hears all the feedback, the trainer invites him/her to make comments regarding the role play and the comments of others. In this way, he/she can learn to evaluate the effectiveness of his/her skill enactment in the light of evidence from others as to its success or lack of success.

In all aspects of feedback, it is crucial that the trainers maintain the behavioral focus of Structured Learning. Trainer comments must point to the presence or absence of specific, concrete behaviors, and not take the form of general evaluative comments or broad generalities. Feedback, of course, may be positive or negative in content. Negative comments should always be followed by a constructive comment as to how a particular fault might be improved. At minimum, a "poor" performance (major departures from the behavioral steps) can be praised as "a good try" at the same time as it is being criticized. Trainees should be given the opportunity to rerole play these same behavioral steps after receiving corrective feedback. At times, as a further feedback procedure, we have audio taped or video taped entire role plays. Giving trainees later opportunities to observe themselves on tape can be an effective aid to learning, enabling them to reflect on their own behavior.

Since a primary goal of Structured Learning is skill flexibility, role play enactment that departs markedly from the behavioral steps may not be "wrong." That is, a different approach to the skill may in fact "work" in some situations. Trainers should stress that they are trying to teach effective alternatives, and that the trainees would do well to have the behavioral steps in their repertoire of skill behaviors available to use when appropriate. As the final optional feedback step, after all role playing and discussion is completed, the trainers may enact one additional modeling vignette or replay portions of the modeling tape. This step, in a sense, summarizes the session and leaves trainees with a final review of the behavioral steps.

Transfer of Training

Several aspects of the training sessions we have described above have, as their primary purpose, augmenting the likelihood that learning in the training setting will transfer to the youngster's real-life environment. We would suggest, however, that even more forthright steps need to be taken to maximize transfer. When possible, we would urge a homework technique which we have found to be successful with most groups. Trainees should first be told how important (i.e., the most important step of all) this transfer aspect is, and instructed in how best to implement it. Trainees should be instructed to try, in their own real-life settings, the behaviors they have practiced during the session. The name of the person(s) with whom they will try it, the day, the place, etc., are all discussed. The trainee is urged to take notes on his/her first transfer attempt on the Homework Report form provided by the trainers. This form requests detailed information about what happened when the trainee attempted the homework assignment, how well he/she followed the relevant behavioral steps, the trainee's evaluation of his/her performance and his/her thoughts about what the next assignment might appropriately be.

It has often proven useful to start with relatively simple homework behaviors and, as mastery is achieved, work up to more complex and demanding assignments. Often it is best to make a first homework assignment something that can be done close by; i.e., in the school, community center, or wherever the class is meeting. It may then be possible to forewarn and prepare the person(s) with whom the youngster is planning to try out the new skill, in order to ensure a positive outcome. For example, a trainee's homework assignment might be to ask the gym teacher a particular question. The trainer might then tell the gym teacher to expect the trainee's question so that he/she is prepared to answer in a positive way. Trainers should be cautioned, however, that breach of confidentiality can damage a teenager's trust in the trainer. If persons outside of the group are to be informed of specific training activities, youngsters should be told of this, and their permission should be asked, early in the group's life.

These experiences of success at beginning homework attempts are crucial in encouraging the trainee to make further attempts at real-life skill use. The first part of each session is devoted to presenting and discussing these homework reports. When trainees make an effort to complete their homework assignments, the trainers should provide social reinforcement (praise, approval, encouragement). Trainers should meet trainee's failure to do their homework with some chagrin and expressed disappointment. It cannot be stressed too strongly that without these, or similar attempts to maximize transfer, the value of the entire training effort is in severe jeopardy.

External Support and Self-Reward

Of the several principles of transfer training for which research evidence exists, the principle of performance feedback is clearly most consequential. A youngster can learn very well in the training setting and do all his/her transfer homework, and yet the training program can be a performance failure. "Learning" concerns the question: Can he do it? "Performance" is a matter of: Will he do it? Trainees will perform as trained if, and only if, there is some "payoff" for doing so. Stated simply, new behaviors persist if they are rewarded, diminish if they are ignored or actively challenged.

We have found it useful to implement several supplemental programs outside of the Structured Learning training setting which can help to provide the rewards or reinforcements trainees need so that their new behaviors are maintained. These programs include providing for both external social reward (provided by people in the trainee's real-life environment) and self-reward (provided by the student him/herself).

In several settings, we have actively sought to identify and develop environmental or external support by holding orientation meetings for school staff and for relatives and friends of youngsters—i.e., the real-life reward and punishment givers. These meetings acquaint significant others in the youngster's life with Structured Learning, the skills being taught, and the steps which make up these skills. The most important segment of these sessions involves presenting the procedures whereby staff, relatives, and friends can encourage and reward trainees as they practice their new skills. We consider these orientation sessions to be of major value for transfer of training. In such sessions, the trainers should provide the significant others with an overview of Structured Learning, much like the overview previously described for use with a new group of trainees. An accurate picture of what goes on in a Structured Learning class—what procedures are typically used, and why—should be provided. Most important, participants should be informed as to how they might help in the transfer effort, and why their contributions are so necessary to the success of the program. Typically, such potential reward givers should be given instructions in how to reinforce appropriate behaviors, or the approximations of such behaviors. One might tell them what specific responses on their part would be appropriate for the skills being covered in the Structured Learning class. It is often worthwhile to engage these significant others in role playing the kinds of responses they might make, so thay can have practice and feedback in these behaviors.

Frequently, environmental support is insufficient to maintain newly learned skills. In fact, many real-life environments in which youngsters work and live actually actively resist a youngster's efforts at behavior change. For this reason, we have found it useful to include in our transfer efforts a method through which students can learn to be their own rewarders—the method of self-reinforcement or self-reward.

Once a new skill has been practiced through role playing, and once the trainee has made his/her first homework effort and gotten group feedback, we recommend that trainees continue to practice their new skill as frequently as possible. It is at this time that a program of self-reinforcement can and should be initiated. Trainees can be instructed in the nature of self-reinforcement and encouraged to "say something and do something nice for yourself" if they practice their new skill well. Self-rewards may be both things that one says to one's self and things that one does for one's self. The trainee should be taught to evaluate his/her own performance, even if his/her efforts don't meet with the hoped for response from others. For example, if the youngster follows all of the steps of a particular skill well, he/she might be taught to reward him/herself by saying something (e.g., "I'll play basketball after school") as a special reward. It is important that these self-rewards are indeed special; i.e., not things that are said or done routinely, but things that are done to acknowledge and reinforce special efforts. Trainees' notes can be collected by the trainer in order to keep abreast of independent progress made by trainees, without consuming group time. A trainer should advance a trainee to this level of independent practice only when it is clear that he/she can successfully do what is being asked.

As an additional aid to transfer, it is important to acknowledge the power of peer group pressure on the behaviors of adolescents. The natural peer leader often is far more influential in a youngster's life than any adult trainer could hope to be. In this regard, it is sometimes possible to capitalize on the natural leadership qualities of some adolescents. Hence, the trainer may want to select a peer (adolescent) co-trainer who can be trained and used instead of a second adult trainer. If a peer co-trainer is selected, it is important, of course, that he/she be proficient in the particular skill being taught.

RESEARCH EVALUATION

We have conducted a number of investigations designed to examine the skill acquisition efficacy of Structured Learning with adolescents. In most of these studies, the youngsters involved were aggressive, disruptive or, in similar ways, antisocial. Table 9.1 presents the substance of this research program. As can be seen from this information, consistently positive findings have emerged. Structured Learning successfully trains adolescents in such prosocial skills as empathy, negotiating, assertiveness, following instructions, self-control, and perspective taking.

Beyond initial demonstrations that Structured Learning "works" with aggressive adolescents, these beginning studies have also highlighted other aspects of the teaching of prosocial behaviors. D. Fleming (1976), in an effort to capitalize upon adolescent responsiveness to peer influence, demonstrated that gains in negotiation skill are as great when the Structured Learning group leader is a respected peer as when the leader is an adult. Litwack (1977), more concerned with the skill-enhancing effects of an adolescent anticipating that he will later serve as a peer leader, showed that such helper role expectation increases the degree of skill acquired. Apparently, when the adolescent expects to teach others a skill, his own level of skill acquisition benefits, a finding clearly relevant to Reissman's helper therapy principle (1965). Trief (1976) demonstrated that successful use of Structured Learning to increase the perspective-taking skill (i.e., seeing matters from other people's viewpoint) also leads to consequent increases in cooperative behavior. The significant transfer effects both in this study and in the Golden (1975), Litwack (1976), and Raleigh (1977) investigations have been important signposts in planning further research on transfer enhancement in Structured Learning.

As in our earlier efforts with adult trainees, we have begun to examine the

Table **9.1.** Structured Learning Research with Adolescent and Preadolescent Trainees

Investigator	Target skill	Trainees	Setting	Results
Berlin, 1976	Empathy	Aggressive adolescents (JI) and PINS[a] ($N = 58$) $\bar{x}$ age $= 13.6$	Residential Center	1. SL with conflict content $>$ SL with nonconflict content 2. SL with conflict content $>$ no treatment 3. I level 3 and 4 $>$ I level 2
D. Fleming, 1976	Negotiation	Aggressive preadolescents ($N = 80$) $\bar{x}$ age $= 10.5$	Regular classes in elementary urban school	1. No difference between high and low self-esteem trainees 2. No difference between adult led and peer-led SL groups 3. All SL groups: significant acquisition but nonsignificant transfer
L. Fleming, 1976	Negotiation	Aggressive ($N = 48$) and passive ($N = 48$) educable mentally retarded preadolescents $\bar{x}$ age $= 10.5$	Special education classes in urban elementary school	SL $>$ Attention control for aggressive and passive trainees
Greenleaf, 1977	Self-control	Aggressive preadolescents ($N = 60$) $\bar{x}$ age $= 14.6$	Regular classes in urban junior high school	In progress (testing the effect of peer reinforcement of skill behavior on transfer)
Golden, 1975	Resistance reduction with authority figure	Aggressive adolescents ($N = 60$) $\bar{x}$ age $= 15.2$	Regular classes in urban senior high school	1. SL $=$ Discrimination training ("good" versus "bad" models) 2. SL $>$ No treatment control on acquisition and transfer criteria
Hummel, 1977	Self-control	Aggressive adolescents ($N = 60$) $\bar{x}$ age $= 15.8$	Regular classes in rural senior high school	In progress (testing the effect of training in self-instructional skills on transfer)
Jennings, 1975	Interviewee behaviors (initiation, elaboration, etc.)	Emotionally disturbed adolescents ($N = 40$) $\bar{x}$ age $= 13.7$	Children's unit of state mental hospital	1. SL $>$ Minimal treatment control on subskills of initiation and termination of silence

274

Table 9.1. Structured Learning Research with Adolescent and Preadolescent Trainees

Investigator	Target skill	Trainees	Setting	Results
Litwack, 1976	Following instructions	Passive resistive adolescents (N = 53) $\bar{x}$ age = 14.10	Regular classes in urban junior high school	2. SL > Minimal treatment control on attractiveness to interviewer SL + anticipate serving as peer trainer > SL alone > No treatment on both acquisition and transfer criteria
Raleigh, 1976	Assertiveness	Aggressive (N = 37) and passive (N = 37) adolescents $\bar{x}$ age = 13.5	Regular classes in urban junior high schools	SL (in groups) > SL (individual), discussion (groups), discussion (individual), no treatment on assertiveness or acquisition and transfer criteria
Swanstrom, 1977	Self-control	Aggressive preadolescents (N = 42) $\bar{x}$ age = 9.0	Regular classes in urban elementary school	1. SL = Structured discussion 2. SL > No treatment control on acquisition criteria
Trief, 1976	Perspective-taking (Pt.) cooperation[b]	Aggressive adolescents (JD PINS)[a] (N = 58) $\bar{x}$ age = 15.5	Residential center	1. SL (affective + cognitive focus) > SL placebo control and brief instruction control on PT[b] 2. SL (affective focus) > SL placebo control and brief instruction control on PT[b] 3. SL (cognitive focus) > SL placebo control and brief instruction control on PT[b] 4. SL (combined focus) > SL placebo control and brief instruction control on cooperation
Wood, 1977	Assertiveness	Aggressive and passive adolescents (N = 70) $\bar{x}$ age = 14	Regular classes in urban senior high school	In progress (testing the effect of "identical elements" between SL and application setting on transfer)

[a]JD = juvenile delinquents; PINS = persons in need of supervision.
[b]Acquisition and transfer.

value of teaching certain skill combinations. Aggression-prone adolescents often get into difficulty when they respond with overt aggression to authority figures with whom they disagree. Golden (1975), responding to this type of event, successfully used Structured Learning to teach such youngsters "resistance-reducing behavior," defined as a combination of reflection of feeling (the authority figure's) and assertiveness (forthright but nonagressive statement of one's own position). Others in our research group have examined Structured Learning in other ways relevant to aggressive adolescents. Jennings (1975) was able to use Structured Learning successfully to train adolescents in several of the verbal skills necessary for satisfactory participation in more traditional, insight-oriented psychotherapy. And Guzzetta (1974) was successful in providing means to help close the gap between adolescents and their parents by using Structured Learning to teach empathic skills to parents.

In similar studies in progress or being planned, we are seeking to teach other prosocial skills listed in figure 9.1. In these investigations, we are attempting to further implement two experimental design strategies characteristic of our completed studies, both of which we feel are highly desirable components of treatment evaluation research with delinquent and aggressive populations. The first concerns the inclusion of procedures designed to increase the transfer of the newly learned skills from the therapy setting to real-life settings. The second is use of factorial designs in order to define change-enhancing prescriptive matches of treatments, trainers, and trainees.

REFERENCES

Achenbach, T.M. The classification of children's psychiatric symptoms: A factor-analytic study. *Psychological Monographs, 80,* 1966, (Whole No. 615).

Achenbach, T.M. *Developmental psychopathology.* New York: Ronald Press, 1974.

Achenbach, T.M. & Edelbrock, C.S. The classification of child psychopathology: A review and analysis of empirical efforts. *Psychological Bulletin, 85,* 1978, 1275-1301.

Adams, S. Assessment of the psychiatric treatment program, phase I: Third interim report. *Research Report No. 21. California Youth Authority,* 1961.

Adams S. The PICO project. In N. Johnson; L. Savits; & M.E. Wolfgang (Eds.), *The sociology of punishment and correction.* New York: Wiley, 1962.

Bailey, W. Correctional outcome: An evaluation of 100 reports. Unpublished manuscript, University of California at Los Angeles, 1966.

Berlin, R.J. Teaching acting-out adolescents prosocial conflict resolution through structured learning training of empathy. Unpublished doctoral dissertation, Syracuse University, 1976.

Bernal, M.E., Duryee, J.S., Pruett, H.L. & Burns, B.J. Behavior modification and the brat syndrome. *Journal of Consulting and Clinical Psychology, 32,* 1968, 447-456.

Braukmann, C.L. & Fixsen, D.L. Behavior modification with delinquents. In M. Herson; R.M. Eisler; & P.M. Miller (Eds.), *Progress in behavior modification.* New York: Academic Press, 1976.

California Department of the Youth Authority. James Marshall treatment program: Progress report, 1967.

Carney, F.J. Summary of studies on the derivation of base expectance categories for predicting recidivism of subjects released from institutions of the Massachusetts Department of Corrections. Boston: Massachusetts Department of Corrections, 1966.

Craft, M.; Stephenson, G.; & Granger, C. A controlled trial of authoritarian and self-governing regimes with adolescent psychopaths. *American Journal of Orthopsychiatry, 34,* 1964, 543-554.

Cronbach, L.J.; & Snow, R.E. *Aptitudes and instructional methods.* New York: Irvington, 1977.

Drabman, R.S.; Spitalnik, R.; & O'Leary, K.D. Teaching self-control to disruptive children. *Journal of Abnormal Psychology, 82,* 1973, 10-16.

Dreger, R.M.; Lewis, P.M.; Rich, T.A.; Miller, K.S.; Reid, M.P.; Overlade, D.C.; Taffel, C. & Flemming, E.L. Behavioral classification project. *Journal of Consulting Psychology, 28,* 1964, 1-13.

Empey, L.T. Contemporary programs for convicted juvenile offenders: Problems of theory, practice and research. In Mulvihill, D.J. & Tumin, M.M. (Eds.), *Crimes of violence,* Vol. 13. Washington, D.C.: U.S. Government Printing Office, 1969.

Fleming, D. Teaching negotiation skills to pre-adolescents. Unpublished doctoral dissertation, Syracuse University, 1976.

Fleming, L. Training passive and aggressive educable mentally retarded children for assertive behaviors using three types of structured learning training. Unpublished doctoral dissertation, Syracuse University, 1976.

Garrity, D. The effects of length of incarceration upon parole adjustment and estimation of optimum sentence. Washington State Correctional Institution. Unpublished doctoral dissertation, University of Washington, 1956.

Golden, R. Teaching resistance-reducing behavior to high school students. Unpublished doctoral dissertation, Syracuse University, 1975.

Goldstein, A.P. (Ed.) *Prescriptions for child mental health and education.* Elmsford, N.Y.: Pergamon Press, 1978.

Goldstein, A.P. & Kanfer, F.H. *Maximizing treatment gains: Transfer enhancement in psychotherapy.* New York: Academic Press, 1979.

Goldstein, A.P.; Sprafkin, R.P.; & Gershaw, N.J. *Skill training for community living.* Elmsford, N.Y.: Pergamon Press, 1976.

Goldstein, A.P.; Sprafkin, R.P.; Gershaw, N.J.; & Klein, P. *Skill-streaming the adolescent: A structured learning approach to teaching prosocial behavior.* Champaign, Ill.: Research Press, 1979.

Goldstein, A.P. & Stein, N. *Prescriptive psychotherapies.* Elmsford, N.Y.: Pergamon Press, 1976.

Greenleaf, D. Peer reinforcement as transfer enhancement in Structured Learning Therapy. Unpublished masters thesis, Syracuse University, 1977.

Group for the Advancement of Psychiatry, Psychopathological disorders in childhood: Theoretical considerations and a proposed classification: *GAP Report No. 62,* 1966.

Guzetta, R.A. Acquisition and transfer of empathy by the parents of early adolescents through structured learning training. Unpublished doctoral dissertation, Syracuse University, 1974.

Harrison, R.M. & Mueller, P. Clue hunting about group counseling and parole outcome. Sacramento: California Department of Corrections, 1964.

Hewitt, L.E. & Jenkins, R.L. *Fundamental patterns of maladjustment: The dynamics of their origins.* Springfield, Ill.: State of Illinois, 1946.

Hummel, J.W. An examination of Structured Learning Therapy, self-control, negotiation training and variation in stimulus conditions. Unpublished doctoral dissertation, Syracuse University, 1977.

Hunt, D.E. *Matching models in education: The coordination of teaching methods with student characteristics.* Toronto: Ontario Institution for Studies in Education, 1971.

Jennings, R.L. The use of structured learning techniques to teach attraction enhancing interviewee skills to residentially hospitalized, lower socioeconomic emotionally disturbed children and adolescents: a psychotherapy analogue investigation. Unpublished doctoral dissertation, University of Iowa, 1975.

Kassenbaum, G.; Ward, D.; & Wilner, D. *Prison treatment and its outcome.* New York: Wiley, 1972.

Klausmeier, H.J.; Rossmiller, R.A.; & Saily, M. (Eds.) *Individually guided elementary education.* New York: Academic Press, 1977.

Knight, D. The Marshall program: assessment of a short-term institutional treatment program. Sacramento: Department of the Youth Authority, Research Report 56, 1969.

Litwack, S.E. The use of the helper therapy principle to increase therapeutic effectiveness and reduce therapeutic resistance: Structured learning therapy with resistant adolescents. Unpublished doctoral dissertation, Syracuse University, 1977.

Manster, G.J. *Adolescent development and the life tasks.* Boston: Allyn & Bacon, 1977.

Martinson, R. What works? Questions and answers about prison reform. *The Public Interest,* 1974, 22-54.

McClintock, F. *Attendance centres.* London: Macmillan, 1961.

McCorkle, L.W.; Elias, A.; & Bixby, F. *The Highfields story.* New York: Holt, Rinehart and Winston, 1958.

O'Connor, R.D. Relative efficacy of modeling, shaping, and the combined procedures for modification of social withdrawal. *Journal of Abnormal Psychology, 79,* 1972, 327-334.

Palmer, T. Final report to the California Community Treatment Project. Sacramento: California Youth Authority, 1976.

Patterson, G.R. & Anderson, D. Peers as social reinforcers. *Child Development, 35,* 1964, 951-960.

Patterson, G.R. & Reid, J.B. Intervention for families of aggressive boys: A replication study. *Behavior Research & Therapy, 11,* 1973, 383-394.

Peterson, D.R.; Quay, H.C.; & Cameron, G.R. Personality and background factors in juvenile delinquency as inferred from questionnaire responses. *Journal of Consulting Psychology, 23,* 1959, 392-399.

Peterson, D.R.; Quay, H.C.; & Tiffany, T.L. Personality factors related to juvenile delinquency. *Child Development, 32,* 1961, 355-372.

Quay, H.C. Dimensions of personality in delinquent boys as inferred from the factor analysis of case history data. *Child Development, 35,* 1964, 479-484.

Quay, H.C. Patterns of aggression, withdrawal and immaturity. In H.C. Quay & J.S. Werry (Eds.), *Psychopathological disorders of childhood.* New York: Wiley, 1966.

Quay, H.C. & Quay, L.C. Behavior problems in early adolescence. *Child Development, 36,* 1965, 215-220.

Raleigh, R. Individual vs. group structured learning therapy for assertiveness training with senior and junior high school students. Unpublished doctoral dissertation, Syracuse University, 1977.

Reissman, F. *The Culturally deprived child.* New York: Harper, 1965.

Robinson, J. & Smith, G. The effectiveness of correctional programs. In R. Giallombardo (Ed.), Juvenile delinquency. New York: Wiley, 1976.

Ross, A.O.; Lacey, H.M.; & Parton, D.A. The development of a behavior checklist for boys. *Child Development, 36,* 1965, 1013-1027.

Sealy, A. & Banks, C. Social maturity, training, experience and recidivism amongst British borstal boys. *British Journal of Criminology, 11,* 1971, 245-264.

Slavson, S.R. *A textbook in analytic group psychotherapy.* New York: International Universities Press, 1964.

Stein, N. & Bogin, D. Individual child psychotherapy. In A.P. Goldstein (Ed.), Prescriptions for child mental health and education. Elmsford, N.Y.: Pergamon Press, 1978.

Stumphauser, J.S. Increased delay of gratification in young prison inmates through imitation of high-delay peer models. *Journal of Personality and Social Psychology, 21,* 1972, 10-17.

Swanstrom, C. Training self-control in behavior problem children. Unpublished doctoral dissertation, Syracuse University, 1977.

Trief, P. The reduction of egocentrism in acting-out adolescents by structured learning therapy. Unpublished doctoral dissertation, Syracuse University, 1976.

Vinter, R. & Janowitz, M. Effective institutions for juvenile delinquents: A research statement. *Social Service Review, 33,* 1959, 118-130.

Vorrath, H.H. & Brendtro, L.K. *Positive peer culture.* Chicago: Aldine, 1974.

Wahler, R.G. Setting generality: Some specific and general effects of child behavior therapy. *Journal of Applied Behavior Analysis, 2,* 1969, 239-246.

Warren, M.Q. Classification for treatment. Presented at Seminar on the Classification of Criminal Behavior. Washington, D.C.: National Institute of Law Enforcement and Criminal Justice, 1972.

Wood, M. Adolesent acquisition and transfer of assertiveness through the use of structured learning therapy. Unpublished doctoral dissertation, Syracuse University, 1977.

Appendix:
Resource Materials
For Teaching Social Skills

The following section presents materials that could be employed by the teacher or clinician as stimuli to set the stage for social skills instruction, as vehicles for teaching, or as ways to provide practice and generalization of skills. The list is organized into categories corresponding to the principal medium through which the material is presented. These include: Games, Audio-Visual Presentations, Printed Materials and Books. Dramatic Play Materials, Pictorial and Display Materials, and Kits. The latter represent combinations of media. The list is organized as nearly as possible into age levels. The list is not exhaustive, and the intent is to make the reader aware of materials available rather than to endorse any specific items.

GAMES/GAME CONSTRUCTION

1. Let's Make Faces Game
    Elementary. Eight multiracial heads and interchangeable plastic eyes and mouths for making different expressions. Also gives experiences in eye-hand coordination, visual discrimination, and left-right progression. Exploration of feelings and emotions. Trend Enterprises, Inc.

2. Talking-Feeling-Doing Game
    Elementary. A board game primarily for use in counseling or therapy with children and also has some potential for social skills training. Creative Therapeutics.

3. Feelin'
    Grades 5-12. Classroom game based on recognition of feelings as one of the first steps to understanding self, communicating, and improving relationships. From 1-6 players can participate. Argus Communications.

4. Social Security
    Ages 6-adult. An exercise in communication skills for classrooms, youth groups, and families. For 2-6 players. Set consists of playing board, spinner, six decks of cards, pawns, and a die. Opportunities for Learning, Inc.

5. Roll-a-Role
    Ages 8-adult. A communications game based on role playing. A pair of players roll the character cubes and have three minutes to act out a situation or subject. Set consists of plastic character cubes, a talk topic deck of cards, where-it-happens chart, and a timer. For large or small groups. Opportunities for Learning, Inc.

6. Human Relations Games
    Secondary. Includes transparencies and games dealing with the following concepts: self-awareness, self-esteem, semantics, nonverbal communication, decision making, problem solving, cooperation and competition, etc. Set consists of: 21 transparencies, game manual, class worksheets, and supplements. Lansford Publishing Co., Inc.

7. Grow Power—Decision Making and Personality Development Game
    Intermediate-Junior High. Board game exposes students to many common behavior and decision situations. Discussion leads to mental, emotional, and social growth. Up to 6 people can play. Educational Activities, Inc.

8. No. 158 Creative Games for Learning: Games for Parents and Teachers to Make
    Ages 3 to 8 years. 50 games to make that promote social, motoric, cognitive, and academic learning. Includes objective for each game, drawing of game, materials needed, steps for construction, and rules for playing. Spiral-bound, 160 pp. The Council for Exceptional Children.

9. Game Maker Set
    Elementary. Includes all things for making your own games: wipe-off spinner, 40 cards and game field, 15 game pieces, 4 dice, crayons, and idea book. Packed in storage carton. Helpful for individualizing for special needs. Constructive Playthings.

10. Wipe-Off Game Boards
    Elementary. Set of 4 boards. Each is sturdy 14″ × 22″ plastic coated board and wipes clean. Use together with game pieces to create games for individualized and small group learning. Constructive Playthings.

PICTORIAL AND DISPLAY MATERIALS

1. Dial-a-Face
    Preprimary-Primary. Kit contains situation cards with one or more faces missing and manila tag dials containing faces showing happiness, anger, sadness, etc. Children pick appropriate expression from dial to fit scene on situation card. Ideal School Specialty Supply.

2. Social Development Picture Packet
    4-9 year olds. Full color pictures stimulate social and language development. Each set includes 12 pictures, and teacher's resource sheet. Constructive Playthings.

3. Moods and Emotions
    K-3. Sixteen dramatic photographs (12¼″ × 17″) and 40-page teacher's manual help children deal with emotions. Lyons.

4. Social Development
    K-3. Twelve full-color pictures (10¾″ × 13¾″) and 12 resource sheets help develop good social attitudes. Lyons.

5. Mental Health (Emotions)
    Elementary. Transparency series helps children gain a better understanding of their emotions. Titles include: Individual Differences, Family Composition, A New Baby Comes Home, Handling Anger, Disappointment, Rejection and/or Shyness, Happiness, Things That Make Us Happy & Things That Make Us Sad. Set includes 9 transparencies and manual. Gamco Industries, Inc.

6. Understanding Our Feelings
    Elementary. Twenty-eight picture photographs of children and adults expressing a wide variety of positive and negative feelings. Stimulates discussion of feelings. Constructive Playthings.

7. Our Feelings
    Elementary. Set of four large three-dimensional cutouts of children expressing a variety of emotions. Instructo/McGraw-Hill.

8. Friendship Jubilee
    Elementary, junior high. Five illustrated color resolutions. Emphasis is made on social relationships. Figures range to 27″ high. Nasco Learning Fun.

9. Consequences
   Junior and Senior High. 12″×6″ colorful illustrated cards present 71 problems of social responsibility. Some issues dealt with are personal safety, concern for "left-out" people, one-to-one cooperation, furthering welfare of all society, and protecting the environment. Teacher's manual included. Developmental Learning Materials.

10. Points of View
    Secondary. Sixty-three full-color cards in size 8″×9½″ show situations involving people with conflicting views based on differences in age, race, sex, culture, politics, and personal behavior. Teacher's manual included. Developmental Learning Materials.

11. Nonverbal Communication
    Secondary. Transparencies, with the use of pictorial aids, show importance of nonverbal communication and awareness of unsuspected messages. Covers grooming, mannerisms, gestures, audio, tactile, and visual clues, and double messages. Includes 15 transparencies and teacher guide. Lansford Publishing Co., Inc.

12. Effective Listening
    Secondary. Discusses problems of effective listening and suggestions for improvement. Topics include: need for effective listening, speaker and listener roles, problems with listening, steps to improve listening, puzzle of communication, how to listen accurately, checks for good listening, hearing is not listening, and filters. Set includes 12 transparencies, teacher guide, supplements, and workbook. Lansford Publishing Co., Inc.

DRAMATIC PLAY MATERIALS

1. Hand Puppets
   Preprimary-primary. Each puppet is hand washable and encourages conversation or story telling. Teacher's guide is included. Special Education Early Learning.

2. Face Puppets
   Preprimary-primary. Six large, easy to hold, chipboard puppets. Each character is colorful and encourages conversation, role playing, drama, etc. Characters coincide with hand puppets. Special Education Early Learning.

3. Paddle Masks
Four masks, 10½" diameter, with handles 5½" long × 3" wide, made of chipboard. Also a box of six assorted plastic markers for making faces on masks is included. Paddlemasks can be used for dramatic play, personal and social awareness, and body-space awareness. Special Education Early Learning.

4. People Puppets
Elementary. Set of eight cotton puppets, includes father, mother, boy, girl, policeman, farmer, and fireman. Constructive Playthings.

5. Family Face Puppets
Elementary. Set of six 12" hardboard masks. Included are mother, father, sister, brother, grandmother, and grandfather. Children can role play their feelings with these props. Constructive Playthings.

6. Puppet Enrichment Program—Personal and Social Development
Elementary and preprimary. Kit includes four puppet sleeves designed for use with interchangeable features, story starter picture card book, 33⅓ rpm record with songs, plays, and stories for puppets, two cassette tapes with duplicator worksheets, and teacher's manual. Children make puppets and participate in record activities. Open-ended program. Special Education Early Learning.

PRINTED MATERIALS AND BOOKS

1. Social-Emotional Program
Special Education-Preschool. Provides suggestions for teaching social and emotional skills for infancy to 5 years and means for determining mastery of skills. Consists of 120 = page, 8" × 5½", spiral-bound (card format) volume, placement test, and data sheet masters for 40 skills objectives. Walker Educational Book Corp.

2. Working Together: A Socialization Skills Primer
3-6 year olds. Eighty small group activities that promote cooperation among children. Some skills taught are: taking turns, exchanging objects, praising each other's efforts and abilities, asking for help, and making things together. For groups of about 9 children. Communication Skill Builders, Inc.

3. Step Text
Preschool. Twenty-two book sequenced program designed to develop

cognitive skills, language ability and social adaptability in children, ages 3-6. Teacher's guide and self-storing container included. Contains 400 color, photographic illustrations. Some titles are: *My feelings, All about me, friends, and Rainy day pals.* Advanced Learning Concepts, Inc.

4. What Does It Mean?
    Preschool. Series of six books help young children understand and deal with a variety of experiences and feelings. Each book has 32 pages, is 6½″×7″, and contains color illustrations. Set of books: *Afraid, Angry, Help!, Sharing, Sorry,* and *Success.* Children's Press.

5. Together
    Preschool-grade 3. Book that fosters awareness of interrelationships. Includes full-color photographs and easy text. Actual size is 10¼″×8¼″ and 40 pages. Children's Press.

6. Transition
    K-2. Set of four books about a child's initial school experiences. Each book is 32 pages (8″×9¼″), and has color illustrations.
    1. *I'd rather stay home*—about child's fear of leaving home
    2. *Are we still best friends?*—examines feelings in a relationship
    3. *Sometimes I hate school*—about child's feelings when a secure teacher/student relationship is disrupted
    4. *Doing things together*—about children's relationship with parents, peers, and teachers
    Children's Press.

7. Identity I
    Elementary. Set of four books about feelings and emotions in a child's everyday situation. Each book has 32 pp., is 8″×9½″ and has color photographs.
    1. *Feelings between brothers and sisters*
    2. *Feelings between kids and parents*
    3. *Feelings between friends*
    4. *Feelings between kids and grown-ups*
    Children's Press.

8. Identity II
    Elementary. Set of four books, each 32 pp., 8″×9½″, and color photographs, about feelings of young children in everyday situations.
    1. *Being alone, being together*

    2. *Big sister, little brother*
    3. *A friend can help—About a child who's parents divorce*
    4. *A new baby*
Children's Press.

9. Identity III
Elementary. Set of four books about the feelings of young children in everyday situations. Each book is 32 pp., 8″×9½″ and has color and black and white photographs.
    1. *Daydreams and night fantasies and nightmares*
    2. *I'm not going—Moving to a new home*
    3. *Tracy—Girl with cerebral palsy*
    4. *Why me?*—Vignettes about dreams, chosen last, teaser, and
       poor reader
Children's Press.

10. I Can Read About Good Manners
Grades 2-4. A read-along unit for reluctant readers to help them learn good manners in real-life situations. Set of 10 books, cassette, and guide. Troll Associates.

11. Basic Skills Enrichment
K-6. Illustrated, reproducible worksheets suitable for individuals, small groups, or entire class; and activity cards that provide a variety of learning and role-playing experiences. Designed to extend and enrich skills in self-awareness, values clarification, decision making, career education, and multicultural awareness. Each set includes two books of spirit masters and two sets of activity cards. Opportunities for Learning, Inc.

12. Will I Ever Be Good Enough?
K-3. Book about a young girl who develops self-confidence in her own abilities and overcomes the jealousy she feels toward her friend. Book has 32 pages, 8″×9½″, and is illustrated. Children's Press.

13. Handling Your Ups and Downs
Primary. A Children's Book About Emotions. Word Books.

14. I'm Running Away
K-3. Book about the emotions of a young child who decides to run away from home. Book is 32 pp., 8″×9½″, and illustrated. Children's Press.

15. New Neighbors
    K-3. Book about the feelings of a young child who feels left out. Book is 32 pp., $8'' \times 9\frac{1}{2}''$, and illustrated. Children's Press.

16. Feeling Angry
    Preschool-grade 3. Book about a girl who is feeling angry because of a new baby brother. Book is 32 pages, $7\frac{1}{4}'' \times 9\frac{1}{2}''$, and has color illustrations. Children's Press.

17. How Do You Feel?
    Preschool-grade 3. Book about emotions such as love, fear, pride, anger, and joy. Accompanied by full-color photographs of children in Press.

18. How I Feel
    Preschool-grade 3. Book about emotions such as love, fear, pride, anger, and joy. Accompanied by full-color photographs of children in action. Book is $10\frac{1}{4}'' \times 8\frac{1}{4}''$ and 40 pages. Children's Press.

19. I'll Get Even
    K-3. Book about a young boy who feels anger and frustration when he can't help build a kite. Book is 32 pp., $8'' \times 9\frac{1}{2}''$, and illustrated. Children's Press.

20. I Have Feelings
    4-9 years. Pictures and narrative of boy experiencing different emotions. Human Sciences Press, Inc.

21. Homer and the Homely Hound Dog
    7-11 years. The book uses a dog character to convey how irrational thoughts can lead to negative feelings and self-defeating behavior. 33 pages and illustrated. Institute for Rational Living, Inc.

22. Social Responsibility: A Teachable Skill
    Elementary. Handbook for elementary teachers. Includes activities dealing with respect for work, citizenship, people of other cultures, people of all ages, people with a handicap, being a wise consumer, and environment. Ohio Department of Education.

23. Happy Thinking
    Elementary. Forty-two reproducible activity cards help increase a child's awareness and appreciation of the positive in his surroundings.

Suitable for individuals, small groups, or entire class. Opportunities for Learning, Inc.

24. Developing Social Acceptability
Special Education-all ages. Training program for helping the handicapped child interact smoothly in the community. Emphasis is placed upon personal health care and grooming and basic social skills. Includes a 208 page manual and 67 picture cards. Primarily designed for parents. Walker Educational Book Corp.

25. People Need Each Other
Special Education. A variety of activities teach social awareness and the interdependence of people in modern society. Opportunities for Learning, Inc.

26. Manners Matter
All grades. Good manners in everyday situations are illustrated by the young people in this set. Spanish captions available. Cutouts range to 27″. Trend Enterprises, Inc.

27. Everywhere We Go
Grade 4. Part of National Forum Developmental Guidance Series. This textbook provides a nondirective approach to topics of family, friends, teachers, leisure, school activities, group relationships, jobs, and community life. American Guidance Service.

28. It's Your Life
Grades 5-9. An easy-to-read (5.5 grade level) and understand approach that stresses understanding oneself and others, improving communications, analyzing personal goals and values, and improving human relations. Each book contains an introduction, chapter and unit end materials, clarification of unfamiliar terms, and suggested activities. Benefic Press.

29. Getting Along With Others
Grades 6-9. Illustrated guidance booklet. Contains 40 pages, paperbound. Science Research Associates.

30. How To Get Along With Others
Grades 6-9. Forty-page booklet providing personal and social guidance for young people. Science Research Associates.

31. Nice Nifty Innovations for Creative Expression
    Elementary-junior high. Book contains ideas, activities, games, and learning centers for enhancing self-concept and more positive interpersonal relationships. Includes individual, small group, and class activities. Love Publishing Company.

32. Better Personal Relationships Through Honest Communication
    Grades 7-12. Program helps students come to a better knowledge and understanding of self through dialogue with parents, friends, and teachers. Focuses on ability to share emotions, feelings, and ideas. Includes paperback and 40 spirit masters. Argus Communications.

33. Planned Group Guidance
    Secondary. Group discussion manual focusing on teenagers' interests in four areas: relationships with others, orientation to self, orientation to school, and planning for the future; 38 discussion sections included. American Guidance Service.

34. Coping With Series
    Secondary. Twenty-three books deal with serious ethical and personal problems and everyday problems of school, home, and friendship. Attention is given to the many different kinds of relationships. Titles include *Easing the scene, To like and be liked, You always communicate something, Can you talk with someone else?* Includes manual. American Guidance Service.

35. Human Relations Fundamentals
    Secondary. Covers verbal and nonverbal communication, self concept role enactment, responsibility, active listening, supportive and defensive climates for interaction, and self expression. Set of 22 transparencies, teacher guide, article reprints. Lansford Publishing Co., Inc.

36. Getting It Together: A Reading Series About People
    Secondary. Presents a mature, high-interest text available at three different reading levels. Program consists of a text, a student resource book, answer key, and a teacher's guide. The text includes 50 stories about real-life problems that students confront in their everyday lives. Book helps improve reading skills, provides information for coping with personal problems and conflicting attitudes, and for finding sources of help. Science Research Associates, Inc.

37. Improving Self-Esteem and Relationships
    Secondary. Materials are set up so that almost anyone can facilitate

nonthreatening group sessions with youth and/or adults for the purpose of learning to like oneself, to identify and communicate his or her own needs and feelings, and to affirm potentials in other group members. Unit includes 18 transparencies, two cassettes, and teacher guide. Lansford Publishing Co., Inc.

38. How To Get Rid of Emotions That Give You a Pain in The Neck
Secondary. Book offers 30 exercises to help get priorities in order and take charge of your life. Exercises cover self evaluation, benefiting from criticism, and setting goals. Argus Communications.

39. Elementary. Canfield, Jack and Harold Wells. *100 ways to enhance self-concept in the classroom.* Prentice-Hall, Inc.

40. Elementary. Simon, Sidney, and Sally W. Olds. *Helping your child learn right from wrong: A guide to values clarification.* Simon and Schuster.

41. Elementary. Stawar, Terry. *Teaching children self control: A fable mod manual to deal with behavior problems of elementary school-age children.* Institute for Rational Living, Inc.

42. Elementary. Young, Howard S. *A rational counseling primer.* Institute for Rational Living, Inc.

AUDIO-VISUAL

Filmstrips and Cassettes

1. I Know How You Feel
Preschool. Filmstrip program helps children become aware of their own and others' feelings. Teaches that many behavioral options exist and promotes prediction of probable outcomes of certain behaviors. Titles include: *Ms. Meany and Mr. Look Around, Not everyone likes ice cream, A kid is a kid, On the merrry-go-round, Look at both sides,* and *Your feelings are your own.* Set of six filmstrips, six cassettes, and teacher's manual. Bowmar.

2. How Are You Feeling Today?
Preschool. A filmstrip program illustrating four basic emotions—happiness, sadness, anger, and fear. Helps children recognize facial and

body movement clues to emotions and recognize and express their own emotions. Titles included: *Making faces, Sometimes people feel happy, Sometimes people feel sad, Sometimes people feel angry, Sometimes people feel scared,* and *How are you feeling today?* Set of six filmstrips, six cassettes, and teacher's manual. Bowmar.

3. Tales of the Wise Old Owl
   Primary. Full-color filmstrip series presents animal stories that promote appreciation of human values, social awareness, communication, and reading development. Group I titles are: *Dr. Retriever's surprise, The busy bee, Commencement at the obedience academy, Silly excuses, Chuckie Chipmunk, Speedy the snail.* Set of six filmstrips, three cassettes, and six guides. Group II titles are: *Bushy the squirrel, Corky the crow, Bruss the beaver, School Days in the ocean, House of the wren, Peppy the pup.* Set of six filmstrips, three cassettes, and six guides. Group III titles are: *Bootsie the lamb, The feather that was lost, The wind and the seed, Pearl of great price, The fairy ring,* and *Justus the ant.* Set of six filmstrips, three cassettes and six guides. Society for Visual Education.

4. Personal Development, Growing Up and Knowing What To Do
   K-3. Filmstrip series teaches children how to act and what to do in home, school, and community situations. Helps children develop greater self confidence and awareness of the needs and feelings of others. Titles include: *Learning To listen carefully, Getting lost, Going to school, Learning to help others, Learning to do things for yourself,* and *What to do when you visit.* Set of six filmstrips. Troll Associates.

5. Manners Are Lots of Fun
   K-3. Filmstrip series teaches children how friendliness, courtesy, and cooperation can help make their lives happier and more productive in school, at home, and in the community. Titles include: *School manners, Community manners,* and *Home manners.* Set of three filmstrips and cassettes, Troll Associates.

6. Who Are You?
   K-3. Filmstrip series that explores relationships between children and their families, teachers, and friends. Titles include: *Who am I anyway?, How your parents see you, How your brothers and sisters see you, How your friends see you, How grownups see you,* and *Who I really am!* Set of six filmstrips and three cassettes. Troll Associates.

7. Kindle III: Getting along
   K-3. Five filmstrips introduce children to the concept of relationships

and why they are important to us. Titles include: *It's mine, Sticks "n" stones, Will you be my friend?, Smiles don't just happen,* and *I don't care anyhow.* Unit includes five color filmstrips, records or cassettes, teaching guide, and storage box. Scholastic Instructional Materials.

8. Kindle IV: Mixing In
    K-3. Explores with children some of the individual problems we all have in learning to get along with others. Five filmstrips include: *Do I have to win?, White lies don't count, All alone,* and *Who me?* Unit includes five color filmstrips, records, or cassettes, teaching guide, and storage box. Scholastic Instructional Materials.

9. Families
    K-4. Filmstrip series help young children learn the different needs of families and how these needs are fulfilled. Titles include: *Families need people, Families need homes, Families need food, Families need clothing, Families need money,* and *Families need machines.* Set of six filmstrips and three cassettes. Troll Associates.

10. Kindle V: I Can Tell
    Early childhood K-3. Explores world of nonverbal communication and how it can help us understand ourselves and others better. Filmstrips include: *Talking hands, What faces say, Rainbows and raindrops,* and *Twist "n" turn.* Unit includes five color filmstrips, records or cassettes, teaching guide, and storage box. Scholastic Instructional Materials.

11. Winnie the Witch: Stories About Values
    Primary. Animated people teach about honesty, responsibility, diligence, and forgiveness in fantasy settings. Encourages children to relate their own feelings and experiences. Set of four color filmstrips, four cassettes, and guide. Society for Visual Education.

12. Tales of Winnie the Witch
    Primary-intermediate. Animated creatures teach children the values of love, sharing, being neighborly and unselfish, looking at both sides of a story, and the Golden Rule. Program consists of six color filmstrips, six cassettes, and guide. Society for Visual Education.

13. Winnie the Witch and the Frightened Ghost
    Primary-intermediate. Animated creatures teach children that it's

dumb to be afraid of others just because they're different. Color filmstrip, cassette, and guide. Society for Visual Education.

14. Winnie the Witch and the Friendless Creature
     Primary-intermediate. A creature learns how to make friends when
     Winnie teaches him how to smile. Teaches viewers that to win a
     friend, you have to be a friend. Filmstrip, cassette, and guide. Society
     for Visual Education.

15. Learning About Manners
     Primary-intermediate. Teacher and mixed ethnic group of students
     discuss the importance of showing respect, kindness, and consider-
     ation for others for effective group living. Titles include: *Manners at
     home, Manners at school, Manners on the playground, Manners while
     visiting friends, Manners at the theater, Manners on public transpor-
     tation.* Set of six filmstrips (color), three cassettes, and six guides.
     Society for Visual Education.

16. Understanding Ourselves and Others
     Grades 1-4. Film loops help children understand the causes of fear,
     loneliness, and other emotions, and to accept differences of others.
     Titles include: *Understanding the difference between alone and lonely,
     Fear—Real and imaginary, Why we get angry, People are different,
     aren't they?,* and *Learning when and where.* Set of five film loops.
     Troll Associates.

17. Feelings
     Primary-intermediate. Light-hearted stories help children understand
     and deal with feelings. Appropriate for children with learning prob-
     lems. Each set consists of four color filmstrips with four cassettes.

     Set 1 - Feelings   Set 2 - Feelings
     Outside/inside   *That's not fair*
     When I grow up   *Everybody's afraid of*
     I am many different people   *something*
     Stop acting like a baby   *G-r-r-r-r*
                                   But I don't know how
     ATC Publishing Corporation

18. Understanding Your Feelings
     Elementary. Filmstrips introduce the emotions of anger, fear, sad-
     ness, and happiness. Children learn ways of expressing these emotions
     and are encouraged to discuss their feelings. Opportunities for
     Learning, Inc.

19. Winning and Losing
    Grades 2-5. Filmstrip series helps children put competition into perspective. Reasons for competing in school and at play are presented, and good sportsmanship is emphasized. Titles include: *Why we compete, Any number can play, Winners and losers,* and *It's only a game.* Set of four filmstrips and four cassettes. Troll Associates.

20. Learning to Live With Others
    Primary-intermediate. Full-color filmstrips depict stories designed to help children think for themselves and get along with others. Group I includes: *Learning to be your best self, Learning about listening, Learning what giving is all about,* and *Learning to be responsible.* Set of four filmstrips, two cassettes, and four guides. Group II includes: *Learning to trust people, Learning to keep a promise, Learning about patience,* and *Learning to face up to mistakes.* Set of four filmstrips, two cassettes, and four guides. Society for Visual Education.

21. Developing Basic Values
    Primary-intermediate. Full-color filmstrips illustrate the need for moral and ethical values in everyday living. Titles include: *Respect for property, Consideration for others, Acceptance of differences,* and *Recognition of responsibilities.* Set of four filmstrips, two cassettes and four guides. Society for Visual Education.

22. Making Friends
    Grades 4-6. Captioned filmstrips explore desirable personality and behavior traits. Designed as a unit in personal guidance with review frames and checklists for students to rate themselves. Titles include: *How do you rate at home?, How do you rate at school?,* and *How do you rate with your friends?* Set of three filmstrips (captioned). BFA Educational Media.

23. Responsible Decision Making
    Elementary. Presents experiences in responsible decision making and reinforces social skills, self concept, communication skills, and problem solving techniques. Based on Dreikur's guides. Complete program includes six filmstrips, six cassettes, and teacher's guide. Separate titles are: *Returning other people's things, Listening to directions, Overcoming shyness, Earning friends, Keeping promises,* and *Helping yourself and others.* Individual filmstrip/cassette. Gamco Industries, Inc.

24. Smiles and Frowns
    Elementary. *Looking bird* suggests ways that exceptional students can take responsibility for being good citizens at school and play, e.g., using a litter bag. Complete program includes filmstrip and cassette. Gamco Industries, Inc.

25. Getting Along in School
    Preschool-primary. Filmstrips give children examples of good behavior and work habits to help them do better in classes and with relationships with other children. Titles include: *Being on time, Doing things for yourself, Taking care of things, Working with others, How quiet helps,* and *Listening and following instructions.* Nasco Learning Fun.

26. The Adventures of the Lollipop Dragon
    Primary. Full-color filmstrips illustrate a green dragon helping children become aware of the rights of others and learn that cooperation promotes happier living. Titles include: *How the lollipop dragon got his name, Working together, Avoiding litter, Care of property, Taking turns,* and *Kindness to animals.* Six filmstrips, three cassettes, and guide. Society of Visual Education.

27. The Family
    K-3. Filmstrips show functions of families and deal with the problems of adoption, divorce, separation, and death. Families are depicted with different economic, ethnic, and cultural backgrounds. Titles include: *Family members and their roles, Each family is different, Meeting physical needs, Meeting emotional needs, From childhood to old age,* and *Families from other countries.* Set of six filmstrips and three cassettes. BFA Educational Media.

28. Living With Your Family
    Primary. Full-color filmstrips illustrate the essence of family life: need for love, responsibilities, helping each other, and opportunities for growth and happiness. Provides material for role playing and discussion. Titles include: *What is a family?, The family has a new baby, A day with your family,* and *Family fun.* Set of four captioned filmstrips, two cassettes, and four guides. Society for Visual Education.

29. Little Citizen Series
    Primary. Filmstrips depict the personal attitudes and behavior patterns that contribute to good citizenship. Titles include: *Raggedy Elf* (friendship) *Mighty hunters* (cooperation), *The boy* (understanding),

Bike behavior (traffic safety and courtesy), *The game of might-have-been* (accepting things as they are), and *Little cloud* (sharing). Set of six filmstrips, six cassettes, and six guides. Society for Visual Education.

30. Learning To Be Together
    Grades 9-12. Filmstrip series helps students examine behavior and attitudes that hinder communication between people and find alternate ways to handle feelings and attitudes. Titles include: *Keeping people apart, People are people, Putting people in boxes,* and *Love.* Set of four filmstrips and four cassettes. BFA Educational Media.

31. Understanding Your Relationship With Others
    Grades 7-12. Student acquires a better understanding of himself and others. Explores the interesting differences of people, idea of belonging, and common interests with other people, and fosters a desire to contribute to a group. Set consists of filmstrips and cassettes. The Baker and Taylor Companies.

32. All About Manners
    Secondary. Program includes filmstrips and cassettes. Open-ended questions, brief explanations, situations, and humor are used. Contains five color filmstrips, five audio cassette slides and teacher's manual. Interpretive Education.

33. Social Skills
    Exceptional-adolescent. Teaches correct behavior and attitudes needed for acceptance and social adjustment. Provides guidance for older students who are thinking about "dropping out" of school. Titles include: *Talk! talk! talk!* (using proper language), *Why school?, Hurt* (Golden Rule), *The magic of manners, Who am I?, Here's looking at you* (good grooming), *The boy with blue eyes* (prejudice), and *The justice maker* (guide for behavior when in trouble with law). Complete program includes eight filmstrips, eight cassettes, worksheet, and manual. Gamco Industries, Inc.

34. Get in Touch With Your Emotions
    Grades 3-6. Color filmstrips help students to become more aware of their emotions. Manual contain scripts and discussion questions. Titles include: *It's natural to be angry or afraid, You can show love and affection, Adjusting to unhappiness, The brighter side of life.* Set of four filmstrips, two cassettes, and manual. Kimbo Educational Activities.

35. Values: Making Choices
     Grades 4-6. Filmstrip series present open-ended stories about jealousy, loyalty, trust, and privacy, group comformity vs. individual ideas, and the issue of "what price winning." Titles include: *The tree house, The field trip, The championship game,* and *The class project.* Set of four filmstrips and four cassettes. BFA Educational Media.

36. Healthy Feelings
     Filmstrip series about four teenagers help students learn that certain feelings can cause other feelings, that feelings can be related to physical health, and that a behavior change can affect the way they feel. Titles include: *Feelings: Ours and others, Feelings are made, Feelings: What we do,* and *Feeling good.* Set of four sound filmstrips and four cassettes. BFA Educational Media.

Films

1. Values: Understanding Others
    Elementary. Film that discusses how people are different and encourages children to ask themselves, "How would I feel if I were he?" 8¼ minutes and color. BFA Educational Media.

2. Delicious Inventions from Willy Wonka and the Chocolate Factory
    Elementary. Five children tour Wonka's wonderful factory and receive a sweet lesson in manners. 15 minute color film. Films Incorporated.

3. School Problems: Getting Along With Others
    Elementary. Film about five typical school problems which need decision making. At end of each sequence, viewers are asked to discuss the problem and suggest possible solutions. Film is 10½ minutes and in color. BFA Educational Media.

4. Values: Playing Fair
    Elementary. Film shows examples of playing fair and not playing fair. Children are shown from preschool to junior high age learning to take turns and becoming part of a team. 10 minutes BFA Educational Media.

5. The New Kid
    Elementary. Film about making friends in a new neighborhood. Film is in color and will last 11 minutes. BFA Educational Media.

6. Feelings: Don't Stay Mad
    Elementary. Film about the universality of anger, necessity of expressing it, but in a way that doesn't hurt others. Film is in color, 14¾ minutes. BFA Educational Media.

7. Feelings: What Are You Afraid Of?
    Elementary. Film about fears: universality of fears, expressing fears, and getting help with fears. Film encourages your viewers to talk about their own personal fears. 12½ minutes, color. BFA Educational Media.

8. Getting Angry
    Elementary. Film about boy who takes his new birthday present to school and it is broken on the playground. A chain reaction of anger follows in which many children are involved. Encourages class discussion. 10 minutes, color. BFA Educational Media.

9. Values: Cooperation
    Elementary. Film that shows three friends helping each other and having lots of fun in the process of cooperating. Color and 11 minutes. BFA Educational Media.

10. Disappointment: A Day That Didn't Happen
    Intermediate-Junior High. Jennie receives disappointment that a favorite uncle calls to cancel his planned visit. Provokes discussion on anger, hurt, emptiness. Color, 11 minutes, video cassette. Xerox films.

11. Worry: I'm In Big Trouble Now
    Intermediate-Junior High. Billy, who is in charge of his little brother, Chris, loses him while exploring a barn with a friend. Provokes discussion on responsibility, guilt, fear, and worry. Color, 12 minutes, video cassette. Xerox Films.

12. The Transformation of Mabel Wells
    Intermediate-Junior High—Secondary. A cranky old woman returns from the hospital to find get-well cards and gifts from many people. Provokes discussion of loneliness, helping, and friendship. Color, 12 minutes. Cine Golden Eagle Award. Xerox Films.

13. Loneliness: The Empty Tree House
    Intermediate Junior. John's best friend moves. Another boy initiates a

friendship but leaves when a group asks them to go sledding. John hesitates to go. 10 minutes. Xerox Films.

14. Jealousy: I Won't Be Your Friend
Intermediate Junior. Tony sees his best friend spending more and more time with a new boy. Provokes discussion on demands we make on friends and how we can prepare for changes in a relationship. 13 minutes. Xerox Films.

15. Who Did What To Whom?
Secondary. Film for improving human relations. Introduces principles of human interaction to almost any group. Principles covered are positive and negative reinforcement, punishment, and extinction. Film shows 40 short scenes that occur every day at home, in school, and around the office. Discussion time is provided after every scene. Film is 16½ minutes in length. Sufficient for a full 2-hour session. Also included is a leader's guide. Research Press.

Records and Cassettes

1. Won't You Be My Friend?
Preschool-primary. Songs guide the child in emotional and social awareness. Included are rhythm games and songs to help learn each other's names, to enrich dramatic play, and to enjoy the experience of taking turns. Titles include: "What Makes Me Happy" "I'm Afraid," "Won't You Be My Friend?," "Angry Song," and "I Want You All to Myself." Lyons.

2. Ideas, Thoughts, and Feelings
Preschool-primary. Emphasis in album is on discovery, problem solving, and independent thinking. Activities can be done in small groups or with partners. Some titles are: "Everybody Has Feelings," "I Like Me," "Making Friends," "I Don't Like Me," and "Things I'm Thankful For." Lyons.

3. Feelin' Free
Preschool, primary. Record encourages young children to use their minds and bodies to express themselves, not only to move but to verbalize feelings. Teacher's guide contains activities, suggestions, and lyrics for each song. Lyons.

4. Songs About My Feelings
Pre K-3. Children relate to their moods and feelings through partici-

pation songs and activities. Deals with human relations concepts such as how we feel about ourselves and others. Includes guide. Lyons.

5. The Learning Party
    Early elementary. Musical album helps the young child understand growing, senses, family, and relating to others. Includes guide. Constructive Playthings.

6. Everybody Cries Sometimes
    Elementary. Album that helps create an atmosphere of understanding and respect for each other. Includes songs: "Everybody Says," "Lonely Blues," "Scarey Things," "Is There Room In the Boat?" Educational Activities, Inc.

7. Good Manners Through Music
    Elementary. Album titles include: "Hang Up Your Clothes," "Share Your Top," "Use Good Manners With Your Pets." 12"-33⅓ rpm record. Nasco Learning Fun.

8. Elementary. Goldsmith, Rachelle C. and Barry Goldsmith. "Relaxation—The Key to Life." Recorded on Kimbo L.P. 9080, Manual-Kimbo Educational, 1973.

9. Peace, Harmony, Awareness
    All ages. Audio program that teaches relaxation, self-confidence and control, and helps improve relationships. Can be used with individuals, groups, and children with special needs. Consists of a manual, six audio cassettes, and seven, 8"×10" color photographs. Teaching Resources Corporation.

10. Effective Communication
    Grades 7-12, college, adult. Involves listening, skills, nonverbal expression, and awareness of feelings for understanding human nature and exchanging ideas. Titles of cassette programs are: "The Art of Listening," "Awareness of Feelings," "Speech Mannerisms," and "Attacking and Defending." Set consists of two cassettes with teacher's guide and spirit master activities. Argus Communciations.

PROGRAMS AND KITS

1. Peabody Early Experience Kit (PEEK)
    Preschool. Promotes cognitive, affective, and oral language develop-

ment of prekindergarten children. 50 percent of activities focus on cognitive, 25 percent on affective, and 25 percent on oral language areas. Materials are designed for a group of 12 children. Materials are stored in two carrying cases; includes teacher's guide; 250 lessons in two hardcover manuals; four cloth puppets; 11″ × 11″ pouch to store daily lesson materials; rubber stamp to act as reinforcer; 17″ × 34″ vinyl chart and collapsible wooden easel; 13-24″ rope sections; 186 crepe rubber beads in three sizes and three shapes; six decks of 52 minicards each; fishing pole to hook cards; eight color posters (21″ × 28″); four cassettes or seven records contain 27 songs and various sounds; 30 familiar small objects, such as buttons and pennies; sound makers consisting of wooden tone block and stick and 80 accompanying color story pictures; 232 shape pictures on the backs of photographs; 27 song cards to accompany recorded songs; 9″ × 10″ cardboard template folder; six plastic tumblers; two cloth balls, and 4-9″ × 11″ sailcloth bags. American Guidance Service.

2.   The Adventures of the Lollipop Dragon Book-Cassettes
Primary. Book-cassettes kits depict the fanciful green dragon who helps children develop positive social attitudes and values. Each kit contains 10 copies of the book and one tape cassette. Titles are: *"How the Lollipop Dragon got his name," "Working together," "Avoiding litter," "Care of property," "Taking turns," "Kindness to animals."* Each title: one cassette, 10 books. Set of six titles, six cassettes, and 60 books. Society for Visual Education.

3.   DUSO Kit D-1
Kindergarten and lower elementary. Activities designed to aid in learning words for feelings; learning that feelings, goals, values, and behavior are dynamically related; and learning to talk more freely about feelings, goals, values, and behavior. Materials are manual, 2 story books, 33 posters with easel, 21 records or five cassettes, six hand puppets, 11 puppet props, two character puppets, 33 puppet activity cards, 5 group discussion cards, 33 role playing activity cards. American Guidance Service Inc.

4.   DUSO Kit D-2
Upper primary - grade 4. Activities to develop understanding and valuing of oneself; understanding of interpersonal relationships and purposive nature of human behavior; understanding of interrelationships among ideas, feelings, beliefs, behavior, and of competence. Materials include: Manual, 33 posters with easel, 17 records or 5 cassettes, 6 hand puppets, 2·character puppets, 33 puppet activity

cards, 33 discussion pictures, 6 discussion guide cards, 8 self and
social development activity cards, 33 role playing activity cards.
American Guidance Service, Inc.

5. Me and Others
Special education. A multimedia program designed to teach students
how to know and live with oneself and others. Specific topics include
evaluation of self and life in a positive manner, recognizing and dealing with different life roles, successful communication, solving personal problems, and being sensitive to feelings and needs. Complete
program consists of 2 color-sound filmstrips, 2 audio cassettes, 24
copies of a 96-page work-a-text, and teacher's manual. Opportunities
for Learning, Inc.

6. Self Identification Set I
Elementary. Set of four bound books, four cassettes, and teacher's
guide contain stories and realistic photographs. Includes reflective
questions. Titles are: *Feelings between brothers and sisters, Between
friends, Between kids and grownups,* and *Between kids and parents.*
Constructive Playthings.

7. Self Identification Set II
Elementary. Includes set of four 32-page books with colored photographs. Four cassettes talk the child through the photographs and
narrate the story line. Titles are: *Being alone, Being together, Big
sister, Little brother, A friend can help* (adjusting to divorced
parents), and *A new baby.* Four books, four cassettes, teacher's
guide.Constructive Playthings.

8. Tales of Winnie the Witch
Upper primary-intermediate. Animated creatures teach children important human values and book-cassette read-along format encourages the practice of reading skills. Stories are written from 2.0-3.0
reading level. Consists of 6 cassettes, 60 books (10 per cassette program), and storage pouches. Society for Visual Education.

9. Social Development
K-20 Cassette learning package helps children recognize social traits
and develop desirable behaviors in the affective domain. No reading is
required. Titles include: Responsibility, Honesty, Cooperation, Respect for Others, and Friendliness. A package includes a 15-20 minute
cassette lesson, 30 four page student response booklets, teacher's
guide, post test, and library cards. Media materials, Inc.

10. My Friends and Me
     Preschool. Kit includes teacher's guide, 2 activity manuals containing instructions for 190 activities; metal carrying case; 24″ × 32″ free-standing activity board; 6-23″ × 29″ full-color activity pictures; 59 magnetic shapes in various forms and colors; 2-10″ × 12″ story books with 40 stories and 232 color illustrations; 2 fuzzy 12″ dolls; 3 inked print blocks of adults, children, and above-mentioned doll figures; 5 cassettes or 12-7″ records containing 16 recorded activities, narration, dialogue, and 23 songs; miscellaneous equipment of ink pad, ink, sponge, 4 liquid-chalk pens, eraser; song cards (7″ × 9¾″); and spirit masters of 38 illustrated family activities. Kit assists personal and social development. American Guidance Service.

11. Social Perceptual Training Kit For Community Living
     Upper elementary-prevocational. Kit contains book with 50 lessons for developing social comprehension, 425 photographic slides, cassette, 31 drawings for preparation of spirit masters or transparencies. Subunits include:

     • introduction to signals,
     • numbers as signals,
     • places as signals,
     • making a good impression,
     • shopping-buying,
     • a big store,
     • living on our own,
     • getting and keeping a job,
     • after hours, and
     • getting along with others.

     Complete kit. Educational Activities, Inc.

12. Transition
     Elementary and junior high. Emphasizes social and emotional growth of middle school and junior high school student. Appreciation of human differences is stressed by presenting a wide range of racial, ethnic, and economic groups and physical handicaps. Students write out and act out scenarios about personal conflicts and decision making; simulated encounters; directed observation and analysis of human behavior; and large and small group discussions. Program consists of five units entitled: (1) Communication and Problem Solving Skills; (2) Encouraging Openness and Trust; (3) Verbal and Nonverbal Communication of Feelings; (4) Needs, Goals, and Expectations; and (5) Increasing Awareness of Values. Ninety-one lesson-activities of 20 minutes each are included. Materials are 5 sets, each stored in its

own box; manual to accompany each set; cartoon posters (color); cassettes of stories; duplicating masters; discussion cards for units 1, 3, 4; a gavel; measuring tape; 28 illustrations (9½″×14″) for unit 3; "feeling word" cards for unit 3; and chart on steps in interviewing for unit 4. American Guidance Service.

13. Nonverbal Communication and Interaction
     Secondary. Includes: (1) what is nonverbal communication?; (2) functions of nonverbal communication; (3) body motion; (4) language of distance' (5) voice language; (6) environmental language; (7) physical characteristics; (8) artifacts; (9) tactile communication; (10) written communication; and (11) importance of nonverbal communication. Games are also included. Set consists of 14 transparencies, cassette tape, games, teacher guide, and other supplementary material. Lansford Publishing Co., Inc.

14. Should I
     Secondary. A set of 6″×8″ booklets about personal decisions by ordinary people affect and are affected by events of global importance. Argus Communications.

15. Behavior Modification for the Classroom Teacher
     All grades. Kit containing indexed file of over 100, 4″×6″ cards that present techniques of behavior modification, activities for dealing with specific behavior problems, socio-techniques, and samples of forms for recording student behavior. A dramatized cassette tape for teacher use is also included that deals with the method for setting up a behavior modification plan and principles of behavior management. Opportunities for Learning, Inc.

LISTING OF PUBLISHERS

Advanced Learning Concepts
211 W. Wisconsin Avenue
Milwaukee, Wisconsin 53203

American Guidance Service
Publisher's Building
Circle Pines, Minnesota 55014

Argus Communications
7440 Natchez Avenue
Niles, Illinois 60648

ATC Publishing Corporation
J.S. Latta, Inc.
P.O. Box 1276
Huntington, West Virginia 25715

BFA Educational Media
2211 Michigan Avenue
P.O. Box 1795
Santa Monica, California 90406

The Baker and Taylor Companies
Drawer Z
Momence, Illinois 60954

Benefic Press
1900 N. Narragansett
Chicago, Illinois 60639

Bowmar/Noble
4563 Colorado Blvd.
Los Angeles, California 90039

Children's Press
1224 W. Van Buren
Chicago, Illinois 60607

Communication Skill Builders, Inc.
817 East Broadway
P.O. Box 6081-D
Tucson, Arizona 85733

Constructive Playthings
1040 East 85th Street
Kansas City, Missouri 64131

The Council for Exceptional Children
1920 Association Drive
Reston, Virginia 22091

Creative Therapeutics
155 Country Road
Cresskill, New Jersey 07626

Developmental Learning Materials
7740 Natchez Avenue
Niles, Illinois 60648

Educational Activities
P.O. Box 392
Freeport, New York 11520

Films Incorporated
733 Green Bay Road
Wilmette, Illinois 60091

Gamco Industries, Inc.
P.O. Box 1862 K
Big Spring, Texas 79720

Human Sciences Press
72 Fifth Avenue
New York, New York 10011

Ideal School Specialty Supply Company
P.O. Box 1327
Salina, Kansas 67401

Institute for Rational Living
45 East 65th Street
New York, New York 10021

Instructo/McGraw-Hill
Cedar Hollow and Matthews Hill Road
Paoli, Pennsylvania 19301

Interpretive Education
2306 Winters Drive
Kalamazoo, Michigan 49002

Kimbo Educational
P.O. Box 477
Long Branch, New Jersey 07740

Lansford Publishing Company
P.O. Box 8711
San Jose, California 95155

Love Publishing Company
6635 East Villanove Place
Denver, Colorado 80222

Lyons
5030 Riverview Avenue
Elkhart, Indiana 46514

Media Materials, Inc.
Department W 87654
2936 Remington Avenue
Baltimore, Maryland 21211

Nasco Learning Fun
901 Janesville Avenue
Fort Atkinson, Wisconsin 53538

Ohio Department of Education
Division of Educational
   Design and Renewal
65 South Front Street
Room 1004
Columbus, Ohio 43215

Opportunities for Learning, Inc.
8950 Lurline Avenue
Department 9AB
Chatsworth, California 91311

Prentice-Hall
Englewood Cliffs
New Jersey 07632

Research Press
Box 317730
Champaign, Illinois 61820

Scholastic Instructional Materials
904 Sylvan Avenue
Englewood Cliffs, New Jersey 07632

Science Research Associates
155 North Wacker
Chicago, Illinois 60606

Simon and Schuster
1230 Avenue of the Americas
New York, New York 10020

Society for Visual Education
1345 Diversey Parkway
Chicago, Illinois 60614

Special Education Early Learning
Cleo Learning Aids
2573 Noble Road
Cleveland, Ohio 44121

Teaching Resources Corp.
100 Boylston Street
Boston, Massachusetts 02116

Trend Enterprises
P.O. Box 3073
St. Paul, Minnesota 55165

Troll Associates
320 Rt. 17
Mahwah, New Jersey 07430

Walker Educational Book Corp.
720 Fifth Avenue
New York, New York 10019

Word Books
Word Incorporated
P.O. Box 1790
Waco, Texas 76703

Xerox Films
245 Long Hill Road
Middletown, Connecticut 06457

Author Index

Subject Index

About the Editors and Contributors

Gwendolyn Cartledge is an Assistant Professor at Cleveland State University in the College of Education, where her primary responsibility is training teachers to work with children with special needs. She received her B.S. and M.Ed. from the University of Pittsburgh and Ph.D. in Special Education from The Ohio State Universtiy. She has been a classroom teacher and supervisor of programs for learning disabled and emotionally disturbed children. Professional interests center on developing academic and social skills in handicapped learners. Previous publications include a chapter on teaching strategies for children with learning disabilities and "The Case for Teaching Social Skills in the Classroom: A Review" in the *Review of Educational Research,* which she coauthored.

JoAnne F. Milburn is Director of Starr Commonwealth of Columbus, a children's mental health program which includes residential and day treatment as well as outpatient counseling services. She received her B.A. from Stanford University, M.S.W. from U.C.L.A., and Ph.D. in Special Education from The Ohio State University. She has worked with children in several settings, has served on the faculty of the College of Social Work, and holds an adjunct appointment on the Faculty for Exceptional Children at The Ohio State University. She has been a reviewer for Contemporary Psychology and coauthored "The Case for Teaching Social Skills in the Classroom: A Review" in *The Review of Educational Research.*

Mary Ann S. Bash (M.A., University of Northern Colorado) is Director of the Title IV-C Cognitive Program Solving: "Think Aloud" Project in Denver Public Schools. Her major area of interest is in developing K-12 reading and language programs.

Bonnie W. Camp (Ph.D., Indiana University; M.D., University of Colorado) is Associate Professor of Pediatrics and Psychiatry at the University of Colorado School of Medicine. Her major research interests are in development of self-control processes and effects on learning.

N. Jane Gershaw (Ph.D., Syracuse University) is Chief of the Syracuse VA Mental Hygiene Clinic and holds academic rank as Adjunct Assistant Professor of Psychology at Syracuse University and Clinical Assistant Professor of Psychology at the SUNY Upstate Medical Center. She has been involved in research and clinical application of behavioral techniques in group psychotherapy.

Arnold P. Goldstein (Ph.D., Pennsylvania State University) is Professor of Psychology at Syracuse University. His major research interest is the teaching of prosocial behavior to antisocial, aggressive populations.

Paul Klein (M.S., State University of New York at Cortland) is a consulting teacher on special assignment with the Syracuse School District for programs for severely emotionally disturbed children in resource classrooms. He has directed alternative school programs for adolescents and preadolescents for the Syracuse School District, and has served as a consultant in behavior management techniques for other school districts within the central New York area.

Sherri Oden (Ph.D., University of Illinois) is Assistant Professor of Education and Human Development and Psychology at the University of Rochester.Her current research is on identifying processes in social skill and relationship development. Her major research has focused on the role of instructions with children who are not accepted by peers or lack friendships.

Mara Sapon-Shevin (Ed.D., University of Rochester) is Visiting Professor of Special Education at Cleveland State University. Her major research interests are in the areas of mainstreaming, teaching social skills to young children, and the development of cooperative instructional activities.

Stuart Schleien (M.Ed., University of Georgia) is Instructor of Special Education and Recreation at Virginia Commonwealth University in Richmond, Va. He is heavily involved in leisure skills curriculum development, technical assistance, and behavioral research with mentally retarded individuals.

Robert P. Sprafkin (Ph.D., Ohio State University) is Coordinator of the Syracuse VA Day Treatment Center, as well as Adjunct Associate Professor of Psychology at Syracuse University and Clinical Associate Professor of Psychology at the SUNY Upstate Medical Center. He has been involved in the development of psychoeducational training programs for diverse groups.

Paul Wehman (Ph.D., University of Wisconsin-Madison) is Assistant Professor of Special Education at Virginia Commonwealth University in Richmond, Va. His current research interests are in leisure education for severely handicapped individuals and job placement for the severely disabled.